FROMMER'S
EasyGuide

TO W9-COW-338

LIMA, CUSCO &
MACHU PICCHU

By
Nicholas Gill

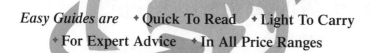

Easy Guides are ✦ Quick To Read ✦ Light To Carry
✦ For Expert Advice ✦ In All Price Ranges

FrommerMedia LLC

Published by
FROMMER MEDIA LLC

ISBN 978-1-62887-246-0 (paper), 978-1-62887-247-7 (e-book)

Editorial Director: Pauline Frommer
Development Editor: Michael Kelly
Production Editor: Lynn Northrup
Cartographer: Liz Puhl
Indexer: Maro Riofrancos

For information on our other products or services, see www.frommers.com.

Frommer Media LLC also publishes its books in a variety of electronic formats. Some content that appears in print may not be available in electronic formats.

Manufactured in the United States of America

5 4 3 2 1

FROMMER'S STAR RATINGS SYSTEM

Every hotel, restaurant, and attraction listed in this guide has been ranked for quality and value. Here's what the stars mean:

★ Recommended
★★ Highly recommended
★★★ A must! Don't miss!

AN IMPORTANT NOTE

The world is a dynamic place. Hotels change ownership, restaurants hike their prices, museums alter their opening hours, and buses and trains change their routings. And all of this can occur in the several months after our authors have visited, inspected, and written about these hotels, restaurants, museums, and transportation services. Though we have made valiant efforts to keep all our information fresh and up-to-date, some few changes can inevitably occur in the periods before a revised edition of this guidebook is published. So please bear with us if a tiny number of the details in this book have changed. Please also note that we have no responsibility or liability for any inaccuracy or errors or omissions, or for inconvenience, loss, damage, or expenses suffered by anyone as a result of assertions in this guide.

CONTENTS

ABOUT THE AUTHOR

Food and travel writer **Nicholas Gill** lives in Lima, Peru, and Brooklyn, New York. His work appears in *The New York Times*, *The Wall Street Journal*, *Fool*, *New York Magazine*, and *Roads & Kingdoms*, among others. He is the co-founder of NewWorlder.com, a website dedicated to exploring food and travel in the Americas.

ABOUT THE FROMMER'S TRAVEL GUIDES

For most of the past 50 years, Frommer's has been the leading series of travel guides in North America, accounting for as many as 24 percent of all guidebooks sold. I think I know why.

Though we hope our books are entertaining, we nevertheless deal with travel in a serious fashion. Our guidebooks have never looked on such journeys as a mere recreation, but as a far more important human function, a time of learning and introspection, an essential part of a civilized life. We stress the culture, lifestyle, history, and beliefs of the destinations we cover, and urge our readers to seek out people and new ideas as the chief rewards of travel.

We have never shied from controversy. We have, from the beginning, encouraged our authors to be intensely judgmental, critical—both pro and con—in their comments, and wholly independent. Our only clients are our readers, and we have triggered the ire of countless prominent sorts, from a tourist newspaper we called "practically worthless" (it unsuccessfully sued us) to the many rip-offs we've condemned.

And because we believe that travel should be available to everyone regardless of their incomes, we have always been cost-conscious at every level of expenditure. Though we have broadened our recommendations beyond the budget category, we insist that every lodging we include be sensibly priced. We use every form of media to assist our readers, and are particularly proud of our feisty daily website, the award-winning Frommers.com.

I have high hopes for the future of Frommer's. May these guidebooks, in all the years ahead, continue to reflect the joy of travel and the freedom that travel represents. May they always pursue a cost-conscious path, so that people of all incomes can enjoy the rewards of travel. And may they create, for both the traveler and the persons among whom we travel, a community of friends, where all human beings live in harmony and peace.

Arthur Frommer

THE BEST OF LIMA, CUSCO & MACHU PICCHU

Peru may be inseparable from Machu Picchu and the legacy of the Inca Empire, but a scratch beneath the surface reveals a fascinating and dynamic country that preserves its Andean traditions. Cosmopolitan types dive into Lima's world-class dining, while travelers in Gore-Tex outdoor gear gather at pubs around Cusco's 500-year-old Plaza de Armas in anticipation of ruins treks. Yet even in this cross-section of some of Peru's highlights, there's much more. In Sacred Valley markets, artisans haggle over handwoven alpaca textiles. On the desert coast, a 5,000-year-old city is being excavated as you read this. There are beaches for surfing, fervent religious processions, and highland celebrations with surreal masks.

Sightseeing   **Cusco** revels in its Andean traditions, with exquisite Inca stonemasonry on nearly every street. Take a train though the **Sacred Valley** to the Inca town of **Ollantaytambo** and legendary **Machu Picchu.** The fast-paced capital, **Lima,** has revitalized its colonial quarter to go along with its sophisticated nightlife and shopping. Visit the ancient pyramid complex of **Caral,** which parallels the ones in Egypt, or surf some of South America's most consistent waves at **Punta Hermosa.**

Eating & Drinking   The word's out: Contemporary Peruvian cuisine is one of the world's most surprising and sophisticated. Get a heaping plate of tuna, sliced into Asian-inflected *tiradito* right off the boat, or savor **ceviche** at a hip, open-air restaurant. The highlands are famed for what the Incas ate: 300 varieties of potatoes and grains like **quinoa.** There are giant river fish such as *paiche* and exotic tropical fruits from the Amazon and *ají* **peppers** that spice up all kinds of dishes. Taste a coca or passion-fruit sour—mixologists' takes on the classic **pisco sour.**

Nature   Even in this small selection of terrain, Peru's natural diversity is astounding: bold **Andes** mountains running down the middle of the country, a 3,220km (2,000-mile) **Pacific coast,** and the lush rainforest at the edge of the **Amazon,** which surrounds Machu Picchu. Whether you're into extreme sports, birding, or photography, you'll find islands full of sea lions, snowcapped mountains, raging rivers, and hillsides blanketed with orchids.

History   Peru wears its complex web of pre-Columbian cultures and Spanish colonialism on its hand-woven sleeve. From Inca ruins such as the mammoth **Sacsayhuamán** fortress overlooking Cusco and pre-Inca archaeological sites like **Caral,** to colonial mansions built by conquistadors over Inca palaces in **Cusco** and the Republican-era houses turned art galleries and boutique hotels in Lima's **Barranco** neighborhood, you don't have to look far for a thrilling history lesson.

THE best AUTHENTIC EXPERIENCES

o **Exploring the Catacombs of San Francisco (Lima):** Beneath this colonial church and convent in the center of Lima, an estimated 75,000 bodies were interred until a main cemetery was built. There's no creepier or fascinating experience in Peru than wandering through this maze of eerily arranged human bones. See p. 59.

o **Eating ceviche (Lima):** A staple of Peruvian coastal cuisine, ceviche has taken the world by storm. A tantalizing dish of raw fish and shellfish marinated in lime juice and hot chili peppers, it's wonderfully refreshing and spicy. It's traditional for lunch, and best at a seaside *cevichería.* See p. 72.

o **Hopping on an Andean train:** The train to Machu Picchu from Cusco is a thrilling journey through the sacred Urubamba Valley, filled with anticipation, while the train south to Lake Titicaca is full of transfixing highland scenery, also with a giant payoff at the end. See p. 200.

o **Marveling at Machu Picchu:** Cradled by the Andes and swathed in clouds, the ruins of the legendary "lost city of the Incas" are one of the world's most spectacular sites. Despite its enormous popularity, the site remains a thrilling experience, especially at sunrise, when rays of light creep over the mountaintops. See p. 198.

o **Self-medicating with *mate de coca:*** Coca-leaf tea, a legal local beverage and centuries-old tradition, gives you a break when dealing with the high altitude of the Andes—which can make your head spin and your body reel. Rural highlanders chew coca leaves, as the Incas did, but you can get nearly the same relief from coca tea. See p. 119.

o **Soaking up the sun on the southern beaches (Side Trips from Lima):** Some call the playas of Asia Peru's version of the Hamptons. During summer weekends, the city's wealthy make the 100km (62-mile) drive south from Lima to swim in beaches far superior to the capital. An entire satellite city appears with many of the same restaurants, shops, and nightspots as in the capital city. See p. 103.

- **Staring at the stars (Sacred Valley):** On a clear night, it's not hard to perceive the Incas' worship of the natural world, in which the moon was a deity. If your visit coincides with a full moon in that gargantuan sky and you identify the Southern Cross, you'll be talking about it back home for months. See p. 190.

- **Worshiping the sun at Inti Raymi (Cusco):** One of the continent's most spectacular pageants, the Festival of the Sun celebrates the winter solstice, honoring the Inca sun god with colorful Andean parades, music, and dance. The event envelops Cusco and transforms the Sacsayhuamán ruins overlooking the city into a majestic stage. See p. 136.

- **Searching for seals and penguins:** Spend a morning on a boat or yacht sailing to the Islas Ballestas near Paracas or the Islas Palomino near Callao, groups of tiny islets that are like a mini-Galapagos. Short excursions put you face to face with sea lions, Humboldt penguins, and Peruvian boobies, as well as other colonies of rare seabirds. See p. 108.

THE best ACTIVE ADVENTURES

- **Hiking the Inca Trail (Machu Picchu):** An arduous 4-day trek to Machu Picchu leads across astonishing Andean mountain passes and through some of the greatest attractions in Peru, including dozens of Inca ruins, dense cloud forest, and breathtaking mountain scenery. The trek has a superlative payoff: a sunrise arrival at the glorious ruins of Machu Picchu, shrouded in mist at your feet. See p. 212.

- **Soaring over the Costa Verde (Lima):** Lima rising from the coastal cliffs over the Pacific is perhaps the city's most emblematic visual. Get an even better look while catching a gust of wind from a Miraflores park and paragliding over the Pacific Ocean. See p. 68.

- **Trekking to really remote ruins (Sacred Valley):** Notch bragging rights by making arduous journeys to ruins you'll have virtually to yourself. Choquequirao is an Inca site still only 30 percent uncovered; it takes 4 or 5 days on foot to get there and back. Some think of it as the new Machu Picchu. See p. 220.

- **Walking in the serene Sacred Valley:** You don't have to join the crowds on the strenuous 4-day Inca Trail to Machu Picchu. Ollantaytambo and Yucay are the best bases for easy walks in the pretty countryside of the Urubamba Valley. The trek from the Inca site Moray to the ancient Salineras salt mines is particularly beautiful. See p. 179.

- **Running big-time white water:** Just beyond Cusco are some excellent river runs, ranging from mild to world-class; novices can do 1-day trips to get their feet (and more) wet, while more experienced rafters can take multiday trips that sail from the highlands into the Amazon. See p. 176.

- **Surfing the waves (Pacific Coast):** Wave connoisseurs are sweet on Peru's long Pacific coastline and a great variety of left and right reef breaks, point breaks, and big-time waves. Northern Peru, best from October to March, is the top choice of most, and surfers hang out in the easygoing fishing villages of Huanchaco and Máncora. See p. 103.

THE best RESTAURANTS

o **Astrid y Gastón (Lima):** For two decades this restaurant and its famed chef Gastón Acurio have brought more international attention to Peruvian cuisine than any other. Now set in a sprawling and historic San Isidro building with multiple dining rooms and kitchens, it is one of the world's great restaurant spaces. See p. 73.

o **Central (Lima):** This tasting-menu-only restaurant, a few blocks from the sea in Miraflores, is widely considered the best in all of Latin America. Dishes are based not just around altitude, but also on the ecosystems of rare and mostly unknown ingredients found at that altitude. See p. 73.

o **Cicciolina (Cusco):** Andean ingredients get paired with farm-to-table ethos and Mediterranean recipes at this Cusco restaurant that continues to thrive despite flashier neighbors. The quaint second-level space with exposed beams and hanging bushels of garlic gets our vote for Cusco's most romantic restaurant. See p. 140.

o **El Huacatay (Sacred Valley):** This garden-side restaurant in a mud wall compound in Urubamba has an international take on Andean ingredients, such as gnocchi made with coca flour and alpaca lasagna. It's the perfect place for a long, relaxing meal after a day of touring the valley. See p. 183.

o **La Chomba (Cusco):** *Picanterías* are rustic restaurants specializing in regional home cooking, a tradition perhaps best explored in the crisp air of Cusco, such as this no-frills eatery. Inside, giant portions of *chicharrón* (fried pork) or *cuy* (guinea pig) are washed down with giant glasses of *frutillada,* a low-alcohol maize beer livened up with strawberries. See p. 144.

o **La Mar (Lima):** Not only does this groundbreaking *cevichería* know what region their fish is being sourced from, they know exactly who the fisherman is who caught it. While La Mar has spawned satellite locations around the world, the Lima flagship continues to be a model of sustainable seafood and one of the most continually popular restaurants in town. See p. 76.

o **La Picantería (Lima):** Modeled after the rustic *picanterías* found along Peru's northern coast, this laid-back, lunch-only spot is in an out-of-the-way neighborhood, yet still lures the foodie set. Food is served family-style, primarily by choosing one of a handful of fish caught that morning and how you would like it prepared. Portions are big and hearty. See p. 79.

o **Maido (Lima):** Mitsuharu Tsumura's Miraflores restaurant has pushed Nikkei food, a natural fusion of Peruvian and Japanese cuisines, further than any other chef thus far. Don't think of it as a Japanese restaurant; this is 100 percent Peruvian that utilizes the country's diverse set of ingredients. See p. 74.

- **The Tree House (Machu Picchu):** The best restaurant in Aguas Calientes is hidden up a set of steps, just off the main plaza. Inside, a fireplace burns and a chalkboard lists Peruvian fusion dishes like pork ribs glazed with elderberry and tamarind sauce and alpaca *anticuchos*. See p. 225.

THE best HOTELS

- **Hotel B (Lima):** Originally built for a prominent Lima family by a renowned French architect as a seaside retreat, this Belle Epoque mansion is now Barranco's hippest hotel. The art-filled property, attached to Lima's hottest gallery, has helped redefine the city's hotel scene. See p. 98.
- **Hotel Monasterio (Cusco):** Simply put, this is one of the world's great hotels. Set in a former monastery that dates to 1592, a national monument, it was built over an Inca palace. From the Baroque chapel to the cloistered courtyard to the Spanish colonial artwork, every turn makes you feel like you are in a living museum. See p. 154.
- **Libertador Tambo del Inka (Sacred Valley):** Designed by iconic Lima architect Bernardo Fort-Brescia, this cushy Urubamba property has upped the hotel game in the Sacred Valley. Aside from one of the largest spas in the entire region, it has an indoor/outdoor pool and its own rail station to Machu Picchu. See p. 186.
- **Skylodge Adventure Suites (Sacred Valley):** You need to climb or zipline to get into these glass capsules on the side of a mountain. Each suite has a private bathroom and runs on solar power. It's the world's first hanging lodge, and it offers absolutely spectacular 300-degree views of the Sacred Valley. See p. 195.
- **Country Club (Lima):** This grande dame was built in 1927 and has been a center of Limeño high society ever since. Fronting the exclusive Lima Golf Club, this classic hacienda-style hotel is decorated with artwork on loan from one of the city's finest museums, plus swanky leather chairs and stained-glass windows. See p. 93.
- **Inkaterra Machu Picchu Pueblo Hotel (Machu Picchu):** Few realize that the area surrounding Machu Picchu is such diverse cloud forest. This upscale ecolodge makes sure you know any time you leave, with its 372 different native species of orchids, spectacled bear rehabilitation project, and cock-of-the-rock lek. See p. 227.
- **Second Home Peru (Lima):** With Costa Verde views, this Tudor mansion, the former home of Peruvian sculptor Victor Delfin, is one of Lima's most overlooked hotels. Family-run with a large collection of art and original details, some of the rooms even have ocean-facing terraces. See p. 99.
- **Machu Picchu Sanctuary Lodge (Machu Picchu):** There is one reason why this hotel makes this list: Machu Picchu. It's literally right outside. While all of the other nearby hotels are down in the village below, here you can see the ruins from some of the bedroom windows. It's just you and the people who have hiked the Inca Trail who are first in line for a sunrise visit. See p. 228.

o **La Lune (Cusco):** What? A hotel with just one suite? What? It has spalike bathrooms and a fireplace? What? It can fit an entire family? What? It includes all your meals at the French restaurant downstairs? Yes. Yes. Yes. And yes. See p. 156.

o **Westin Hotel & Convention Center (Lima):** For a time, this glitzy glass tower was the tallest building in all of Peru, only to be eclipsed by one next door. Lima's most modern hotel is a wonder, with state-of-the-art electronics, smart technology, and a forward-thinking wellness program. See p. 94.

THE best ARCHITECTURAL LANDMARKS

o **Ollantaytambo:** Ollanta's fortress ruins have some of the Incas' finest stonemasonry, including 200 stone steps straight to the top. Another engineering genius is the grid of 15th-century *canchas,* or city blocks, that form the old town. Canals ripple alongside the stone streets, carrying water down from the mountains. See p. 189.

o **Inca masonry (Cusco):** Monumental Inca walls, constructed of giant granite blocks so well carved that they fit together without mortar like jigsaw puzzle pieces, dominate historic Cusco. Down alleyways lined with polygonal stones, kids can pick out the famous 12-angled stone and a series of stones that forms the shape of a large puma. See p. 128.

o **Sacsayhuamán (Cusco):** Among the Incas' greatest ruins, these zigzagged defensive walls—with some blocks weighing as much as 300 tons—are an unexpected delight for kids. Some large stones have time-worn grooves, which children have discovered make great slides. And nearby is a stone funhouse of claustrophobia-inducing tunnels. See p. 132.

o **Colonial Lima:** The original core of Lima, once the Americas' richest settlement, preserves a wealth of handsome colonial-era architecture that has survived fires, earthquakes, and decades of neglect. Visit baroque churches and monasteries and restored colonial mansions with long carved-wood balconies. See p. 58.

o **Caral-Supe (Side Trips from Lima):** The first constructions at the settlement of Caral-Supe in the desert north of Lima date as far back as 2600 B.C., leading many to call it the oldest city in the Americas. Excavations are still ongoing, but many of the plazas and residential buildings have already been reconstructed. Still, few international tourists even know it exists. See p. 101.

o **The Bridge of Sighs (Lima):** Barranco was a seaside retreat for wealthy Limeños during the Republican era, and they built mansions along wide, leafy streets. The neighborhood's architectural centerpiece is the Puente de los Suspiros, a wooden bridge crossing a sloping boardwalk that runs down to the beach below. See p. 63.

UNDISCOVERED PERU

o **Crossing cultures at Fiesta de la Cruz:** The Festival of the Cross isn't as solemnly Catholic as it sounds. Best in Lima, Cusco, and Ica, the festival features vibrant cross processions as well as folk music and dance, the highlight being the famed and daring "scissors dancers," who long ago performed on top of churches. See p. 47.

o **Going wild at Virgen del Carmen (Paucartambo):** The minuscule, remote Andean colonial village of Paucartambo hosts one of Peru's wildest festivals. The 3 days of dance, drinking, and frightening costumes pack in thousands, who camp all over town and then wind up (only temporarily, one hopes) at the cemetery. See p. 47.

o **Hitting a purple patch at El Señor de los Milagros (Lima):** Prince would love this highly religious procession—the largest procession in South America—with tens of thousands of reverent followers clad in bright purple. The Lord of Miracles lasts an entire day and venerates a painting of Jesus Christ, created by an Angolan slave and a lone survivor of the devastating 1746 earthquake. See p. 48.

o **Raising an eyebrow at Larco Herrera (Lima):** Peru's great museums are almost all in Lima, and this archaeology collection includes 45,000 pieces of pre-Columbian art from the Moche dynasty (A.D. 200–700). Pornographic ceramics, with massive phalluses in compromising positions in the Moche Sala Erótica may give you a jolt. See p. 62.

o **Sampling *chifa* and Nikkei:** Large Chinese and Japanese immigrant populations have greatly influenced modern Peruvian cooking. Go upscale with raw fish at Costanera 700, or try what's become a Peruvian staple: *chifa,* a local variant of Chinese. See p. 71.

o **Trying Andean delicacies and libations:** *Chicha,* home-brewed beer made from fermented maize, is served at modest taverns or homes flying the *chicha* flag—a long pole with a red flag or balloon letting people know there's *chicha* inside. Served lukewarm in plastic tumblers, it's not to many foreigners' liking. Equally hard to swallow is *cuy,* or guinea pig, an inexplicable local delicacy with more teeth and bones than meat. See p. 33.

THE best MARKETS & SHOPPING

o **Barrio de San Blas (Cusco):** Cusco's most flavorful shopping zone is the picturesque neighborhood of San Blas, which rises into the hills and bursts with the workshops of artists and artisans, art galleries, and ceramics shops. Duck into studios and see artists at work. See p. 125.

o **Chinchero's handicrafts market:** Less known than Pisac's market, but more authentic and with higher-quality artisanal goods. Sellers from remote mountain populations still wear traditional garments. But be warned: The altitude is as dizzying as the textiles. See p. 182.

o **Mercado de Artesanía (Pisac):** Though the country's most popular market, this lively institution—awash in colorful Andean textiles, including rugs, sweaters, and ponchos—still cannot be missed. It takes over the central plaza and spills across adjoining streets. See p. 173.

o **Mercado de San Pedro (Cusco):** It's only a few blocks from Cusco's Plaza de Armas, yet few tourists even realize it is there. Cusco's central market is a wonderland of strange Andean products, especially the rows upon rows of different native tubers. There are also natural medicines, wood kitchen utensils, handicrafts, local cheeses, and juice bars using fruits trucked in from the Amazon. See p. 130.

o **Miraflores (Lima):** The upscale Miraflores neighborhood is full of shops stocked to the rafters with handicrafts, silver jewelry, and antiques from around Peru. For one-stop shopping, *artesanía* mini-malls not far from Parque Kennedy have the country's widest selection of ceramics, textiles, and art. For contemporary goods, there's the Larcomar shopping center, hanging off the cliffs of the Costa Verde, with a mix of local and international designer stores. See p. 53.

o **Pablo Seminario (Urubamba):** The ceramicist Pablo Seminario operates out of a laid-back place that's equal parts home, workshop, zoo, and storefront—easily one of the coolest ceramics shops in Peru. His work features funky pre-Columbian motifs. See p. 179.

o **Visiting Surquillo food market (Lima):** It's not the fanciest market, but if you want to get a feel for where Lima's top chefs and local families shop for fresh produce, seafood, and meats, don't miss this lively, redolent market at the edge of Miraflores, a fascinating food-shopping and cultural experience. See p. 83.

SUGGESTED LIMA, CUSCO & MACHU PICCHU ITINERARIES

Y ou want to get the most out of your trip to Peru in the time that you have available. Here are some ideas for structuring your travels. Unless you have a solid month to spend, you probably won't get to see as much of Peru as you'd wish, at least on a first trip. Peru is deceptively large, and at least as important are the considerable geographic and transportation barriers that complicate zipping around the country. Some regions require difficult travel by land, with no air access. It's ill-advised to try to do too much in too short a period; in addition to travel distances and transportation routes, you've got to take into account other factors—such as jet lag and acclimatization to high altitude—that require most visitors to slow down. Of course, slowing down is never a bad thing, so feel free to trim the itinerary, too—particularly since several of the itineraries are go, go, go—and add days in a particularly relaxing place, such as the Sacred Valley or the beaches south of Lima.

REGIONS IN BRIEF

Peru shares borders with Ecuador and Colombia to the north, Brazil and Bolivia to the east, and Chile to the south. It lies just below the Equator and is the third-largest country in South America—larger than France and Spain combined, covering an area of nearly 1,300,000 sq. km (500,000 sq. miles). Peruvians will tell you that their country comprises three distinct geological components: coast, *sierra* (highlands), and *selva* (jungle). The capital, Lima, and most major cities are on the coast, but the Amazon rainforest, which makes up nearly two-thirds of Peru, and the bold Andes mountain range dominate its topography.

The Central Coast   The Pacific coastal region is a narrow strip that runs from one end of the country to the other (a distance of some 2,200km/1,400 miles) and is almost entirely desert. Lima, the capital, lies about halfway down the coast. To the south, in one of the driest areas on Earth, are Pisco, Ica, and Paracas, the cradle of several of Peru's most important ancient civilizations, as well as the Ballestas Islands, promoted locally as "Peru's Galápagos" for their diverse indigenous fauna. The area is especially prone to earthquakes, such as the devastating one that struck the region in August 2007.

Cusco & the Sacred Valley   The dramatic Andes mountains in south-central Peru contain the country's most famous sights, including the former Inca capital of Cusco and scenic highland villages that run the length of the beautiful Sacred Valley. Cusco sits at an elevation of some 3,400m (11,000 ft.). The valley is dotted with singularly impressive Inca ruins, of which Machu Picchu (and the Inca Trail leading to it) is undoubtedly the star. Indigenous culture is particularly strong in the region.

Machu Picchu   You immediately get a sense of how quickly the landscape can change on the train ride between Cusco and Machu Picchu when you suddenly have the need to take off your jacket. The ancient city is found in the high jungle 2,430m (7,972 ft.) above sea level, a meeting point between the Andes and the Amazon Basin. The sparsely populated surrounding region is home to various tropical microclimates teeming with rare flora and fauna that includes countless species of orchids, as well as spectacled bears, condors, and the Andean cock-of-the-rock.

THE BEST OF PERU IN 2 WEEKS

This 2-week itinerary will allow you to experience many of Peru's biggest attractions, from its historic colonial cities to its natural wonders. You will start and end your journey in the capital of Lima, though the primary check on everyone's bucket list, of course, are the lively ancient Inca capital Cusco and that empire's legendary lost city, Machu Picchu. After your fill of adventuring in the highlands, a few days on the beach will be waiting, though you wouldn't be the first to find it irresistible to linger in Cusco and the Sacred Valley (especially if you want to hike the Inca Trail or do another highland trek).

Day 1: Touch Down in Lima

All international flights arrive into the capital, Lima, and even though most people are headed elsewhere, you may want or find yourself obligated to spend at least a day in Lima. Make the most of it by touring the revitalized **colonial quarter** of Lima Centro (p. 58), or perhaps visiting one of the country's outstanding museums, such as the **Museo Rafael Larco Herrera** archaeology museum (p. 62), and hitting either a great *cevichería* or a cutting-edge *novo andino* restaurant.

The Best of Lima, Cusco & Machu Picchu in 2 Weeks

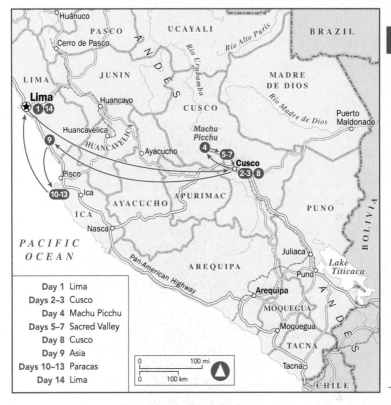

Huánuco

PASCO
Cerro de Pasco

UCAYALI

Río Alto Purús

BRAZIL

LIMA
JUNIN

Lima
① ⑭

Huancayo

Huancavelica

HUANCAVELICA

Ayacucho

Pisco

⑩-⑬ Ica

AYACUCHO

ICA

Nasca

PACIFIC
OCEAN

Pan-American Highway

Río Urubamba

ANDES

CUSCO

Machu
Picchu
④ ➤ ⑤-⑦

MADRE
DE DIOS

Río Madre de Dios

Puerto
Maldonado

Cusco
②-③ ⑧

APURIMAC

AREQUIPA

Juliaca

Puno

Arequipa

MOQUEGUA

Moquegua

TACNA

Tacna

PUNO

BOLIVIA

Lake
Titicaca

ANDES

CHILE

Day 1 Lima
Days 2–3 Cusco
Day 4 Machu Picchu
Days 5–7 Sacred Valley
Day 8 Cusco
Day 9 Asia
Days 10–13 Paracas
Day 14 Lima

0   100 mi
0   100 km

Then move on your way to Peru's most famous Inca attractions. (If you're able to get an overnight flight that puts you into Lima early in the morning, you may want to consider an immediate connection to Cusco to save time and avoid the hassles of Lima, buying yourself an extra day elsewhere.)

Days 2 & 3: Cusco, Inca Capital

Although your goal might be to hit Cusco running, the city's lofty altitude, more than 3,400m (11,000 ft.), prohibits that. Spend a couple of days seeing the old Inca capital at a relaxed pace, making sure to hang out around the **Plaza de Armas** and visit **La Catedral (Cathedral), Convento de Santa Catalina (Santa Catalina Convent),** and **Qoricancha (Temple of the Sun).** Cusco is one of the best places in Peru to shop, eat, and party, so make sure to squeeze those vital activities in with sightseeing.

Day 4: The Stuff of Legend: Machu Picchu

Though Machu Picchu really deserves an overnight stay, if you're trying to see the best of Peru in 2 weeks, you can't afford the time. So take the morning train from Cusco to Machu Picchu **(Aguas Calientes),** South America's number-one attraction. Spend the middle part of the day exploring the **ruins** here (p. 207), spending the night in town.

Days 5–7: Soaking Up the Sacred Valley

Take a morning train from Aguas Calientes direct to the **Sacred Valley** (p. 189), the heartland of the Incas and home to many important architectural and cultural attractions. Base yourself at one of the country-style lodges in **Urubamba** (p. 185), giving yourself ample time to make short trips to the market and ruins at **Pisac** (p. 173), the **Salineras de Maras** and terraces of **Moray** (p. 179), and the fortress of **Ollantaytambo** (p. 190). Make time to go mountain biking, hiking, or horseback riding, as well as to participate in a *pachamanca,* a ritual feast where food is cooked in an earthen oven.

Day 8: Back in Cusco

If you weren't able to catch an archaeology museum in Lima, or even if you did, check out the beautifully designed **Museo de Arte Precolombino** (**MAP;** p. 126). Enjoy some of the lively cafes, bars, and restaurants of Cusco; you'll find plenty while strolling around the **Barrio de San Blas** (p. 125). If you have time and plenty of energy, catch a cab (or walk up) to the fantastic Inca ruins overlooking the city, **Sacsayhuamán** (p. 132).

Day 9: Heading South

From Cusco, catch an early flight back to Lima, renting a car at the airport upon landing and head south along the Pan-American Highway. Make a pit stop for ice cream made from lúcuma at **Helados OVNI** (p. 106), a roadside stand in Chilca, but then continue on to the beaches of **Asia** (p. 104), a satellite city at Km 100 that appears during the summer months, where you can find a hotel or resort on one of the nearby beaches.

Days 10–13: Paracas

In recent years, the resort area along Paracas Bay has become one of the most activity-rich destinations in coastal Peru. Over the next few days, while basing yourself in one of a handful of recently opened resort-style hotels, your options of things to do are seemingly endless: kitesurfing in the bay, riding dune buggies or sandboarding on sand dunes, visiting pisco distilleries near Ica, or just relaxing by the pool or at the spa. Additionally, the Islas Ballestas Marine Reserve (p. 108), filled with colonies of sea lions and seabirds, is just a short boat ride away. Return to Lima the final afternoon.

Day 14: Final Morning in Lima, and Then Home

Arequipa is Peru's top spot for fine alpaca goods. Spend the morning shopping for sweaters, shawls, and scarves before flying to **Lima,** where you'll catch your flight back home.

CUSCO HIGHLANDS IN 1 WEEK

With a single week in Peru, it's best to concentrate on a manageable regional trip. For first-timers, there's one place almost everyone has absolutely got to see: Machu Picchu. I certainly have no problem with that; it's perhaps the top sight in South America. In one week, you can experience Cusco, the Inca capital that's become a dynamic travelers' hub; the empire's once-thought-lost imperial city; and the serene Urubamba Valley that the Incas held sacred.

Day 1: Through Cusco to the Sacred Valley

All international flights arrive in Lima, but try to arrange it so that an overnight flight gets you there very early in the morning, with time enough to get an 8 or 9am flight to Cusco (note that flights are occasionally delayed by weather in Cusco, so the earlier the flight, the better). With only a week in Peru, there's little need to linger in Lima unless you want a day to take it easy and see the colonial quarter of Lima Centro and have lunch at a *cevichería.*

Because the altitude in Cusco (more than 3,400m/11,000 ft.) is so daunting, head first to the lower Sacred Valley and save the capital city for the end of your trip. Relax at a country hotel in the Sacred Valley (most can arrange a pickup at Cusco airport); see Chapter 7 for options.

Day 2: Pisac's Market & Inca Ruins

If possible, schedule your trip so that Day 2 is a market day (Tuesday, Thursday, or, best of all, Sunday). Take a *combi* or taxi to Pisac and check out the lively **artisans' market** in the Plaza de Armas. Have lunch at **Ulrike's Café** (p. 175), right on the main square. After lunch visit the great **Inca ruins** (p. 173) looming above town; either hike up to them (this may be very challenging for those who've just arrived) or take a taxi. Pisac's ruins will give you a taste of what you're about to see in Ollantaytambo and Machu Picchu. Head a little farther along in the valley (again by taxi or *combi*) to a rustic country hotel near **Urubamba** or **Yucay,** where you'll have dinner and spend the night.

Day 3: On to Ollantaytambo

Wake early and take a *combi* or taxi to **Ollantaytambo** (p. 189) to explore the spectacular **Fortress Ruins** (p. 190) before the busloads arrive. Then grab lunch at **Café Mayu** (p. 192) by the train station and wander the Inca **Old Town** (p. 192). Energetic travelers can climb the path up to old Inca granaries for great views of Ollanta and the valley. Or take a taxi back toward Urubamba and hike along the river to **Salineras de Maras** (p. 179), the ancient salt mines, or catch a *combi* and then taxi to **Moray,** an enigmatic Inca agricultural site.

If you don't mind moving around, you could transfer to a hotel in Ollanta to enjoy it at night when there are few tourists (and be there early for the train the next morning to Machu Picchu). Otherwise, head back to your hotel in the valley around Urubamba.

Cusco Highlands in 1 Week

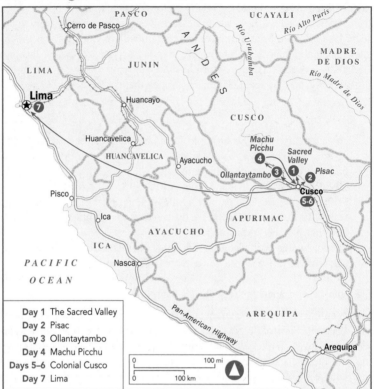

Day 1	The Sacred Valley
Day 2	Pisac
Day 3	Ollantaytambo
Day 4	Machu Picchu
Days 5–6	Colonial Cusco
Day 7	Lima

Day 4: What You Came for: Machu Picchu

Catch an early-morning train from Ollantaytambo to **Aguas Calientes** (p. 189). Catch the bus up to the ruins and spend the day exploring the site (hiking up to the **Huayna Picchu peak** for panoramic views, if you're in shape; p. 209). Have lunch at the Machu Picchu Sanctuary Lodge next to the ruins and stay until late in the afternoon, after the large tour groups have left. Spend the night either next to the ruins (if you've got very deep pockets) or back down in Aguas Calientes (which is actually more fun). Hit the bars along the railroad tracks to share stories with some of the backpackers who've survived the Inca Trail.

Days 5 & 6: Colonial Cusco

Sticking to the area near the Plaza de Armas, visit the **Cathedral** (p. 122) and the **Santa Catalina Convent** (p. 127) in the morning. After lunch, see the stunning **Qoricancha** (**Temple of the Sun;** p. 129), the site that best illustrates Cusco's clash of Inca and Spanish cultures. Take a walk along the **Calles Loreto** and **Hatunrumiyoc** to see some more magnificent Inca stonework. In Plaza Nazarenas, check out the beautifully designed **Museo** de **Arte Precolombino** (**MAP;** p. 126) and some of the upscale alpaca goods shops on the square. Then stop for a celebratory dinner at **MAP Café** (p. 138), the chic restaurant in the museum's courtyard, or **Limo,** for sushi and superb views of the Plaza de Armas (p. 141). End the evening with a pisco sour at one of the lively cafes or bars near the Plaza de Armas.

The next morning, pop into a few alpaca and silver jewelry shops around the Plaza de Armas and Plaza Nazarenas. Hike up to the hilly **San Blas** (p. 125) neighborhood, site of dozens of cool shops and art galleries, and do some shopping for handicrafts, souvenirs, and art. Have a relaxing lunch at **Jack's Café Bar** (p. 143), a popular gringo hangout. After lunch, catch a cab (or walk) up to **Sacsayhuamán** (p. 132), the fantastic ruins overlooking the city. For dinner, try **Cicciolina** (p. 140) or **ChiCha,** a star chef's take on local Cusqueña cuisine (p. 140). Later, get a taste of Cusco's hopping nightlife at one of the pubs or nightclubs around the Plaza de Armas.

Day 7: To Lima & Home

Have a final stroll around Cusco before catching a flight to Lima. You'll probably have an evening flight back home, so you may have enough time for a ceviche lunch in Lima and, if you're ambitious, a short tour of colonial **Lima Centro** (p. 58) in the late afternoon.

FOODIE LIMA IN 3 DAYS

Lima's culinary scene is so vibrant and strong—many put it on the same level as a place like Paris or Tokyo—that many travelers just forgo all other sightseeing and focus on the food. This short itinerary takes in the best restaurants, markets, *cevicherías, chifas,* pisco bars, and breweries in Lima, from street food stalls to the eateries of some of the world's finest chefs.

Day 1: Ceviche & Rare Ingredients

Start your day with a light snack at **Pan de la Chola,** an artisan bakery that uses flours from native wheat and grain, as well as serves fair trade coffee from Peruvian producers. Lay out your map and plot your day. Your first stop will be at **La Mar** (p. 76), Gastón Acurio's famed *cevichería,* a restaurant that helped turn Peru's national dish into a worldwide phenomenon. It's one of the most transparent seafood restaurants anywhere as it traces the catch back to the very fisherman who caught it. Make this your first taste of ceviche, as well as other coastal dishes like *tiradito,* thinly sliced raw seafood in lime and chile sauce, or *pulpo al oilvo,* octopus in a purple olive sauce. Swing by **Nuevo Mundo Draft Bar** (p. 84) for a pint of Peruvian and spend the next few hours strolling along the Miraflores *malecón* (pier) to burn a few calories. Rest and clean up before dinner at **Central** (p. 73) for an elaborate tasting menu based on altitude from internationally renowned chef Virgilio Martinez. Follow up with drinks at the bar of **Amaz** (p. 74), an Amazonian-themed restaurant that has one of the city's best bar programs, often infusing pisco with Amazonian fruits and herbs.

Day 2: Markets, Chifa & Nikkei

Wake up early to see the **Terminal de Chorrillos** (p. 53) in full swing. As the painted wooden boats return from sea, you'll get the sense that this intimate fish market at the southern edge of Lima is a small coastal village rather than a big city suburb. Catch a taxi to the **Mercado de Surquillo** (p. 83), a neighborhood market with a varied collection of unique fruits and vegetables from the Andes, Amazon, and coast. Step up to a juice bar for a glass filled with the pumpkin- and maple-tasting *lúcuma,* or the high-in-vitamin-C *camu camu.* Hop on the Metropolitano, the mass transit bus line to downtown Lima, and explore Lima's historic center, eventually ending up in the Barrio Chino, Lima's Chinatown. Have lunch on the pedestrian-only Calle Capón at one of the many *chifas,* Peruvian Chinese restaurants, such as **Salón de la Felicidad** (p. 71). Afterward, walk about 7 blocks, passing the Plaza de Armas, to **Bar Maury,** where the pisco sour was invented in the 1930s. Spend the rest of the afternoon around the plaza visiting attractions or return to your hotel and rest. End the day tasting Nikkei food, a fusion of Peruvian ingredients with Japanese cooking techniques, at **Maido** (p. 74) in Miraflores.

Day 3: Coffee & Criolla

Start your day on Parque Kennedy in Miraflores at **La Lucha** (p. 77) to try a favorite Peruvian breakfast, *pan con chicharrón,* a sandwich with fried pork and slices of boiled sweet potato topped with onion relish. Wash it down with a glass of granadilla, a type of passion fruit. Jump on the Metropolitano to the bohemian neighborhood of Barranco, walking past the plaza to **Café Bisetti** (p. 80), a roaster that specializes in native Peruvian coffees. Spend the middle part of the day visiting art galleries or strolling across the Puente de los Suspiros, the neighborhood's iconic wooden bridge. When ready, **Isolina** (p. 80), a two-level *criolla taberna,* is waiting. Here you can order classic Limeño dishes like *tacu tacu* (refried rice and beans) or *cau-cau* (a tripe and potato stew). While there is still daylight, catch a taxi down to the beach to **La Rosa Nautica** (p. 75), a Victorian-style seafood restaurant and bar on a pier set over the Pacific Ocean. Order a pisco sour in the lounge area as the sun is setting. If you are still hungry, the dining room is just a few steps away.

TWO WEEKS OF OUTDOOR ADVENTURES IN PERU

Few places pack the kind of outdoor bounty and natural beauty into their borders the way Peru does. This itinerary is designed for high-octane thrill-seekers, to take in some of Peru's most scenic natural areas as well as give a taste of some unusual ways to tackle the outdoors. For a pure adrenaline rush, it's hard to beat incredible Andean treks, white-water rafting, mountain biking past ancient ruins, and board surfing on towering sand dunes.

Two Weeks of Outdoor Adventures in Peru

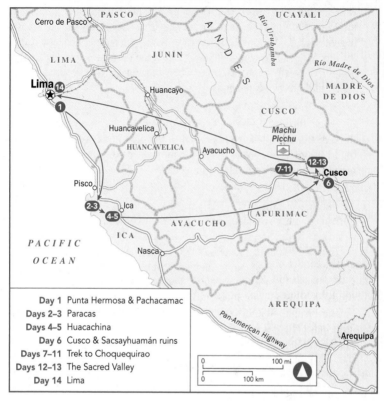

Day 1   Punta Hermosa & Pachacamac
Days 2–3   Paracas
Days 4–5   Huacachina
Day 6   Cusco & Sacsayhuamán ruins
Days 7–11   Trek to Choquequirao
Days 12–13   The Sacred Valley
Day 14   Lima

Day 1: South of Lima

Spend your first day in the country just south of Lima. Make your way to **Punta Hermosa** (p. 104), one of the most reliable surf spots on Peru's central coast. Either rent a board or take a lesson with a local pro in the chilly waters. After a lunch of ceviche at one of the no-frills beach shacks, join a bike tour of **Pachacámac** (p. 102) in the valley of the Lurín River, a place of organic farms and a sizable pyramid complex that dates back more than 1,000 years. You can either return to Lima that night or camp down in a small hotel in the area.

Days 2 & 3: Paracas

Spend the following morning driving south to **Paracas,** several hours south of Lima, camping down in a coastal resort on the waterfront. In the afternoons when the winds pick up, this sheltered bay becomes a hotspot for **wind or kitesurfing,** and most hotels can provide equipment or give lessons. In the morning when the wind is calmer, you can **kayak** in the bay, keeping your eyes open for the occasional dolphin or sea lion.

Days 4 & 5: Huacachina

Check into a small hotel near the oasis of **Huacachina** outside of Ica. Rent a sandboard from one of the shops around the lagoon or join a dune buggy tour through the dunes for the rest of the day. Early the next morning, hike up to the top of the dunes to watch the sunrise. For the rest of the day, you can go with a guide to search the desert for fossilized shells and shark teeth, remnants from when the region was covered by the ocean millions of years ago.

Day 6: A Breather in Cusco

Fly back through Lima and on to Cusco. In the afternoon, hike up through the San Blas neighborhood to the grand **Sacsayhuamán ruins** (p. 132), one of the Incas' finest monuments. Take it easy getting acclimatized on what is essentially a rest day.

Days 7–11: Trek to Choquequirao

An alternative to the Inca Trail, embark on this 4-day trek to **Choquequirao** (p. 220), spectacular but rarely visited Inca ruins high above the Apurímac River. The route descends to a campsite next to the river, only to climb 1,219 vertical meters (4,000 ft.) the next day. (Choquequirao is just one of several stunning multi-day treks in the Cusco highlands; if you've never been to Peru before, you may want to opt for the grand-daddy of them all, the Inca Trail, which takes you right to the foot of Machu Picchu.) White-water fanatics might prefer to trade a 4-day rafting trip for the trek to Choquequirao.

Days 12 & 13: The Sacred Valley

After your trek down from Choquequirao, come back to earth in the serene Sacred Valley of the Incas. Here you can do one day's **white-water rafting** on the Urubamba River, or if you'd prefer to keep your hiking boots on, do a day hike and walk from the Inca site of Moray down to the **Salineras salt mines** at Maras (p. 179; 3 hr.).

Day 14: Above the Fray in Lima

Although there's adventure enough in Lima just dodging murderous traffic, there's one last opportunity for outdoors adventure before your flight out. If you're lucky, you'll have a chance to catch a thermal current and get up in the air in a **paraglider,** soaring out over Miraflores and the Costa Verde (p. 68).

LIMA, CUSCO & MACHU PICCHU FOR FAMILIES IN 8 DAYS

Despite how exotic the country can feel to many visitors, with some minimal planning, Peru can also be quite family friendly. In this 8-day itinerary, there is more than enough to keep children of multiple ages stimulated without ever stepping off the beaten path.

Day 1: Urban Exploring

Get your children's attention right from the start of the trip. Take them to **Lima's historic center,** making a beeline for the **Convento de San Francisco de Asis** (p. 59), a colonial-era church and convent with a spectacular library of old books, which will not blow their minds nearly as much as the catacombs beneath the complex, where tens of thousands of bones are spookily arranged in intricate patterns. Afterward, stroll over to the **Plaza Mayor** (p. 58), making sure to catch the changing of the guards at the **Palacio de Gobierno** (p. 58), precisely at noon. After lunch in the **Barrio Chino,** taxi to **Huaca Pucllana** (p. 67) in Miraflores, where your kids will love exploring a 4th-century pyramid complex and dining at a restaurant overlooking the site.

Day 2: Out on the Water

From the district of **Callao,** spend the day on a boat trip to the **Islas Palomino,** where you'll spot nesting seabirds such as Peruvian boobies and Inca terns, as well as Humboldt penguins. Some tours will even allow groups to jump in the water with a wetsuit and snorkel to swim with sea lions. Return to your hotel in the afternoon, and then end the day at the **Larcomar Shopping Center** (p. 83), a mall and entertainment complex peering over Lima's coastal cliffs.

Days 3 & 4: Ahhh! Stimulation Everywhere!

With the city's high altitude, keep Cusco plans light and flexible. Take your time strolling through museums like the very visual and interactive **Museo Machu Picchu Casa Concha** or the **Museo de Arte Precolombino (MAP)** (p. 126), which will give kids a history lesson and build up their excitement for their upcoming trip to Machu Picchu. Spend some time hanging out on the **Plaza de Armas** and visit **La Catedral** (p. 58), then move uphill to pedestrian-only Calle Hatunrumiyoc and point out the 12-angled stone outline of the puma immersed in the wall. Plan an afternoon for **Sacsayhuamán** (p. 132), not just the ruins but the huge rocks with slick grooves that make for superb slides, plus a meal at Gastón Acurio's burger joint **Papacho's** (p. 143), which will be familiar enough for the kids and have enough booze to keep parents happy. Save some time for shopping distractions that will undoubtedly arise.

Day 5: Crowd-Pleaser Machu Picchu

Take a train from Poroy, Cusco's nearest rail station, to Aguas Calientes at the base of Machu Picchu. Plan on spending the night in town, giving you ample time to explore the **ruins** (p. 205) at the pace the kids can handle, rather than rushing in and out.

Days 6 & 7: Soaking Up the Sacred Valley

Allow everyone to sleep in (or if they're up for it, take an early walk along the riverfront) and then catch a train to the **Sacred Valley,** checking in to the **Aranwa Sacred Valley Hotel** (p. 186) outside Urubamba, where the family can spend the next 2 nights enjoying the pool and spa, taking excursions to the market and ruins at **Pisac** (p. 173), and touring the **Salineras de Maras.**

Day 8: Back to Lima

Catch a morning flight back to Lima. Spend your last day picking up any souvenirs you haven't bought at the **Mercado Indio** (p. 82) close to Parque Kennedy in Miraflores. Prepare for your flight home.

PERU IN CONTEXT

P eru has a habit of turning virtually every visitor into an amateur archaeologist or outdoors enthusiast. Intriguing ruins, the legacies of the Incas, and even more ancient pre-Columbian cultures fire the imagination, and outstanding museum collections of ceramics, textiles, and remarkably preserved mummies weave a complex tale of some of the world's most advanced cultures. Dense tracts of Amazon rainforest and forbidding Andes summits are known to only a select few adventurers. And yet—Machu Picchu's immense popularity notwithstanding—with so many sites still being excavated, and ruins almost continually discovered in remote jungle regions, Peru still has the rare feeling of a country in the 21st century that hasn't been exhaustively explored.

The third-largest country in South America (after Brazil and Argentina), Peru has grown immensely as a travel destination over the past decade—though it still seems comparatively undervalued, given all it has to offer. With spectacular Andes Mountains and highland culture, Amazon rainforest second only to Brazil, a rich array of wildlife, and some of the Americas' greatest ruins of pre-Columbian cultures, Peru deserves to be experienced by so many more people.

When the Spanish conquistador Francisco Pizarro and his fortune-hunting cronies descended on Peru in 1528, they found not only vast riches, but also a highly sophisticated culture. The Spaniards soon overpowered the awed and politically weakened Inca Empire, but they didn't discover the Incas' greatest secret: the imperial city of Machu Picchu, today acclaimed as the pinnacle achievement of the continent's pre-Columbian societies.

Most people still know Peru only as the land of the Incas. Yet today it is a land of dynamic, cosmopolitan cities with world-class restaurants; indeed, Peru's tantalizing regional cuisines have taken many parts of the world by storm, on the shoulders of a few celebrity chef-ambassadors. Mountain bikers and surfers, ice climbers and mountaineers, birders and naturalists are flocking to Peru's vast jungle, desert, coast, and mountains.

While it embraces its traditions and storied pre-Columbian past, Peru is undeniably a country on the move. Just a couple of decades removed from military dictatorships, extreme poverty, and homegrown terrorism, Peruvians are proud of their nation's new incarnation as a stable democracy with enviable economic growth. The novelist Mario Vargas Llosa, winner of the 2010 Nobel Prize for Literature, has extolled his country's economic and social progress: "I do not remember—and I'm 75 years old—a time when Peru has had such a good image abroad."

Peru's fascinating history is in evidence everywhere: in mortarless Inca stones that serve as foundations for colonial churches, in open graves with bits and pieces of ancient textiles, and in traditional dress, foods, and festivals, as well as strongly held Andean customs and beliefs. Visitors to Peru will discover a country and a people rooted in a glorious past but looking forward to a future of new possibilities.

PERU TODAY

Peru's recent history of suffering—2 decades of political mayhem and corruption, hyperinflation, surprise attacks from homegrown Maoist "Shining Path" terrorists, cocaine trafficking, and violent street crime—is well documented. Throughout the 1980s and early '90s, Peruvians fled the capital and the countryside, fearful of attack; few travelers were brave enough to plan vacations in the troubled nation.

Though Peru is rich in artifacts and culture, it remains poor and a society dominated by elites. Although a third of the population lives at or below the poverty line, in recent years the level of extreme poverty has dropped considerably, to 4.3 percent. The horrendous violence of 2 decades ago has now almost completely abated, and outside of areas deep in the jungle, there are no areas where visitors should not feel welcome to travel. Rumors of a Shining Path revival have not been borne out, even though at least two major attacks in the last decade, including a bombing near the U.S. Embassy in Lima, have been attributed to the group.

The disgraced and now ailing former president Alberto Fujimori, who fled the country to live in exile in Japan, was arrested in Chile in 2005 attempting to return to Peru in a surprise bid to run for president. Extradited to Peru and jailed, Fujimori was convicted on charges of ordering the murders of suspected Shining Path guerrillas and their collaborators by death squad (he remains in a jail in Lima for his role in ordering death squads, along with three other concurrent sentences, including for abuse of power, bribery, and illegal wiretapping of phones). The trial marked the first time in Peruvian history that a former president has been tried for crimes committed during his administration.

With the 2001 election of Alejandro Toledo, the country's first president of native Indian origin, many Peruvians believed that the country had finally turned a corner and that the 21st century would bring stability, progress, and prosperity. Although the economy initially grew at an impressive rate, the road to a safer and more stable Peru ran into more than a few bumps along the way. Like previous governments, Toledo's administration was plagued by instability, abuse of power, and poor management, opening the door for former president Alan García, who returned from exile abroad and improbably captured the 2006 presidential election. García positioned himself as a centrist, seeking to put a clamp on inflation and aggressively pursuing free-market policies. Most notably, he pushed aggressively for a free-trade agreement with the United States, a treaty entered into force in 2009. The Peruvian economy recorded a robust growth rate of 9.2 percent in 2008, a 15-year high and one of the most impressive in the world.

But Peru's political realities continue to be unique, if not surreal. The former army officer Ollanta Humala was elected in 2011, defeating Keiko Fujimori, the right-wing daughter of former (and you'll recall, jailed) Alberto Fujimori. Humala, previously a firebrand and outspoken nationalist, battled Shining Path guerrillas, led a military uprising against Fujimori in 2000, and is saddled with a controversial family (including a brother jailed for kidnapping and killing police officers). But he posited himself as a non-ideological reformer in the model of Brazil's transformative former president Luiz Inacio Lula da Silva, a one-time leftist labor union leader who oversaw Brazil's rise to global economic prominence. Like Lula, Humala argued that he was poised to cement Peru's economic and social transformation into a modern, stable democratic nation.

The Peruvian economy has continued to expand, dropping off slightly in recent years as demand for raw products has slowed. Although much of that growth has been stimulated by foreign investment in mining and other sectors, from which few Peruvians benefit, there is a growing sense of optimism. Tourism growth has averaged 10 percent annually, with record-setting numbers of travelers (1 million plus) embarking on ecotourism in Peru's protected natural areas, and a dizzying number of swank new hotels (both Peruvian and internationally owned) springing up across the country, including in far-flung places like the banks of Lake Titicaca, Colca Canyon, and the formerly ramshackle, hippie beach destination Máncora. Peru is poised to become the second-largest coffee producer in South America, and is projected to register one of the highest growth rates and lowest inflation rates in the Americas, just behind the region's juggernaut, Brazil. The capital Lima, experiencing a real-estate boom, has undertaken construction of a better mass transit network. Mario Vargas Llosa, Peru's most famous novelist (and former presidential candidate), won the Nobel Prize for Literature in 2010, becoming the first Peruvian to do so, and also for the first time, a Peruvian film, "The Milk of Sorrow," was nominated for an Academy Award for Best Foreign Film. The acclaimed Afro-Peruvian singer Susana Baca was named Peru's Minister of Culture in 2011 (becoming the first black minister in Peru's history), and major international pop stars like Bono of U2 have descended on Cusco, Machu Picchu, and Tambopata National Reserve, validating Peru's rising profile.

WATCH YOUR language

The term *cholo* is often used to describe Peruvians of color and obvious Amerindian descent, usually those who have migrated from the highlands to the city. It is frequently employed as a derogatory and racist term by the Limeño population of European descent, but former President Alejandro Toledo claimed the term for himself and all *mestizos* (those of mixed race) of Peru, to demonstrate pride in their common culture and to take the sting out of the term.

Afro-Peruvians are more commonly called *morenos(as)* or *negros(as)*. Using any of these terms can potentially be a complicated and charged matter for foreigners, especially those who have little experience in the country or fluency in the language. It's best for gringos (foreigners; almost always not a derogatory term) simply to steer clear of such linguistic territory. It's better to refrain from making distinctions among races and colors than to risk offending someone.

Though there's an incipient national swagger that's been sorely missing for decades, based on the prospects of prosperity for some and the renewed growth of a middle class, in Peru the divide between rich and poor, coastal elites and indigenous highlanders, and modern and traditional, continues to loom large. Without a doubt, a newly confident Peru is more welcoming than ever for visitors. All those unfortunate years of corrupt politicians, lawlessness, and economic disarray may have clouded but never eclipsed the beauty and complexity of this fascinating Andean nation.

THE MAKING OF PERU

Peru is littered with archaeological discoveries of many civilizations, from highland to coast. Two decades ago, a National Geographic team discovered Juanita the Ice Maiden, an Inca princess sacrificed on Mount Ampato more than 500 years ago. Only in the last decade, archaeologists unearthed more than 2,000 extraordinarily well-preserved mummies from one of Peru's largest Inca burial sites, found under a shantytown on the outskirts of Lima. Researchers describe Caral, a site in central Peru believed to date to 2600 B.C., as the oldest city in the Americas, and archaeologists recently celebrated the discovery of a 4,000-year-old temple on the northern coast.

First inhabited as many as 20,000 years ago, Peru was the cradle of several of the most ancient and sophisticated pre-Columbian civilizations in the Americas. The Chavín, Paracas, Nazca, Huari, Moche, and Incas, among others, form a long line of complicated, occasionally overlapping, and frequently warring cultures stretching back to 2000 B.C. Before the Incas, two other civilizations, the Chavín and the Huari-Tiahuanaco, achieved pan-Andean empires. Most of what is known about pre-Columbian cultures is based on the unearthing of temples and tombs because none possessed a written language. Further complicating matters is the fact that, as one culture succeeded a previous one, it imposed its values and social structure on the vanquished but also assimilated features useful to it, making distinction among some early cultures exceedingly difficult.

Prehistory (20 000 B.C.–6000 B.C.)

Early societies were located mainly in the coastal areas and highlands. Many fell victim to warfare, cyclical floods, extended drought, and earthquakes. Evidence of pivotal pre-Columbian cultures—including ruined temples; spectacular collections of ceramics, masks, and jewelry; and tombs found with well-preserved mummies—is everywhere in Peru, and some sites are only now being excavated and combed for clues.

The first inhabitants are thought by most historians to have crossed the Bering Strait in Asia during the last ice age, worked their way across the Americas, and settled in the region around 20 000 B.C. (although this migratory pattern has been disputed by some scholars). They were nomadic hunter-gatherers who lived along the central and northern coasts. The Pikimachay cave, which dates to 12 000 B.C., is the oldest known inhabited site in Peru. The earliest human remains, discovered near Huánaco in highland Peru, are from around 7000 B.C. Early Peruvians were responsible for cave paintings at Toquepala (Tacna, 7000 B.C.) and houses in Chillca (Lima, 5000 B.C.). Experts say that recent analysis of findings at the coastal site Caral, in the Supe Valley, demonstrates the existence of the earliest complex civilization in the Americas. The city was inhabited as many as 4,700 years ago, 1,000 years earlier than once believed.

Pre-Inca Cultures (6000 B.C.–A.D. 1100)

A long line of equally advanced cultures preceded the relatively short-lived Inca Empire. Over several thousand years, civilizations up and down the south Pacific coast and deep in the highlands developed ingenious irrigation systems, created sophisticated pottery and weaving techniques, and built great pyramids, temples, fortresses, and cities of adobe. Early peoples constructed mysterious cylindrical towers and the even more enigmatic Nazca Lines, giant drawings of animals and symbols somehow etched into the desert plains for eternity.

Over the course of nearly 15 centuries, pre-Inca cultures settled principally along the Peruvian coast and highlands. Around 6000 B.C., the Chinchero people along the southern desert coast mummified their dead, long before the ancient Egyptians had thought of it. By the 1st century B.C., during what is known as the Formative, or Initial, period, Andean society had designed sophisticated irrigation canals and produced the first textiles and decorative ceramics. Another important advance was the specialization of labor, aided in large part by the development of a hierarchical society.

> ### Center of the World
>
> The word *Inca* means "Children of the Sun," while *Cusco* is literally "navel," a reference no doubt to its central place in the continent-spanning Inca Empire.

The earliest known Peruvian civilization was the **Chavín culture** (1200–400 B.C.), a theocracy that worshiped a feline, jaguar-like god and settled in present-day Huántar, Ancash (central Peru). Over 8 centuries, the Chavín, who never developed into a military empire, unified groups of peoples across Peru. The most spectacular remnant of this culture, known for its advances in stone carving, pottery, weaving, and metallurgy, is the Chavín de Huántar temple, 40km (25 miles) east of Huaraz. The ceremonial center, a place of pilgrimage, contained wondrous examples of religious carving, such as the Tello Obelisk and the Raimondi Stella. The temple demonstrates evidence of sophisticated engineering and division of labor.

A subsequent society, the **Paracas** culture (700 B.C.–A.D. 200), took hold along the southern coast. It is renowned today for its superior textile weaving, considered perhaps the finest example of pre-Columbian textiles in the Americas. The Paracas peoples were sophisticated enough to dare to practice trepanation, a form of brain surgery that consisted of drilling holes in the skull to cure various ailments and correct cranial deformation. You can see fine examples of Paracas textiles and ceramics at the Julio C. Tello Museum in Paracas.

The Classical period (A.D. 200–1100) was one of significant social and technological development. Likely descendants of the Paracas, the Moche and Nazca cultures are among the best studied in pre-Columbian Peru. The **Moche** (or **Mochica**) civilization (A.D. 200–700), one of the first true urban societies, dominated the valleys of the north coast near Trujillo and conquered a number of smaller groups in building their widespread empire. The Moche were a highly organized hierarchical civilization that created extraordinary adobe platform complexes, such as the Temples of the Sun and Moon near Trujillo (the former was the largest man-made structure of its day in the Americas), and the burial site of Sipán, near Chiclayo, where the remains and riches of the famous Lord of Sipán, a religious and military authority, were unearthed in remarkably preserved royal tombs (remarkably brought to life, as it were, at the Museo de Tumbas Reales in Lambayeque). Moche pottery, produced from molds, contains vital clues to their way of life, down to very explicit sexual representations. Its frank depictions of phalluses, labia, and nontraditional bedroom practices might strike some visitors as pre-Columbian pornography. The best spot to view the extraordinary (in all senses of the word) ceramics of the Moche is the Rafael Larco Herrera Museum in Lima; see p. 62.

The **Nazca** culture (A.D. 300–800) established itself along the coastal desert south of Lima. Nazca engineers created outstanding underground aqueducts, which permitted agriculture in one of the most arid regions on Earth, and its artisans introduced polychrome techniques in pottery. But the civilization is internationally known for the enigmatic **Nazca Lines,** geometric and animal symbols etched indelibly into the desert, elements of an agricultural and astronomical calendar that are so vast that they can only really be appreciated from the window of an airplane.

The **Huari** (also spelled **Wari**) culture (A.D. 600–1100), an urban society that was the first in Peru to pursue explicitly expansionist goals through

PERU IN CONTEXT | The Making of Peru

Chakana, the Inca Cross

The ever-present Inca cross, the **Chakana** (consisting of four symmetrical sides of three steps each and a hole in the middle) is the very symbol of Inca civilization and its complex cosmology. Represented in it are three levels of existence or worlds: *Hana Pacha*, the higher world of the *apus*, or gods; *Kay Pacha*, the middle world of man's everyday existence; and *Ucu Pacha*, the lower world inhabited by spirits of the dead and ancestors. The hole in the center of the cross is both the axis through which a shaman might travel to other worlds and states of consciousness, and representative of Cusco, the center of the Incan empire. Some believe the Chakana to be a compass or calendar. The familiar motif of three steps is seen repeatedly in Inca constructions, from Machu Picchu to the Temple of the Sun in Cusco.

3

PERU IN CONTEXT | The Making of Peru

military conquest, settled the south-central *sierra* near Ayacucho. Along with the **Tiahuanaco** people, with whom they shared a central god figure, the Huari came to dominate the Andes, with an empire spreading all the way to Chile and Bolivia. Both cultures achieved superior agricultural technology in the form of canal irrigation and terraces.

Separate regional cultures, the best known of which is the **Chimú** culture (A.D. 700), developed and thrived over the next 4 centuries. The Chimú, adroit metallurgists and architects, built the monumental citadel of Chan Chan, a compound of royal palaces and the largest adobe city in the world, near the northern coastal city Trujillo. The Chimú were the dominant culture in Peru before the arrival and expansion of the Incas, and they initially represented a great northern and coastal rivalry to the Incas. Other cultures that thrived during the same period were the **Chachapoyas,** who constructed the impressive Kuélap fortress in the northern highlands; the **Ica** (or **Chincha**), of Lima; and the *altiplano* (high plains) that built the finely crafted *chullpa* towers near Puno and Lake Titicaca. The **Sicán** (or **Lambayeque**) culture, which built great temple sites and buried its dead with extraordinary riches, fell to the Chimú near the end of the 14th century. The Chimú themselves were, in turn, conquered by the Incas.

The Inca Empire (1200–1532)

Though Peru is likely to be forever synonymous with the Incas, who built the spectacular city of Machu Picchu high in the Andes and countless other great palaces and temples, the society was merely the last in a long line of pre-Columbian cultures. The Inca Empire (1200–1532) was relatively short-lived, but it remains the best documented of all Peruvian civilizations. Though the height of its power lasted for little more than a century, the Inca Empire extended throughout the Andes, all the way from present-day Colombia down to Chile—a stretch of more than 5,635km (3,500 miles). At its apex, the Inca Empire's reach was longer than even that of the Romans.

The Incas were a naturalistic and ritualistic people who worshiped the sun god Inti and the earth goddess Pachamama, as well as the moon, thunder, lightning, and the rainbow, all regarded as deities. The Inca emperors were believed to be direct descendants of the sun god. The bold Andes Mountains were at least as important in their system of beliefs: The dwelling places of respected spirits, the 7,000m (22,960-ft.) peaks were the sites of human sacrifices. The Incas founded Cusco, the sacred city and capital of the Inca Empire (which they called Tahuantinsuyo, or Land of Four Quarters). The ruling sovereign was properly called the Inca, but today the term also refers to the people and the empire.

The Incas' Andean dominance was achieved through formidable organization and a highly developed economic system. The Incas rapidly expanded their empire first through political alliances and absorption, and then by swift military conquest. Though the Incas imposed their social structure and way of life, they also assimilated useful skills and practices, even granting administrative positions to defeated nobles of the Chimú and other cultures. The Incas thus succeeded in achieving political and religious unification across most of their domain.

The Incas recorded an astounding level of achievement. They never developed a system of writing, but they kept extraordinary records with an accounting system of knots on strings, called *quipus*. They laid a vast network of roadways, nearly 32,200km (20,000 miles) in total across the difficult territory of the Andes, connecting cities, farming communities, and religious sites. A network of runners, called *chasquis,* operated on the roads, relaying messages and even transporting foodstuffs from the coast to the Andes. *Tambos,* or way stations (such as Tambo Colorado near Paracas; see p. 106), dotted the highways, serving as inspection points and shelters for relay runners. The Inca Trail was a sacred highway, connecting the settlements in the Urubamba Valley to the ceremonial center, Machu Picchu.

The Incas' agricultural techniques were exceedingly skilled and efficient, with advanced irrigation systems and soil conservation. The Incas were also extraordinary architects and unparalleled stonemasons. Inca ruins reveal splendid landscaping and graceful construction of perfectly cut stones and terraces on inaccessible sites with extraordinary views of valleys and mountains.

A rigid hierarchy and division of labor ruled Inca society. At the top, just below the Inca sovereign (who was also the chief military and religious figure and considered a descendant of the sun), was the ruling elite: nobles and priests. Tens of thousands of laborers provided the massive manpower necessary to construct temples and palaces throughout the empire. The Inca kept chosen maidens, or Virgins of the Sun (*acllas*), who serviced the Inca sovereign and Inca nobles.

Extraordinarily tight community organization was replicated across the empire. At the heart of the structure was the Inca's clan, the *panaca,* composed of relatives and descendants. Spanish conquistadors chronicled a dynasty that extended to 12 rulers, from **Manco Cápac,** the empire's founder in 1200 who was said to have risen out of Lake Titicaca, to **Atahualpa,** whose murder in Cajamarca by Spanish conquerors spelled the end of the great power.

The Inca **Pachacútec** ruled from 1438 to 1463, and he is considered the great builder of Inca civilization. Under his rule, Cusco was rebuilt, and some of the most brilliant examples of Inca architecture were erected, including Cusco's Qoricancha (Temple of the Sun; see p. 129), the Ollantaytambo and Sacsayhuamán fortresses (see p. 190 and p. 132), and, of course, the famed religious retreat Machu Picchu. Pachacútec also initiated the empire's expansion. It was Pachacútec's successor, **Tupac Yupanqui** (1463–93), however, who achieved dominance from Ecuador to Chile. A great conqueror, he defeated his Chimú rivals in northern Peru.

After the death of the Inca **Huayna Cápac** in 1525, civil war ensued, brought on by the empire splitting between his two sons, Atahualpa and Huáscar. The Spaniards, arriving in northern Peru in 1532, found a severely weakened empire—a pivotal reason the Incas so swiftly succumbed to a small band of invading Spaniards. Another key was the Spaniards' superior military technology. Against cannons and cavalry, the Incas' slings, battle-axes, and cotton-padded armor stood little chance. But their defeat remains puzzling to most visitors to Peru, not to mention many scholars.

Spanish Conquest & Colonialism (1532–CA 1800)

Columbus and his cohorts landed in the Americas in 1492, and by the 1520s, the Spanish conquistadors had reached South America. Francisco Pizarro led an expedition along Peru's coast in 1528. Impressed with the riches of the Inca Empire, he returned to Spain and succeeded in raising money and recruiting men for a return expedition. In 1532, Pizarro made his return to Peru over land from Ecuador. After founding the first Spanish city in Peru, San Miguel de Piura, near the Ecuadorian border, he advanced upon the northern highland city of Cajamarca, an Inca stronghold. There, a small number of Spanish troops—about 180 men and 30 horses—cunningly captured the Inca emperor Atahualpa. The emperor promised to pay a king's ransom of gold and silver for his release, offering to fill his cell several times over, but the Spaniards, having received warning of an advancing Inca army, executed the emperor in 1533. It was a catastrophic blow to an already weakened empire.

Pizarro and his men massacred the Inca army, estimated at between 5,000 and 6,000 warriors. The Spaniards installed a puppet Inca, Tupac Huallpa, the brother of Huáscar, who had died while Atahualpa was being held. They then marched on Cusco, capturing the capital city on November 15, 1533, and emptying the Sun Temple of its golden treasures. After the death of Tupac Huallpa en route, a new puppet was appointed, Manco Inca.

Two years later Pizarro founded the coastal city of Lima, which became the capital of the new colony, the Viceroyalty of Peru. (For a taste of Lima's colonial riches, stroll the historic quarter of Lima Centro; see p. 58.) The Spanish crown appointed Spanish-born viceroys the rulers of Peru, but Spaniards battled among themselves for control of Peru's riches, and the remaining Incas continued to battle the conquistadors. A great siege was laid to Cusco in 1536, with Manco Inca and his brothers directing the rebellion from the fortress Sacsayhuamán (see p. 132). Pizarro was assassinated in 1541, and the indigenous insurrection ended with the beheading of Manco Inca, who had escaped to Vilcabamba, deep in the jungle, in 1544. Inca Tupac Amaru led a rebellion in 1572 but also failed and was killed.

Over the next 2 centuries, Lima gained in power and prestige at the expense of the old Inca capital and became the foremost colonial city of the Andean nations. The Peruvian viceroyalty stretched all the way from Panama to Tierra del Fuego. Cusco focused on cultural pursuits and became the epicenter of the Cusco School of painting (Escuela Cusqueña), which incorporated indigenous elements into Spanish styles, in the 16th and 17th centuries.

Independent Peru (1821–1942)

By the 19th century, grumbling over high taxes and burdensome Spanish controls grew in Peru, as it did in most colonies in the Americas. After liberating Chile and Argentina, José de San Martín set his sights north on Lima in 1821 and declared it an independent nation the same year. Simón Bolívar, the other hero of independence on the continent, came from the other direction. His successful campaigns in Venezuela and Colombia led him south to Ecuador and finally Peru. Peru won its independence from Spain after crucial battles in late 1824. Though Peru mounted its first civilian government, defeat by Chile in the War of the Pacific (1879–83) left Peru in a dire economic position.

Several military regimes ensued, and Peru finally returned to civilian rule in 1895. Land-owning elites dominated this new "Aristocratic Republic." In 1911, the Yale historian Hiram Bingham happened upon the ruins of the imperial city Machu Picchu—a discovery that would begin to unravel the greatness of the Incas and forever associate Peru with the last of its pre-Columbian civilizations.

Peru launched war with Ecuador over a border dispute—just one of several long-running border conflicts—in 1941. Though the 1942 Treaty of Río de Janeiro granted the area north of the River Marañon to Peru, Ecuador would continue to claim the territory until the end of the 20th century.

Present-Day Peru (1945–Present Day)

Peru's modern political history has been largely a turbulent mix of military dictatorships, coups d'état, and disastrous civilian governments, engendering a near-continual cycle of instability. Particularly in the 1980s and 1990s, Peru became notorious for government corruption at the highest levels—leading to the exile of two recent presidents—and widespread domestic terrorism fears.

Peru shook off 2 decades of dictatorship in 1945 after a free election (the first in many decades) of José Luis Bustamante y Rivero. Bustamante served for just 3 years. General Manuel A. Odría led a coup and installed a military regime in 1948. In 1963, Peru returned to civilian rule, with Fernando Belaúnde Terry as president. The armed forces overthrew Belaúnde in 1968, but the new military regime (contrary to other right-leaning dictatorships in Latin America) expanded the role of the state, nationalized a number of industries, and instituted agrarian reform. The land-reform initiatives failed miserably. Reelected in 1980, Belaúnde and his successor, Alan García (1985–90), faced, and were largely unsuccessful in dealing with, hyperinflation, massive debt, nationwide strikes, and two homegrown guerrilla movements—the Maoist Sendero Luminoso (Shining Path) and the Tupac Amaru Revolutionary Movement (MRTA)—that destabilized Peru with violent terror campaigns throughout the late 1980s and early 1990s. Peruvians fled the capital and the countryside, fearful of attack; few travelers were brave enough to plan vacations in the troubled nation. Meanwhile, Peru's role on the production end of the international cocaine trade grew exponentially.

García refused to pay Peru's external debt (which prompted both the IMF and World Bank to cut off support) and then fled into exile after being charged with embezzling millions. With the economy in ruins and the government in chaos, Alberto Fujimori, the son of Japanese immigrants, defeated the Peruvian novelist Mario Vargas Llosa and became president in 1990. In 1992, Fujimori's government arrested key members of both the MRTA and the Shining Path (catapulting the president to unprecedented popularity). His administration turned authoritarian, however, shutting down Congress in 1992, suspending the constitution, and decreeing an emergency government that he effectively ruled as dictator. There was a massive abuse of power on the part of the police and military, who engaged in systematic repression that led to kidnappings and killings of suspected terrorists. Many were overt political targetings of innocents.

Austerity measures got Peru on the right track economically, with reforms leading to widespread privatizations, annual growth of 7 percent, and a drop in inflation from more than 10,000 percent annually to about 20 percent. Many Peruvians reluctantly accepted Fujimori's overturn of democracy. Having pushed to get the constitution amended so that he could run for successive terms, Fujimori was reelected in 1995. Fujimori resigned the presidency in late 2000 and escaped into exile in Japan after a corruption scandal involving his shadowy intelligence chief, Vladimiro Montesinos. Videotape of Montesinos bribing a congressman and subsequent investigations (including a daily barrage of secret videotapes broadcast on national television) revealed a government so thoroughly corrupt that it was itself involved in the narcotics trade that it was ostensibly stamping out. Fujimori had funneled at least $12 million to private offshore accounts. Montesinos escaped to Venezuela, where he was harbored by the government until found and returned to Peru for imprisonment. Fujimori remains in a jail in Lima for his role in ordering death squads, along with three other concurrent sentences, including for abuse of power, bribery, and illegal wiretapping of phones. The 2009 trial marked the first time in Peruvian history that a former president was tried for crimes committed during his administration.

Alejandro Toledo, a political newcomer from a poor Indian family, won the 2001 election and became Peru's first president of the 21st century. The U.S. State Department Human Rights Report named Peru among the success stories of the year, praising the country for meeting international standards for free elections and addressing past abuses and corruption under the Fujimori administration. Toledo had labeled himself an "Indian rebel with a cause," alluding to his intent to support the nation's native Andean populations, or *cholos.* A shoeshine boy and son of peasants who went to Harvard and Stanford, became a World Bank economist, and ultimately wrestled the top office from a corrupt leader was the very embodiment of the dream of social mobility—in a country where there is little upward movement by non-whites. Toledo offered an encouraging symbol of hope to both Peruvians and the international community. Yet, like previous governments, Toledo's administration was plagued by instability, abuse of power, and poor management.

Peru had been engaged in a longstanding dispute with Yale University in the United States over the possession of thousands of valuable pre-Columbian artifacts removed from Peru during the archaeological expeditions of Hiram Bingham, the Yale professor credited with rediscovering Machu Picchu in 1911 and publicizing it to the world. Peru claimed it had merely loaned the artifacts to Yale and even sought the intervention of U.S. President Barack Obama in the matter. In 2010, Yale finally stopped asserting its claim and agreed to return the bulk of the artifacts, long held in the Peabody Museum in New Haven, Connecticut, by the end of 2012 in anticipation of the creation of a new museum in Cusco (on which Yale will advise).

Peru's 30 million people are predominantly *mestizo* (of mixed Spanish and indigenous heritage) and indigenous Andean, but the population is a true melting pot of ethnic groups. Significant minority groups of Afro-Peruvians (descendants of African slaves, living mainly in the coastal area south of Lima), immigrant Japanese and Chinese populations among the largest in South America, and smaller groups of European immigrants, including Italians and Germans, help make up Peru's population of 30 million. In the early days of the colony, Peruvian-born offspring of Spaniards were called *criollo,* though that term today refers mainly to coastal residents and Peruvian cuisine.

After Bolivia and Guatemala, Peru has the largest population by percentage of Amerindians in Latin America. Perhaps half the country lives in the *sierra,* or highlands, and most of these people, commonly called *campesinos* (peasants), live in small villages or rural areas. Descendants of Peru's many Andean indigenous groups in remote rural areas continue to speak the native languages Quechua (made an official language in 1975) and Aymara or other Amerindian tongues, and for the most part, they adhere to traditional regional dress. However, massive peasant migration to cities from rural highland villages has contributed to a dramatic weakening of indigenous traditions and culture across Peru. (The early-2000s government of Alejandro Toledo, himself a proud *cholo,* or person of direct Andean Indian roots, committed itself to a valorization and preservation of native language and traditions, though.)

Peruvians are a predominantly Roman Catholic people (more than 90 percent claim to be Catholic), although Protestant evangelical churches have been winning converts, a fact that is worrisome to the Catholic Church. Animistic religious practices (worship of deities representing nature), inherited from the Incas and others, have been incorporated into the daily lives of many Peruvians and can be seen in festivals and small individual rituals such as offerings of food and beverages to Pachamama, or Mother Earth.

Until recently a rather well-guarded secret, Peruvian cuisine is among the most accomplished and diverse cuisines found anywhere. As a dining city, the cosmopolitan capital, Lima, is on par with some of the finest eating cities in the world. But it's far from the only place one can expect to eat very well. Arequipa has its own very distinguished cuisine with liberal and creative use of *ajíes,* or hot peppers. Cusco's dining scene used to be comparatively bland, but no more; today it, too, thrives with innovative restaurants. And northern coastal cooking, particularly that of Chiclayo and Lambayeque, is quickly earning its own adherents.

EATING & DRINKING

Peruvian cuisine is among the finest and most diverse cuisines found in Latin America and, indeed, the world. As knowledge of Peruvian food spreads, more and more travelers are even making focused gastronomic pilgrimages to Peru—for many travelers, the cuisine will rank among the highlights of their visit.

Peruvian cooking differs significantly by region, and subcategories mirror exactly the country's geographical variety: coastal, highlands, and tropical. The common denominator among them is a blend of indigenous and Spanish (or broader European) influences, which has evolved over the past 4 centuries. Traditional Peruvian coastal cooking is often referred to as *comida criolla,* and it's found across Peru. The other main types of cuisine are *andino,* or *Andean* (highlands), and *novo andino* (creative or haute twists on and updates of traditional highlander cooking). Several celebrity chefs, including Gastón Acurio, Mitsuharu Tsumura, and Virgilio Martinez, are leading the charge of contemporary Peruvian cuisine with their restaurants landing on *Restaurant* magazine's prestigious World's 50 Best list.

Coastal preparations concentrate on seafood and shellfish, as might be expected. The star dish, and the most exported example of Peruvian cuisine, is **ceviche,** a classic preparation of raw fish and shellfish marinated (not cooked) in lime or lemon juice and hot chili peppers, served with raw onion, sweet potato, and toasted corn. Ceviche, often spelled *cebiche,* has been around in some form since the time of some of Peru's earliest civilizations, though the modern form did not appear until Japanese chefs in Lima began experimenting with it in the 1970s. *Cevicherías,* traditionally open only for lunch, usually serve several types of ceviche as well as a good roster of other seafood. *Tiradito* is finely sliced fish marinated with lime juice and *ají* peppers, essentially Peruvian sashimi or carpaccio. Other coastal favorites include *pulpo al olivo* (a tasty pairing of thinly sliced octopus and a sauce made of purple olives), *conchitas* (scallops), and *corvina* (sea bass). Land-based favorites are *cabrito* (roast kid) and *ají de gallina* (a tangy creamed chicken and chili dish).

Highlanders favor a more substantial style of cooking. Corn and potatoes were staples of the Incas and other mountain civilizations before them. Meat, served with rice and potatoes, is a mainstay of the diet, as is trout (*trucha*) in some areas. *Lomo saltado,* strips of beef mixed with onions, tomatoes, peppers, and french-fried potatoes and served with rice, seems to be on every menu. *Rocoto relleno,* a hot bell pepper stuffed with vegetables and meat, and *papa rellena,* a potato stuffed with meat or veggies and then fried, are just as common (but are occasionally extremely spicy). Soups are excellent.

In the countryside, you might see people in the fields digging small cooking holes in the ground. They are preparing *pachamanca,* a roast cooked over stones. It's the Peruvian version of a picnic; on weekends, you'll often see families outside Cusco and other places stirring smoking fires in the ground while the kids play soccer nearby. *Cuy* (guinea pig) is considered a delicacy

DATELINE

Pre-Columbian

20 000– 10 000 B.C.	The earliest settlers, most likely migrants from Asia, arrive.
1000 B.C.– 900 B.C.	Establishment of Chavín de Huántar.
700 B.C.	Rise of Paracas culture in the southern desert.
300 B.C.– A.D. 700	Nasca Lines created.
A.D. 200	Consolidation of Moche dynasty in northern Peru.

CA. 300	Burial of Lord of Sipán.
1150	Construction of Chan Chan begins.

Colonial Era & Independence

1200	Manco Cápac becomes the first Inca (emperor) and founds Inca Empire.
1438	Reign of the Inca Pachacútec; Sacsayhuamán and Machu Picchu built.
1460–65	Inca conquest of southern desert coast;empire extends to Ecuador.

in many parts of Peru, especially the Andes, though to many it tastes just like chicken. It comes roasted or fried, with head and feet upturned on the plate.

In the Amazon jungle regions, most people fish for their food, and their diets consist almost entirely of fish such as river trout and *paiche* (a huge river fish, now considered endangered). Restaurants feature both of these, with accompaniments including *yuca* (a root), *palmitos* (palm hearts) and *chonta* (palm-heart salad), bananas and plantains, and rice *tamales* known as *juanes*. Common menu items such as chicken and game are complemented by exotic fare such as caiman, wild boar, turtle, monkey, and piranha fish—but even though some locals eat some items that are endangered and illegal to serve in restaurants, it doesn't mean that you should.

In addition to Peruvian cooking, visitors will find plenty of international restaurants, including a particularly Peruvian variation, *chifas* (restaurants serving Peruvian-influenced Chinese food, developed by the large immigrant Chinese population), a mainstay among many non-Chinese Peruvians. *Chifas* are nearly as common as restaurants serving *pollo a la brasa* (spit-roasted chicken), which are everywhere in Peru.

Drinking is less of an event in Peru. While Peruvian wines from the coastal desert are improving, they still can't really compare with superior examples found elsewhere on the continent (Chile and Argentina, predominantly). Most wines in better restaurants come from these three countries, along with Spain. Yet one indigenous drink stands out: **pisco,** a powerful spirit distilled from grapes. The pisco sour (a cocktail mixed with pisco, egg whites, lemon juice, sugar, and bitters) is effectively Peru's margarita: tasty, refreshing, and ubiquitous. New takes on the pisco sour have sprung up at sophisticated mixology bars: *maracuyá* (passion fruit) sours, coca sours (made with macerated coca leaves), and other cocktails highlighting indigenous tropical fruits, such as *lúcuma*. Pisco is also taken straight.

1527	Inca civil war.
1532	Atahualpa defeats brother to gain control of the Inca Empire. Pizarro captures Atahualpa.
1533	Spaniards assassinate Atahualpa; Cusco sacked and burned by Spaniards.
1535	Francisco Pizarro establishes Lima and names it capital of the Viceroyalty of Peru.
1541	Pizarro killed in Lima.
1572	Tupac Amaru, the last Inca emperor, captured and executed.
1780	Tupac Amaru II leads failed revolt against Spanish.
1821	General José de San Martín captures Lima and proclaims Peru's independence.
1824	Peru defeats Spain and becomes the last colony in Latin America to gain its independence.
1849–74	Chinese workers (100,000) arrive in Peru as menial laborers.
1870s	Rubber boom in the Peruvian Amazon.
1879–83	Chile defeats Peru and Bolivia in the War of the Pacific; Peru loses southern territory to Chile.

continues

Peruvians everywhere (but especially in the highlands) drink *chicha*, a tangy, fermented brew made from maize and inherited from the Incas. Often served warm in huge plastic tumblers, it is unlikely to please the palates of most foreign visitors, although it's certainly worth a try if you come upon a small, informal place with the *chicha* flag (often a red balloon) flying in a rural village (it means something akin to "get your fresh *chicha* here"). *Chicha morada*, on the other hand, is nothing to be afraid of. It is a delicious but sweet nonalcoholic beverage, deep purple in color, prepared with blue corn and served chilled, the perfect accompaniment to ceviche. *Masato* is a drink made from fermented *yuca*, typical of the Amazon region.

Dining Customs

Among the more interesting dining customs—beyond the eating of guinea pig—is the lovely habit of offering a sip of beer or *chicha* before the meal to Pachamama, or Mother Earth. Many Peruvians in the Andes still ritualistically thank the earth for its bounty, and they show their appreciation by spilling just a bit before raising the drink to their own mouths.

Restaurants range from the rustic and incredibly inexpensive to polished places with impeccable service and international menus. Set three-course meals are referred to by a variety of terms: *menú del día, menú económico, menú ejecutivo,* and *menú turístico.* They are all essentially the same thing and can sometimes be had for as little as 10 *soles* (the Peruvian currancy; see p. 253) in rural areas. Informal eateries serving Peruvian cooking are frequently called *picanterías, huariques, quintas,* and *chicherías.*

Fixed-price lunch deals are referred to as *menús del día* (or simply *menú*). The majority of restaurants include taxes and services in their prices, and your bill will reflect the menu prices. Others, however, separate taxes and services, and the bill can get pretty byzantine, especially when it comes to imported wine. You

---

20th Century

1948 Coup d'état installs military government.

1963 Peru returns to civilian rule; Fernando Belaúnde Terry becomes President.

1968 Civilian government ousted in coup led by General Juan Velasco Alvarado.

1969 Large-scale land reform and nationalization programs initiated.

1970 Disastrous landslide kills 20,000 in Yungay (Ancash).

1975 Velasco ousted in coup.

1980 Peru returns to civilian rule with re-election of Fernando Belaúnde. Maoist terrorist organization, Sendero Luminoso (Shining Path), and a smaller group, Tupac Amaru (MRTA), launch armed guerrilla struggle.

1982 Debt crisis; deaths and "disappearances" escalate following military crackdown on guerrillas and drug traffickers.

1985 Alan García wins presidency, promises to rid Peru of military and police "old guard." Belaúnde first elected president to turn

might see a subtotal, followed by a 10 percent service charge and a 19 percent IGV (general sales tax). It's primarily only higher-end restaurants that do this.

Note: Some upscale restaurants will place a couple of small plates of cheese, sausage, olives, or other tidbits on your table to nibble on as you wait for your meal. In almost all cases, you will be charged for these items, called a *cubierto,* or cover. Usually, it'll add S/5 to S/20 to your bill. If you don't touch the stuff, in theory you shouldn't have to pay for it because you didn't order it, but many restaurants automatically tack on the charge—and few are the customers who don't consider the *cubierto* part of the cost of eating out.

Dining hours are not much different from typical mealtimes in cities in North America or Great Britain, except that dinner (*cena*) is generally eaten after 8pm in restaurants. Peruvians do not eat nearly as late as Spaniards. Although lunch (*almuerzo*) is the main meal of the day, for most visitors, it generally is not the grand midday affair it is in Spain, unless it is the weekend and you are dining at a *cevichería* or *quinta,* where most locals linger over lunch for a couple of hours.

If you invite a Peruvian to have a drink or to dine with you, it is expected that you will pay (the Spanish verb *invitar* literally connotes this as an invitation). Do not suggest that a Peruvian acquaintance join you in what will certainly be an expensive restaurant or cafe for him or her, and then pony up only half the tab.

PERU IN POP CULTURE
Music

There is evidence of music in Peru dating back 10,000 years, and musical historians have identified more than 1,000 genres of music in the country. Traditional instruments include *pututos* (trumpets made from seashells) and many other wind instruments crafted from cane, bone, horns, and precious

over power to a constitutionally elected successor since 1945.

1988 Hyperinflation and bankruptcy rock Peru. Shining Path's guerrilla bombing and assassination campaign intensifies.

1990 Human rights groups estimate as many as 10,000 political murders (including thousands of *campesinos*) in Peru. Alberto Fujimori, son of Japanese immigrants, runs on anticorruption platform and defeats Mario Vargas Llosa, Peru's best-known novelist.

1992 Fujimori dissolves Congress, suspends the constitution, and imposes censorship. Shining Path leader Abimael Guzmán arrested and sentenced to life in prison.

1994 6,000 Shining Path guerrillas surrender to authorities.

1996 Tupac Amaru guerrillas seize 490 hostages at the residence of the Japanese ambassador. The American Lori Berenson convicted of treason by a secret military court and sentenced to life in prison for plotting with Tupac Amaru Revolutionary Movement.

continues

metals, as well as a wide range of percussion instruments. Exposure to Western cultures has introduced new instruments such as the harp, violin, and guitar to Peruvian music. But Peruvian music can still be identified by its distinctive instruments, and there are many besides the basics of highland music.

The *cajón* is a classic percussion instrument, typical in *música criolla* and *música negra,* as well as *marinera.* A simple wooden box with a sound hole in the back, the *cajón* is played by a musician who sits on top and pounds the front like a bongo. The *cajón* has been introduced into flamenco music by none other than the legendary flamenco guitarist Paco de Lucía. Another popular instrument is the *zampoña,* which belongs to the panpipe family and varies greatly in size. The *zampoña* is never absent at festivals in southern Peru, particularly Puno.

Many travelers may be at least superficially familiar with the dominant strains of Peruvian music. Anyone who has traveled in Europe, South America, or even Asia is likely to have seen and heard roving bands of street musicians decked out in highlander garb (ponchos and *chullo* hats) playing the *música folclórica* that emanates from high in the Andes Mountains. Known for its use of the *quena* (pan flute, played like a recorder), *charango* (from the lute family), and mandolin, the distinctive sounds of this Peruvian music—similar to that heard in other Andean countries, such as Bolivia and Ecuador—were widely sampled in the Simon and Garfunkel song "El Cóndor Pasa." That song was based on a melody by a Peruvian composer, Daniel Alomía Robles, who himself had appropriated a traditional Quechua *huayno* folk melody.

I'd point adventurous ears with an interest in ethnomusicology toward a handful of Andean *música folclórica* recordings released by the Smithsonian Folkways Series. *Mountain Music of Peru,* a two-volume series released in the early 1990s, includes recordings, celebratory and religious in nature, that

1997 Peruvian special forces launch an attack and free hostages held at the Japanese ambassador's residence. El Niño—the worst of the century—causes severe drought in Peru.

American missionaries shot down by Peruvian military. Alejandro Toledo becomes Peru's first president of native Indian origin. Massive earthquake rocks Arequipa and southern Peru.

Modern Times

2000 Fujimori re-elected by landslide to a third 5-year term. His chief of intelligence, Vladimiro Montesinos, caught on videotape bribing an opposition politician. Fujimori resigns, goes into exile in Japan.

2001 Montesinos captured in Venezuela. Plane carrying

2002 Peru seeks to extradite former president Fujimori from Japan.

2003 Toledo declares state of emergency. Interpol issues arrest warrant for Fujimori and Congress requests Fujimori's extradition from Japan.

2005 Fujimori arrested in Chile; jailed next year in Peru (where he remains).

were made in mountain villages in the 1960s. As such, they are raw and lack studio polish. Smithsonian also issues other volumes covering the traditional regional music of Peru, from *Cajamarca and the Colca Valley (Vol. 3)* to *The Region of Ayacucho (Vol. 6)*. Though its song selections aren't specifically Peruvian, listeners may also enjoy the *Rough Guide to the Music of the Andes* compilation.

Just as there is a notable divide in Peruvian cuisine, with radically different takes in the *sierra* (mountains) and *costa* (coast), so, too, is Peruvian music divided along these lines. In coastal areas, principally Lima and communities just south, such as El Carmen, the most distinctive music came from the Afro-Peruvian population, descendants of slaves. Black Peruvians created a unique mix of African rhythms and Spanish and other European influences, called *música criolla*. Percussion is fundamental, in addition to strings and vocals, but the music is frequently bluesier than its jazz-inflected Afro counterparts that developed in Brazil and Cuba. A great place to start exploring is the compilation, selected by David Byrne and released on his Luaka Bop label, *Afro-Peruvian Classics: The Soul of Black Peru*, featuring the influential singers and groups Eva Ayllón, Susana Baca, Perú Negro, Chabuca Granda, Nicomedes Santa Cruz, and others. Those same stars (but no repeat songs) are also featured on *The Rough Guide to Afro Peru*.

Chicha is a relatively new addition to the list of musical genres. A hybrid of sorts of the *huayno* (see the "Dance" section, below) and Colombian *cumbia*, *chicha* is an extremely popular urban dance, especially among the working class. It has spread rapidly across Peru and throughout Latin America. A good compilation of vintage *cumbia* is *Peru Maravilloso* (2013), which includes rare tracks from many of the top artists.

The former Minister of Culture, Susana Baca, has reached an audience of American and international ears through her recordings on the Luaka Bop

2006	Former President Alán García elected President after return from exile.
2007	7.9 earthquake devastates southern desert coast (Pisco and Ica).
2010	Mudslides in Sacred Valley strand 2,000 tourists at Machu Picchu and kill 5. Mario Vargas Llosa becomes first Peruvian to be awarded Nobel Prize for Literature. Lori Bensen released from prison after 15 years.
2011	Ollanta Humala is elected President. The Afro-Peruvian singer Susana Baca is named Minister of Culture, becoming Peru's first black minister in more than 200 years.
2012	Joran van der Sloot, who became notorious as the prime suspect in the disappearance of Natalee Holloway in Aruba in 2005, pleads guilty to the 2010 murder of Peruvian woman Stephanny Flores.
2014	Six-year maritime dispute between Chile and Peru is settled when the International Court of Justice in The Hague rules largely in favor of Peru, stripping Chile of economic rights over a swath of the Pacific Ocean.

label. Look for her eponymous album or *Ecos de Sombra.* Both are superb. In Peru, Eva Ayllón is even more of a megastar. A good recording available worldwide is *Eva! Leyenda Peruana.* Another long-time female Afro-Peruvian performer is Chabuca Granda; a greatest hits collection of her work is called *Latinoamericana.* Perú Negro's albums *Sangre de un Don* and *Jogorio,* recorded after the death of the group's founder Ronaldo Campos in 2001, are both widely available.

A taste of Peruvian music serves either as great preparation for a trip to Peru or as a fond souvenir after the fact. But nothing equals grooving to live Peruvian coastal *música criolla* in a nightclub, at a stylish Lima jazz bar, or in a *peña*—a one-time social club now frequented by locals and tourists for live music—or hearing highlands' *música folclórica* during an Andean festival or stumbling upon it in a town square. The renaissance of Peru's indigenous musical forms is a hugely welcome development in this culturally rich country.

Dance

Dances associated with Afro-Peruvian music include lively and sensual *festejo* dances, in which participants respond to the striking of the *cajón,* one of Afro-Peruvian music's essential instruments. The **alcatraz** is an extremely erotic dance. Females enter the dance floor with tissue on their posteriors. The men, meanwhile, dance with lit candles. The not-so-subtle goal on the dance floor is for the man to light the woman's tissue (and thus become her partner).

Peruvian tourism authorities produce a guide to festivities, music, and folk art, and the guide features a diagram of native dances in Peru. Especially up and down the coast, and in the central corridor of the Andes, the map is a bewildering maze of numbers indicating the indigenous dances practiced in given regions. Two dances, though, have become synonymous with Peru, the *huayno* and *marinera.*

The **huayno** is the essential dance in the Andes, with pre-Columbian origins fused with Western influences. Couples dancing the *huayno* perform sharp turns, hops, and taplike *zapateos* to keep time. *Huayno* music is played on *quena, charango,* harp, and violin. The **marinera,** a sleek, sexy, and complex dance of highly coordinated choreography, is derivative of other folkloric dances in Peru, dating back to the 19th century. There are regional variations of the dance, which differ most from the south coast to the northern highlands. Dancers keep time with a handkerchief in one hand. *Marinera* music in Lima is performed by guitar and *cajón,* while a marching band is de rigueur in the north. *Marinera* festivals are held across Peru, but the most celebrated one is in Trujillo in January.

One of the most attention-getting dances in Peru, though, is that performed by **scissors dancers.** Their *danza de las tijeras* is an exercise in athleticism and balance. Dancers perform gymnastic leaps and daring stunts to the sounds of harp and violin. The main instrument played to accompany the dance is the pair of scissors, made up of two independent sheets of metal around 25cm (10 in.) long. The best places to see scissors dancers are Ayacucho, Arequipa, and Lima.

Textiles

Woven textiles have to be considered among the great traditional arts of Peru. Peru has one of the most ancient and richest weaving traditions in the world; for more than 5,000 years, Peruvian artisans have used fine natural fibers for hand weaving, and the wool produced by alpacas, llamas, and vicuñas is some of the finest in the world, rarer even than cashmere. The most ancient textiles that have been found in Peru come from the Huaca Prieta temple in Chicama and are more than 4,000 years old. In pre-Columbian times, handwoven textiles, which required extraordinary patience and skill, were prized and extremely valuable; distinctive textiles were indicators of social status and power. They were traded as commodities. Paracas, Huari, and Inca weavings are among the most sophisticated and artful ever produced in Peru. The Paracas designs were stunningly intricate, with detailed animals, human figures, and deities against dark backgrounds. Huari weaving features abstract figures and bold graphics. The Incas favored more minimalist designs, without embroidery. The finest Inca textiles were typically part of ritualistic ceremonies—many were burned as offerings to spirits.

Whereas pre-Columbian civilizations in Peru had no written language, textiles were loaded with symbolic images that serve as indelible clues to the cultures and beliefs of textile artists. Worship of nature and spiritual clues are frequently represented by motifs in textiles. Many of the finest textiles unearthed were sacred and elaborately embroidered blankets that enveloped mummies in burial sites. Found in tombs in the arid coastal desert, one of the world's driest climates, the textiles are remarkably preserved in many cases.

Contemporary Peruvian artisans continue the traditions, sophisticated designs, and techniques of intricate weaving inherited from pre-Columbian civilizations, often employing the very same instruments used hundreds of years ago and still favoring natural dyes. The drop spindle (weaving done with a stick and spinning wooden wheel), for example, is still used in many regions, and it's not uncommon to see women and young girls spinning the wheel as they tend to animals in the fields. Excellent-quality woven items, the best of which are much more than mere souvenirs, include typical Andean *chullo* wool or alpaca hats with earflaps, ponchos, scarves, sweaters, and blankets.

Books & Literature

The classic work on Inca history and the Spanish conquistadors is *The Conquest of the Incas* (Harvest Books, 2003) by John Hemming, a readable narrative of the fall of a short-lived but uniquely accomplished empire. *Lost City of the Incas* (Phoenix Press, 2003) is the travelogue and still-amazing story of Hiram Bingham, the Yale academic who brought the "lost city" to the

What They Say
"There is an incompatibility between literary creation and political activity." **—Mario Vargas Llosa**, Nobel Prize–winning novelist and former candidate for president

world's attention in 1911. Bingham's book is an interesting read, especially after so many years of speculation and theory about the site. Also available by Bingham is *Inca Land: Explorations in the Highlands of Peru* (National Geographic, 2003, although originally published in 1922), detailing four expeditions into the Peruvian Andes.

The Incas and Their Ancestors (Thames and Hudson, 2001) by Michael Moseley is a good account of the Inca Empire and, importantly, its lesser-known predecessors. For most readers, it serves as a good introduction to Peru's archaeology and the sites they will visit, although some people find that it reads too much like a textbook. Illustrations include black-and-white photographs of Inca drawings and a few color photos. A terrific story of a recent archaeological find is *Discovering the Ice Maiden: My Adventures on Ampato* (National Geographic Society, 1998) by Johan Reinhard. The account of Reinhard's discovery of a mummified Inca princess sacrificed 500 years ago on a volcano summit in southern Peru details the team's search and its race to save what is considered one of the most important archaeological discoveries in recent decades. The book contains excellent color photographs of the maiden, who can now be viewed in Arequipa. Reinhard's *The Ice Maiden: Inca Mummies, Mountain Gods, and Sacred Sites in the Andes* (National Geographic, 2005) is a memoir of archaeological adventures and the impact of his discovery of Juanita (both on him personally and the interpretation of Peruvian history).

The Peru Reader: History, Culture, Politics (Duke University Press, 1995), edited by Orin Starn, is one of the finest primers on Peru's recent history and political culture. It includes essays by several distinguished voices, including Mario Vargas Llosa.

The Madness of Things Peruvian, Democracy Under Siege by Alvaro Vargas Llosa (Transaction Publishers, 1994) isn't easy to find, and it chronicles only up to the mid-'90s, but it is a well-rendered analysis of the failings of Peruvian democracy. Robin Kirk's *The Monkey's Paw: New Chronicles from Peru* (University of Massachusetts Press, 1997) is a story of the impact of social and economic upheaval in Peru on marginalized peoples, with the homegrown guerrilla movements taking center stage.

Naturalists and birders might want to pick up *A Field Guide to the Birds of Peru* (Ibis Pub Co., 2001) by James F. Clements, although it is perhaps not the comprehensive field guide that a country as biologically diverse as Peru deserves. Many serious birders prefer *A Guide to the Birds of Colombia* (Princeton University Press, 1986) by Steven Hilty and William Brown, probably the definitive regional guide (and covering many of the birds also found in Peru). Also of interest is *A Parrot Without a Name: The Search for the Last Unknown Birds on Earth* (University of Texas Press, 1991) by Don Stap, an account of John O'Neill and LSU scientists documenting new species in the jungles of Peru.

Peru: The Ecotravellers' Wildlife Guide (Academic Press, 2000) by biologists David Pearson and Les Beletsky is a 500-page handbook survey of

Peruvian flora and fauna, including information about conservation, habitats, national parks, and reserves. It's a good introduction for readers ready to explore the Peruvian outdoors, from the Andes to the Amazon, and other repositories of Peru's magnificent animal and plant life. The book is nicely illustrated and useful for identification purposes.

Peter Frost's *Exploring Cusco* (Nuevas Imágenes, 1999) is one of the best-detailed local guides, with excellent historical information and frank commentary by the author, a long-time Cusco resident, on the ancient Inca capital, the Sacred Valley, and, of course, Machu Picchu. *Trekking in Peru: 50 of the Best Walks and Hikes* (Bradt Publications, 2014) by Hilary Bradt is a trusty guide, with a collection of classic and off-the-beaten-path treks around Peru. It's a good all-around guide for trekkers and walkers.

The Cloud Forest: A Chronicle of the South American Wilderness (Ingram, 1996) is a travelogue by Peter Matthiessen, who trekked some 10,000 miles through South America, including the Amazon and Machu Picchu. Matthiessen found larger-than-life characters and ancient trails deep in the jungle, experiences that led to the author's fictional novel *At Play in the Fields of the Lord* (Vintage Books, 1991). Set in the unnamed Peruvian jungle, it's a thriller about the travails of the missionary Martin Quarrier and an outsider, Lewis Moon, a mercenary who takes a much different tack while immersing himself in a foreign culture. Both are displaced outsiders whose lives have an irreversible impact on native Amerindian communities deep in the Amazon.

Another good travelogue on Peru is *The White Rock* (Overlook, 2003) by Hugh Thomson, an absorbing account of Thomson's 20 years traveling throughout the Andes of Peru, Bolivia, and Ecuador in search of lost Inca cities.

The towering figure in contemporary Peruvian fiction is Mario Vargas Llosa, Peru's most famous novelist and a winner of the Nobel Prize in Literature, who was nearly elected the country's president back in 1990. It's difficult to choose from among his oeuvre of thoroughly praised works; *Aunt Julia and the Scriptwriter* (Penguin, 1995) is one of his most popular works, but it's without the heft of others, such as *The Real Life of Alejandro Mayta* (Noonday Press, 1998), a dense meditation on Peruvian and South American revolutionary politics that blurs the lines between truth and fiction, or *Death in the Andes* (Penguin, 1997), a deep penetration into the contemporary psyche and politics of Peru. Another side of the author is evident in the small erotic gem *In Praise of the Stepmother* (Penguin, 1991), a surprising and beautifully illustrated book. His powerful book *The Feast of the Goat* (Farrar Straus & Giroux, 2001), about the Dominican dictator Rafael Trujillo, made the year-end best lists of many critics in 2001. Vargas Llosa might be a difficult and "heavy" writer, but he is an unusually engaging one.

Alonso Cueto is one of the next generation's most ballyhooed novelists; he won several international awards for *La Hora Azul (The Blue Hour;* Editorial Anagrama, 2005). *El Susurro de la Mujer Ballena (The Whisper of the Whale Woman;* Planeta, 2007) is his latest.

César Vallejo, born in Peru in 1892, is one of the great poets of Latin America and the Spanish language. His *Complete Posthumous Poetry* (University of California Press, 1980), in translation, and *Trilce* (Wesleyan University Press, 2000), a bilingual publication, are the best places to start. Vallejo wrote some of the poems in *Trilce,* a wildly creative and innovative avant-garde work that today is considered a masterpiece of modernism, while in prison. Vallejo later fled to Europe and immersed himself in the Spanish Civil War.

Culinary books are becoming increasingly popular as Peruvian cuisine becomes more internationally known. *Peru: The Cookbook* (Phaidon, 2015), by Gastón Acurio, features 500 traditional recipes from around the country. *Ceviche: Peruvian Kitchen* (Ten Speed Press, 2014), from London restaurateur Martin Morales, has a mix of classic and contemporary Peruvian recipes.

Film

Peru's film industry trails far behind those of its neighbors Argentina and Brazil, though a recent Oscar nomination may begin to change that. In a historic achievement for Peruvian film, *La Teta Asustada (The Milk of Sorrow)* by Claudia Llosa was nominated for an Academy Award for Best Foreign Language Film in 2010 (it also received the Golden Bear award at the Berlin International Film Festival in 2009). Less exalted but also reaching an international audience was *Máncora* (Maya Entertainment Group, 2009), a sexy Peruvian road movie set in part in the Pacific surfing resort along the northern coast, which debuted at the Sundance Film Festival in 2009.

The best-known films about or featuring Peru are foreign. Two documentaries try to untangle the lasting impact of disgraced former president Alberto Fujimori. *The Fall of Fujimori: When Democracy and Terrorism Collide* (Stardust Productions, 2006) is a portrait of the eccentric ex-president and his controversial war against guerrilla movements in Peru. *State of Fear* (Skylight Pictures, 2006), based on the findings of the Peruvian Truth Commission, chronicles the 2-decade-long reign of terror by Shining Path. It doesn't shy away from documenting the abuses of the government in fighting terrorism.

Touching the Void (IFC Films, 2004), available on DVD, is the harrowing dramatic reenactment (based on the book by Joe Simpson) of a climber's disastrous and near-fatal accident climbing in the Andes Mountains near Huaraz. It is gripping, but may derail any mountaineering plans you had.

The Dancer Upstairs (Fox Searchlight, 2003), a drama directed by John Malkovich and starring Javier Bardem, is a political thriller loosely based on the hunt for Abimael Guzman, the Shining Path leader, and the complicated story of the American Lori Benson, implicated and imprisoned as a terrorist collaborator in Peru (though the movie is set in an unnamed South American nation). *The Motorcycle Diaries* (MCA Home Video, 2005), an excellent film by Walter Salles about the young Che Guevara, is, in large part, a travelogue of Argentina, Chile, Colombia, and Venezuela, but Machu Picchu plays a scene-stealing role.

On a slightly less artistic note, the last installment in the Indiana Jones series, *Indiana Jones and the Kingdom of the Crystal Skull* (Paramount Home Entertainment, 2008) takes place in part in Peru, including the Nazca Lines and (ostensibly) the Peruvian jungle (actually filmed in Hawaii).

Peter Matthiessen's novel *At Play in the Fields of the Lord* (1991) was later made by Hector Babenco into an occasionally pretty but silly movie starring John Lithgow, Daryl Hannah, and Tom Beringer with a bowl-cut and face paint, and relocated from the Amazon basin of Peru to Brazil.

WHEN TO GO

Peak travel season for foreigners is, in great part, determined by the weather. Peru experiences two very distinct seasons, wet and dry—terms that are much more relevant than "summer" and "winter." Peru's high season for travel coincides with the driest months: May through October, with by far the greatest number of visitors in July and August. May and September are particularly fine months to visit much of the country. Airlines and hotels also consider the period from mid-December through mid-January as peak season.

From June to September (winter in the Southern Hemisphere) in the highlands, days are clear and often spectacularly sunny, with chilly or downright cold nights, especially at high elevations. For trekking in the mountains, including the Inca Trail, these are by far the best months. This is also the best time of the year to visit the Amazon basin: Mosquitoes are fewer, and many fauna stay close to the rivers (although some people prefer to travel in the jungle during the wet season, when higher water levels allow for more river penetration). Note that Peruvians travel in huge numbers around July 28, the national holiday, and finding accommodations in popular destinations around this time can be difficult.

Climate

Generally, May through October is the dry season; November through April is the rainy season, and the wettest months are January through April. In mountain areas, roads and trek paths can become impassable. Peru's climate, though, is markedly different among its three regions. The coast is predominantly arid and mild, the Andean region is temperate to cold, and the eastern lowlands are tropically warm and humid.

On the desert **coast,** summer (Dec–Apr) is hot and dry, with temperatures reaching 77°F to 95°F (25°C–35°C) or more along the north coast. In winter (May–Oct), temperatures are much milder, though with high humidity. Much of the coast, including Lima, is shrouded in a gray mist called *garúa.* Only extreme northern beaches are warm enough for swimming.

In the **highlands** from May to October, rain is scarce. Daytime temperatures reach a warm 68°F to 77°F (20°C–25°C), and nights are often quite cold (near freezing), especially in June and July. Rainfall is very abundant from

Lima's Average Temperatures & Precipitation

	JAN	FEB	MAR	APR	MAY	JUNE	JULY	AUG	SEPT	OCT	NOV	DEC
Avg. High (°F)	77	79	79	75	70	66	63	63	63	66	68	73
Avg. High (°C)	25	26	26	24	21	19	17	17	17	19	20	23
Avg. Low (°F)	66	68	66	65	61	59	57	56	56	57	61	63
Avg. Low (°C)	19	20	19	18	16	15	14	13	13	14	16	17
Wet Days	1	0	0	0	1	1	1	2	1	0	0	0

Cusco's Average Temperatures & Precipitation

	JAN	FEB	MAR	APR	MAY	JUNE	JULY	AUG	SEPT	OCT	NOV	DEC
Avg. High (°F)	66	66	67	68	68	67	67	68	68	70	69	68
Avg. High (°C)	19	19	19	20	20	19	19	20	20	21	21	20
Avg. Low (°F)	44	44	44	41	37	34	34	34	39	42	43	43
Avg. Low (°C)	7	7	7	5	3	1	1	1	4	6	6	6
Wet Days	12	11	10	6	4	3	4	3	2	2	1	5

December to March, when temperatures are slightly milder—64°F to 68°F (18°C–20°C), dropping only to 59°F (15°C) at night. The wettest months are January and February. Most mornings are dry, but clouds move in during the afternoon and produce heavy downpours.

Although the Amazon **jungle** is consistently humid and tropical, with significant rainfall year-round, it, too, experiences two clearly different seasons. During the dry season (May–Oct), temperatures reach 86°F to 100°F (30°C–38°C) during the day. From November to April, there are frequent rain showers (which last only a few hours at a time), causing the rivers to swell; temperatures are similarly steamy.

Current Weather Conditions   The best place to head online for a detailed weather forecast is www.wunderground.com/global/PR.html.

When You'll Find Bargains   The cheapest time to fly to Peru is usually during the off season: from late October to mid-December and from mid-January through April. Though that coincides with the rainy season in the highlands and jungle, it's the peak of summer along the coast, and many Peruvians vacation in coastal resorts December through February. Remember that weekday flights are often cheaper than weekend fares.

Rates generally increase in June, then hit their peak in high travel seasons between July and September, and in December for the run-up to Christmas and New Year. July and August are also when most Europeans take their holidays, so besides higher prices, there are more crowds and more limited availability of the best hotel rooms.

You can avoid crowds, to some extent, by planning trips for October through April, though you should be mindful of the trade-off in weather conditions. In general, the shoulder seasons (April to June, late September through October) are the best combination of fewer crowds and relatively lower prices. Be mindful of major Peruvian holidays, particularly at places like Cusco and Machu Picchu, which are also major destinations for Peruvians as well as international travelers.

Calendar of Events

For additional information on major festivals, see www.infoperu.com.pe/en/informacion_fest. php. For additional information about regional festivals, see individual destination chapters.

JANUARY

Entrega de Varas, Cusco. Community elders (*yayas*) designate the highest authorities of their villages in this pre-Columbian festival, which is celebrated with *chicha* (fermented maize beer) and *llonque* (sugar-cane alcohol); elders give the mayor the *vara* (a staff, or scepter) as a symbol of his position of authority. January 1.

FEBRUARY

Carnaval. Lively pre-Lenten festivities. (Look out for balloons filled with water—or worse.) Cajamarca is reputed to have the best and wildest parties; Puno and Cusco are also good. The weekend before Ash Wednesday.

MARCH

Festival Internacional de la Vendimia (Wine Festival), Ica. A celebration of the grape harvest and the region's wine and pisco brandy, with fairs, beauty contests, floats, and musical festivals, including Afro-Peruvian dance. Second week of March.

Semana Santa. Handsome and spectacularly reverent processions mark Easter week. The finest are in Cusco and Ayacucho. Late March/early April.

Lord of the Earthquakes, Cusco. Representing a 17th-century painting of Christ on the cross that is said to have saved the city from a devastating earthquake, the image of the Lord of Earthquakes (*El Señor de los Temblores*) is carried through the streets of Cusco in a reverential procession, much like the Incas once paraded the mummies of their chieftains and high priests. Easter Monday, late March or early April.

APRIL

Peruvian Paso Horse Festival, Pachacámac. The Peruvian Paso horse, one of the world's most beautiful breeds, is celebrated with the most important annual national competition at the Mamacona stables near Pachacámac, 30km (19 miles) south of Lima. April 15 to April 20.

MAY

Fiesta de la Cruz. The Festival of the Cross features folk music and dance, including "scissors dancers," and processions in which communities decorate crosses and prepare them for the procession to neighboring churches. The *danzantes de tijeras* (scissors dancers) re-create old times, when they performed on top of church bell towers. Today the objective is still to outdo one another with daring feats. Celebrations are especially lively in Lima, Cusco, and Ica. May 2 and 3.

Qoyllur Rit'i, Quispicanchis, near Cusco. A massive indigenous pilgrimage marks this ritual, which is tied to the fertility of the land and the worship of Apus, the spirits of the mountains. It forms part of the greatest festival of native Indian nations in the hemisphere: Qoyllur Rit'i. The main ceremony is held at the foot of Mount Ausangate, with 10,000 pilgrims climbing to the snowline along with dancers in full costume representing mythical characters. Others head to the summit in search of the Snow Star and take huge blocks of ice back down on their backs—holy water for irrigation purposes. First week in May.

JUNE

Corpus Christi, Cusco. A procession of saints and virgins arrives at the Catedral to "greet" the body of Christ. Members of nearby churches also take their patron saints in a procession. An overnight vigil is followed by a new procession around the Plaza de Armas, with images of five virgins clad in embroidered tunics and the images of four saints: Sebastian, Blas, Joseph, and the Apostle Santiago (St. James). Early June.

Virgen del Carmen, Paucartambo. In a remote highland village 4 hours from Cusco, thousands come to honor the Virgen del Carmen, or Mamacha Carmen, patron saint of the *mestizo* population, with 4 days of splendidly festive music and dance, as well as some of the wildest costumes in Peru.

Dancers even perform daring moves on rooftops. The festival ends in the cemetery in a show of respect for the souls of the dead. Pisac also celebrates the Virgen del Carmen festival, almost as colorfully. June 15 to June 18.

Inti Raymi, Cusco. The Inca Festival of the Sun—the mother of all pre-Columbian festivals—celebrates the winter solstice and honors the sun god with traditional pageantry, parades, and dances. One of the most vibrant and exciting of all Andean festivals, it draws thousands of visitors who fill Cusco's hotels. The principal event takes place at the Sacsayhuamán ruins and includes the sacrifice of a pair of llamas. General celebrations last several days. June 24.

San Juan, Cusco and Iquitos. The feast day of St. John the Baptist, a symbol of fertility and sensuality, is the most important date on the festival calendar in the entire Peruvian jungle. John the Baptist has taken on a major symbolic significance because of the importance of water as a vital element in the entire Amazon region. Events include fiestas with lots of music and regional cuisine. In Iquitos, don't miss the aphrodisiac potions with suggestive names. June 24 in Cusco; June 25 in Iquitos.

San Pedro/San Pablo, near fishing villages in Lima and Chiclayo. The patron saints of fishermen and farmers, Saint Peter and Saint Paul, are honored at this festival; figures of the saints are carried with incense, prayers, and hymns down to the sea and are taken by launch around the bay to bless the waters. June 29.

JULY

Fiestas Patrias. A series of patriotic parties mark Peru's independence from Spain in 1821. Official parades and functions are augmented by cockfighting, bullfighting, and Peruvian Paso horse exhibitions in other towns. The best celebrations are in Cusco, Puno, Isla Taquile, and Lima. July 28 and 29.

AUGUST

Santa Rosa de Lima, Lima. Major devotional processions honor the patron saint of Lima. August 30.

OCTOBER

El Señor de los Milagros, Lima. The Lord of Miracles is the largest procession in South America, and it dates from colonial times. Lasting nearly 24 hours and involving tens of thousands of purple-clad participants, it celebrates a Christ image (painted by an Angolan slave) that survived the 1746 earthquake and has since become the most venerated image in the capital. October 18.

NOVEMBER

Todos Santos & Día de los Muertos. Peruvians salute the dead by visiting cemeteries carrying flowers and food. Families hold candlelit vigils in the cemetery until dawn. The holiday is most vibrantly celebrated in the highlands. November 1 and 2.

DECEMBER

Santuranticuy Fair, Cusco. One of the largest arts-and-crafts fairs in Peru—literally, "saints for sale"—is held in the Plaza de Armas. Artisans lay out blankets around the square, as in traditional Andean markets, and sell figurines and Nativity scenes as well as ceramics, carvings, pottery, and *retablos* (altars). Vendors sell hot rum punch called *ponche.* December 24.

Public Holidays

National public holidays in Peru include New Year's Day (Jan 1), Three Kings Day (Jan 6), Maundy Thursday and Good Friday (Easter week, Mar or Apr), Labor Day (May 1), Fiestas Patrias (July 28–29), Battle of Angamos (Oct 8), All Saints' Day (Nov 1), Feast of the Immaculate Conception (Dec 8), and Christmas (Dec 24–25).

LIMA

Founded in 1535, Lima was the Spanish crown's "City of Kings," the richest and most important city in the Americas and considered to be the most beautiful colonial settlement in the region. Lima was home to some of the Americas' finest baroque and Renaissance churches, palaces, and mansions, as well as the continent's first university. Today's modern capital, with a population of nearly 9 million—about one-third of Peru's population—sprawling and chaotic Lima thoroughly dominates Peru's political and commercial life. Although many travelers used to give it short shrift, Lima is newly welcoming to visitors. The historic *centro* is being spruced up, and spread across the capital are the country's most creative restaurants, finest museums, and most vibrant nightlife. Limeño cuisine is the subject of growing international buzz, and foodies bent on a gastronomic tour of Peru are flocking to Lima's diverse restaurant scene.

History Peculiar in a modern capital, evidence of pre-Columbian culture exists throughout the city, with the remains of adobe pyramids next to high-rises. Founded by the conquistador Francisco Pizarro and for 2 centuries the headquarters of the Spanish Inquisition, the city's colonial wealth and importance are on view throughout Lima Centro.

Sightseeing Concentrate on colonial *casonas* and baroque churches in the historic center, as well as Peru's finest collection of archaeology museums. Then see a gentler side of the city in outer suburbs such as Barranco, a former fishing village along the coast.

Eating & Drinking Lima is not just the dining capital of Peru but the best eating city in South America. From *cevicherías* serving the city's signature dish and neighborhood *huariques* (holes-in-the-wall) to some of the world's top restaurants and Japanese and Chinese fusion cuisines, Lima's got it all. It also has Peru's best pisco bars; the pisco sour was born here, after all.

Arts & Culture The city's impressive art and archaeology museums serve as perfect introductions to the rich history and culture you'll encounter elsewhere in Peru; not to be missed are Rafael Larco Herrera Museum, with the world's largest private collection of pre-Columbian art, and Museo de la Nación, which traces the history of Peru's ancient civilizations.

Shopping Lima is Peru's shopping mecca, with superb regional handicrafts from across the country, ranging from excellent handmade textiles and colonial-style artwork to altarpieces from Ayacucho. Most head straight to the big markets in Miraflores, but a better experience is browsing small boutiques and galleries run by collectors and connoisseurs, especially in Barranco.

THE BEST TRAVEL EXPERIENCES IN LIMA

o **Delving into a pre-Columbian past:** Lima's first-class museums are a great introduction to Peru's complex ancient civilizations, from the Moche to the Chimú. But an unexpected tie to the past are the ancient adobe pyramids (such as Huaca Pucllana) plunked down in residential neighborhoods. See p. 67.

o **Strolling colonial Lima:** Newly safe and spruced-up Lima Centro is home to many of Peru's best colonial and republican-era palaces and mansions, baroque and Renaissance churches. Strolling through the historic quarter makes plain the city's great early importance. See p. 58.

o **Savoring ceviche:** Peru's signature dish is a tantalizing plate of raw fish and/or shellfish marinated in lime or lemon juice and *ajíes,* or chili peppers. A plate of tangy ceviche served at an informal neighborhood restaurant—a *huarique* to locals—is an unforgettable Limeño experience. See p. 72.

o **Kicking back in Barranco:** This easygoing former seaside village with colorfully painted old houses is the place to go to get away when you're feeling overwhelmed by Lima's big-city chaos. Famous for its happening nightlife, increasingly it's home to boutique hotels and terrific restaurants. See p. 53.

o **Rocking a *peña:*** Lima's vibrant *criolla* music culture is on display at its *peñas,* lively music clubs where folkloric and Afro-Peruvian music and dance, emphasizing both percussion and audience participation, go deep into the night. You've got to hit at least one in Lima. See p. 58.

ESSENTIALS

Getting There

By Plane Lima is the gateway for most international arrivals to Peru; see "Getting There" and "Getting Around" in Chapter 9 for more detailed information. All flights from North America and Europe arrive at Lima's **Aeropuerto Internacional Jorge Chávez** (www.lap.com.pe; © 01/595-0666), located 16km (10 miles) west of the city center. Lima is connected by air with all major cities in Peru; there are regular flights to Ayacucho, Cusco, Puerto Maldonado, Juliaca, Arequipa, Tacna, Cajamarca, Chiclayo, Trujillo, Pucallpa, Iquitos, Tarapoto, Tumbes, and Piura. The major domestic airlines are **Avianca** (www.avianca.com; © 01/511-8222), **LAN** (www.lan.com; © 212/582-3250 in the U.S., or **01/213-8200**), **LC Péru** (www.lcperu.pe; © 01/619-1313),

Peruvian Airlines (www.peruvian.pe; ✆ **01/716-6000**), and **Star Perú** (www.starperu.com; ✆ **01/705-9000**).

The airport has a tourist information booth (in the international terminal only), two 24-hour currency-exchange windows, three banks, ATMs, a post office, and car-rental desks, including **Avis** (www.avis.com; ✆ **01/575-1637,** ext. 4155), **Budget** (www.budget.com; ✆ **01/575-1674**), **Hertz** (www.hertz. com; ✆ **01/575-1390**), **National Car Rental** (www.nationalcar.com.pe; ✆ **01/578-7878**), and **Thrifty** (www.thriftyperu.com; ✆ **01/484-0749**). The tourist information booth can help with hotel reservations. The arrival and departure terminals can be very congested, especially when a number of international flights arrive at once, and early in the morning when many flights depart Lima for Cusco. Be very mindful of your luggage and other belongings at all times. To get through large groups of travelers and relatives all hovering about, you might need to forget about being polite and simply push your way through the crowd.

Remember to reconfirm your flight at least 48 hours in advance and arrive at the airport with ample time before your flight. *Flights are frequently overbooked,* and passengers who have not reconfirmed their flights or who arrive later than (usually) 45 minutes before scheduled departure risk being bumped from the flight. Flights to Cusco are especially popular; make your reservations as far in advance as possible. Also check to be sure that you will have enough time to make your connecting flight if coming from overseas.

To get from the airport to Lima—either downtown or to suburbs such as Miraflores, San Isidro, and Barranco (the sites of most tourist hotels)—you can take a taxi or private bus. When you exit with your luggage, you will immediately be besieged with taxi offers; the ones nearest the door are invariably the most expensive. **Taxi companies** (who have plenty of representatives hawking their services) are inside the security area at the international and domestic arrivals terminal, though Taxi Green is the most reliable. They charge S/50–S/55 to Miraflores (about 30 minutes to 1 hour from the airport) and S/40–S/45 to downtown Lima (Lima Centro)—though they'll almost certainly begin by asking for more. *Tip:* You get 15 minutes of free Wi-Fi on your smartphone at the airport, which is just enough time to order an Uber (www.uber.com), whose cars are always waiting outside, tend to be cheaper, and are GPS-enabled (this helps in a traffic jam).

Private **limousine taxis** (*taxis ejecutivos* or *remises*) also have desks in the airport; their fares are about $55 one-way. One to try is **MitsuTaxi** (✆ **01/261-7788**).

By Bus Lima is connected by bus to neighboring countries and all major cities in Peru. No central bus terminal exists, however; the multitude of bus companies serving various regions of the country all have terminals in Lima, making bus arrivals and departures exceedingly confusing for most travelers. Many terminals are located downtown, although several companies have their bases in the suburbs. Most bus terminals have nasty reputations for thievery and general unpleasantness; your best bet is to grab your things and hop into a cab pronto. Of the dozens of bus companies servicing the capital and points around the country, the largest with frequent service in and out of Lima are **Ormeño,** at Av. Javier Prado Este 1059, San Isidro (www.grupo-ormeno.com. pe/ormeno.php; ℂ **01/472-5000**); **Cruz del Sur,** Av. Javier Prado Este 1101, La Victoria (www.cruzdelsur.com.pe; ℂ **01/311-5050**); **Excluciva,** Av. Javier Prado Este 1155, La Victoria (www.civa.com.pe; ℂ **01/418-1111**); and **Oltursa,** Av. Aramburú 1160, San Isidro (www.oltursa.com.pe; ℂ **01/708-5000**).

Visitor Information

A 24-hour tourist information booth, **iPerú** (ℂ **01/574-8000**), operates in the international terminal at the Jorge Chávez International Airport. The most helpful **iPerú** office is in Miraflores, at the **Larcomar** shopping mall, Módulo 10, Av. Malecón de la Reserva 610 (ℂ **01/445-9400**), open Monday through Friday from 11am to 1pm and 2 to 8pm. The **Oficina de Información Turística** in Lima Centro is at Pasaje Los Escribanos 145, just off the Plaza de Armas, in Lima Centro (ℂ **01/427-6080**); it's open Monday through Saturday from 9am to 6pm.

One of the best private agencies for arrangements and city tours, as well as general information, is **Lima Tours,** Jr. Junín 211 (www.limatours.com.pe; ℂ **01/619-6900**), with a downtown office at Nicolás de Piérola 589, 18th floor. Another excellent spot for information and advice, particularly on outdoor and adventure travel in Peru, such as trekking, mountaineering, and rafting, is the office of **South American Explorers,** Enrique Palacios 956, Miraflores (www.saexplorers.org; ℂ **01/445-3306**). The organization is legendary among veteran South American travelers, and it's not a bad idea to become a member ($60) before traveling so that you can take advantage of its resources (you can also join on the spot). The clubhouse in Lima maintains a library of maps, books, trail information, trip reports, and storage facilities. It's open Monday through Friday from 9:30am to 4:30pm and Saturday from 9:30am to 1pm. There are also clubhouses in Cusco and Quito, Ecuador.

City Layout

Lima is an exceedingly diffuse city, so it's complicated to get around. The city center, known as Lima Centro, abuts the Río Rímac and the Rímac district across the river. The city beyond central Lima is a warren of ill-defined neighborhoods; most visitors are likely to set foot in only San Isidro, Miraflores, and Barranco, which hug the coast and the circuit of urban beaches leading to the so-called "Costa Verde." Major thoroughfares leading from the city center to outer neighborhoods are Avenida Benavides (to Callao); Avenida Brasil (to Pueblo Libre); Avenida Arequipa, Avenida Tacna, and Avenida Garcilaso de la Vega (to San Isidro and Miraflores); Paseo de la República (also known as Vía Expresa) and Avenida Panamá (to Miraflores and Barranco); and Avenida Panamericana Sur (to San Borja and south of Lima).

Neighborhoods in Brief

Lima Centro Lima Centro is the historic heart of the city, where the Spaniards built the country's capital in colonial fashion. It has repeatedly suffered from earthquakes, fires, and neglect, so although it was once the continent's most important colonial city, stunning examples of the original town are less prevalent than one might expect. Much of Lima Centro is dirty, unsafe, crowded, and chaotic, although city officials are slowly getting around to much-needed restorations of the remaining historic buildings and have drastically upgraded police presence in the city center (making it just about as safe as anywhere in the city during the day). The great majority of visitors stay in outer suburbs rather than Lima Centro; most hotels are small *hostales* (inns) aimed at budget travelers and backpackers. The absolute heart of the Lima Centro is the Plaza de Armas, site of La Catedral (cathedral) and government palaces, and nearly all the colonial mansions and churches of interest are within walking distance of the square. Several of Lima's top museums are in **Pueblo Libre,** a couple of kilometers southwest of Lima Centro, while **San Borja,** a couple of kilometers directly southeast of Lima Centro, holds two of the finest collections in all of Peru.

Miraflores & San Isidro San Isidro and Miraflores, the city's most exclusive residential and commercial neighborhoods, are farther south (5–8km/3–5 miles) toward the coast. These districts are now the commercial heart of the city, having usurped that title from Lima Centro some years ago. San Isidro holds many of the city's top luxury hotels and a slew of offices and shopping malls. Miraflores is the focus of most travelers' visits to Lima; it contains the greatest number and variety of hotels, bars, and restaurants, as well as shopping outlets. A number of the city's finest hotels are along the *malecón* (boulevard) in Miraflores. Although San Isidro and Miraflores are middle-class neighborhoods, both are congested and not entirely free of crime.

Barranco Barranco, several kilometers farther out along the ocean, is a tranquil former seaside village that is the city's coolest and most relaxed district, now known primarily for its nightlife. It is where you'll find many of Lima's best restaurants and especially bars, and live-music spots, frequented by Limeños and visitors alike. Though there are only a few boutique hotels and hostels in Barranco, increasingly it's becoming a cool place to stay, especially for the young and sophisticated. The next district south along the beach is **Chorrillos,** a residential neighborhood known primarily for the Club de Regattas, a pricey beach club, as well as Morro Solar, a cluster of brown hills that form the southern end of the city. A controversial statue, Cristo del Pacifico, a 37m (121-ft.) statue of Christ, stands here, privately funded by former president Alan García, and can be seen glowing in the night from across the city. Beyond the Morro Solar are the *Pantanos de Villa,* swamps that are rich with flora and fauna.

Getting Around

Navigating Lima is a complicated and time-consuming task, made difficult by the city's sprawling character (many of the best hotels and restaurants are far from downtown, spread among three or more residential neighborhoods), heavy traffic and pollution, and a chaotic network of confusing and crowded *colectivos* and unregulated taxis.

By Taxi Taxis hailed on the street are a reasonable and relatively quick way to get around in Lima. However, taxis are wholly unregulated by the government: All anyone has to do to become a taxi driver is get his hands on a vehicle—of any size and condition, although most are tiny Daewoo

"Ticos"—and plunk a cheap TAXI sticker inside the windshield. Then he is free to charge whatever he thinks he can get—with no meters, no laws, and nobody to answer to except the free market. One has to counsel visitors to be a bit wary of taking taxis in Lima, even though I personally have never had problems greater than a dispute over a fare. (If you're not fluent in Spanish, and even if you are but you have an obviously non-Peruvian appearance, be prepared to negotiate fares.) Limeños tell enough stories of theft and even the occasional violent crime in unregistered cabs to make hailing one on the street inadvisable for older visitors or for those with little command of Spanish or experience traveling in Latin America. If the issue of getting into quasi-official cabs makes you nervous, by all means call a registered company—especially at night (even though the fare can be twice as much).

Registered, reputable taxi companies—the safest option—can be called from your hotel or restaurant, or you can call direct to **Alo Taxi** (✆ **01/217-7777**), **Taxi Móvil** (✆ **01/422-3322**), and **Taxi San Borja** (✆ **01/225-8600**). Whether you call or hail a taxi, you'll need to establish a price beforehand—so be prepared to bargain. Most fares range from S/5 to S/25. From Miraflores or San Isidro to downtown, expect to pay S/20 to S/25; and from Miraflores to Barranco, S/12 to S/15. Note that when you hail a taxi on the street, the fare requested will surely be a bit higher; it makes sense to try to haggle. Only pay upon reaching your destination.

As an alternative, taxis hailed from smartphone apps like **Uber** or **Easy Taxi** are a secure alternative, and prices tend to be cheaper than hailing in the street. In neighborhoods such as Barranco, Miraflores, or San Isidro, most will have a car at your location within 5 to 10 minutes upon ordering.

By Bus The biggest advancement in public transportation in Lima's history was the 2010 inauguration of the modern, clean, and very efficient **Metropolitano Bus** (www.metropolitano.com.pe; ✆ **01/203-9000**), which travels along the Vía Expresa and Paseo de la República, connecting Lima Centro to Miraflores, Barranco, and as far south along the coast as Chorrillos. It is most convenient for traveling to Lima Centro, Miraflores, and Barranco, although the single, straight line of stops will still leave you a long walk or short taxi ride from many destinations (six new routes are planned for the future). Fares are S/1.50, deducted from a minimum fare card of S/5. The buses run daily from 6am to 9:50pm. The major stops are as follows: in Lima Centro: Tacna and Jr. de la Unión; in San Isidro: Javier Prado, Canaval y Moreyra, and Aramburú; in Miraflores: Angamos, Ricardo Palma, Benavides, and 28 de Julio; and in Barranco: Balta and Bulevar.

Other than the Metropolitano, *micros, colectivos,* and *combis* (all names for varying sizes of buses that make both regular and unscheduled stops) are very inexpensive means of transportation in the city, but are very confusing for most visitors, can be dangerous, and in general are not recommended. (See the "*Combi* or *Carro*? Getting Around in and out of Town" box in Chapter 9 for more info about *micros* and *combis*.) Routes are more or less identified by signs with street names placed in the windshield, making many trips confusing for those unfamiliar with Lima. Some do nothing more than race up and down long avenues (for example, the bus labeled TODO AREQUIPA travels the length of Avenida Arequipa). For assistance, ask a local for help; most Limeños know the incredibly complex bus system surprisingly well. Although the buses sometimes seem to hurtle down the street, because they make so many stops, trips from the outer suburbs to downtown can be quite slow. Most *micros* and *combis* cost S/3, and slightly more after midnight and on Sunday and holidays. When you want to get off, shout *baja* (getting off) or *esquina* (at the corner). From Lima Centro to Miraflores, look for buses with signs in the windows indicating LARCO–SCHELL–MIRAFLORES (or some combination thereof). From Miraflores to downtown Lima, you should hop on a bus headed along WILSON/TACNA. Buses to Barranco have signs that read CHORILLOS/HUAYLAS.

By Foot Lima can be navigated by foot only a neighborhood at a time (and even then, congestion and pollution strongly discourage much walking). Lima Centro and Barranco are best seen by foot, and, although large, Miraflores is also walkable. Between neighborhoods, however, a taxi is essential.

By Car For getting around Lima or the immediate region, this is not even a consideration.

[FastFACTS] LIMA

ATMs/Banks Peruvian and international banks with currency-exchange bureaus and ATMs are plentiful throughout Lima Centro, especially in the outer neighborhoods such as Miraflores, San Isidro, and Barranco, which are full of shopping centers, hotels, and restaurants. Money-changers (sometimes in smocks with obvious "$" insignias) patrol the main streets off Parque Central in Miraflores and central Lima with calculators and dollars in hand.

Dentists For English-speaking dentists in Lima, try **Peru Dental** at 355 Monterrey St., 4th Floor, Chacarilla (www.perudental. com; ✆ 01/202-2222), or **Smiles Peru** at Av. José Prado 575, office 201 in Miraflores (www.smilesperu. com; ✆ 01/242-2152).

Doctors & Hospitals The U.S. and British embassies (see "Embassies & Consulates") provide lists of English-speaking doctors, dentists, and other health-care personnel in Lima. English-speaking medical personnel and 24-hour emergency services are available at the following hospitals and clinics: **Clínica Anglo-Americana,** Alfredo Salazar, Block 3, San Isidro (✆ 01/712-3000); **Clínica San Borja,** Guardia Civil 337, San Borja (✆ 01/475-4000); **Maison de Santé,** Calle Miguel Adgouin 208 (✆ 01/619-610), near the Palacio de Justicia (✆ 01/428-3000, emergency 01/427-2941); and **Clínica Ricardo Palma,** Av. Javier Prado Este 1066, San Isidro (✆ 01/224-2224). For an ambulance, call **Alerta**

Médica at ✆ 01/470-5000 or **San Cristóbal** at ✆ 01/440-0200.

Embassies & Consulates U.S., Avenida La Encalada, Block 17, Surco (✆ 01/434-3000); **Australia,** Víctor A. Belaúnde 147/Vía Principal 155, office 1301, San Isidro (✆ 01/222-8281); **Canada,** Calle Bolognesi 228, Miraflores (✆ 01/319-3200); **U.K.** and **New Zealand,** Av. Jose Larco 1301, Miraflores (✆ 01/617-3000).

Emergencies In case of an emergency, call the 24-hour **traveler's hotline** (✆ 01/574-8000) or the **tourist police,** OR POLTUR (✆ 01/460-1060 in Lima, or 01/460-0965). The **INDECOPI** 24-hour hotline can also assist in contacting police to report a crime

01/224-7888 in Lima, 01/224-8600, or toll-free 0800/42579 from any private phone).The general **police** emergency number is ℂ **105;** for **fire,** dial ℂ **116.**

Internet Access Public Wi-Fi has overtaken Internet *cabinas* (booths) and cyber-cafes as the most common form of Internet access in Lima. There is free Wi-Fi access almost everywhere if you have a smartphone, laptop, or tablet. You'll find it in shopping centers, public parks, restaurants, cafes, and nearly every hotel in Lima.

Mail & Postage Lima's main post office (*Central de Correos*) is on the Plaza de Armas at Camaná 195 (ℂ **01/427-0370**) in central Lima. The Miraflores branch is at Petit Thouars 5201 (ℂ **01/445-0697**); the San Isidro branch is at Calle Las Palmeras 205 (ℂ **01/422-0981**). Letters and postcards to North America or Europe take between 10 days and 2 weeks, and cost S/7–8 for postcards, S/9–10 for letters. A **DHL/Western Union** office is at Nicolás de Piérola 808 (ℂ **01/424-5820**).

Pharmacies A pharmacy chain with a number of storefronts across Lima is **InkaFarma.** Miraflores locations include Av. Benavides 1921 (ℂ **01/271-4796**) and Av. José Pardo 620 (ℂ **01/243-4711**). This and other pharmacies have 24-hour delivery service.

Police The **Policía Nacional de Turismo (National Tourism Police)** has staff members that speak English and are specifically trained to handle the needs of foreign visitors. The main office in Lima is at Av. Javier Prado Este 2465, 5th Floor, San Borja (next to the Museo de la Nación); the 24-hour tourist police line is ℂ **01/574-8000.** Also see "Emergencies" above.

Safety Lima neighborhoods such as Miraflores and San Isidro are as safe and as calm as most North American cities, though in Lima Centro and some of the city's residential areas, the risk of street crime remains. Although carjackings, assaults, and armed robberies are not routine, they're not unheard of either. Armed attacks at ATMs have also occurred. Use ATMs during the day, with other people present. Most thefts occur on public transportation, such as buses and *combis*. There have been several reports of thieves who've boarded buses in and out of Lima to cities both north and south of the capital, relieving passengers at gunpoint of their valuables. Be very careful with your belongings; leave your passport and other valuables in the hotel safe, and use a money belt. Public street markets are also frequented by thieves, as are parks (especially at night) and the beaches in and around Lima. Although the large-scale terrorist activities of the local groups Sendero Luminoso and MRTA were largely stamped out in the early 1990s, there are occasionally reports of a possible resurgence. Neither group, however, is currently active in any of the areas covered in this book.

Telephone Lima's area code is 01. It need not be dialed when making local calls within Lima, but it must be dialed when calling Lima from another city.

EXPLORING LIMA

Many visitors to Lima are merely on their way to other places in Peru, and few spend more than a couple of days in the capital. But because nearly all transport goes through Lima, most people take advantage of layovers to see what distinguishes the city: its colonial old quarter—once the finest in the Americas—and several of the finest museums in Peru, all of which serve as magnificent introductions to Peruvian history and culture.

Much of the historic center has suffered from sad neglect; the municipal government is committed to restoring the aesthetic value, but, with limited

What to See & Do in Lima Centro

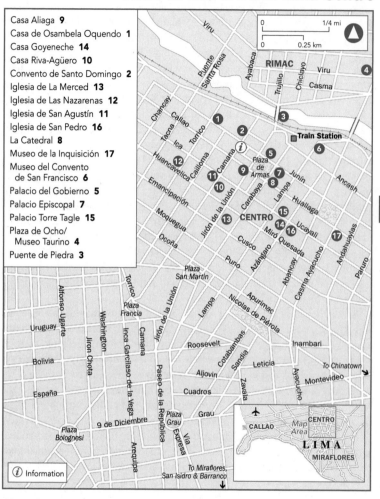

Casa Aliaga **9**
Casa de Osambela Oquendo **1**
Casa Goyeneche **14**
Casa Riva-Agüero **10**
Convento de Santo Domingo **2**
Iglesia de La Merced **13**
Iglesia de Las Nazarenas **12**
Iglesia de San Agustín **11**
Iglesia de San Pedro **16**
La Catedral **8**
Museo de la Inquisición **17**
Museo del Convento
  de San Francisco **6**
Palacio del Gobierno **5**
Palacio Episcopal **7**
Palacio Torre Tagle **15**
Plaza de Ocho/
  Museo Taurino **4**
Puente de Piedra **3**

(i) Information

funds, it faces a daunting task. Today central Lima has a noticeable police presence and is considerably safer than it was in years past. A full day in Lima Centro should suffice; depending on your interests, you could spend several days traipsing through Lima's many museum collections, many of which are dispersed in otherwise unremarkable neighborhoods. But for those with a couple of extra days in the city, when Lima's traffic and grit get to you, head to the artsy coastal neighborhood, Barranco, home to Lima's best nightlife and the site of a handful of excellent small museums. It will likely greatly improve your impressions of the capital.

Lima Centro: Colonial Lima

Lima's grand **Plaza de Armas ★** (also called the **Plaza Mayor,** or **Main Square**), the original center of the city and the site where Francisco Pizarro founded the city in 1535, is essentially a modern reconstruction. The disastrous 1746 earthquake that initiated the city's decline leveled most of the 16th- and 17th-century buildings in the old center. The plaza has witnessed everything from bullfights to Inquisition-related executions. The oldest surviving element of the square is the central bronze fountain, which dates from 1651. Today the square, although perhaps not the most beautiful or languid in South America, is still rather distinguished beneath a surface level of grime and bustle (and it has been named a UNESCO World Heritage Site). The major palaces and cathedral are mostly harmonious in architectural style and color. (The facades are a mix of natural stone and a once-bold yellow color now dulled by smog and mist.) On the north side of the square is the early-20th-century **Palacio del Gobierno (Presidential Palace),** where a changing of the guard takes place daily at noon; free guided visits of the palace are offered Monday through Friday from 10am to 12:30pm. The **Municipalidad de Lima (City Hall)** is on the west side of the plaza. Across the square is **La Catedral (Cathedral),** rebuilt after the earthquake, making it by far the oldest building on the square, and, next to the cathedral, the **Palacio Episcopal (Archbishop's Palace),** distinguished by an extraordinary wooden balcony.

A block north of the Plaza de Armas, behind the Presidential Palace, is the Río Rímac and a 17th-century Roman-style bridge, the **Puente de Piedra** (literally, "stone bridge"). It leads to the once-fashionable **Rímac** district, today considerably less chic—some would say downright dangerous—although it is the location of a few of Lima's best *peñas,* or live *criolla* (Creole/coastal) music clubs. The **Plaza de Acho bullring,** once the largest in the world, and the decent **Museo Taurino (Bullfighting Museum)** are near the river at Hualgayoc 332 (© **01/482-3360**). The museum is open Monday through Friday from 9am to 3pm and Saturday from 9am to 2pm, and admission is S/6. The ring is in full swing during the Fiestas Patrias (national holidays) at the end of July; the regular season runs October through December.

Five blocks southwest of Plaza de Armas is Lima Centro's other grand square, **Plaza San Martín.** Inaugurated in 1921, this stately square with handsome gardens was recently renovated. At its center is a large monument to the South American liberator, José de San Martín.

Lima's **Barrio Chino,** the largest Chinese community in South America (200,000 plus), is the best place to get a taste of the Peruvian twist on traditional Chinese cooking in the neighborhood's *chifas.* For recommendations, see the "Peruvian *Chifas*" box on p. 71. The official boundary of Chinatown is the large gate on Jirón Ucayali.

THE TOP ATTRACTIONS

Catedral de Lima ★ CATHEDRAL Lima's baroque cathedral, an enlargement of an earlier one from 1555, was completed in 1625. It suffered damages in earthquakes in 1687 and was decimated by the big one in 1746.

The present building, again damaged by tremors in 1940, is an 18th-century reconstruction of the early plans. Twin yellow towers sandwich an elaborate stone facade. Inside are several notable *churrigueresque* (Spanish baroque) altars and carved wooden choir stalls, but the cathedral is best known for the chapel where Francisco Pizarro lies and a small **Museo de Arte Religioso (Museum of Religious Art)** housed in the rear of the church.

Immediately to the right after you enter the church is a chapel decorated in magnificent Venetian mosaics and marble. In case you don't know whose earthly remains are inside the tomb, letters in mosaic tiles over the arch of the chapel spell out FRANCISCO PIZARRO. The founder of Lima and killer of the Incas' emperor was himself assassinated in the Plaza de Armas in 1541, but his remains weren't brought to the cathedral until 1985. (They were discovered in a crypt in 1977.) Look closely at the mosaic on the far wall, which depicts his coat of arms, Atahualpa reaching into his coffer to cough up a ransom in the hopes of attaining his release, and other symbols of Pizarro's life. The museum has a few fabulous painted-glass mirrors from Cusco, a collection of unsigned paintings, and a seated sculpture of Jesus, with his chin resting pensively on his hand; it's as bloody a figure of Christ as you're likely to see. Allow about an hour for a visit.

Plaza de Armas. www.arzobispadodelima.org. © **01/427-9647.** Admission to cathedral and museum S/10 adults, S/5 students. Guides available in English and Spanish (voluntary tip). Mon–Sat 10am–5pm.

Museo de la Inquisición ★ MUSEUM Across the street from Congress, this elegant 16th-century colonial mansion once belonged to the family considered the founders of Lima, but it became the site of a tribunal for the notorious Spanish Inquisition. The museum soberly addresses this phase of religious intolerance in Lima, where at least 32 Peruvians died and countless others were tortured during the Inquisition, which persisted until 1820. The unfortunate history is plainly evident in the catacombs, which served as prison cells; on view are several instruments of torture. The guided tour lasts about an hour. Be sure to take note of the intricately carved ceiling of the Tribunal room, which was home to the National Senate during republican times.

Plaza Bolívar (Junín 548). www.congreso.gob.pe/museo.htm. © **01/428-7980.** Free admission. Guided tours in English, Spanish, French, and Portuguese. Daily 9am–5pm.

Museo del Convento de San Francisco de Asis de Lima ★★★ CONVENT/MUSEUM The yellow and white 17th-century Convent of Saint Francis is one of the most striking of Lima's Colonial-era churches, not to mention one of the few that survived the 1746 earthquake. A mandatory guided tour takes visitors through many highlights, such as an extraordinary library with 20,000 books, many of them centuries old, and a museum of religious art with a series of portraits of the apostles by the studio of famed Spanish painter Francisco Zurbarán. You'll also find carved *mudéjar* (Moorish-style) ceilings, and cloisters lined with *azulejos* (glazed ceramic tiles) from Seville. The most memorable aspect of a visit is without a doubt what lies underneath the compound. Beginning in 1546, before the main cemetery

A "MAGIC" water PARK

One of Centro's most colorful attractions, the fountains of the **Circuito Mágico del Agua** water park ★ is a great place to take the kids and beat the summer heat. The best time to visit the 13 fountains shooting into the sky and a tunnel kids will love to carouse beneath is at night, when the spectacle of colorful effects and dancing waters set to music is delightful (shows at 7:15, 8:15, and 9:30pm). The centerpiece, the Magic Fountain, propels a stream 76m (250 ft.) into the air, a Guinness record. The water park (✆ **01/427-1993**) is located at Parque de la Reserva (Av. Petit Thouars at Jr. Madre de Dios), in the Santa Beatriz district. It's open Wednesday through Sunday, 3–10:30pm; admission is S/4, free for children under 4.

was built, this was a burial ground for priests and some other original residents of Lima. As many as 25,000 bodies were interred here, and a walk through the catacombs reveals creepy displays of bones, like a round well neatly lined with skulls and femurs. Allow 1½ hours to see it all, including waiting time for an English-language tour.

Ancash s/n (Plaza de San Francisco). www.museocatacumbas.com. ✆ **01/426-7377.** Admission S/7 adults, S/3.50 students. Guides available in English and Spanish. Daily 9:30am–5:30pm.

COLONIAL CHURCH ROUNDUP ★★

Lima Centro has a number of fine colonial-era churches worth visiting. Most are open Monday through Saturday for visits, and most have free admission.

Directly south of La Catedral on Azángaro at Ucayali, **San Pedro** ★ (✆ **01/428-3017**), a Jesuit church that dates to 1638, is perhaps the best-preserved example of early colonial religious architecture in the city. The exterior is simple and rather austere, but the interior is rich with gilded altars and balconies. The bold main altar, with columns and balconies and sculpted figures, is particularly impressive. There are also some beautiful 17th- and 18th-century baroque *retablos* (altars) of carved wood and gold leaf. A small museum of colonial art is to the right of the entrance of the church, which is open Monday through Saturday from 7am to noon and 5 to 8pm; admission is free.

Iglesia de La Merced, Jr. de la Unión at Miró Quesada (✆ **01/427-8199**), 2 blocks southwest of the Plaza de Armas, was erected on the site of Lima's first Mass in 1534. The 18th-century church has a striking carved baroque colonial facade. Inside, the sacristy, embellished with Moorish tiles, and the main altar are excellent examples of the period. The church also possesses a nice collection of colonial art. Yet it is perhaps most notable for the devoted followers of Padre Urraca, a 17th-century priest; they come daily in droves to pay their respects, praying and touching the large silver cross dedicated to him in the nave on the right, and leaving many mementos of their veneration. The church is open Monday through Saturday from 8am to noon and 4 to 8pm.

Practically destroyed during an 1895 revolution, **San Agustín,** at the corner of Jr. Ica and Jr. Camaná (℡ **01/427-7548**), is distinguished by a spectacular *churrigueresque* facade, one of the best of its kind in Peru, dating to the early 18th century. San Agustín's official hours are daily from 8 to 11am and 4:30 to 7pm, but, in practice, it's frequently closed. The **Convento de Santo Domingo,** at the corner of Conde de Superunda and Camaná, toward the River Rímac (℡ **01/427-6793**), draws many Peruvians to visit the tombs of Santa Rosa de Lima and San Martín de Porras. It is perhaps of less interest to foreign visitors, although it does have a very nice main cloister. It's open Monday through Saturday from 9am to 12:30pm and 3 to 6pm; admission is S/3.

Las Nazarenas, at the corner of Huancavelica and Avenida Tacna on the northwest edge of the colonial center (℡ **01/423-5718**), has a remarkable history. It was constructed in the 18th century around a locally famous painting of Christ by an Angolan slave. Known as "El Señor de los Milagros," the image, painted on the wall of a simple abode in 1651 (many slaves lived in this area on the fringes of the city), survived the massive 1655 earthquake, even though everything around it crumbled. The site was abandoned for 15 years until someone rediscovered it and began to build a shrine around it. People began to flock to the painting, and soon the Catholic Church constructed a house of worship for it. Behind the altar, on the still-standing wall, is an oil replica, which is paraded through the streets on a 1-ton silver litter during the El Señor de los Milagros festival; this is one of Lima's largest festivals and is held on October 18, 19, and 28 and November 1. Everyone wears purple during the procession. Las Nazarenas is open Monday through Saturday from 6:30am to noon and 5 to 8:30pm.

COLONIAL PALACE ROUNDUP ★

The historic quarter of Lima, the old administrative capital of Spain's South American colonies, once boasted many of the finest mansions in the hemisphere. Repeated devastation by earthquakes and more recent public and private inability to maintain many of the superb surviving *casas coloniales,* however, has left Lima with only a handful of houses open to the public.

Casa Riva-Agüero, Camaná 459 (ira.pucp.edu.pe; ℡ **01/626-6600**), is an impressive 18th-century mansion with a beautiful green-and-red courtyard that now belongs to the Catholic University of Peru. It has a small folk-art

Me Ama, No Me Ama, Me Ama . . .

A curious park along the ocean at the edge of Miraflores, much beloved by Limeños looking to score, is the **Parque del Amor** (literally, "Love Park"), designed by the Peruvian artist Victor Delfín with a nod to Antoni Gaudí's Parque Güell in Barcelona, Spain. It features good views of the sea (when it's not shrouded in heavy fog), benches swathed in broken-tile mosaics, and, most amusingly, a giant, rather grotesque statue of a couple making out—which is pretty much what everyone does nearby. Benches are inscribed with sentimental murmurs of love, such as *vuelve mi palomita.* If it's Valentine's Day, stand back.

museum in the restored and furnished interior. The house is open Monday through Friday from 10am to 5pm; admission is S/2. **Casa Aliaga ★★**, Jr. de la Unión 224 (www.casadealiaga.com; ✆ **01/427-7736**), is the oldest surviving house in Lima, dating from 1535. It is also one of Lima's finest mansions, with an extraordinary inner patio and elegant salons, and it continues to be owned and lived in by descendants of the original family. The house is open Monday through Friday from 9:30am to 5pm (by advance reservation only); admission is S/30. On Thursday evenings, the house accepts reservations for tasting menu dinners cooked by descendant Jeronimo de Aliaga, who has trained in many of Peru and Spain's finest restaurants. The house can also be visited as part of a city tour (S/75) conducted by **Lima Tours** (www.lima tours.com.pe; ✆ **01/619-6900**). A worthy alternative if you don't want to spring for a guided tour is **Casa de Osambela Oquendo,** Conde de Superunda 298 (✆ **01/428-7919**). The tallest house in colonial Lima, today it belongs to the Ministry of Education. Although it's still not officially open for visits, the caretaker will usually show visitors around, including up four levels to the baby-blue *cupola-mirador* for views over the city. (The original owner built the house so he could see all the way to the port.) The Osambela house has a spectacular patio, 40 bedrooms, and eight wooden balconies to the street, a sure sign of the owner's great wealth. It's open daily from 9am to 5pm; admission is free, but tips are accepted.

A couple of blocks east of the Plaza de Armas at Ucayali 363 is **Palacio Torre Tagle ★**, the most famous palace in Lima and one of the most handsome in Peru. Today the early-18th-century palace, built by a marquis who was treasurer of the Royal Spanish fleet, belongs to the Peruvian Ministry of Foreign Affairs and, sadly, can no longer be visited by the public (though it may be worth inquiring at the Ministry, next door at Ucayali 318). Its exterior, with a gorgeous baroque stone doorway and carved dark-wood balconies, is very much worth a look (and you might get a peek inside the courtyard if a group of dark suits enters or leaves when you're passing by). Across the street from Torre Tagle, **Casa Goyeneche** (also called **Casa de Rada**) is another impressive 18th-century mansion, with distinct French influences; it's also not open to the public (although you might be able to manage a peek at the patio). Those with a specific interest in colonial architecture might also want to have a look at the facades of **Casa Negreiros,** Jr. Azángaro 532; **Casa de las Trece Monedas,** Jr. Ancash 536; **Casa Barbieri,** Jirón Callao at Rufino Torrico; **Casa de Pilatos,** Jr. Ancash 390; and **Casa la Riva,** Jr. Ica 426.

THE TOP MUSEUMS

Museo Arqueológico Rafael Larco Herrera ★★★ MUSEUM If you have to choose only one museum to visit in Lima, the Museo Larco is it. Founded in 1926 and set in a modernized 18th-century colonial building, this museum has the largest private collection of pre-Columbian art in the world. Rafael Larco Hoyle, who named the museum after his father, is considered the godfather of Peruvian archaeology, and his museum leaves very few stones uncovered. The highlights are pieces from the Moche dynasty (A.D. 200–700),

Although a residential neighborhood and not immediately thought of as having many tourist sights, apart from the small but excellent Museo Pedro de Osma (p. 66), the charming seaside district of Barranco is still one of the highlights of Lima. Its serenity and laid-back artiness is a welcome contrast to the untidy and seedy character of the rest of the city, and a stroll around the tranquil side streets of brightly colored bungalows is the best way to restore your sanity. It's little wonder that artists and writers have long been drawn to Barranco. Beneath the poetically named wooden footbridge Puente de los Suspiros (Bridge of Sighs) is a gentle passageway, La Bajada de Baños, which leads to a sea lookout and is lined with lovely, squat single-family houses, spindly trees, and stout cacti. During the daytime, the barrio is mellow and tropical-feeling, with sultry breezes coming in from the sea, but at night the area is transformed into Lima's hedonistic hot spot, with locals and visitors flocking to the discos and watering holes here—much to the dismay of local residents who don't own a bar or restaurant.

which flourished on the north coast of Peru near present-day Trujillo and Chiclayo. The civilization is best known for its art, particularly ceramics, and there are 45,000 pieces from the culture here, with fine textiles, jewelry, and stonework providing incredible insight into many elements of Moche society. Healing practices, architecture, transportation, dance, agriculture, music, and religion are all explored. The most celebrated section is the Sala Erótica, which displays a vast collection of erotic ceramics, featuring a near-endless variety of sexual acts, often in explicit ways. Travelers with young children can avoid awkward questions, as this part of the museum is outside and across a garden from the main space. Plan at least 2 to 3 hours to see the entire collection.

An excellent and attractive on-site restaurant, **Café del Museo ★**, with an Italian-Peruvian menu and a full bar, makes a great lunch or an early dinner spot, so you might want to plan your visit around dining here.

Av. Bolívar 1515, Pueblo Libre. www.museolarco.org. ⓒ **01/461-1312.** Admission S/30 adults, S/25 seniors, S/15 students. Private guides available in English and Spanish (tip basis, minimum S/10). Daily 9am–10pm. Take a taxi or the TODO BRASIL *colectivo* to Avenida Brasil, and then another to Avenida Bolívar. If you're coming from the Museo Nacional de Arqueología, Antropología e Historia del Perú (p. 64), walk along the blue path.

Museo de la Nación ★ MUSEUM   Few places on earth have a timeline as complex and varied as Peru and this national history museum, set in a hulking, brutalist structure that was originally the Ministry of Fisheries. Unfortunately, the permanent exhibitions, which include some of the most important pieces of Peruvian history, like the famed Lanzón de Chavín (a carved stone statue from the central highlands), have been closed since 2014 as the museum undergoes massive renovation. It is unclear if it will ever be a museum in the same sense that it was, and there's ongoing debate over where the artifacts will end up. Temporary exhibitions are open to the public, however.

Av. Javier Prado Este 2465, San Borja. © **01/476-9878.** Free admission. Tues–Sun 9am–6pm. You can get here by *colectivo* along Av. Prado from Av. Arequipa, but it is much simpler to take a taxi from Lima Centro or Miraflores/San Isidro.

Museo Nacional de Arqueología, Antropología e Historia del Perú ★ MUSEUM   While Peru's National Museum of Archaeology, Anthropology, and History is not nearly as impressive as Lima's other museum with vast displays of pre-Columbian artifacts, the Museo Larco, there are some excellent pieces here. As a whole, this institution serves as a good primer for those who really want to dig into Peruvian history. Set partly in the 19th-century Quinta de los Libertadores mansion, where independence heroes José San Martín and Simón Bolívar once lived, the museum traces Peruvian civilization from prehistoric times to the colonial and republican periods. Entire rooms are dedicated to the Nazca, Paracas, Moche, and Chimú cultures. Be on the lookout for a replica of the great granite Tello Obelisk. The original was found at Chavín de Huantar near Huaraz in 1919 and kept in Lima until recently, and is one of the most complex stone carvings of its time. There are several interesting mummies wrapped in burial blankets, as well as some nicely preserved textiles. Most descriptions are in Spanish. Allow about an hour for your visit. From the museum, you can follow a walking path along a painted blue line to the Rafael Larco Herrera Museum. It's about a mile away, or 20 minutes straight into traffic on Antonio de Sucre, and most travelers pair visits together.

Plaza Bolívar s/n, Pueblo Libre. http://mnaahp.cultura.pe. © **01/321-5630.** Admission S/10 adults, S/5 seniors and students. Private guides available in English and Spanish for S/20. Tues–Sat 8:35am–5pm, Sun 8:45am–3:30pm. Take a taxi here, or take the Todo Brasil *colectivo* to Avenida Vivanco, and then take a 15-min. walk.

OTHER MUSEUMS

Asociación Mario Testino (MATE) ★★ GALLERY   Until nonprofit cultural center MATE opened in July 2012, there were relatively few places to see the work of world-renowned fashion photographer Mario Testino, a Lima native known for his images of the British Royal family and nearly every major fashion darling and Hollywood celebrity. Set in a restored 1898 republican-era mansion decorated with ornate tiles and century-old ironwork, this beautiful space is a major contribution to the city's quickly expanding arts scene. On display are rotating exhibitions of Testino's work, as well as paintings and photography from other Peruvian and international artists. There's also an excellent attached cafe with locally sourced coffees and an art store. Plan for an hour or two here.

Pedro de Osma 409, Barranco. www.mate.pe. © **01/251-7755.** Admission S/20. Tues–Sat 11am–8pm, Sun 11am–6pm. By *colectivo* from Av. Tacna to Barranco.

El Lugar de la Memoria, la Tolerancia y la Inclusión Social (LUM) ★ MUSEUM   This striking museum, dedicated to the legacy of Peru's decades-long internal conflict, opened in 2015 overlooking the Costa Verde. Translated to "The Space of Memory, Tolerance and Social Inclusion," the three-level museum includes a wide range of multimedia exhibits designed to honor the victims of the bloody and protracted war between the Maoist Shining Path and MRTA rebel groups and Peru's armed forces, which began in 1980 and raged across the country for 20 years. "Yuyanapaq," which means "To Remember" in Quechua, is a deeply moving exhibition created by Peru's Truth and Reconciliation Commission that outlines the conflict in devastating images.

Bajada San Martín 151, Miraflores. www.lum.cultura.pe. ℂ **01/719-2065.** Free admission. Tues–Sun 10am–6pm. By taxi only.

Fundación Museo Amano ★ MUSEUM   In 2014, this excellent private pre-Colombian textile museum founded by single collector, Yoshitaro Amano, opened to a public audience (for the previous 50 years, it had been only open by appointment during limited hours). The astounding collection includes more than 40,000 artifacts, primarily textiles representing the entire history of cultural development in ancient Peru. The pieces showcase the styles and techniques of the Chavín, Paracas, Moche, Nazca, Huari, Sihuas, Chimú, and Inca cultures. A highlight is the extensive collection of weavings of the Chancay from the northern coast, of which you would be hard-pressed to find more than a piece or two anywhere else. Exhibitions are found in four elegantly laid out rooms that include a chronological sequence of textiles and a room dedicated to raw materials.

Calle Retiro 160, Miraflores. www.museoamano.org. ℂ **01/441-2909.** S/30 admission. Tues–Sun 10am–5pm (guided tour in Spanish for S/30 per group). Take a taxi to the 11th block of Av. Angamos Oeste/Av. Santa Cruz.

Museo de Arte Contemporáneo (MAC) ★ MUSEUM   Long put on the backburner despite having a stellar collection ready to go, the Instituto de Arte Contemporáneo finally was able to garner enough support to launch a formal contemporary art museum in 2013. The minimalist glass and cement square space, beside a reflecting pool, rotates exhibitions every 3 months. The collection of works, which spans from 1950 to the present, includes pieces from mostly Latin American artists, ranging from optical art and abstract expressionism to geometric art and pop art.

Av. Grau 1511, Barranco. www.maclima.pe. ℂ **01/514-6800.** Admission S/10 adults, S/6 students. Tues–Sun 10am–5pm.

Museo de Arte de Lima (MALI) ★ MUSEUM   Lima's largest art museum displays 3,000 years of Peruvian art, ranging from Chavín and Paracas ceramics and weavings to modern-day video installations. There's an extensive collection of paintings from the Cusqueña school, dating back to colonial times, along with watercolors by famous milieu painter Pancho Fierro, and a well-detailed history of photography going back to its introduction to Peru in 1842. The building's history is as storied as some of the pieces. Italian architect Antonio Leonardi designed the neo-Renaissance-style Palacio de la Exposición, which was inaugurated in 1872 by then-president José Balta for the International Exposition of Lima to celebrate 50 years of Peruvian independence. It later served as a blood bank and garrison, before becoming a permanent exhibition space in 1961. A multi-year renovation, concluded in 2010, completely overhauled every exhibition room, brightening up the parquet and black-and-white checkered tile floors. Plan for a few hours here.

Paseo Colón 125. www.mali.pe. ℰ **01/204-0000.** Admission S/30 adults, S/15 students and seniors. Tues–Fri and Sun 10am–8pm (Sat only until 5pm).

Museo Oro del Perú ★ MUSEUM   The privately held Museo Oro del Perú (Gold Museum) was created from the private collection of a man named Miguel Mujica Gallo, who pieced together thousands of glittering gold ceremonial objects from many pre-Colombian cultures in Peru. A decade ago the National Institute of Culture and the Tourism Protection Bureau declared that many of the pieces were fake, though the museum has since replaced the pieces at issue. The collection spans dozens of Inca and pre-Inca cultures, and includes such items as funerary masks and gold-plated arms from the Sicán, a gold-plated weasel from the Frias, and Nazca shin protectors. There are also mummies, ceramics, and textiles, though to some, the museum's most interesting collection is the section of the museum called "Weapons of the World," which features tens of thousands of different weapons from across the globe, from spears and stone clubs from prehistoric tribes to guns and swords from recent centuries.

Av. Alonso de Molina 1100, Monterrico. www.museoroperu.com.pe. ℰ **01/345-1292.** Daily 10:30am–6pm. Admission S/33 for adults, S/16 for students. A taxi is the most direct way here; coming by *colectivo* involves taking at least two buses along Arequipa to Avenida Angamos, changing to one marked UNIVERSIDAD DE LIMA, and asking the driver to let you off at the Museo Oro del Perú.

Museo Pedro de Osma ★ MUSEUM   This stately Barranco museum began as the private collection of Don Pedro de Osma Gildemeister, who explored Peru gathering art objects from the 16th to 19th centuries. On display in the ornate mansion (Palacio de Osma) are paintings, sculptures, altarpieces, silver pieces, Huamanga stone carvings, and furniture, mostly from Arequipa, Ayacucho, and Cusco. The house is as impressive as the colonial art, with gardens and a separate building with a collection of silver pieces, mostly of religious use. Plan on spending an hour here.

Pedro de Osma 421, Barranco. www.museopedrodeosma.org. ℰ **01/467-0063.** Admission S/20 adults, S/10 students (guided tours in Spanish and English included in admission). Tues–Sun 10am–6pm. By *colectivo* from Av. Tacna to Barranco.

Organized Tours

Lima is a large, sprawling, and confusing city, so if you want to make quick work of a visit, an organized tour of the major sights might be the best option. Standard city tours are offered by innumerable agencies. Among the most dependable is **Lima Tours,** Nicolás de Piérola 589, 18th floor (www.lima tours.com.pe; ℰ **01/619-6900**). A standard half-day tour of Lima Centro costs

ARCHAEOLOGICAL sites IN LIMA ★

Lima is hardly the epicenter of pre-Columbian Peru, and few visitors have more than the museums featuring ancient Peruvian cultures on their minds when they hit the capital. Surprisingly, there are a handful of *huacas*—adobe pyramids—that date to around A.D. 500 and earlier interspersed among the modern constructions of the city. The archaeological sites are junior examples of those found in northern Peru, near Chiclayo and Trujillo. If you're not headed north, Lima's *huacas*, which have small museums attached, are worth a visit.

In San Isidro is **Huaca Huallamarca** (also called Pan de Azúcar, or "Sugar Loaf"), at the corner of Avenida Nicolás de Rivera and Avenida El Rosario. The perhaps overzealously restored adobe temple of the Maranga Lima culture has several platforms and is frequently illuminated for special presentations. It's open Tuesday through Sunday from 9am to 5pm; admission is S/5 for adults and S/3 for students. **Huaca Pucllana ★★** is a sacred pyramid, built during the 4th century and still undergoing excavation, in Miraflores at the corner of calles General Borgoño (Block 8) and Tarapacá, near Avenida Arequipa (http://huacapucllana miraflores.pe; ✆ 01/445-8695). It has a small park, a terrific restaurant (p. 75), and an *artesanía* gallery. From the pyramid's top, you can see the roofs of this busy residential and business district. It's open Wednesday through Monday from 9am to 5pm; admission is S/12 and S/6 for students. Guides are available in English or Spanish for S/20 per group, tours last 45 to 60 minutes.

S/120. Lima Tours also offers visits to Pachacámac as part of its "Lima Arqueológica" tours, as well as highlights packages across Peru.

Limavision, Jr. Chiclayo 444, Miraflores (www.limavision.com; ✆ 01/447-7710), offers half-day sightseeing tours of Lima, including a choice of excursions, for S/115, as well as daylong trips to Caral for S/515 or a half-day at Pachacamac for S/115. **Fertur Perú ★** (www.fertur-travel.com; ✆ 877/247-0055 in the U.S.) is a highly professional outfit, run by a Peruvian-American couple, with reasonably priced city tours and multi-day packages to sights across Peru. **Class Adventure Travel (CAT) ★**, Grimaldo del Solar 463, Miraflores (www.cat-travel.com; ✆ 877/240-4770), is an excellent all-purpose agency run by a knowledgeable and friendly Dutch couple in the U.S.; it offers a 3-day city tour and travel arrangements around Peru.

Free short **walking tours** of Lima are frequently offered by the Municipalidad de Lima (Town Hall). For the latest schedule, call ✆ 01/427-4848.

Mirabus (www.mirabusperu.com; ✆ 01/242-6699) is a double-decker bus that leaves from Parque Kennedy and offers several tours, from Lima Centro, to a night tour and even a dinner buffet tour, to visits outside of town to Pachacámac and Caral. Tours range from S/70 for a 4-hour downtown colonial tour to S/160 for a night tour with dinner and a show. Although it sounds a bit uncomfortably close to those stag or bachelorette bus parties where everyone drinks his or her way across town, **El Bus Parrandero,** Av. Benavides 330, Of. 101, Miraflores (www.elbusparrandero.com; ✆ 01/445-4755), is a colorful party bus promoting gregarious evening tours of Lima, with unlimited drinks, snacks, and live music. Tours are given Monday through Saturday from 8 to 11pm, departing from Larcomar shopping mall; the party ride costs S/90. Perfect if you've got your heart set on reliving (or continuing) your college days while you're in Lima.

Outdoor Activities & Spectator Sports

Beaches   Although Lima is perched on the Pacific coast, Río de Janeiro it's not. Still, several beaches in Miraflores and Barranco are frequented by locals, especially surfers, in the summer months. They are in a constant state of improvement, with new boardwalks, restaurants, and landscaping appearing each year. There's even talk of a Hyatt hotel being installed below Larcomar. Regardless, the beaches are unfit for swimming. The waters are heavily polluted and plagued by very strong currents. Although the beaches aren't that appealing in and of themselves, they might serve those with an interest in people-watching: The sands are very much frequented by Limeños in the summer (Dec–Mar). Much nicer and cleaner beaches are located immediately south of Lima (see Chapter 5, "Side Trips from Lima").

Biking & Jogging   Given Lima's chaotic traffic, jogging is best confined to parks. Probably the best area is the bicycling and jogging paths along the *malecón* in Miraflores, near the Marriott and Belmond Miraflores Park hotels, as well as in Parque El Olivar in San Isidro or along the Costa Verde. Tour operator **Peru Bike** (www.perubike.com; 🕿 01/260-8225) offers several day trips around Lima and south of the city in Pachacamac. A site with good information about biking in Lima is **www.cicloturismoperu.com,** which lists places where bikes can be rented, bike-friendly routes around town, and tours to join.

Bullfighting   Bullfighting, less of a national craze here than in Spain or Mexico, is held in July and in the main season from October to December at the 18th-century **Plaza de Acho,** Jr. Hualgayoc 332, in Rímac (🕿 **01/315-5000**), the third-oldest ring in the world. Events are held Sunday afternoon. The *fiestas taurinas* bring matadors from Spain and take place at the same time as the Señor de los Milagros in October. Tickets, which range from about S/60 to S/300 for a single event (depending on whether seats are in the shade), can be obtained at the box office at the bullring. They can also be purchased at **Teleticket** (www.teleticket.com.pe; 🕿 01/613-8888), which has booths in all Wong and Metro grocery stores. Inquire about advance tickets by sending an e-mail to plazadeacho@peru.com.

Golf   Golf courses in Lima aren't open to nonmembers. Your best bet for golf is to stay at one of the exclusive hotels with golf privileges at the elite Lima Golf Club (www.limagolfclub.org.pe; 🕿 01/277-7090) in San Isidro: **Country Club Lima Hotel** (p. 93) and **Sonesta Hotel El Olívar Lima** (p. 96).

Paragliding   A sport that has quite literally taken off in Lima is paragliding (*parapente*). Look along the cliffs of the Costa Verde in Miraflores and points south and, on propitious days, you're likely to spot a paraglider soaring high above (as high as 200 to 500m [about 650–1,650 ft.] above ground). No experience is required; novices can team up for a tandem ride with an instructor for a good introduction to the thrill of motorless soaring for 270 soles for a 20-minute flight. A booth on the *malecón* operated by the municipality, just north of the Parque de Amor beside a small *parapuerto* (little more than a small piece of park grass), collects payment and sends out flights at regular intervals while the level of wind is safe. Flights are usually from about 11am to 5pm and no reservations are needed. Everyone gets a video taken from a helmet camera downloaded on a flash drive for free. Companies to contact include **Aeroextreme Paragliding School** (www.aeroxtreme.com), **Fly Adventure** (www.flyadventure.net), and **PeruFly** (www.perufly.com).

Peruvian Pacing Horses Peruvian Paso horses (*caballos de paso*), which have a unique four-beat lateral gait, are considered by many to be the world's smoothest riding horse and also one of the showiest of all horse breeds. If you're already a fan of the breed, or just a fan of horses in general, seeing them on their home turf could be exciting. There are *concursos* (show events) scheduled at different times of the year; there's a big one in April (free admission). Information about exhibitions is available from the **Asociación Nacional de Caballos Peruanos de Paso,** Bellavista 546, Miraflores (www. ancpcpp.org.pe; ⓒ **01/447-6331**).

Soccer The most important league and national *fútbol* (soccer) matches are held at the Estadio Momunmental, designed by Uruguayan architect Walter Lavalleja Sarriés in the district of Ate as the home of team Club Universitario de Deportes, better known as "La U." It has more than 80,000 seats, making it one of South America's largest stadiums—and an obvious choice for World Cup qualifying matches. Other games are held at the venerable **Estadio Nacional,** Paseo de la República, Blocks 7–9, located just 5 minutes from the city center. It underwent a major renovation in 2011 and is the home of the local team. Tickets (S/20–S/125) for most matches can be purchased the same day at the stadium or from **Teleticket** (www.teleticket.com.pe; ⓒ **01/613-8888**).

Surfing The best beaches near Lima are south of the city—Punta Hermosa, Punta Rocas (highly recommended), Cerro Azul, and Pico Alto (see Chapter 5, "Side Trips from Lima," for more information). Still right off the Costa Verde within the city limits are good breaks, including beside the pier at La Rosa Nautica restaurant in Miraflores, as well as at Barranquita, El Triangulo, Redondo, and Ala Moana. The biggest wave is at La Herradura in Chorrillos, though only advanced surfers should even attempt it. Pick up locally made gear like **Boz wetsuits** at Av. Angamos Oeste 1130, Miraflores (www.wet suitsboz.com; ⓒ **01/440-0736**) and **boards** from **Wayo Whilar,** Alameda Las Garzas Reales, Mz.FA-7, Urb. Brisas de Villa, Chorrillos (www.wayowhilar. com.pe; ⓒ **01/254-1344**). **Pukana Surf School** at Playa Makaha in Miraflores (www.pukanasurf.com; ⓒ **01/9808-22946**) gives private and small group lessons, and also rents boards.

Surfing in central Peru is best from April through December (and at its peak in May); surfers who hit the waves year-round usually do so in wetsuits.

Especially for Kids

At first glance, busy Lima may not seem like the most kid-friendly city. The best breaks from sightseeing are the **Circuito Mágico del Agua** (p. 60), a water park with colored fountains and a nightly light show; and the **Miraflores** *malecón,* or boulevard (p. 68), where you're likely to spot paragliders taking off for tandem flights above the coastline. Older kids might enjoy some of Lima's more offbeat attractions, such as the ancient (4th c. A.D.) adobe pyramid **Huaca Pucllana** (p. 67); **Museo Arqueológico Rafael Larco Herrera** (p. 62), the world's greatest collection of pre-Columbian ceramics (though you might wish to exercise discretion when faced with showing the children the Sala Erótica's explicit forms); and the catacombs at **Convento de San Francisco** (p. 59), with neat stacks of thousands of human bones that kids will find either creepy or cool, or perhaps both. For those enamored of horses, check out the **Peruvian Paso horses** (p. 69) and shows of this unique, prancing breed (information from **Asociación Nacional de Caballos Peruanos de Paso**). If the city center becomes overwhelming, do as many Limeños do and head to the more easygoing seaside districts of **Barranco** and **Chorrillos** (p. 53).

WHERE TO EAT

Lima is the most cosmopolitan dining city in all of Peru, and perhaps the greatest food city in Latin America, with restaurants of all budgets and a wide range of cuisines—from upscale seafood restaurants and *comida criolla* (coastal Peruvian cooking), to Chinese, incredible street food, and plenty of Italian, French, and other international restaurants. Lima is also the top spot in the country to sample truly creative gastronomy, as well as the dish Peru is perhaps best known for: ceviche. Although there are more restaurants classified as "very expensive" than anywhere else in Peru, diners coming from North American and European capitals should recognize that while not inexpensive, Lima's top restaurants are the equal of many top dining capitals but comparatively much less expensive than high-end restaurants in New York, London, Paris, or Rome.

Many of the best restaurants are concentrated in Miraflores, and to a lesser extent San Isidro, though recent years have seen the map expanding. There's superb northern coastal cuisine in Surquillo. One of the best *criolla* restaurants is in Barranco. Even way out in La Molina, there are chefs and restaurants making waves. Still, it's difficult to eat poorly anywhere in Lima. The bar is high. In Lima Centro, around the *Barrio chino,* there are excellent *chifas,* Chinese-Peruvian restaurants. In Chorrillos, you will find some of the best traditional *cevicherías.* In Miraflores there are sandwich shops and grills set up on street corners selling *anticuchos,* skewered beef heart. Even food courts in the malls have excellent food. Like anywhere, Lima has its share of fast food, both local and international chains, but for those with a willingness to try something new, the options are endless.

Chinatown (*Barrio chino*), southeast of the Plaza de Armas and next to the Mercado Central (beyond the Chinese arch on Jirón Ucayali), is a good place to sample the Peruvian take on Chinese food. These *chifas*, inexpensive restaurants with similar menus, are prolific in the small but dense neighborhood. Among those worth visiting (generally open daily 9am–10pm or later) are **Wa Lok** ★ (see below), probably the best known in the neighborhood; **Salón de la Felicidad** ★, Jr. Paruro 795 (✆ **01/426-4516**), with lots of Cantonese classics; and **Salón Capon**, Jr. Paruro 819 (www.saloncapon.com; ✆ **01/426-9286**), which has dim sum carts.

Restaurants here, predictably, are most crowded in the early evening, especially Thursday through Saturday, as well as weekends during lunch time. In the business districts of Miraflores and San Isidro, lunch can also get quite busy—at least in the nicer restaurants that are popular with local and international businessmen. To locate restaurants in Lima Centro, Miraflores, and San Isidro, see the maps "Where to Stay & Dine in Lima Centro" (p. 91), "Where to Stay & Dine in Miraflores" (p. 93), and "Where to Stay & Dine in San Isidro" (p. 95).

Lima Centro
MODERATE
El Rincón Que No Conoces ★ PERUVIAN Legendary chef Teresa Izquierdo Gonzáles, the godmother of Peruvian cuisine, is no longer with us, but her legacy lives on at her famous *huarique* (a no-frills traditional restaurant) at the edge of Lima's center. The old-school *criolla* haunt with red bricks and yellow walls is the place to come for Doña Teresa's classic preparations of *causa rellena* (yellow potato casserole layered with shrimp or tuna), *ají de gallina* (shredded chicken in spicy sauce), and *picarones* (squash fritters). You won't find any foams or fusion here, just simple, home-cooked Peruvian food made with lots of love and soul. Many loyal Limeños have been coming here for years. There is a different menu each day of the week, with Wednesdays sporting a buffet that includes a pisco sour. Though the cozy two-level restaurant is close to nowhere, it's an institution, and worth the detour.

Bernardo Alcedo 363, alt. cuadra 20 de Petit Thouars. www.elrinconquenoconoces.pe. ✆ **01/471-2171.** Main courses S/20–S/32. Tues–Sun noon–4:30pm.

Kañete ★ PERUVIAN Chef-owner Israel Laura studied in Barcelona before opening up several restaurants in Lima with fresh takes on *criolla* food. After a long absence, he's back on the scene with this casual bistro set in the same bright, cozy spot he started out in. The menu, written out on a standing chalkboard beside the open kitchen, lists simple, soulful, always changing dishes based on what's fresh and in season. A catch of the day can be served in ceviche, while there are usually a few hearty meat courses, like rabbit in white wine sauce, which are cooked for such long times that they can be cut with a spoon.

Jr. Cañete 550. ✆ **01/330-1639.** Main courses S/22–S/45. Tues–Sun noon–5pm.

CEVICHERÍAS

You can't really go to Peru—especially Lima—without sitting down for an irresistibly fresh plate of ceviche (also written *cebiche*), the tantalizing plate of raw fish and shellfish that's marinated in lime juice and chili peppers and served with toasted corn, sweet potato, and raw onion. The citrus juice "cooks" the fish, so it's not really raw the way sushi is. Plenty of restaurants of all stripes—from lowly neighborhood joints to snooty fine-dining spots popular with government bureaucrats and visiting businessmen—offer ceviche, but you really have to go to an authentic *cevichería* for the true experience. In addition to **Canta Rana** (p. 80), another worth checking out is **Hijo de Olaya,** Av. Comandante Espinar 849, in Miraflores near Ovalo Gutierrez (✆ **01/241-0941**), with a short menu of excellently prepared ceviches. There's also **Punta Sal,** Malecón Cisneros, block

3, at the corner of Trípoli in Miraflores (✆ **01/242-4524**), one of a small chain of informal *cevicherías,* and the iconic **Sonia,** at La Rosa Lozano y Tirado 173, in Chorrillos (www.restaurantsonia.com; ✆ **01/251-6693**), founded by a fisherman and his wife who are credited with creating several now-national Peruvian recipes such as *pescado a la chorrillana* (fish in a spicy garlic and tomato sauce). Hip takes on the *cevichería* include Gastón Acurio's **La Mar Cebichería** (p. 76), **El Mercado** (p. 76), and **Pescados Capitales** (p. 77). Peruvians view ceviche as a daytime dish, and most *cevicherías* aren't even open for dinner (the high acidity makes for difficult nighttime digestion for many); for the full experience, go at lunchtime and order a classic pisco sour to start, followed by *chicha morada* (or, if you're feeling kinky, a bottle of curiously neon-yellow Inka Cola).

L'Eau Vive ★ FRENCH   Though the food is rather simple, there are plenty of other reasons to make a stop at L'Eau Vive. An order of French Carmelite nuns runs the restaurant and donates the proceeds to charity. The location, inside an 18th-century palace across the street from one of Lima's most important mansions, is quite convenient if you are sightseeing around the Plaza Mayor. Lunchtime visitors get a basic set menu with Peruvian-inflected French dishes that change often. Dinners feature elegant international courses like prawn bisque or trout baked in cognac. The sisters happily serve wine with the meals. A free show comes around 9pm, when the nuns sing a moving rendition of "Ave Maria."

Ucayali 370. ✆ **01/427-5612.** Main courses S/12–S/43. Mon–Sat 12:30–3pm and 7:30–9:30pm.

T'anta ★ CAFE/PERUVIAN   This casual Peruvian bistro from Gastón Acurio has locations around town, though this Centro location is particularly convenient as it is just off the Plaza Mayor, fronting a pedestrian-only passage, and open early. Stylish yet totally laid back despite being always busy, the restaurant serves a full range of Peruvian classics and international specialties. The menu is huge, covering sandwiches, pastas, rice dishes, stews, and lots of sweets. If you can't find anything to eat here, you might as well just fly home.

Nicolás de Rivera 142, Centro. www.tantaperu.com. ✆ **01/428-3115.** Reservations not accepted. Main courses S/19–S/44. Mon–Sat 9am–10pm, Sun 9am–6pm.

INEXPENSIVE

El Chinito ★ SANDWICHES   This Chinese-Peruvian sandwich shop has been around since the 1960s, though only recently has it gained something of a cult following, expanding to new neighborhoods around town, including Barranco, Miraflores, and San Isidro. The simple shop slings out several traditional Peruvian sandwiches, such as their famous *chicharrón* (fried pork), as well as *chancho asado* (roasted pork), *pavo* (roasted turkey), *butifarra* (sausage), and several others.

Jr. Chancay 894, Lince. www.elchinito.com.pe. ℂ **01/423-2197.** Sandwiches S/15–S/16. Mon–Sat 8am–9pm, Sun 8am–1pm.

Wa Lok ★ CHINESE   Along with dim sum parlor Salon Capon around the corner, Wa Lok is one of the oldest and most famous *chifas* (Chinese-Peruvian restaurants) near Calle Capón, the center of Lima's Barrio China, or Chinatown. Tile floors and clunky wood tables make up the decor. The colossal menu—more than 100 dishes strong—ranges from simple Cantonese favorites like pork dumplings and fried rice to dim sum to more elaborate fare like Peking duck. There's a louder second location in Miraflores at Av. Angamos Oeste 700, attached to a casino.

Jr. Paruro 878, Centro. www.walok.com.pe. ℂ **01/427-2750.** Main courses S/15–S/35. Mon–Sat noon–11:15pm, Sun noon–10:30pm.

Miraflores & San Isidro

VERY EXPENSIVE

Astrid y Gastón Casa Moreyra ★★★ PERUVIAN/AVANT-GARDE   If any single restaurant could be credited with revolutionizing Peruvian cuisine, it would be this one. In the late 1990s, chef Gastón Acurio and his German wife and partner Astrid Gutsche made the transition from contemporary French cuisine to Peruvian. At the time, native ingredients from the Andes and Amazon were looked down upon in the capital. In the years since, food has become the biggest single factor in uniting Peruvians, and Acurio—now with dozens of restaurants across the globe—has become the face of the cuisine. After 20 years in its original Miraflores location, in early 2014 Astrid y Gastón moved to the historic Casa Moreyra, a beautifully renovated and modernized colonial hacienda. Many of the original frescoes and interior details were preserved and have meshed beautifully with modern details like glass and contemporary art. Gardens and five kitchens were also added. The sprawling compound is home to a more casual restaurant serving Peruvian standards and small plates with pisco-based cocktails, as well as a more formal, high-end, tasting-menu-only restaurant with wine pairings. Reservations are a must.

Casa Moreyra, Av. Paz Soldán 290. www.astridygaston.com. ℂ **01/242-5387.** Main courses S/45–S/85, tasting menu approximately S/500, including wine pairing. Tues–Sat 1:30–3pm and 7–11pm.

Central ★★★ PERUVIAN/AVANT-GARDE   Peru's most important young culinary star is without a doubt Virgilio Martínez, who recently received a Michelin star at his U.K. restaurant, Lima London. Martinez's Central, opened in 2009, has quickly grown a following for its high-end approach to rare and unusual Peruvian ingredients. Additionally, Martinez runs Mater Inciativa, a cooperative of culinary types that includes Martinez's wife Pía León and his sister Malena, who is Central's executive chef. The cooperative travels around the country investigating new products and working with local producers. Many of the products, like Amazonian fish and high-altitude algae, make their way onto the menu here, including placement on a phenomenal altitude-based tasting menu that pairs beautifully with one of Lima's best wine programs. The beautiful space, always buzzing, is as impressive as the food, with high ceilings, towering stone walls, an open kitchen, and a rooftop garden. Many consider this to be the best restaurant in Peru, if not all of Latin America, and one that the prestigious World's Best Restaurant list has ranked as high as #4. Reservations are a must.

Calle Santa Isabel 376. www.centralrestaurante.com.pe. © **01/242-8515.** Tasting menu S/500. Mon–Fri 12:45–3:30pm and 7:45–11pm, Sat 7:45–11pm.

Maido ★★★ NIKKEI/SUSHI   Nikkei food, the natural fusion of Japanese and Peruvian, is having its moment in Lima and around the world. Maido and its talented chef Mitsuharu Tsumura, aka "Micha," are at the epicenter of the movement. The minimalist, three-level space here is decorated with shoji screens that conceal several private rooms and lounges. It's not overly formal, with lots of wood and glass. While most Nikkei restaurants in Lima lean toward more traditional, Maido is innovative, incorporating Amazonian fish like *paiche* and combining national plates like *tacu tacu with chaufa* (fried rice) and crispy pork belly. Lovers of sushi, sashimi, and *tiradito* will find plenty on the menu to explore, though for those really expecting to be knocked off their feet, the elaborate tasting menus are the way to go. There's a superb wine list as well as artisanal Peruvian beers.

Calle Colón 192. www.maido.pe. © **01/444-2568.** Main courses S/30–S/65. Daily 12:30–4pm and 7:30–11pm.

EXPENSIVE

Ámaz ★★ AMAZONIAN   Opening a serious Amazonian restaurant is not a simple task. It takes years to build up a network of producers, and even then getting fresh products to the coast is another challenge. Somehow chef Pedro Miguel Schiaffino, whose more formal restaurant Malabar is one of the city's best, managed to pull it off. Stepping inside trendy Ámaz, on an up-and-coming restaurant row beside the Miraflores Hilton, is like stepping into the rainforest. Fiber lampshades made from *bejuco* and *tamish* (Amazonian plants) look like leaves, hanging wooden pegs resemble a jungle canopy, and there's a mural of gold, glimmering snakes with glowing eyes. Ámaz is what the Rainforest Cafe should look like. As exotic as some of the ingredients are—macambo seeds, giant Amazonian snails, cocona fruit—many are presented in such familiar ways that even picky eaters will be pleased. As many dishes use indigenous names and preparations unfamiliar to most diners, including Limeños, waiters are well-versed in describing what is what. Usually they'll suggest a few dishes to share family-style, with Amazonian fried rice and fried finger foods as a safety net.

Av. La Paz 1079. www.amaz.com.pe. © **01/221-9393.** Main courses S/35–S/65. Mon–Sat 12:30–11pm, Sun 12:30–4:30pm.

Fiesta Chiclayo Gourmet ★★ NORTHERN PERUVIAN   This restaurant has single-handedly taken northern coastal cuisine to new levels. It started in the city of Chiclayo, where it still has a location, though chef Hector Solís, the driving force, is based in Lima. The hearty, heavy food of the region stands out for its different ingredients (goat, duck, cilantro, grouper, and so on) and pre-Colombian influences (Moche), resulting in unique and flavorful combinations. There are a handful of ceviches, focused on the fish of the region, including a hot one that gets grilled over a corn husk. Don't miss specialties like *arroz con pato a la Chiclayana* (Chiclayo-style rice with duck) or *tortilla de raya* (a Spanish omelet with skate).

Av. Reducto 1278, Miraflores. www.restaurantfiestagourmet.com. © **01/242-9009.** Reservations recommended. Main courses S/39–S/65. Daily 12:30–5pm and 8–11pm.

La Rosa Nautica ★ SEAFOOD   Even though busload after busload of tourists regularly fill this decades-old city landmark, it's still one of the best dining experiences in Lima. A rambling Victorian building with a maze of rooms does the hosting, set on a pier in the middle of the Pacific Ocean. Diners can look out the many windows and see surfers on the waves and the misty cliffs of the Costa Verde towering above. Impeccable service and a lengthy menu are just a couple of the reasons the restaurant has expanded to Colombia and Argentina. There are a few meat and pasta dishes, but seafood is the specialty, prepared every which way you can imagine: raw, grilled, steamed, fried, baked, as sushi, as ceviche, in a stew, or in a sauce. The sunsets, especially when paired with a potent pisco sour, are some of the best around.

Espigon 4 Circuito de Playas. www.larosanautica.com. © **01/445-0149.** Main courses S/35–S/60. Daily noon–midnight.

Restaurant Huaca Pucllana ★ PERUVIAN   This is nothing less than one of the most incredible restaurant settings anywhere in the world, nestled within the compound of a 1,500-year-old adobe pyramid. The rustic atmosphere inside, with red walls and rough-hewn wood beams, is pleasant enough, but try to snag a seat on the covered terrace so you can peer out at the pre-Columbian structure as you eat. You'll find more exciting food elsewhere in town, though the contemporary *criolla* dishes like *humitas verdes* (tamales) and *lomo saltado* (stir-fried beef and potatoes) won't disappoint. Expect to be surrounded almost entirely by other tourists. At night, the walkways and the pyramid complex are illuminated, and diners are welcome to tour the grounds after dinner.

Huaca Pucllana, General Borgoño, Block 8. www.resthuacapucllana.com. © **01/445-4042.** Main courses S/32–S/60. Mon–Sat 12:30pm–midnight, Sun 12:30–4pm.

MODERATE

Cosme ★ ECLECTIC   On a residential street, amid condo towers, this funky eatery is a superb destination for those who are looking to just kick back with a good cocktail and food in a lively atmosphere. The setting feels like a piece of pop art: There are multicolored recycled plastic bottles lining the ceiling, a backlit image of a vulture glows at one end, and photos show old-school Lima street scenes. The chef, James Berckemeyer, who has worked in several Michelin three-star restaurants in Spain, has put together an eclectic menu of mostly small plates like Chinese steamed buns with pork belly, octopus with quinoa, and beef cheeks that are cooked over low heat for 36 hours. Cocktails are driven by house-made sodas, which are infused with ingredients like *camu camu* or ginger and basil.

Tudela y Varela 162, San Isidro. www.cosme.com.pe. *C* **01/421-5228.** Main courses S/25–S/50. Tues–Sun 12:30–5pm.

El Mercado ★★ SEAFOOD/FUSION   Chef Rafael Osterling (the man behind the more formal Rafael) is one of Peru's biggest celebrity chefs, and this high-energy, lunchtime-only restaurant has been one of the city's most popular eateries since opening a few years ago. The indoor-outdoor space with a long bar, industrial-seek aesthetic, and beachy decor fills up with Lima's pretty people who don't seem to mind that there is usually a wait (it doesn't accept reservations). The food continues to get better and better and everything has a touch of Asian-Mediterranean flair, which Osterling is known for. Seafood dominates the menu, coming in the form of ceviches, four types of seafood rice, *jalea* (deep-fried seafood), and grouper cheeks.

Hipólito Unánue 203, Miraflores. www.rafaelosterling.com. *C* **01/221-1322.** Reservations not accepted. Main courses S/25–S/55. Tues–Sun 12:30–5pm.

La Mar ★★★ SEAFOOD   Though Gastón Acurio put Peruvian cuisine on the map with Astrid y Gastón, it was only when he launched this upscale *cevichería* in 2005 that the trend went worldwide. The original La Mar, on Avenida La Mar near a dozen other top *cevicherías,* thrust Peru's national dish into the spotlight, with the restaurant subsequently exported to places like San Francisco and Bogota. The concept is simple: high-quality seafood in an unpretentious setting. The large, casual dining area, always lively, is open to the elements, aside from a bamboo ceiling that allows rays of sun to occasionally break through. The menu is lengthy, with 10 or so variations on ceviche ranging from a classic *mixto* (fish and shellfish) to the more exotic Nikkei, with tuna and tamarind. Other favorite seafood plates make use of ingredients like *erizo* (sea urchin), *pulpo* (octopus), *conchitas* (scallops), and dozens of types of fish. La Mar only serves what is fresh. Like most *cevicherías,* this one is open for lunch only.

Av. La Mar 770. www.lamarcebicheria.com. *C* **01/421-3365.** Main courses S/25–S/65. Daily noon–5pm.

Madam Tusán ★★ CHINESE   While there's an inexpensive *chifa* (local slang for a Chinese restaurant) on almost every street in Lima, many of them use low-quality ingredients and prepare basic, uninspired Cantonese dishes.

This upscale take, from celebrity chef and restaurateur Gastón Acurio, does a superb job of infusing Peruvian ingredients and keeping the quality high and consistent. The dramatic space features a hanging red acrylic dragon from sculptor Marcelo Wong. Intimate family booths line both walls of the main dining room. In keeping with traditional *chifa* fashion, the menu is massive, incorporating expected classics like *siu mai* (dumplings) and *pollo chi jau kay* (breaded chicken in oyster sauce), while adding more exotic dishes like *pekin cuy* (Peking-style guinea pig) and roasted pork. There's also a beautiful list of original cocktails that combine pisco with Asian fruits and flavors, worthy of a trip all its own. Another location at 28 de Julio 1045, at Paseo de la República, serves Peruvian-style dim sum on weekend mornings from 9am to noon.

Av. Santa Cruz 859. www.madamtusan.pe. © **01/505-5090.** Main courses S/29–S/45. Daily noon–midnight.

Pescados Capitales ★ SEAFOOD   One of Lima's first upscale *cevicherías,* Pescados Capitales is still the most famous, now with a satellite location in San Borja. The name is a play on the phrase for "original sin" (in Spanish, *pescado,* or "fish," is one letter removed from *pecado,* or "sin"), and the menu expands the notion by giving plates like ceviche and *arroz con mariscos* names like "guilt," "pride," or "envy." The space centers around a wooden terrace with umbrella-shaded seating, with two additional dining areas enclosed by a glass and bamboo roof. The restaurant is extremely popular with Lima's well-to-do, and the waits can get particularly long on weekends. This is one of the few *cevicherías* that open for dinner, which is usually quieter and more laid-back than the daytime. A second location has been added in San Borja.

Av. La Mar 1337. www.pescadoscapitales.com. © **01/717-9470.** Main courses S/28–S/48. Daily 12:30–5pm and 8–11pm.

INEXPENSIVE

El Pan de la Chola ★★ CAFE/BAKERY   This brick-walled shop decorated with blackboard specials began as a summer pop-up on the Asia beach boulevard and has since blossomed into one of Lima's finest cafes and bakeries. Model and actor Jonathan Day, who studied artisan baking while traveling around the U.S. and Europe, is best known for his *pan de la chola,* a seeded, whole-wheat bread that he bakes fresh each morning. Visitors buy it by the loaf, as part of a gourmet sandwich, or with spreads like hummus or tapenade. A handful of other rotating breads—all organic—are also served, as well as Greek yogurt, juices, brownies, and a full variety of great specialty coffees made from fair-trade Peruvian beans.

Av. La Mar 918. No phone. Main courses S/10–S/20. Tues–Sat 8am–10pm, Sun 9am–6pm.

La Lucha Sangucheria ★★ SANDWICHES   Most visitors to Peru get so caught up with ceviche that they don't realize just how big of a sandwich culture Lima has. While most of the sandwich shops are rather basic or just a stand in front of a bar, La Lucha brings a gourmet touch to classics like the *butifarra* (country ham with onion relish) and *chicharrón* (fried pork with

Before the turn of the millennium, few people outside of Peru had ever heard of its cuisine. That has all changed. Chef Gastón Acurio, one of the first Peruvian chefs to begin pairing European-cooking techniques with Peruvian ingredients, has launched a chain of *cevicherías* (La Mar), regional restaurants (ChiCha), *chifas* (Madam Tusán), and even a Peruvian-themed burger joint (Papacho's), among several other concepts, many of which are now found throughout Latin America and the world. His flagship restaurant, Astrid y Gastón in San Isidro, has earned him a spot on the prestigious World's Best Restaurant list, as have Central from Virgilio Martínez and Maido from Mitsuharu Tsumura. Lima has quickly become one of the world's great food cities, and foodie visitors are flocking to the city at increasing rates to dine at top restaurants and explore the markets. There is perhaps no more exciting time of year for the culinary-inclined than during Mistura (www.mistura.pe), an annual food festival, the world's largest, which is open to the public and takes place for about 10 days in early September, attracting hundreds of thousands of visitors. It's Peruvian food in Disneyland form. In recent years it has been held on the beach in Magdalena del Mar. Even if you are not here in September, there are ways to get more involved in Peru's food scene than simply going out to eat. Culinary tours of the capital and cooking classes are increasingly popular. I recommend Delectable Peru gourmet food tours ★★ (www.delectableperu.com; 𝒞 **239/244-2336** in the U.S.) run by English-speaking Ericka LaMadrid, who sets up custom tours of street food, markets, or top restaurants, or tours focusing on a specific dish or type of food, such as ceviche or Nikkei. She can also set up cooking classes with some of Lima's best chefs at their restaurants.

sweet potatoes). They can be ordered with a side of beautifully crisp fries made from *huayro* potatoes, some of Lima's best. There's also a full juice bar with regional flavors like *granadilla* (a type of passionfruit), *cocona* (an acidic type of tomato), and *aguaymanto* (gooseberry). The Parque Kennedy location, with open-air sidewalk seating and a small dining area with checkered tiled floors, is the original, though it's become so popular that branches at Óvalo Gutiérrez and the Larcomar shopping center food court have been added.

Benavides 308. www.lalucha.com.pe. 𝒞 **01/241-5953.** Sandwiches S/8–S/20. Daily 7am–1am.

Peru Pa'Ti ★ FOOD HALL/CAFE   This is Peru's version of a food hall, with a handful of small purveyors that include a bakery, coffee shop, bar, restaurant, and sweets shop. The hip space changes as you move from one spot to the next. Pick up a plastic card when you enter the space, each vendor will swipe it every time you want something, and then you just pay on your way out the door. I'm fond of the Peruvian coffees from Harry Neira, as well as the bakery and sandwiches from Renato Peralta's Barra Migas. This is a great place to just hang out to check your e-mail or read a book.

Parque Armendariz 546, Miraflores. 𝒞 **01/445-5099.** Main courses S/10–S/25. Tues–Sat 8am–11pm, Sun 8am–8pm.

Surquillo

MODERATE

La Picantería ★★★ NORTHERN PERUVIAN   After the success of his restaurants Fiesta Gourmet, Chiclayo, and Trujillo, chef and owner Hector Solís went back to his roots with this rustic, lunch-only eatery, based on the famed *picanterías* of Peru's northern coast. Like its inspirations, the restaurant serves oversized, family-style portions of traditional northern coastal dishes like *cebiche de pato* (duck ceviche) and *asado de tira* (beef short ribs). The house specialty is the fish that is brought in each morning and sold by the size and preparation you desire, with options like steamed, fried, breaded, or stuffed. All are phenomenal. This is one of the few Lima establishments to sell *chicha,* a fermented maize beer with a strong, sour flavor that is sweetened up with fruits like peach and strawberry. Designers have done a fine job of re-creating the bare-bones feel of an authentic *picanterías* here, with picnic-style tables and cane ceiling panels.

Av. Francisco Moreno 388. www.picanteriasdelperu.com. © **01/241-6676.** Main courses S/25–S/55. Tues–Sun 11am–5pm.

Barranco

MODERATE

Amor Amar ★ SEAFOOD/INTERNATIONAL   For those who can find it—even taxi drivers have a difficult time locating the obscure side street it is situated on—Amor Amar has one of the most special atmospheres of any restaurant in Lima. Within a walled Barranco compound is a republican-era mansion that holds an art gallery, an open-air bar with trendy pisco cocktails, and an exposed dining area with a canopy warmed by standing heaters when it gets chilly. The whole place feels like some secret compound for food and wine aficionados. As you might expect from the name, seafood is the specialty here, mostly classic Peruvian dishes with touches of the Mediterranean, though there are also whole-animal *asados* (slow-cooked meats) prepared in a brick oven.

Jiron Garcia y Garcia 175. www.amoramar.com. © **01/619-9595.** Main courses S/30–S/65. Mon–Sat 12:30–4pm and 8pm–midnight, Sun 12:30–5pm.

Cala ★ PERUVIAN   Aside from the very touristy Rosa Nautica, few restaurants have taken advantage of Lima's beachfront. Trendy Cala helped change the game when it opened in 2006 on Playa Barranquita, so close to the Pacific Ocean that waves roll right up to the bar and open-air dining terrace. Though it has gone through a few chef changes and a redesign, the two-level space with wood floors and white curtains still packs in a crowd of pretty people. The menu is quite playful, hopping from classic Peruvian seafood plates like ceviche and grilled octopus to a long list of risottos and cuts of Wagyu beef. Some hit the mark. Some don't. The downstairs turns almost club-like during weekend nights, with top DJs spinning electronic music and the bar serving a full range of original pisco-based cocktails.

Playa Barranquito. www.calarestaurante.com. © **01/252-9187.** Main courses S/25–S/65. Mon, Wed–Thurs noon–midnight, Sat noon–2am, Sun noon–6pm.

Canta Rana ★ SEAFOOD   This neighborhood *cevichería* is one of Barranco's most beloved lunch spots. Extremely informal, the bare-bones interior reflects the Argentina-born owner's love of *fútbol,* with every spare inch of wall space emblazoned with logos and flags and old match photos. The "Singing Frog" is known for its excellent seafood and large portions. There are more than a dozen types of ceviche, served in heaping bowls with purple onions, *choclo* (maize), and slices of *camote* (sweet potato). Many linger here for hours, ordering snacks like *conchas a la parmesana* (scallops on the half-shell with melted Parmesan) and clay pots of *langostinos al ajillo* (shrimp with garlic), washing it down with pitchers of beer or *chicha morada* (a juice made from purple corn).

Génova 101. ✆ **01/247-7274.** Main courses S/20–S/40. Tues–Sat 11am–11pm, Sun–Mon 11am–6pm.

Isolina ★★ CRIOLLA   *Criolla*-style food is what most Limeños eat at their house or what they think of when remembering what their grandmothers made. Yet, it's rare that *criolla* cooking appears at a restaurant, and when it does, it's usually at a place that's very simple. Enter Isolina, which opened in 2015. This cool, two-level restaurant with painted tile floors and reclaimed wood from the original Barranco *casona* it is set in has brought newfound recognition to these hearty, soulful dishes, many of which include offal. From its ceviche (sole with fried octopus) to its *tacu tacu* that uses black beans like in the old days to a *cau-cau* (tripe and potato stew) that shares a plate with *sangrecita* (boiled, fried, and seasoned chicken blood), all of it is delicious and beautifully executed.

Av. San Martín 101. www.isolina.pe. ✆ **01/247-5075.** Main courses S/25–S/55. Sun–Mon 10am–5pm, Tues–Sat 10am–11pm.

INEXPENSIVE

Tostaduría Bisetti ★ CAFE   This intimate roaster and coffeehouse is maybe the center of Peru's coffee movement. Aside from having access to the best coffee beans being produced from top *fincas* in Peru's high jungle regions, the servers can handle geeky brewing tools like siphons or a chemex. Occasionally the cafe holds cuppings in its back laboratory, though most guests are happy to just kick back and read a magazine by the couches or wood tables.

Pedro de Osma 116, Barranco. www.cafebisetti.com. ✆ **01/713-9565.** Snacks S/5–S/10. Mon–Sat 8am–10pm, Sun 2–9pm.

SHOPPING

The Peruvian capital has the greatest variety of shopping in the country, from tiny boutiques to handicraft and antiques shops. Although shopping at markets in *sierra* villages and buying direct from artisans in the highlands or on the islands of Lake Titicaca are superior cultural experiences, don't discount the fact that, unless you ship the loot home, you'll most likely have to lug it back to Lima. In Lima, you can find traditional handicrafts from across Peru; prices are not usually that much higher, and the selection might be even better than in the regions where the items are made. One exception is fine alpaca goods, which are better purchased in the areas around Cusco, Titicaca, and Arequipa, both in terms of price and selection.

Miraflores is where most shoppers congregate, although there are also several outlets in Lima Centro and elsewhere in the city; Barranco is also growing as a shopping destination with many independent boutiques. Most shops are open daily from 9:30am to 12:30pm and 3 to 8pm.

Antiques & Jewelry

Look for silver jewelry and antiques along Avenida La Paz in Miraflores. In particular, there's a little pedestrian-only passageway at Av. La Paz 646 that's lined with well-stocked antiques shops, many with nice religious art, including **La Línea del Tiempo ★** (✆ **01/241-5461**). Other Miraflores antiques shops include **La Relique,** Prado 187 (✆ **01/9647-2299**) and **Kerubin,** Ugarte 233 (www.elkerubin.com; ✆ **01/241-9191**). Another great shop is **La Casa Azul ★**, Alfonso Ugarte 150 (✆ **01/446-6380**), which specializes in colonial furniture, religious art, and other fantastic decorative pieces. The friendly owners can help arrange shipping and assist with getting export approval for especially valuable pieces.

Ilaria ★★, Av. Larco 1325 in Miraflores (www.ilariainternational.com; ✆ **01/444-2347**), as well as in the Larcomar shopping center nearby, is the granddaddy of Peruvian jewelry stores. With dozens of shops across the country, it's tops in terms of design in elegant silver art objects, jewelry, and decorative items. Many designs are based on traditional, antique Peruvian designs.

Lorena Pestana ★ at Av. Borgoño 770 (www.lorenapestana.pe; ✆ **01/446-4033**) spent time in a small Amazonian village studying weaving and handicraft techniques, as well as the ancestral art of the Chavin culture, all of which she uses as inspiration. Many of the creative pieces pair silver with organic materials such as feathers or seashells.

Additional *platerías* and *joyerías* (silver and jewelry shops) worth a visit are **El Tupo,** La Paz 553, Miraflores (www.eltupo.com.pe; ✆ **01/444-1511**) and in downtown Lima, **Joyería Gold/Gems Perú,** Pasaje Santa Rosa 119 (✆ **01/426-7267**), which stocks Colombian emeralds and fashionable, inexpensive Italian steel jewelry.

Fashion

High-end designers are mostly found in independent storefronts in San Isidro, especially along Avenida Conquistadores, which is the closest thing Lima has to a Rodeo Drive. The sister of fashion photographer Mario, designer **Giuliana Testino** has a showroom at Av. Pérez Araníbar 2132 in San Isidro (www.giulianatestino.com; ✆ **01/264-3874**), where she sells items from some of her most recent collections of upscale women's wear. **Sumy Kujon's** creations, which often blend her Chinese-Peruvian heritage, are seen on runways from New York to Paris, but in Lima you can visit her at her San Isidro boutique, inside of a residential building at Av. Pardo y Aliaga 382 #301 (www.sumykujon.com; ✆ 01/441-9106). In an adobe house from the 1900s at Atahualpa 479 in Miraflores, **Alessandra Petersen** (www.alessandrapetersen.com; ✆ 01/242-5374) sells original dresses and jackets, mostly using natural materials such as Peruvian pima cotton, alpaca wool, and silk.

Shoemaker **Botería Negreiros,** at Calle Las Casas 041 in San Isidro (✆ 01/442-0599), makes and sells a variety of leather boots and sandals for women, including knee-high equestrian and Hiram Bingham–style boots. With notice, the retailer can even create custom shoes based on designs you pick.

Handicrafts & Textiles

Miraflores is home to the lion's share of Lima's well-stocked shops, which overflow with handicrafts from around Peru, including weavings, ceramics, and silver. Several dozen large souvenir and handicrafts shops are clustered on and around Avenida Ricardo Palma (a good one is **Artesanías Miraflores,** no. 205) and Avenida Petit Thouars (try **Artesanía Expo Inti,** no. 5495). **Indigo** ★, Av. El Bosque no. 260, San Isidro (www.galeriaindigo.com.pe; ✆ 01/440-3099) is one of Lima's top handicrafts and gift stores, with thoughtfully selected original designs from most regions across Peru. You'll find items here that you won't find in the big, multi-booth markets. Handicrafts shops elsewhere in Miraflores include **Agua y Tierra,** Diez Canseco 298 (✆ 01/445-6980), and **Silvania Prints,** Diez Canseco 378 (www.silvaniaperu.com; ✆ 01/242-0667).

For fine alpaca goods, head to **Kuna** ★★, Av. Larco 671, Miraflores (✆ 01/447-1623), one of the most original and highest-quality purveyors of all things alpaca, with excellent contemporary designs for men and women. Other locations include the Larcomar shopping mall, the Larco Herrera museum, and the Westin. Other alpaca shops include **Alpaca Mon Repos** ★, Centro Comercial Camino Real (✆ 01/221-5331); **Alpaca Peru,** Diez Canseco 315 (✆ 01/241-4175); and **All Alpaca,** Av. Schell 375 (✆ 01/427-4704).

For artisan furniture and decorative art objects skillfully handcrafted from wood, don't miss **Artesanos Don Bosco** ★★★, Av. San Martín 135 (www.artesanosdonbosco.pe; ✆ 01/265-8480), which recently opened a storefront/gallery in Barranco in a beautiful 19th-century *casona.* A nonprofit organization begun by an Italian priest in the Andes near Huaraz, in north-central Peru, these artisans (trained in poor, remote highlands communities) create extraordinary, unique pieces, with a tongue-and-groove technique and many with curved forms. Each piece is the work, start to finish, of a single artisan. The organization operates a charity promoting development efforts among indigenous communities throughout the Americas.

One of the largest shops, which stocks a huge range of Peruvian handicrafts from all over the country, is **Peru Artcrafts** ★ in the Larcomar shopping mall, Malecón de la Reserva 610 (✆ 01/446-5429). Although it's considerably more expensive than other shops (all prices are in dollars), it's perhaps the best for last-minute and one-stop shopping. A giant *artesanía* market with dozens of stalls is the **Mercado Indio** ★, Av. Petit Thouars 5245 (at General Vidal),

Miraflores. (In fact, almost all of Avenida Petit Thouars, from Ricardo Palma to Vidal, is lined with well-stocked handicrafts shops.) For most visitors to Lima, this is one-stop shopping for Peruvian handcrafts, arts, gifts, and souvenirs from around the country. Another good spot for handicrafts from around Peru, in Lima Centro, is the **Santo Domingo** *artesanía* **arcades,** across the street from the Santo Domingo convent on Conde de Superunda and Camaná.

In Barranco, the finest upscale purveyor of crafts and home furnishings is **Dédalo ★★★**, Saenz Peña 295 (*℃* **01/477-0562**). If you arrive here around midday and hungry, you'll be happy to find a little cafe out back in the garden, serving salads, sandwiches, and tamales. A superb selection of folk art and handicrafts from across Peru can be found at **Las Pallas ★★★**, Cajamarca 212 (*℃* **01/477-4629**); the owner, a British woman named Mari Solari, has been collecting Peruvian folk art for 3 decades and displays it all in several rooms of her fine Barranco house.

Markets & Malls

Lima Centro's crowded **Mercado Central (Central Market),** open daily from 8am to 5pm, is south of the Plaza Mayor, at the edge of Chinatown. You'll find just about everything there, but you should take your wits and leave your valuables at home. The **Feria Artesanal** (Artisans' Market, occasionally called the Mercado Indio, or Indian Market, but not to be confused with the Mercado Indio in Miraflores) has a wide variety of handicrafts of varying quality, but at lower prices than most tourist-oriented shops in Lima Centro or Miraflores (quality might also be a bit lower than at those shops). Haggling is a good idea. The large market is located on Avenida de la Marina (blocks 6–10) in Pueblo Libre and is open daily from noon to 8pm. Small handicrafts markets, open late to catch the bar and post-dinner crowds, are situated in the main squares in both Miraflores and Barranco.

One of my favorite markets in Lima is the fascinating and diverse **Mercado de Surquillo ★★** (Avenida Paseo de la Republica at Ricardo Palma, Miraflores/Surquillo), where Limeños and many of the top chefs in town go to get fresh produce, seafood, meats, and a wide array of kitchen implements. It's a terrific food-shopping and cultural experience, and in recent years, several really nice food stands have opened in and around the market.

Jockey Plaza Mall (*℃* **01/437-4100**) is a modern, American-style shopping mall—the biggest and best in Lima—with department stores, restaurants, movie theaters, a supermarket, and some 200 exclusive shops, plus bars and a food truck court. It's next to the Jockey Club of Peru at Hipódromo de Monterrico, at the intersection of Javier Prado and Avenida Panamericana Sur in Surco. Most stores are open daily from 11am to 9pm. **Centro Comercial Larcomar ★★** (*℃* **01/445-7776**) in Miraflores, along the *malecón* and Parque Salazar (near the Marriott hotel), is one of the swankiest malls in Lima, with a slew of restaurants, movie theaters, and upscale shops overlooking the ocean. It's open daily from 10am to 8pm and is a weekend destination for many Limeños.

ENTERTAINMENT & NIGHTLIFE

Bars & Pubs

Barranco   The delightful area around the Puente de los Suspiros in Barranco has some of the coolest watering holes in Lima. There's **Santos** ★, Jr. Zepita 203 (*℃* **01/247-4609**), a hip joint with an inventive decor, easygoing vibe, and slender balcony with views out to the ocean; the place is packed on weekend nights. Right across the bridge is the slick upscale bar and restaurant **Picas** ★, Bajada de Baños 340 (www.picas.com.pe; *℃* **01/252-8095**), serving great (if pricey) cocktails to a well-dressed crowd. Nearby, **La Posada del Mirador,** Pasaje La Ermita 104 (*℃* **01/477-1120**) occupies an old house overlooking the ocean in a verdant setting with indoor and outdoor garden seating. **Posada del Angel,** Av. Pedro de Osma 164 and 222 (*℃* **01/247-0341**) is a baroque cafe-bar with two locations on the same street and occasional live jazz and folk music. **Ayahuasca** ★★, Prolongación San Martín 130 (*℃* **9810-44745**), is one of Barranco's hottest—and biggest—nightspots, a stylish and usually packed bar in a stately colonial mansion with swank furnishings, art exhibits, and great cocktails, including an impressive array of pisco sours. Brewpub **Barranco Beer Company,** at Av. Almirante Miguel Grau 308 (www.barrancobeer.com; *℃* **01/247-6211**), just off the plaza, has a long list of artisanal beers, available in pints or flights, made in the back of the bar.

Lima Centro   There are two good pubs downtown owned by the same folks. One is **Rincón Cervecero,** a German-style bier hall, at Jr. de la Unión 1045 (www.rinconcervecero.com.pe; *℃* **01/428-1422**). The other, next door, is **Estadio Fútbol Club,** Jr. de la Unión 1047 (www.estadio.com.pe; *℃* **01/428-8866**), and strictly for *fútbol* fans: It's a three-level bar (and disco on weekends) that amounts to a museum of the sport, and with dozens of big-screen TVs, it can get pretty rowdy when a big Peruvian or international game is on. Just beyond Lima Centro, in Pueblo Libre, is **Antigua Taberna Queirolo** ★★, Av. San Martín 1090 (at Av. Vivanco) (www.antiguatabernaqueirolo.com; *℃* **01/460-0441**), a local institution. The atmospheric pisco bar and winery, with a long marble-topped bar, is one of the oldest in Peru, now into its second century. Taste one of the house piscos, accompanied by good snacks (*piqueos*) and more substantial Peruvian specialties such as *rocoto relleno* (stuffed hot pepper).

Miraflores   **Bar Huaringas** ★★★, Bolognesi 472 (www.huaringas.com; *℃* **01/243-8151**), the elegant upstairs at the restaurant Brujas de Cachiche, is one of the top spots in the country for a pisco sour, the national cocktail. The list of piscos is impressive, and the mixologists pour perfect variations on pisco sours, beginning with a coca or *maracuyá* sour. For top-notch cocktails, several restaurant bars, such **Ámaz** (p. 74), which uses Amazonian fruits and herbs to mix with pisco, or **Central** (p. 73), with one of the most varied collections of liquor in the city, are good choices if it's an earlier night. For craft beer, look no further than **Nuevo Mundo Draft Bar** (www.nuevomundo cerveceria.com; *℃* **01/249-5268**), at Av. Larco 421 near Parque Kennedy, operated by the owners of Nuevo Mundo brewery, though the beers of other artisanal Peruvian brewers are on its nine taps, too. It's open until 3am on the weekends. **Art Déco Lounge ★★**, Manuel Bonilla 227 (www.artdecolima. com; ✆ 01/242-3969), a handsome conversion of an older home in Miraflores, takes its colorful and detailed Deco interiors very seriously, as it does the menu of cocktails and nicely selected wine list. **La Esquina Winebar,** Berlín 920 (www.laesquina.com.pe; ✆ 01/242-2456) is a nice little wine bar/restaurant in a city that has very few of them. There's a new second location in Barranco, at Jr. Centenario 165 (✆ 01/248-7387). **Murphy's Irish Pub,** Shell 619 (✆ 01/242-1212) is a longtime favorite drinking hole with a small menu of pub grub. Expect a pool table, darts, Guinness on tap, and Brits and Irishmen hoisting it. Murphy's also hosts live music on Thursday.

Casinos

Peruvians are big on casinos, and many of the larger upscale hotels in Lima have casinos attached. Some of the better ones are the Stellaris Casino at the **JW Marriott Hotel** (p. 90); **Fiesta Casino** at the Thunderbird Hotel at Av. Alcanfores 475, Miraflores (www.fiesta-casino.pe; ✆ 01/616-3131); and **Sheraton Hotel & Casino,** Paseo de la República 170, Centro (✆ 01/433-3320). Most casinos are open Monday through Thursday from 5pm to 2am, and Friday through Saturday from 5pm to 5am.

Cinema

Most foreign movies in Lima are shown in their original language with subtitles. Commercial movie houses worth checking out include **Multicines Larcomar,** Malecón de la Reserva 610, Miraflores (✆ 01/446-7336); **Multicines Starvisión El Pacífico,** Av. José Pardo 121, near the roundabout at Parque Central, Miraflores (✆ 01/445-6990); and **Cinemark Perú Jockey Plaza,** Av. Javier Prado 4200 (✆ 01/435-9262). Art and classic films are shown at the **Filmoteca de Lima** in the Lima Museo de Arte, Paseo Colón 125, Lima Cercado (✆ 01/423-4732), and **El Cinematógrafo,** Pérez Roca 196, Barranco (✆ 01/477-1961). Most theaters in the suburbs cost more than the ones in Lima Centro, but they're more modern and better equipped. Several have matinee prices and discounts on Tuesday. For a list of films *subtituladas* (with subtitles), consult the Friday edition of *El Comercio.* The term *doblada* means "dubbed." Tickets run from S/12 to S/30.

Dance Clubs

Many of Lima's discos are predominantly young and wild affairs. Cover charges range from S/15 to S/50. The main drags in Barranco, Avenida Grau and Pasaje Sánchez Carrión (a pedestrian alley off the main square), are lined with raucous clubs that go late into the evening and annoy Barranco residents.

Two very chic and popular discotheques, **Gótica ★★** (www.gotica.com.pe; ✆ 01/445-6343) and **Aura ★★** (www.aura.com.pe; ✆ 01/242-5516) face each other in the Larcomar shopping center, Malecón de la Reserva 610 in

Miraflores, and feature interconnected open-air terraces, great sea views, and dance music ranging from electronica to the Latin specialty, *pachanga.* Also check out **Bizarro,** at Calle Francisco De Paula Camino 220 in Miraflores (www.bizarrobar.com; ℭ **01/446-3508**), another late-night dance spot with top DJs that attracts pretty 20- to 30-somethings with money to spare on bottle service. At **Deja-Vu,** Av. Grau 294 (www.dejavu.com.pe; ℭ **01/247-6989**), the decor is based on TV commercials, and "waitress shows" tease horny patrons. It's a dancefest from Monday to Saturday; the music trips from techno to trance. **Bar Kitsch,** Bolognesi 743, Barranco (ℭ **01/242-3325**) is one of Lima's hottest bars—literally, sometimes it turns into a sweatbox—with over-the-top decor and recorded tunes that range from 1970s and 1980s pop to Latin and techno.

Gay & Lesbian

Although Peru as a whole remains fervently Catholic, and many gay and lesbian Peruvians feel constricted in the expression of their lifestyle, Lima is the most progressive city in the country, with the most facilities and resources for gays and lesbians, including a significant number of nightclubs. Among the most popular is **Downtown Vale Todo** ★, Pasaje los Pinos 160, Miraflores (www.mundovaletodo.com; ℭ **01/444-6433**), which has closed down a couple of times but always seem to open back up. It puts on occasional shows with strippers. Then there's **Legandaris,** Calle Berlin 363 in Miraflores (ℭ **01/446-3435**), with drag shows and strippers. **La Cueva,** Av. Aviación 2514, San Borja (ℭ **01/224-3731**), is a lively disco with an eclectic soundtrack and large dance floor. All are generally open Wednesday through Saturday; cover charges range from S/15 to S/40.

Live Music Clubs

Barranco   My vote for best live-music club in Lima is **La Noche** ★★, Bolognesi 307 (www.lanoche.com.pe; ℭ **01/477-1012**). Despite its prosaic name, this sprawling multilevel club feels like a swank treehouse, with a great stage and sound system and good bands every night that run the gamut of styles (although it's frequently jazz), plus a hip, mixed crowd of Limeños and internationals. Monday-night jam sessions (no cover charge) are particularly good; otherwise, cover charges range from S/5 to S/40. There's also a La Noche outpost in Lima Centro, at the corner of Jirón Camaná and Jirón Quilca. **La Estación de Barranco** ★, Pedro de Osma 112 (www.laestaciondebarranco.com; ℭ **01/247-0344**) is another nice place, housed in an old train station, with live music Tuesday through Saturday and a slightly more mature crowd (both locals and tourists); the music on tap is often *criolla.* Covers vary from S/5 to S/20. The upstairs bar **The Lion's Head** ★, Av. Grau 268 (www.lionsheadperu.com; ℭ **01/247-1499**), schedules live rock 'n' roll on most nights. **El Dragón** ★, Av. Nicolás De Pierola 168 (www.eldragon.com.pe; ℭ **01/221-4112**), is a cool late-night music and dance spot with live reggae, Latin jazz, and electronic music, depending on the night. There's not always a cover, but when there is it's usually from S/20 to S/40.

Miraflores   Satchmo ★, Av. La Paz 538 (☎ **01/444-4957**), is a sophisticated joint with a variable roster of live bands, including jazz combos—as the
name would indicate. It's a good date spot. Cover charges range from S/20
to S/50. Another great spot for live jazz (as well as bossa nova and Afro-
Peruvian evenings) is **Jazz Zone** ★★, Av. La Paz 656, Pasaje El Suche
(www.jazzzoneperu.com; ☎ **01/241-8139**); covers from S/10 to S/35.
Cocodrilo Verde ★, Francisca de Paula 226 (www.cocodriloverde.com;
☎ **01/445-7583**), has jazz on Wednesday and a variable program of live music
on weekends, with cover charges ranging from S/10 to S/30.

Peñas

The classic Limeño night outing is a *peña,* a performance at a *criolla* music
club that quite often inspires rousing vocal and dance participation. A visit to
Lima really isn't complete until you've seen one.

Barranco   De Rompe y Raja ★, Manuel Segura 127 (www.derompeyraja.
pe; ☎ **01/247-3271**), is a favorite of locals that's open Thursday to Saturday
nights. Look for the popular Matices Negros, an Afro-Peruvian dance trio.
The cover is usually around S/35. **Peña del Carajo!** ★, Calle Catalino
Miranda 158 (www.delcarajo.com.pe; ☎ **01/247-7023**), is another cool *peña*
with good live music, percussion, and dance shows Tuesday through Saturday
starting at 10pm. Covers range from S/20 to S/40. **La Candelaria,** Bolognesi
292 (www.lacandelariaperu.com; ☎ **01/247-1314**), is a comfortable club celebrating Peruvian folklore. It's open Friday and Saturday from 9pm onward;
the cover is normally around S/40. **Don Porfirio** ★★, Manuel Segura 115
(☎ **01/477-3119**), is a bit more downscale than most *peñas* and preferred by
locals, an amiable, hidden-away spot invites participation in its good-quality
music-and-dance shows. Cover is generally S/20.

Lima Centro   Brisas del Titicaca ★★, Jr. Tarapaca 168, the first block of
Avenida Brasil, near Plaza Bolognesi (www.brisasdeltiticaca.com; ☎ **01/332-
1901**), is a cultural institution featuring *noches folclóricas*—indigenous
music-and-dance shows—that are some of the finest in Lima. Shows are
Tuesday and Wednesday at 8pm, Thursday at 9:15pm, and Friday and Saturday at 10:15pm. You can even catch a dance show with lunch, Friday and
Saturday from noon to 6pm. Covers range from S/40 to S/70.

Miraflores   Sachún, Av. del Ejército 657 (www.sachunperu.com;
☎ **01/441-4465**), is favored by tourists and middle-class Limeños who aren't
shy about participating with their feet and vocal cords. The cover ranges from
S/25 to S/50.

Theater & the Performing Arts

Lima's **Teatro Municipal** (www.teatromunicipal.pe; ☎ **01/632-1300**), the
pride of the local performing-arts scene and the primary locale for theater,
ballet, opera, and symphony performances, burned to the ground in 1998 and
sat vacant for years, but was finally resurrected in late 2010 (with updated
fireproofing and anti-seismic technology). It was been restored in dramatic

fashion, with Juan Diego Flórez performing *The Barber of Seville*. Once again it is home to the National Symphony Orchestra and the National Ballet. The 1940s-era **Teatro Segura,** Huancavelica 265 (℅ **01/426-7206**), has mostly theater and dance performances, as well as opera and music concerts. Frequent cultural events, including films and music recitals, are held every week at the **Centro Cultural Ricardo Palma,** Larco Herrera 770, Miraflores (℅ **01/446-3959**) and the **British Council,** Calle Alberto Lynch 110, San Isidro (℅ **01/221-7552**). The **Instituto Cultural Peruano Norteamericano,** at the corner of Angamos and Arequipa in Miraflores (℅ **01/446-0381**), hosts theater, jazz, classical, and folk music. See the daily newspaper *El Comercio* (www.elcomercio.pe) for updated lists of live performing-arts events in Lima (in Spanish only).

Lima has a good theater scene, although, as one might expect, nearly all plays are in Spanish. Two of Lima's best theaters are **Teatro Canout,** Av. Petit Thouars 4550, Miraflores (www.teatrocanout.com.pe; ℅ **01/422-5373**) and **Teatro Auditorio Miraflores,** Av. Larco 1036, Miraflores (℅ **01/447-9378**). Tickets are available at the box offices.

WHERE TO STAY

Lima Centro has a handful of hotels and budget inns, but most people head out to the residential neighborhoods of Miraflores and, to a growing extent, Barranco. San Isidro is the prime business district of Lima and full of hotels primarily, if not exclusively, designed for business and luxury travelers. These *barrios* (San Isidro in particular) have less in the way of official sights, but they are more convenient for dining, nightlife, and shopping, and probably safer, if not necessarily much quieter.

Hotel rates in Lima are the highest in the country, especially at the top end. There are plenty of mid-range and budget choices, although comparatively few have the charm of affordable *hostales* in other cities. Particularly at the top echelon, hotels tack on taxes and service charges to quoted rates, whereas most moderate and less-expensive inns quote rates that already include all taxes and service charges. Be on the lookout for any hotel that tries to charge you the 19 percent IGV (sales tax) on the basic room rate in addition to a 10 percent service charge, though; foreigners and nonresidents with the passport to prove it are exempt from the IGV (but not the service charge). Most *hostales* in Lima—unlike in Cusco, Arequipa, and a few other highland towns— do feature reliable 24-hour hot water.

Airport/Callao
EXPENSIVE
Costa del Sol Wyndham Airport ★   Early-morning flights to Cusco or late arrivals at Jorge Chavez occur with such regularity that it's a wonder it took so long for a proper hotel to be built beside the airport. Operated by national brand Costa del Sol along with Wyndham, this perfectly functional and convenient property saves passengers from making the sometimes

hour-long ride to Miraflores or San Isidro. The rooms are just what you would expect from a mid-range American airport hotel: carpeted floors, a dresser with a small TV, and little decoration.

Av. Elmer Faucett s/n, Aeropuerto Internacional Jorge Chavez. www.costadelsolperu.com. © **01/711-2000.** 192 units. $183 doubles; $248–$284 suites. Rates include breakfast buffet. **Amenities:** Restaurant; cafe; indoor pool; hot tub; Wi-Fi.

Lima Centro
INEXPENSIVE
Hotel España ★   One of the least expensive hotels in Lima sits right in the heart of the UNESCO World Heritage Centre, near the Convento de San Francisco and just 4 blocks from the Plaza de Armas. This popular budget hostel may be basic, but the labyrinthine old building that houses it is filled with quirky charm, from the roaming tortoises and peacock, to the reproduction Roman busts and actual mummies. There's a mix of concrete and creaky parquet floors, with bright walls in the rooms. Note that most of the accommodations come with shared bathrooms. A rooftop terrace with views of the church is a great place to hang and trade travel tales. This isn't a party hostel by any means, so a good night's sleep is easier to find here than at similar properties.

Azángaro 105. www.hotelespanaperu.com. © **01/428-5546.** 30 units. $36 doubles with private bath. Rates include continental breakfast. **Amenities:** Cafeteria.

Posada del Parque ★   While the center of Lima was once the preferred neighborhood to overnight, most travelers moved on to Miraflores and neighboring districts decades ago. Few original accommodations have been maintained, and there's little to do here in the evenings. This excellent little guesthouse with simple amenities in a 1920s *casona* is on a secure street beside similar homes—a rarity for the neighborhood. Facilities are basic, but English-speaking owner Monica Moreno keeps the house clean and the hot water running. Eclectic artwork and homemade pizzas help give the hotel a personal feel.

Parque Hernán Velarde 60. www.incacountry.com. © **01/433-2412.** 9 units. $37–$40 doubles. Rates include continental breakfast. **Amenities:** Wi-Fi (free).

Miraflores
VERY EXPENSIVE
Miraflores Park ★★★   More secluded than the JW Marriott a few blocks away, this posh Belmond property (formerly called Orient Express) has been continually updated since its opening in 1996. It remains one of Lima's preeminent hotels. All of the rooms are suites, starting with spacious junior-level accommodations and ending with butler service in the expansive Presidential Suites. Rooms are tastefully decorated with light, earthy tones and fine wood furniture. Some of the best bathrooms in town are here, with marble floors, rainfall shower heads, and saunas. Just off the *malecón,* the hotel's views across the Costa Verde, particularly from the 11th-floor heated rooftop pool and Observatory Restaurant, are spectacular. Not that it needed it, but in 2010

renowned Peruvian architect Jordi Puig redesigned the ground floor, which now features a sleek fusion restaurant called Tragaluz and an open-air cocktail lounge.

Av. Malecón de la Reserva 1035. www.mirafloresapark.com. © **01/610-4000.** 81 units. $350–$2,030 suites. **Amenities:** 2 restaurants; bar; cafe; concierge; exercise room; small outdoor rooftop pool; spa; squash court; smoke-free rooms; 24-hour room service; Wi-Fi (free).

EXPENSIVE

JW Marriott Hotel Lima ★   Opened in 2000 along the Miraflores *malecón*, across from Parque Salazar and the cliff-side Larcomar shopping center, the Bernardo Fort-Brescia–designed JW Marriott remains one of Lima's top hotels. It's also perhaps the best located: The 25-story, gold-accented glass tower offers absolutely unreal Pacific Ocean views. Every modern amenity one could wish for can be found in the comfortable rooms, which either face the ocean or the city. Those expecting the brand's dependable characteristics won't be disappointed, as the bold color schemes and heavy dark-wood furniture are here as well. At the base of the building is one of the largest casinos in Lima, as well as a few high-end shops. There's an excellent sushi and ceviche bar, as well as an all-day restaurant, La Vista, with a stellar view and one of Lima's best buffets. Rates drop considerably during the weekend, when there aren't as many business travelers taking up the rooms.

Malecón de la Reserva 615. www.marriott.com. © **01/217-7000** or 800/228-9290 in the U.S. and Canada. 300 units. $340–$410 doubles; $465–$485 suites. **Amenities:** 2 restaurants; cafe; concierge; health club; outdoor pool; sauna; Wi-Fi.

MODERATE

Antigua Miraflores Hotel ★   A rare find in the very heart of a modern metropolis, this 1923 mansion with first-floor walls that are made of adobe brick (though now plastered over). It's one of the few independent mid-range hotels in the neighborhood and it takes hospitality seriously, regularly updating rooms and keeping the property spotless. The house is built around a tree-filled courtyard and filled with colonial art, period furnishings, and black-and-white checkered tile floors that lend a historic air. The rooms are spacious, though rather bland, particularly the traditional rooms. The bathrooms are modern, and the colonial rooms have Spanish tiles, giving them some extra life.

Av. Grau 350, Miraflores, Lima. www.peru-hotels-inns.com. © **01/201-2060.** 65 units. $113–$149 doubles. Rates include breakfast selections and airport pickup (2-night stay required). Free parking. **Amenities:** Restaurant; bar; small gym; Jacuzzi; Wi-Fi (free).

Casa Andina Classic Miraflores San Antonio ★   Of mid-range Peruvian brand Casa Andina's four Miraflores hotels, this one is the best value. It's situated in a residential neighborhood on the other side of the Via Expresa highway from most attractions, though just a 15- to 20-minute walk to Larcomar and only steps to the 28 de Julio stop on the Metropolitano. The rooms are standard for the brand, which emphasizes comfort and amenities over price.

What to Stay & Dine in Lima Centro

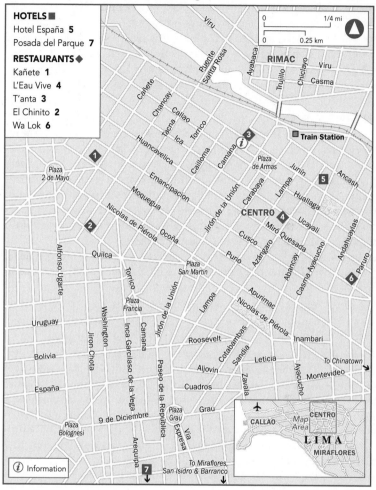

HOTELS ■
Hotel España **5**
Posada del Parque **7**

RESTAURANTS ◆
Kañete **1**
L'Eau Vive **4**
T'anta **3**
El Chinito **2**
Wa Lok **6**

There are marble bathrooms, cheerfully decorated rooms with striped bed-spreads, and a decent breakfast buffet, but otherwise no highs or lows.

Av. 28 de Julio 1088, Miraflores, Lima. www.casa-andina.com. ℂ **866/220-4434** toll-free in the U.S., **08/082-343-805** in the U.K., or **01/213-9739.** 86 units. $79–$99 doubles. Rates include breakfast buffet. **Amenities:** Babysitting; concierge; room service; smoke-free rooms; Wi-Fi.

Casa Andina Private Collection Miraflores ★
When fast-growing Peruvian chain Casa Andina took over the defunct 18-level Hotel César in the heart of Miraflores, many were skeptical. The hulking building, which resembles a series of stacked boxes, had sat empty for several years and was in bad

shape. What a wonder $15 million will do. Opened in 2008, the completely renovated property added an indoor rooftop pool with fantastic views, plus a small spa and art gallery. Though the hotel is part of the chain's high-end Private Collection, the rooms have already begun to feel a tad dated as newer hotels have quickly surpassed it. The location is great, a short walk from some of the best restaurants and nightlife in Miraflores.

Av. La Paz 463. www.casa-andina.com. ☏ **01/213-4300.** 148 units. From $152 doubles; $199–$244 suites. Rates include breakfast. **Amenities:** 2 restaurants; bar; concierge; gym; heated indoor swimming pool; spa; smoke-free rooms; Wi-Fi.

INEXPENSIVE

Hostal El Patio Miraflores ★
In the cookie-cutter world of the Miraflores hotel scene, this intimate, atmospheric little hotel behind an iron gate is a breath of fresh air. The rambling old house is built around a flower-filled Andalusian-style patio and natural light fills the cheerful rooms. The standard rooms are on the small side and far from luxurious, though at this price point you won't find anything better. Standard-plus rooms add kitchenettes, as do suites, which have separate living areas. The staff is friendly and helpful with sightseeing recommendations or getting around town.

Calle Ernesto Diez Canseco 341, Miraflores, Lima. www.hostalelpatio.net. ☏ **01/444-2107.** 25 units. $65 doubles; $80 suite. Rates include continental breakfast. **Amenities:** Wi-Fi (free).

Pariwana Hostel Lima ★
While this hostel, popular with young backpackers and students, doesn't have quite the same spectacular digs as the colonial mansion of its sister location in Cusco (p. 162), the location right on Parque Kennedy could not be better for a fresh face getting to know the city. Dorm rooms are bright and range from 4 to 12 beds. Single women will appreciate the sex-segregated dorm rooms. The private rooms are rather cramped, but there are always lots of group activities, a bar/restaurant, and a rooftop terrace so that regardless of where you sleep, there are places to escape to. The breakfast lasts until 1pm.

Av. Larco 189, Miraflores, Lima. www.pariwana-hostel.com. ☏ **01/242-4350.** 60 units. S/125 doubles w/shared bathroom; S/140 doubles w/bathroom; S/36–S/51 per person in dorm room w/shared bathroom. Rates include breakfast. No credit cards. **Amenities:** Restaurant/bar; lockers; TV room; Wi-Fi (free).

San Antonio Abad Hotel ★
This quaint little hotel in a quiet residential area is a little bit overpriced, though it could do in a pinch. The colonial-style building, near a popular park and within walking distance to the Metropolitano, is clean and comfortable. There's a garden terrace and lounge with a fireplace, though not much else. The rooms are cozy and basic, though all have private modern bathrooms with hot water that works 24 hours a day. The free airport pickup is unusual at this price level.

Av. Ramón Ribeyro 301, Miraflores, Lima. www.hotelsanantonioabad.com. ☏ **01/447-5475.** 24 units. $78 doubles. Rates include breakfast buffet and one-way airport pickup. **Amenities:** Restaurant; bar; Wi-Fi (free).

What to Stay & Dine in Miraflores

RESTAURANTS ◆
Ámaz **10**
Central **16**
Fiesta Chiclayo
  Gourmet **9**
La Lucha Sangucheria **3**
La Rosa Nautica **14**
Maido **11**
Peru Pa'Ti **13**
Restaurant Huaca
  Pucllana **1**

HOTELS ■
Antigua Miraflores Hotel **2**
Casa Andina Classic Miraflores
  San Antonio **8**
Casa Andina Private Collection
  Miraflores **6**

Hostal El Patio Miraflores **5**
JW Marriott Hotel Lima **15**
Miraflores Park **12**
Pariwana Hostel Lima **4**
San Antonio Abad Hotel **7**

4

LIMA | Where to Stay

San Isidro
VERY EXPENSIVE
Country Club Lima Hotel ★★★   This is Lima's classiest hotel. Set beside the Lima Golf Club (guests have special privileges), the property was built in 1927 and has been the center of the city's high society ever since. The hacienda-style hotel feels like an actual country club, with wood paneling and leather armchairs throughout, although service is not at all stuffy. Stained-glass windows, 300 pieces of artwork on loan from the Pedro de Osma Museum, and live piano music wafting through the air on occasion add to the swankiness. The

room layouts are all a bit different, though high wood-beam ceilings, antique furniture, and marble bathrooms with Jacuzzis and separate showers are standard. The clubby, lounge-like English Bar is often recognized for having the top pisco sour in the city, while the two restaurants consistently get rave reviews and attract an outside crowd. A Starbucks, bank, spa, and jewelry store are conveniently located in the attached strip mall. There's live music Friday and Saturday evenings, and social functions are often held in banquet rooms and the sprawling gardens.

Los Eucaliptos 590. www.hotelcountry.com. ✆ **01/611-9000.** 75 units. $279–$309 doubles; $359–$2,350 suite. **Amenities:** 3 restaurants; bar; concierge; fitness center; access to nearby Lima Golf Club; outdoor pool; spa; tennis court; Wi-Fi.

Swissôtel Lima ★ This glitzy high-rise hotel, part of the international Swissôtel chain, has business facilities that rival any other hotel in town, though leisure travelers will appreciate the cushy amenities and the location near Huaca Huallamarca and Parque El Olivar. A recent multimillion-dollar renovation added 12 new meeting rooms, turned the pool indoor-outdoor, and created a modern fitness center. The rooms are spacious and well-appointed. Executive rooms include a work desk, two telephone lines, an espresso machine, and access to an executive lounge/boardroom that has a breakfast buffet and cocktail reception. Rates tend to be cheaper on the weekends.

Vía Central 150 (Centro Empresarial Real), San Isidro, Lima. www.swissotel.com. ✆ **01/421-4400.** 345 units. $190–$290 doubles; $320 and up suites. **Amenities:** 3 restaurants; cafe; bar/lounge; concierge; fitness center; heated indoor/outdoor pool; sauna; spa; Wi-Fi.

The Westin Lima Hotel & Convention Center ★★★ When the Westin opened in 2011, it was the tallest building in all of Peru. Though it has since been surpassed by the neighboring Banco Continental office tower, the 30-story Westin is still one of the most noticeable additions to Lima's skyline in decades, as it sits right at the corner of one of the busiest intersections in the city. For Westin's first foray into South America, the chain went all out, bringing in an all-star team that included national brand Libertador, architect Bernardo Fort-Brescia, and interior designer Tony Chi. In terms of technology and sophistication, this is the most advanced hotel in the country, with smart escalators and electronics at every turn. The glossy interiors are infused with touches of pre-Colombian design, and the oversized rooms feature the brand's signature Heavenly Beds and Heavenly Showers. Lots of shiny metals and leather can be found throughout. Much of the ground floor is dedicated to renowned chef Rafael Piqueras' excellent fine dining restaurant Maras, along with a smaller casual restaurant and a sleek lobby bar and lounge. The second level is home to the Heavenly Spa, *the* spa in Lima, with a thermal circuit and a full range of original treatments.

Calle Las Begonias 450. www.westinlima.com. ✆ **01/201-5000.** 81 units. $161 doubles; $249–$449 suites. **Amenities:** 2 restaurants; 2 bars; concierge; gym; spa; heated indoor pool; Wi-Fi.

What to Stay & Dine in San Isidro

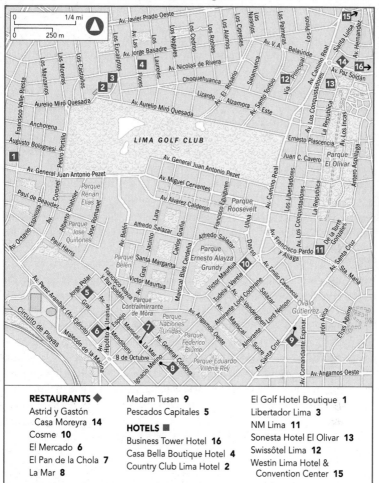

RESTAURANTS ◆

Astrid y Gastón
  Casa Moreyra **14**
Cosme **10**
El Mercado **6**
El Pan de la Chola **7**
La Mar **8**

Madam Tusan **9**
Pescados Capitales **5**

HOTELS ■

Business Tower Hotel **16**
Casa Bella Boutique Hotel **4**
Country Club Lima Hotel **2**

El Golf Hotel Boutique **1**
Libertador Lima **3**
NM Lima **11**
Sonesta Hotel El Olivar **13**
Swissôtel Lima **12**
Westin Lima Hotel &
  Convention Center **15**

EXPENSIVE

Business Tower Hotel ★   Part of a small international chain, the BTH, though centrally located near San Isidro's financial center, and stocked with every possible amenity to assist the business traveler (private taxi services, 24-hr. medical attention, high-speed Wi-Fi), tries its damn hardest not to feel like a business hotel. Each room type has a different theme with different amenities, like the Cosmopolitan series, which adds in-room hot tubs and saunas, or the Business Lofts, with their vaulted ceilings and free airport transfer. All rooms feature stone tile floors, with medium-tone wood paneling and contemporary photography. The downstairs restaurant Quimera and cocktail spot Madbar are far from standard business fare, with elements of molecular gastronomy and a trendy crowd. There's even a hipster barbershop and tattoo parlor called "The Beard."

Av. Guardia Civil 727. www.bth.pe. ℰ **01/319-5300.** 131 units. $123–$180 doubles; $171–$142 suites. Rates include breakfast. **Amenities:** Restaurant; bar; gym; barbershop; tattoo parlor; Wi-Fi.

Libertador Lima ★ Overshadowed by the brand's much larger, newer, and more extravagant Westin hotel, the San Isidro Libertador remains an oldie but a goodie. It's also a great value if all you want is a comfortable place to rest your head in a prime location (near the esteemed Lima Golf Club and far-pricier Country Club hotel). The narrow, 13-floor building is decorated with modern art and kilim rugs. The rooms, whose electronics have been updated (iPod docks, flat-screens, DIRECTV), otherwise suffer from furniture and carpets that are quite dated. All common amenities are on the ground floor, including a quiet restaurant, English-style pub, and small workout room.

Los Eucaliptos 550. www.libertador.com.pe. ℰ **01/518-6300** or 877/778-2281 in the U.S. and Canada. 43 units. $130 doubles; $190 suites. Rates include breakfast. **Amenities:** Restaurant; bar; concierge; gym; Jacuzzi; sauna; Wi-Fi.

NM Lima ★★ With Lima's hotel scene dominated by large chains, it's nice to see an independent hotel that stands out. The NM near Parque El Olivar opened in 2002 and has been attracting steady return visitors, drawn by the design-hotel feel without the over-the-top price. Guests enter through a stark white lobby adorned with avant-garde furniture and sculptures from Peruvian artists. Muted tones and tufted headboards define the smallish rooms. (Those who tend toward claustrophobia should opt for one of the suites.) The ground-floor Atrium Café, with its ornate tiles, and the house Restaurant 300, which packs a nouveau-Victorian vibe, add loads of character.

Avenida Pardo y Aliaga 300. www.nmlimahotel.com. ℰ **01/612-1000.** 126 units. From $242 doubles; $319–$639 suites. Rates include breakfast. **Amenities:** Restaurant; cafe; concierge; gym; Wi-Fi.

Sonesta Hotel El Olivar ★ Though it has much more competition than it did when it opened in the mid-1990s, Sonesta's original Peru property is still quite the charmer. The seven-story hotel, beside the colonial olive groves of Parque El Olivar, is a big hit with business travelers, though leisure travelers won't be disappointed. The rooms are among the largest in Lima, bright and cheery with pastel colors, though they are no longer the most sophisticated in town. The bar and restaurant are a step up from those at most other hotels in town, even if they're not as prominent as they once were. The large outdoor pool, on a roof terrace with stellar views of the park, has enough lounge chairs to feel like a resort.

Pancho Fierro 194. www.sonesta.com. ℰ **800/SONESTA** (766-3782) or 01/712-6000. 134 units. $155–$195 doubles; $220 suite. Rates include breakfast buffet. Children 7

What to Stay & Dine in Barranco

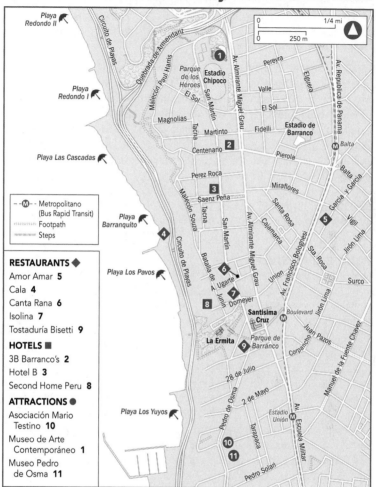

0 _____ 1/4 mi
0 _____ 250 m

Playa Redondo II

Circuito de Playas

Quebrada de Amendanz

Malecón Paul Harris

Parque de los Héroes

Estadio Chipoco

Av. Almirante Miguel Grau

Pereyra

Elguera

Av. Republica de Panama

El Sol

San Martín

Valle

El Sol

Playa Redondo I

Magnolias

Tacna

Martinto

Fidelli

Estadio de Barranco

Centenario **2**

Balta

Playa Las Cascadas

Pierola

Perez Roca

Miraflores

Balta

Garcia y Garcia

3

Saenz Peña

Santa Rosa

Vigil

Jirón Lima

--M-- Metropolitano (Bus Rapid Transit)

Footpath

Steps

Playa Barranquito

Malecón Souza

Tacna

San Martín

Av. Almirante Miguel Grau

Cajamarca

Santa Rosa

STA. Rosa

Av. Francisco Bolognesi

5

Circuito de Playas

4

Batalla de

6

Union

Jirón Lima

Surco

RESTAURANTS ◆

Playa Los Pavos

A. Ugarte

7

Amor Amar **5**

Cala **4**

Canta Rana **6**

Isolina **7**

Tostaduría Bisetti **9**

8

Junín

Domeyer

Santisima Cruz

Boulevard

Juan Pazos

Corpancho

Manuel de la Fuente Chavez

HOTELS ■

3B Barranco's **2**

Hotel B **3**

Second Home Peru **8**

La Ermita

Parque de Barránco

9

ATTRACTIONS ●

Asociación Mario Testino **10**

Museo de Arte Contemporáneo **1**

Museo Pedro de Osma **11**

Playa Los Yuyos

28 de Julio

2 de Mayo

Pedro de Osma

Estadio Unión

Tarapaca

Escuela Militar

Av.

10

11

Pedro Solari

and under stay free in parents' room. **Amenities:** 2 restaurants; cafe; cocktail lounge; bar; concierge; fitness center w/rooftop outdoor pool; Jacuzzi; sauna; Wi-Fi.

MODERATE

Casa Bella Boutique Hotel ★   This small B&B is set in a 1930s San Isidro *casona* just 1 block from the swank Country Club, a neighborhood dominated by business-oriented hotels. Despite renovations, the house still feels like someone's home, with common areas feeling like suburban living rooms. Each room has a singular shape, though they're mostly rooms that are spacious and airy; some have backyard garden views. For the price, you won't find anything of this quality in San Isidro. The hotel has two other locations in Miraflores that are better located if restaurants and shopping are more of what you are looking for.

Las Flores 459, San Isidro. www.casabellaperu.net. © **720/648-3451** in the U.S. or 01/421-7354. 12 units. $69–$75 doubles; $85–$195 suite. Rates include continental breakfast. **Amenities:** Wi-Fi (free).

El Golf Hotel Boutique ★   This true boutique hotel is located on a wonderfully laid-back San Isidro street in a charming townhouse. The property is simple and clean, with unique amenities for a hotel in this price range: a lounge with a fireplace, a terrace with a pool, and even a small bistro-style restaurant that features Peruvian and international dishes. The contemporary rooms are mostly white, with a few splashes of color, and are better equipped than most hotels at double the price. The suites are more spacious, though not terribly different than the rooms.

Valle Riestra 576, San Isidro, Lima. www.elgolfhotelboutiqueperu.com. © **01/677-8888.** 20 units. $110–$150 doubles; $180–$220 suites. Rates include breakfast buffet. **Amenities:** Restaurant; outdoor pool; concierge; 24-hour room service; Wi-Fi (free).

Barranco
VERY EXPENSIVE

Hotel B ★★★   After a long wait and many delays, this 1914 Belle Epoque mansion, originally designed as a seaside retreat for the Garcia Bedoya family by French architect Claude Sahut, redefined Lima's hotel scene when it opened in 2013. Part of the luxe Relais & Châteaux hotel group, Hotel B, as it is sometimes called, is the property that many always dreamed Lima could have. The hotel looks back at its historic past in the ornate facade, open balconies, and raised skylights called *teatinas*. At the same time, there's an eye toward the future in the vertical gardens, a roof deck, and ample modern technology. A Peruvian-Mediterranean restaurant, headed by famed local chef Oscar Velarde, sits on the art-filled ground floor. Guests take their included afternoon tea with finger foods here. Each room is unique, as the original layout was maintained where possible, with original artwork from contemporary Peruvian photographers and painters. Each night at turndown, pillows are topped with a poem and something sweet. The hotel is near the neighborhood's hottest galleries, including the attached Galeria Lucia del Puente, Lima's most renowned contemporary art gallery. The hotel's art concierge can provide special access and private showings for guests.

Saenz Peña 204. www.hotelb.pe. © **01/206-0800.** 17 units. $343–$539 doubles. Rates include breakfast buffet and *lonche* (afternoon tea). **Amenities:** Restaurant; bar; art gallery; library; Wi-Fi.

MODERATE

Second Home Peru ★★   This nicely restored Tudor mansion, formerly the home and gallery of Peruvian sculptor Victor Delfin, is one of the best values for mid-range hotels in Lima. Lima's original boutique hotel, the property sits near the edge of the Costa Verde. Although there are breathtaking views from the terraces and patios, for the most part this place has gone unnoticed. There's an impressive collection of artwork and original detail inside, like Louis XV–style claw-footed bathtubs in every wood-floored room. Reserve in advance for the three Mirador rooms with private ocean-facing terraces. The location is just a short walk from Barranco's famed Puente de los Suspiros, and the Bajada de los Baños, a restaurant-lined walk-way that leads down to the beach.

Domeyer 366. www.secondhomeperu.com. © **01/247-5522.** 8 units. $125–$150 doubles. Rates include breakfast. **Amenities:** Kitchen; outdoor pool; Wi-Fi (free).

3B Barranco's ★   Barranco is undeniably one of Lima's most charming neighborhoods to stay in, but unless you're flush with cash or looking for a dorm bed in a hostel, you don't have many options. 3B is one of the better middle-range possibilities. The white, tile-floored rooms are clean and modern, the furniture is relatively new, and everything works, including the hot water. The hotel doesn't offer much in the way of personality, though for the price and the neighborhood, it's a good value. Discounts are available for longer stays.

Jr. Centenario 130. www.3bhostal.com. © **01/247-6915.** 16 units. $77 doubles. Rates include breakfast. **Amenities:** Kitchen; lounge; rooftop terrace; Wi-Fi (free).

SIDE TRIPS FROM LIMA

A short drive out of Lima seems like entering a different world. Scenic river valleys dotted with small farming communities add a touch of green to the central coast, while to the south, a string of beach communities are a welcome change from the frantic pace of the capital. For those with a few days to explore what the central coast has to offer, you will be pleasantly surprised. Major archeological sites, such as Pachacámac to the south and Caral to the north, pre-date the Incas and reveal some of the oldest civilizations in the Americas. The vast Carretera Panamericana (Pan-American Hwy.), a two-lane strip of asphalt that extends the length of Peru from the Ecuadorian border all the way down to Chile, slices through this section of the desert lowlands, and bus travel is direct, if not always visually stimulating. South of Lima along the coast, the hot and extraordinarily dry desert province of Ica is one of the most arid places on earth. There is sandboarding and dune buggy rides, not to mention vineyards hidden amid the sand dunes, though it is also where the South American Plate collides with the Nazca Plate, one of the most seismically active regions of the world. The most recent tragedy struck in August 2007 when a massive earthquake struck around Pisco and Ica, registering 7.9 on the Richter scale.

History The region forms part of the oldest geological strata in the country; fossils date back as far as the Tertiary or Quaternary era. Caral-Supe is believed to be the oldest city in the Americas, and at 5,000 years old, it parallels the great civilizations of Egypt. In the South, the Paracas and Nazca cultures that took root here (roughly 1300 B.C.–A.D. 700) were two of Peru's most advanced, with exquisite textile weavings and ceramics, among the finest produced by pre-Columbian Peru.

Sightseeing The Reserva Nacional de Paracas (Paracas National Reserve), known for the Ballestas Islands, which locals liken to a smaller version of Ecuador's Galápagos Islands, is the region's biggest attraction; however, there are also a string of beaches frequented by Limeños during the summer weekends, and the Huacachina oasis, a beautiful green-and-blue oasis in the midst of the monochrome desert.

Eating & Drinking   Much like Lima, the cuisine of the coast is that of the *cevichería,* where you can find Peru's national dish and other seafood preparations. Hearty *criolla* dishes from rural country restaurants make an appearance, too. South of the capital, you might even see the occasional vineyard, particularly around Ica, where some of the country's best wines and piscos are produced.

Arts & Culture   The center of Peru's Afro-Peruvian culture is in Chincha, the spiritual home of *criollismo,* a vibrant culture filled with music and dance. Come for the Festival Negro de Chincha in the summer to hear the sounds of the *cajón* and be carried away by the *festejo* or *zapateo.*

THE BEST TRAVEL EXPERIENCES BEYOND LIMA

o **Exploring a pre-Inca world:** Whether you head north to Caral, believed to be the oldest city in the Americas, or south to Pachacámac, which dates to the 1st century, this glimpse of coastal civilizations will have you questioning whether you need to visit Machu Picchu at all. See below.

o **Surfing the waves:** Some of Peru's best surfing takes place south of Lima at beaches like Punta Hermosa, which has a year-round surf scene. You can even visit Cerro Azul, made famous by the Beach Boys in their song "Surfin' Safari." See p. 103.

o **Tasting pisco:** Peru's signature spirit is distilled with eight officially designated grapes, which are grown in vineyards south of Lima, especially between Chincha and Ica. Take a tour of a bodega, then retreat to the tasting room to learn the difference between aromatic and non-aromatic. See p. 112.

o **Taking in Asia's summer scene:** One hundred kilometers (62 miles) south of the capital, a satellite city appears during the summer months on the Boulevard of Asia, not far from the clusters of beach houses, where wealthy Limeños visit many of the same shops, restaurants, and nightspots as back in Lima. See p. 104.

o **Sliding down a sand dune:** Whether you are riding in a dune buggy or strapped into a sandboard, the adrenaline rush from descending a sand dune is hard to top. Head to the Huacachina oasis near Ica to explore some of the biggest dunes. See p. 112.

NORTH OF LIMA

Caral ★

176km (109 miles) N of Lima

Researchers now describe Caral, a site in central Peru, north of Lima, believed to date to 2600 B.C., as the oldest city in all of the Americas, a fact confirmed by carbon dating in 2000. Discovered in 1948, the 66-hectare (163-acre) archaeological site sits on a dusty desert plateau overlooking the Supe River. One of 18 settlements in the valley, the city was built by the Caral-Supe, or Norte Chico, civilization; the city features complex architecture ranging from six large pyramidal structures to sunken circular plazas, many of which have been fully restored. Caral's discovery pushed back the idea of complex societies in Peru more than 1,000 years. While the culture lacked knowledge of ceramics, its residents were believed to have created textiles, and even the *quipu,* a knot system later used by the Incas, has been found at the site. Other findings at the site have included flutes carved from condor and pelican bones, as well as clay figurines. It's believed the city traded regularly for products as far away as Ecuador and the Amazon jungle. Severe droughts likely led to the downfall of the culture. Despite its significance, Caral receives only a few thousand visitors each year, the majority of them Peruvian.

The archeological site (www.zonacaral.gob.pe) is open daily from 9am to 4pm (S/11 per person). Guides can be hired at the entrance for S/20 per group. Plan a half-day at the site. Don't forget sunscreen and insect repellant. There is a small reception area with a souvenir store, a snack bar, and bathrooms. On the weekends, locals from the area sell typical foods to visitors.

GETTING THERE

To reach Caral, you must take the Pan-American Highway north to the town of Huacho, at Km 184, from where you will see signs for Caral on the right. From the highway, the road is quite rough and continues for about 25km (16 miles). Allow about 3½ hours to reach the site from Lima. A 4 × 4 is recommended. Most visitors here come on a long day tour from Lima with a tour agency, such as Lima Tours (www.limatours.com.pe; ✆ **01/619-6900**) or Haku Tours (www.hakutours.com; ✆ **01/983-473-724**), for around $105 per person with four travelers.

While there are rumors of a large hotel being built near Caral, so far nothing has materialized. For visitors who prefer to pace themselves and stay the night nearby, there are small hotels and B&Bs in the coastal towns of Barranca and Supe.

SOUTH OF LIMA

Pachacámac

31km (19 miles) S of Lima

The finest ruins within easy reach of Lima, **Pachacámac,** in the Lurín Valley, was inhabited by several pre-Columbian cultures before the Incas. The extensive site, a sacred city and holy place of pilgrimage, includes plazas, adobe-brick palaces, and pyramidal temples, some of which have been rebuilt by the Peruvian government. It makes for an interesting visit, especially if you're not planning on heading north to Caral or the archaeological sites near Chiclayo and Trujillo.

The earliest constructions here date to the 1st century, although the site reached its apex during the Huari (or Wari) culture (10th c.). Pilgrims came here to pay homage to the feared oracle and creator-god Pachacámac, who was believed to be responsible for earthquakes and matters of state such as war. The Incas conquered the site in the 15th century, and it was one of the most important shrines in the Americas during their rule, although its ceremonial importance began to wane soon afterward. However, two of the most important structures on-site, the Temple of the Sun and the Acllahuasi (or Mamacuña) palace (where "chosen maidens" served the Inca), both date to the Inca occupation. Hernán Pizarro and his gold-hungry troops arrived in 1533 but were disappointed to find a paucity of riches. On the premises is a small museum of pre-Columbian artifacts, including textiles and the dual-personage carved wooden idol of Pachacámac, god of fire and son of the sun god.

The site (✆ **01/430-0168**), which occupies a low hill, is large; allow at least a few hours to visit by foot (the visit from Lima can be completed in a half-day). English-speaking guides are usually available for hire at the entrance if you don't arrive with a guide-led group. The site is open Tuesday to Saturday 9am to 4:30pm. Admission is S/8 for adults, S/4 for students.

Getting There   Pachacámac is about 45 minutes from Lima by car or bus. *Combis* (with signs reading PACHACAMAC/LURIN) leave from Avenida Abancay and the corner of Ayacucho and Montevideo in Lima Centro. The most convenient way to visit—cheaper than hiring a taxi, unless there are several of you—is by a half-day organized tour, offered by Lima Vision, Lima Tours, and others; see "Organized Tours" in Chapter 4. Most tours cost about $50 per person, including transportation and guide. Taxis charge about S/40 to S/50 one-way from Miraflores.

WHERE TO EAT

The drive down to Pachacámac for a weekend lunch is a popular pastime for many families in Lima. There are many relaxed country restaurants, mostly open-air, often attached to their own farm. One of the best is **La Casa de Don Cucho** ★, Calle 8, Hacienda Casa Blanca (www.cuchosazonperuana.com; ✆ **01/231-1415**), run by the jovial TV chef Don Cucho La Rosa, who was instrumental in bringing traditional Peruvian ingredients and cooking styles into the mainstream. Oversized *criolla* dishes and huge cuts of meat in the open-air restaurant are cooked in wood-fired ovens. Nearby, **Chaxras Eco-Restaurante,** Calle 8 (www.chaxras.com; ✆ **01/367-4166**), is more progressive, focusing on organic produce from area producers and sustainably raised meats, plus an herbal cocktail list.

The Southern Beaches

30–70km (19–43 miles) S of Lima

The best beaches easily accessible from Lima line the coast south of the city. Popular spots along the shadeless, arid desert landscape are El Silencio, Punta Hermosa (a good place for ceviche and fresh fish in any number of rustic seafood restaurants), Punta Negra, Santa María, and Pucusana. Probably the best bet is Pucusana, a small fishing village, although it's the farthest beach from Lima. The attractive beaches are very popular with Limeños during the summer months; on weekends, the southern coast is a long line of caravans of sun-seekers.

Note: Even though you can swim in the ocean at this distance from the capital, the currents are very strong, and great caution should be exercised. You should also be careful with your possessions because thieves frequent these beaches. Finally, be forewarned that the beaches are only moderately attractive.

A little farther south along the Panamericana Sur, at Km 97.5, is the trendy recreational area called **Asia** (www.asiasurplaza.com), an entertainment-oriented boulevard packed with fashionable shops, restaurants, bars, and discos, all within easy reach of the beaches Playa Blanca, La Isla, and Las Brisas. This is the center of Peru's southern beaches and real estate, in general; it gets pricier the closer it is to Asia.

Getting There   Unless you have wheels, which is recommended, the best way to reach the beaches south of Lima is to hire a taxi. Taxi Directo (www. taxidirecto.com; © **01/711-1111**) has one-way fares from S/50 to S/80, depending on the beach. *Combis* marked San Bartolo (another one of the beaches) leave from Angamos and Panamericana Sur in Lima; others at Jirón Montevideo and Jirón Ayacucho in Lima Centro will also get you to the beaches. You'll have to tell the driver where you want to get off (or hop off wherever a number of fellow bus travelers do), and then walk a mile or less down to the beach. The ride costs S/5 and takes anywhere from 45 minutes to 2 hours. The beaches and their markers are as follows: El Silencio, Km 42; Punta Hermosa, Km 44; Punta Rocas, Km 45; Punta Negra, Km 46; San Bartolo, Km 52; Santa María, Km 55; and Pucusana, Km 65.

PUNTA HERMOSA

Disregarding the private beach of El Silencio, Punta Hermosa, 10 minutes further down the road, is the first major beach destination south of Lima. During the summer months, beachgoers line the sand and the promenade. There are three lovely beaches here: Playa Norte, Playa Negra, and Playa Blanco. Apartment blocks now huddle around the waterfront, while small restaurants, fishing shacks, and roving vendors are attempting to crowd into any other empty space. The surfing here is some of the best of Peru's central coast, known for consistent swells, big rights, and hollow lefts. The surf scene has given rise to a slew of informal surf camps, surf shops, and surf hostels.

Where to Stay

There are a handful of small hostels and B&Bs in and around Punta Hermosa. One of the most reliable is **Casa Barco,** Av. Punta Hermosa 340 (www.casa barco.com; © **01/230-7081;** $88–$100 doubles), with 25 stylish rooms stacked into a tall house with an outdoor pool overlooking the beach. The family-owned **Punta Hermosa Surf Hostel,** Calle Bolognesi 407 (www. puntahermosasurfhostelperu.com; © **01/230-7732;** S/120 doubles, S/45 per person dorms), is clean and cozy. It's a favorite among surfers as it's cheap and it rents boards and wetsuits.

PUCUSANA

Pucusana is a laid-back traditional fishing village with a small port with hundreds of wooden boats. The bay is quite calm and has several nice beaches, making it ideal for swimming. Playa de las Ninfas, left of the fishing pier, is best and has the clearest water. During the summer, informal boat trips can be arranged to look for dolphins and sea lions around Isla Galápagos, just off shore. Diving is popular along the coastal cliffs. Contact **Peru Divers** (www.perudivers.com; ℂ **01/251-623**), based in Lima, for more information.

ASIA

The Boulevard of Asia, at Km 97.5 of the Pan-American Highway, is a fascinating place. From December to about March, an entire satellite city comes to life here. There are Wong and Metro grocery stores like back in the capital. There are many of the same shops, restaurants, and nightclubs. Outside of those few months, most of it is closed. If you are coming during the summer, keep in mind that traffic will be bumper-to-bumper on Friday and Sunday afternoons. *Note:* Most beaches in the area are accessed through private residential areas.

Where to Stay

Most visitors to Asia are Limeños with weekend homes in private developments located within a 20-minute drive in either direction, though a few hotels have opened in recent years. Right in the middle of the party zone, **Aquavit Hotel** (www.aquavithotel.com; ℂ **01/530-7801;** $170 doubles) is a loud, brash, and sexy hotel with a pool area that is a nonstop fiesta from December to March. Prices drop by 80 percent during the week. At Km 109, a short drive from the boulevard, **Estelar Vista Pacifico Hotel,** Sarapampa (www.hoteles estelar.com; ℂ **01/630-7788;** $180 doubles), is a proper oceanfront resort with 116 rooms, several large pools, and restaurants.

CERRO AZUL

This small fishing village caught the attention of the entire world when the Beach Boys mentioned it in their song "Surfin' Safari." Still renowned for its surfing, particularly around the pier, the village now survives mostly on tourism, particularly from summer residents whose homes now line the shore. The beach is divided by the Puerto Viejo, or old port, and dolphins and sea lions can occasionally be spotted in the water. The town was built over the ruins of the pre-Inca settlement, and some adobe ruins can still be seen, though they have been poorly maintained.

Chincha Alta

200km (124 miles) S of Lima

Afro-Peruvian culture has its center in Chincha Alta, particularly in the El Carmen district. The first Africans here were brought to the area as slaves during the early days of Spanish conquest to work in haciendas and on the guano islands. The mark left on Peruvian food, music, dance, and general culture by Afro-Peruvians cannot be denied. The town is known for its vibrant festivals, like the Festival de Verano Negro, or Black Summer, in late February, which includes pageants, *festejo* and *zapateo* dance contests, parades, and stalls with traditional foods like *sopa seca* (chicken and noodles), *carapulcra* (pork and dehydrated potato stew), and *frijol colado* (bean pudding).

Chincha has been inhabited by hunters and gatherers since about the 10th century. In the 11th century, a warrior group known as the Chincha invaded and installed systems of agriculture and irrigation, using guano from nearby islands to fertilize their fields. They were conquered by the Incas in the mid-1400s.

Getting There Most long-distance buses between Lima and Arequipa will make a stop in Chincha, including **Ormeño** (www.grupo-ormeno.com. pe/ormeno.php; ✆ **01/472-5000**) and **Soyuz** (www.soyuz.com.pe; ✆ **01/205-2307**).

WHERE TO STAY & EAT

If you want to stay the night, there are several good hotels. **Casa Hacienda San Jose,** Km 203 (www.casahaciendasanjose.com; ✆ **056/313-332; $60** doubles), is a historic Spanish colonial property with slave tunnels running underneath. The hacienda was known for its sugar plantation, and it's said that the *anticucho* (beef heart kebab) was invented here by using skewers made from sugar cane. Mid-range chain **Casa Andina,** Km 197.5 (www.casa-andina.com; ✆ **01/213-9718; $69** doubles), has a 50-room property with a large resort-style pool. Chincha makes for a nice stop even if just for a meal. Everyone winds up at **El Batán,** Km 197.5 (www.elbatanchincha.com; ✆ **056/268-050**), right on the highway, which serves many traditional *criolla* dishes like *carapulcra con sopa seca.*

Paracas

260km (162 miles) S of Lima; 75km (47 miles) NW of Ica

Just beyond the port of Pisco, which was badly damaged during the 2007 earthquake, the growing coastal town of Paracas has drawn attention for the natural attractions in abundance at the nearby Ballestas Islands and Paracas National Reserve. It's primarily a tourist town comprised of a growing number of resorts from major international and national hotel brands, tour operators, and *cevicherías.* While there are beaches within the reserve, most of the beaches in the resort area are man-made, and the water tends to be murky, a

---

Ice Cream Break!

On the side of the Pan-American Highway at Km 63.5, in the town of Chilca, is perhaps Peru's most famous ice cream stall. Helados OVNI, marked by a dusty ET and a storefront painted with aliens and UFOs, sells just one flavor of ice cream: *lúcuma.*

This fruit of low-Andean valleys has a green skin and orange, yoke-like pulp. It's rarely eaten raw, though it makes a wonderful addition to sweets. The flavor is something of a cross between maple syrup and pumpkin.

primary reason why the pools are so great. The area can be extremely windy, particularly in the afternoons, which makes the bay ideal for wind- and kitesurfing.

ESSENTIALS

Getting There   There are frequent buses up and down the coast from Lima to Arequipa, with stops in between. From Lima, frequent buses normally take between 3 and 4 hours to reach Paracas. However, because the town is not directly on the Carretera Panamericana, not all coastal buses stop there. Be sure to confirm that the bus won't merely leave you on the side of the road en route to Ica (which would result in the hassle of getting a *combi* to town). **Ormeño** (www.grupo-ormeno.com.pe/ormeno.php; ✆ **01/472-5000**), **Soyuz** (www.soyuz.com.pe; ✆ **01/205-2307**), and **Cruz del Sur** (www.cruzdelsur.com.pe; ✆ **01/311-5050**) all have direct service to Paracas from Lima, continuing on to Ica.

Tours   Most people visit the Paracas National Reserve and Ballestas Islands as part of organized tours. Guides, transportation, and entrance fees are all included in the price. Those who prefer to visit the reserve on their own must pay an entrance fee upon entering the reserve (S/5 for adults and students 14 and older; free for children 13 and under). You can enter the reserve without a guide, but it's highly recommended that you contract one in order to get the most out of a visit. Much that is unique about the area—its climate and conditions, and its migratory wildlife—is not always immediately obvious.

Nearly every Paracas travel agency, as well as those in Lima and Ica, offer a good-value half-day tour of the Islas Ballestas, as well as a half-day tour of the Paracas National Reserve, which are designed so they can be easily paired together. Among locally based operators, **Paracas Explorer** (www.paracas explorer.com; ✆ **056/531-487**) offers standard day trips and half-day trips to the reserve and Islas Ballestas, as well as flyover trips of the Nazca Lines and ATV and bike trips into the desert. Additionally, most resorts will run trips directly.

EXPLORING PARACAS

What is not water in the Paracas National Reserve is hot and dry land, with no transportation to speak of except for independently hired taxis. For this reason, most tourists tend to visit the reserve as part of an organized tour. However, adventurous travelers with plenty of water, sunscreen, and stamina can get to know the peninsula and its rich marine birdlife on their own, camping far from other humans. Safety has become a concern in recent years, though, so camping alone is not a good idea.

Dirt roads crisscross the Paracas Peninsula, and a paved road goes around it, out toward Punta Pejerrey, near the Candelabro. The dirt roads are the most interesting, reaching minuscule fishing villages such as attractive **Lagunillas** and a cliff-top lookout point, **Mirador de los Lobos,** with views of the ocean and lots of sea lions. Sadly, the August 2007 earthquake destroyed the famous **Cathedral** rock and cave formation, one of the National Reserve's great attractions.

Earthquake Aftershocks

The massive 7.9 earthquake that rocked Pisco and Ica in late 2007 destroyed the famous Cathedral rock formation in the Paracas National Reserve, leveled major churches—Ica's Señor de Luren and Pisco's San Clemente—and severely damaged invaluable pre-Columbian artifacts, including mummies and ceramics, in museums in Ica and Pisco. More than 37,000 homes were destroyed, half of them in Pisco. Officials estimated that 85 percent of central Pisco, where most homes in the region were constructed of adobe and incapable of withstanding the tremors, was destroyed. While aid flooded in from around the world, and Peru sent in its military to keep the peace and try to get the most drastically affected communities back on their feet, many who lost their homes were never able to rebuild.

To hike around the peninsula, it's about 21km (13 miles) round-trip to the lookout point (5km/3 miles from the Tello Museum to Lagunillas). Begin at a turnoff left of the paved road beyond the museum. There are few facilities of any kind on the peninsula. You are allowed to camp on the beautiful beaches (where you might see no other humans, just pelicans and other birds), and there are a couple of seafood restaurants in Lagunillas.

Reserva Nacional de Paracas

The Paracas Bay and Peninsula, along with the small Ballestas Islands, compose the Paracas National Reserve, a place of gorgeous unpopulated beaches, strange desert vistas, and spectacular wildlife. Established in 1975, Paracas is the primary marine conservation center in Peru. The 14,504-sq.-km (5,600-sq.-mile) reserve, which can be visited year-round, is about two-thirds ocean, so don't come expecting to see a zoo-like array of plants and animals at every turn—except on the Ballestas, where several thousand sea lions, in addition to many other species, lie about in plain view.

The primary focus of a visit to the reserve is a boat tour of the **Islas Ballestas** (pronounced "Bah-*yes*-tahs"). Although the islands can't possibly live up to locals' touting of them as the "Peruvian Galápagos," the Ballestas do afford tantalizing close-up views (without allowing visitors on the islands) of the habitat's rich roster of protected species, including huge colonies of barking sea lions, endangered turtles and Humboldt penguins, red boobies, pelicans, turkey vultures, and red-footed cormorants. During the summer months (Jan–Mar), baby sea lions are born, and the community becomes even more populous and noisy. The wall-like, cantilevered islands are literally covered with birds; 110 migratory and resident seabirds have been documented, and the bay is a stopover point in the Alaska–Patagonia migration route. Packs of dolphins are occasionally seen slicing through the water; less frequently, humpback whales and soaring Andean condors can also be glimpsed.

The islands are often referred to by locals as *las islas guaneras* because they are covered in bird droppings. ("Guano" is the Quechua word for excrement.) The nitrogen-rich guano is harvested every 10 years and made into fertilizer. (A factory can be seen on the first island.) No humans other than the guano collectors—no doubt a contender for worst job in the world—are allowed on the islands, and all the species in the reserve are protected by law. In practice, however, there are no specially assigned police officers or boats available to enforce protection.

En route to the islands, boats pass the famous **Candelabro,** a giant candelabra-like drawing etched into a cliff overlooking the bay. The huge etching, 126m long and 72m wide (413 × 236 ft.), looks as though it could be a cousin to the Nazca Lines, and it is similarly shrouded in mystery. Some believe that it's a ritualistic symbol of the Paracas or Nazca culture, while others contend that it dates only to the 18th or 19th century, when it served as a protective symbol and navigational guide for fishermen and sailors.

Tours run about S/60 per person, and each boat has an English- or French-speaking guide on board. Most start early in the morning, between 7 and 8am. Visitors are not allowed to set foot on the islands, although boats get close enough for good viewing. Sweaters and windbreakers, hats, and sunscreen are essential.

WHERE TO EAT

Most visitors to Paracas National Reserve dine at their hotels, and both the Doubletree and Hotel Paracas have good restaurants. Informal *cevicherías* at the **El Chaco** waterfront are popular with travelers, and all have basically the same menu and quality.

WHERE TO STAY

Aranwa Paracas ★★   On the northern side of Paracas, this sprawling resort has more amenities than any other hotel in Paracas. Aside from the sparkling beachfront pools, bordered with swim-up rooms on some sides, there are extras like a chapel, convention space, a spa with a saltwater pool for thalassotherapy, and tennis courts. All rooms have ocean views, plus a balcony or patio with a table and chairs, giving them a step up on the competition down the beach, though you'll pay for it.

Av. Paracas S/N. www.aranwahotels.com. © **01/207-0440** for reservations. 116 units. $256–$300 doubles; $320–$544 suites. Rates include breakfast. **Amenities:** Restaurant; 3 bars; 2 pools; tennis courts; spa; Wi-Fi.

Hotel Gran Palma ★   Away from the beach area in the center of town, this relaxed B&B makes a great base for those not looking to spend a lot of money. The rooms are bright and clean, though somewhat cramped. Each has a small balcony with a view of the bay. There is an on-site tour desk that can set up wind- or kitesurfing lessons, tours of the reserve, or transportation to Ica or Lima.

Calle 1 lote 3, El Chaco. www.hotelgranpalma.com. © **01/665-5932** for reservations. 20 units. $82 doubles. Rates include breakfast. **Amenities:** Restaurant; bar; pool; Wi-Fi.

Hotel Paracas ★★★   After the landmark Hotel Paracas was destroyed in the 2007 earthquake, luxe Peruvian chain Libertador, now a part of Starwood hotels, stepped in to turn the setting into one of Peru's poshest resorts. Designed by renowned architect Bernardo Fort-Brescia, the Hotel Paracas might be the best place to stay in all of coastal Peru. The rooms are bright and cushy, with bamboo-covered walls and top-quality electronics, with suites adding a separate living area and balcony or terrace. The real magic happens outside, however, with dreamy daybed-lined pools, multiple restaurants, and a private pier where you can catch a boat to the Islas Ballestas. The 547-square-meter (5,888-sq.-ft.) spa is the region's best, with VIP treatment rooms and a water circuit.

Av. Paracas 173. www.starwoodhotels.com. © **56/581-333** for reservations. 120 units. $160 doubles; $255–$314 suites. Rates include breakfast. **Amenities:** 3 restaurants; bar; 2 pools; spa; kids' club; fitness center; Wi-Fi.

La Hacienda Bahía Paracas ★★   Smaller and more laid-back than the Hotel Paracas and Aranwa, this chic resort is the best value in the area. It doesn't have all the extras that the other hotels have, instead focusing on one large, great pool area and a single restaurant and bar that will serve you pisco sours and ceviche right at your lounge chair. The rooms are bright and airy, and all have a private terrace.

Av. Paracas S/N. www.hoteleslahacienda.com. © **01/213-1010** for reservations. 32 units. $220 doubles; $280 suites. Rates include breakfast. **Amenities:** Restaurant; bar; pool; spa; Wi-Fi.

Ica

300km (186 miles) S of Lima; 75km (47 miles) SE of Paracas

Capital of the department and surrounded by sand dunes, Ica is a surprisingly large and bustling town, given the scorching desert sun its inhabitants have to contend with. The city itself is not worth much exploration, as most of the principal attractions are located beyond the town center. Ica is known primarily for its bodegas, wineries that produce a range of wines and pisco, the white-grape spirit that is the essential ingredient in the national drink, the ubiquitous pisco sour (served as a welcome drink at bars, hotels, and restaurants through-out Peru). Also welcome to travelers in the unrelentingly dry, sandy pampas of the department is the Huacachina Lagoon, a pretty and unexpected oasis amid palm trees and dunes on the outskirts of Ica. In Ica proper is a small collection of interesting colonial mansions and churches as well.

Ica was first settled as early as 10,000 years ago and then inhabited by a succession of advanced cultures, including the Paracas, Nasca, Wari, and Ica civilizations. The Inca Pachacútec incorporated the Ica, Nazca, and Chincha valley territories in the 15th century, but by the mid–16th century, the Spaniards had arrived, and Jerónimo Luis de Cabrera founded the Villa de Valverde del Valle de Ica, which grew in importance as a commercial center for wine and cotton production.

ESSENTIALS

Getting There   There are frequent buses from Lima to Ica (4 hr.), which drop passengers in the center of town. Frequent service also connects Ica to Nazca (2 hr.) and Paracas (40 min). **Cruz del Sur** (www.cruzdelsur.com.pe; ℰ **01/311-5050**) and **Ormeño,** Av. Carlos Zavala 177, Lima (www.grupo-ormeno.com.pe/ormeno.php; ℰ **01/472-5000**) both travel between Lima, Paracas, and points further south. **Soyuz** (www.soyuz.com.pe; ℰ **01/205-2307**) connects Ica with Lima and Pisco and is the fastest and best service (with the most frequent departures) from either city. Bus terminals in Ica are located in the center of town on or just off Jirón Lambayeque, a couple of blocks west of the Plaza de Armas.

   Ica is quite spread out, and getting around town will most likely involve taking inexpensive taxis, which flood the streets. (Most trips in town cost from S/5–S/10.) Taxis are especially useful in visiting the wineries located outside of town. There are also *ciclotaxis,* or bicycle rickshaws, which are cheaper still but less secure. Some visitors enjoy taking them out to Huacachina.

Fast Facts   The **tourist information office** is located at Grau 150 (ℰ **056/227-287**), and the **tourism police** can be found on the Plaza de Armas (ℰ **056/227-673**). **Banco de Crédito,** Av. Grau 109, at the corner of Callao (ℰ **056/233-711**), has an ATM. For medical attention, go to **Hospital Félix Torrealva Gutiérrez,** Bolívar 1065 (ℰ **056/234-798**), or **Hospital de Apoyo,** Camino a Huacachina s/n (ℰ **056/235-231,** or 056/235-101 for emergencies).

EXPLORING ICA

Ica has several colonial churches and mansions of note, even though many have been felled by earthquakes over the years. **Iglesia de la Merced** (also called **La Catedral**), on the southwest corner of the Plaza de Armas, is a late-19th-century colonial church with a handsomely carved altar. **Iglesia de San Jerónimo,** Cajamarca 262, is primarily of interest for its altar mural. **Iglesia de San Francisco,** though constructed in 1950, is notable for its stained glass; it's at Avenida Municipalidad, at Avenida San Martín. The most important church to worshipers, the neoclassical **Templo del Santuario de Luren,** Calle Ayacucho at Piura, was sadly destroyed by the 2007 earthquake that struck the region.

   Among the most attractive of Ica's *casonas,* or colonial mansions, are the **Casona del Marqués de Torre** (today the Banco Continental), on the first block of Calle Libertad; **Casa Mendiola,** on Calle Bolívar; **Casona Alvarado,** a Greco-Roman imitation at Cajamarca 178; and **Casona Colonial El Portón,** Calle Loreto 223.

Huacachina

If you stumble upon this gentle, beautiful oasis in the middle of the desert, surrounded by massive sand dunes and palm trees, you might think it's a mirage. Only 5km (3 miles) southwest of the center of Ica, Huacachina (pronounced "Wah-kah-*chee*-nah") is a small resort village surrounding a small lagoon, in the middle of towering sand dunes, with a few hotels and restaurants. A boardwalk rings the lagoon. The hotels, mostly built during the 1940s, were largely abandoned for decades and opened up again in the 1990s. Most buildings in the area are in poor condition, though as more tourists come to explore the dunes, they are slowly getting fixed up.

Regular buses to Huacachina depart from the Plaza de Armas in Ica. Better yet, you can take an inexpensive and quick taxi or moto taxi; it's best to request one from your hotel and establish the price beforehand (rates run about S/10–S/15).

Sandboarding, a cross between downhill skiing and snowboarding on grainy stuff rather than white powder, is fairly easy to do (or that's what they tell me). You can really build up some speed, and accomplished boarders can maneuver almost like they would on the slopes. It can be very hot, though, and tough going, because there aren't any lifts to transport you back up the dune. After a few spills, you'll be covered in sand. Accidents can occur, so it's best to get some instruction from a local or the outfit renting the boards. You can arrange a boarding excursion, as well as dune buggy rides, through Huacachina Tours (www.huacachina.com; ✆ **956/880-822**).

Vineyards

Dispersed throughout the Ica countryside are some 85 traditional artisanal wineries that produce pisco and wine. Several of the larger bodegas welcome visits; these can be interesting because pisco is such a unique Peruvian product. They don't usually draw big crowds, so visits can be a little homespun and even haphazard. If you don't have your own transportation, the best way to visit the following bodegas is to either take a taxi or check with one of the travel agencies in town about organized tours. Tours given on the premises of the wineries are frequently in Spanish only.

Tacama ★ (www.tacama.com; ✆ **056/228-395**) is about 10km (6¼ miles) northeast of Ica, housed in a 16th-century colonial hacienda. This winery, one of the largest producers in the region, is known internationally and exports its pisco and table wines—some of the finest in Peru—to a number of countries. The Olaechea family has owned the winery since 1889. Despite the farm building's age—it's one of the oldest in the valley—the bodega uses modern technology. The vineyard is still irrigated, incredibly, by the amazing Achirana irrigation canal built by the Incas. Guided tours lasts around 2 hours and end with a tasting.

Just 3km (1¾ miles) north of the center of Ica in the La Tinguiña district, **Bodegas Vista Alegre** (www.vistaalegre.com.pe; ✆ **056/232-919**) is one of the oldest and largest in Peru. It was a Jesuit hacienda until the late 18th century; in 1857, the winery was established by the Picasso brothers, and it's now

No Wine Until Its Time

Ica celebrates a wine-harvest festival (Festival Internacional de la Vendimia) during early March. The second Friday of the month is a major holiday throughout the Ica department. Many activities take place in the vineyards, although around town there are concerts, handicraft fairs, Peruvian *caballos de paso* (step horses) shows, beauty pageants, and cockfighting. (Don't these last two always go together?) It's a great time to get your fill of pisco. The lovely maiden chosen as the Queen of the Festival gets to doff her shoes and squish grapes in a huge wine vat, to the titillation of all.

Another date to remember: July 25 is the Día Internacional del Pisco across Peru, and everybody gets drunk on a national scale.

well-known for its pisco production. To get there on foot, walk on Avenida Grau from the Plaza de Armas, cross over the Ica River, and turn left; the gate entrance to the colonial hacienda is impossible to miss. Call in advance to set up a tour.

Hacienda La Caravedo ★, at Km 291 in the district of Guadalupe (www. piscoporton.com; ✆ 01/711-7800), established in 1864, is the oldest distillery in the Americas. It's home of the internationally famous brand Pisco Portón, and guided tours will walk you through the distillation process and end with a tasting. With advance notice, they can set up Peruvian Paso horse demonstrations and lunch in the vineyard. Reservations are essential.

Harvest time, from late February to April, is by far the best time to visit. At other times, the bodegas can be very quiet; it might be difficult finding someone to give a tour, but you might also have the chance to sit down for a drink with the owner.

WHERE TO EAT

Despite its size, Ica doesn't offer much in the way of fine dining. Most locals and visitors tend to gravitate toward the Plaza de Armas and the handful of sandwich shops, rotisserie-chicken places, and informal restaurants there.

El Otro Peñoncito, Bolívar 422 (✆ 056/233-920), is the nicest restaurant in the city center, with a hugely varied menu of *criolla* (Creole) specialties and basic chicken, meat, and fish dishes, including some vegetarian plates. Sometimes there's live music in the evenings.

WHERE TO STAY

Most of the best hotel options lie beyond the center of Ica; the majority of those in town are rather unappealing budget choices that have inconsistent hot water.

Hostería Suiza ★ This small B&B at the edge of the Huacachina Lagoon, backed by towering sand dunes, has been around for decades. Renovations in recent years have traded the wood floors for white tile and installed cookie-cutter wood furnishings, losing some of the character of the old building, though this is still one of the only clean, reliable options at Huacachina. A beautiful pool area surrounded by gardens is a great retreat from the desert sun.

Balenario Huacachina 264. www.hosteriasuiza.com.pe. © **56/238-762**. 30 units. $72 doubles. Rates include breakfast. **Amenities:** Restaurant; bar; pool; Wi-Fi.

Hotel Casa Sur ★   In a residential area that's a 10-minute drive from the town center or Huacachina, this lovely boutique hotel makes a pleasant base for a night or two. The owners have done a great job of turning this two-story house into a proper small hotel, with a surprisingly large pool area and a superb restaurant. The rooms feature red brick floors and have contemporary art on the walls.

Av. Angostura 367, Residencial La Angostura. www.casasur.pe. © **56/256-101** for reservations. 16 units. $90 doubles. Rates include breakfast. **Amenities:** Restaurant; bar; pool; tour desk; Wi-Fi.

Hotel Las Dunas ★   The largest, most family-friendly Ica resort is located on the north end of town, on a sprawling grassy lot anchored with three enormous pools and a small lake. The facilities are impressive: a spa, a water slide, and tennis courts. Vaulted ceilings with exposed brick, or the flat-screen TVs, are not enough to change the bland corporate feel to the guest rooms. Each has a small balcony or patio facing the pools or gardens.

Av. La Angostura 400. www.lasdunashotel.com. © **56/256-224** for reservations. 130 units. $140 doubles. Rates include breakfast. **Amenities:** Restaurant; bar; 3 pools; spa; tennis courts; Wi-Fi.

Hotel Vinas Queirolo ★★   Surrounded by more than 4 sq. km (1.5 sq. miles) of grapevines near the foothills of the Andes, this hacienda-style hotel is Peru's only true vineyard hotel. The grapes are used by the Queirolo family to make their Intipalka wines at their bodega in Lima. The stylish, sophisticated property is full of wood beams and colonial-style wood furnishings, and decorated with antiques and old clay vessels used to transport pisco. The rooms, simply decorated with stone floors and flat-screen TVs, look out onto a sea of vines. Elsewhere on the property, there's a small pool area to take in the Ica sun, as well as an excellent restaurant and bar.

Carretera a Los Molinos, Km 11. www.hotelvinasqueirolo.com. © **01/205-7170** for reservations. 45 units. $140 doubles. Rates include breakfast. **Amenities:** Restaurant; bar; pool, bike rental; Wi-Fi.

CUSCO

The storied capital of the Inca Empire and gateway to the imperial city of Machu Picchu, Cusco (also spelled Cuzco and Qosqo) ★★★ is one of the highlights of South America. Stately and historic, with stone streets and building foundations laid by the Incas more than 5 centuries ago, the town is much more than a mere history lesson. It is also surprisingly dynamic, enlivened by throngs of travelers who have transformed the historic center around the Plaza de Armas into a year-round hub of South American adventurers. Yet for all its popularity, Cusco is one of those rare places able to preserve its unique character and enduring appeal despite its growing prominence on the tourism radar. Cusco's beautiful natural setting, colorful festivals, sheer number of sights—unparalleled in Peru—and facilities and services organized for travelers make it the top destination in Peru and one of the most exciting places in South America.

History Cusco is a fascinating blend of pre-Columbian and colonial history and contemporary *mestizo* culture. It was the Inca Empire's holy city, the political, military, and cultural center of its continent-spanning empire.

Sightseeing Spaniards razed most of the city, but found some structures so well engineered that they built directly upon the foundations of Inca Cusco. Along with the cathedral, the city's top sights are the many perfectly constructed Inca stone walls, beginning with Quoricancha, the Incas' Temple of the Sun.

Eating & Drinking From Gastón Acurio's creative take on Cusqueña cooking at ChiCha to the no-frills *picanterías* like La Chomba, Cusco has a vibrant dining scene for those who can look beyond the pizzerias. Don't miss a flight of artisanal piscos at the Museo de Pisco or a creative pisco cocktail at the bar at Limo.

Arts & Culture Where Cusco thrives is in its vibrant expressions of Amerindian and *mestizo* culture: June's Inti Raymi, a deeply religious festival that's also a magical display of pre-Columbian music and dance, and raucous Paucartambo in mid-July, are the highlights.

Shopping The handicrafts center of Peru, Cusco's streets and markets teem with merchants and extraordinary textiles, many handwoven in rural mountain communities using the exact techniques of their ancestors. Pick up stylish alpaca fashions, folk art, and silver jewelry at boutiques in San Blas.

THE BEST TRAVEL EXPERIENCES IN CUSCO

o **Drinking in the Plaza de Armas at dusk:** In the early evening, lights cascading up the hills twinkle and street lanterns and the colored fountain glow against a blue-black sky and the silhouettes of the imposing Andes. Cusqueños (residents of Cusco) of all ages parade across the square, window-shop at boutiques under the arcades, and dip into bars with coveted balconies for people-watching. See p. 122.

o **Catching a display of *cultural popular:*** You don't necessarily have to plan your trip to Cusco around Inti Raymi, one of Peru's greatest pageants of Andean culture, to see a spontaneous display, parade, or deeply felt homage to the city's Amerindian roots. See p. 133.

o **Marveling at Inca masonry:** Cusco's streets are a living history lesson, a mesmerizing mash-up of pre-Columbian and colonial cultures. The conquering Spaniards had the good sense to construct their mansions and churches right atop the Incas' brilliant stone foundations. The finest example is Quoricancha, the Temple of the Sun. See p. 129.

o **Strolling hilly San Blas:** Climbing the steep streets of atmospheric San Blas can feel like doing the StairMaster, but the city's most bohemian district is chock-full of art galleries, bars and pubs, and squat, whitewashed colonial buildings with red-tile roofs. See p. 125.

o **Touring Cusco's Inca ruins:** The circuit of fine Inca ruins on the outskirts of Cusco is a terrific primer before heading on to famous ruins in the Sacred Valley. The star is Sacsayhuamán, a fortress of immense granite blocks magnificently perched on a hill overlooking the city. See p. 173.

ESSENTIALS

Getting There

By Plane   Flights arrive from Lima (1 hr.) as well as Arequipa, Juliaca, and Puerto Maldonado, Peru; Santiago, Chile; and La Paz, Bolivia; at **Aeropuerto Internacional Velasco Astete** (⏱ **084/222-611**), 5km (3 miles) southeast of the historic center of Cusco. All major Peruvian airlines fly into Cusco, including **LAN** (www.lan.com; ⏱ **01/213-8200**); **StarPeru** (www.starperu.com; ⏱ **01/705-9000**); **Avianca** (www.avianca.com; ⏱ **01/511-8222**); and **Peruvian Airlines** (www.peruvian.pe; ⏱ **01/716-6000**). Bolivian airline **Amaszonas** (www.amaszonas.com; ⏱ **591/2217-9151**) offers flights between Cusco and La Paz. Chilean airline **Sky Airlines** (www.skyairline.cl; ⏱ **562/2352-5600**) connects Cusco with Santiago. Flights to Cusco are very popular, so make reservations as far in advance as possible during the high season.

Flights to Cusco are popular, so make your reservations as far in advance as possible if you are arriving from another Peruvian city. Flights are occasionally delayed by poor weather or are over-booked, and sometimes from Lima it is necessary to go through Arequipa if direct flights to Cusco are sold out. Although it is possible to arrive from North America on an overnight flight that theoretically will put you into Lima in time for an early-morning flight to Cusco, the window is often quite tight, and a fair number of travelers miss their connecting flights. Also, be sure that your travel agent or airline hasn't inad-vertently booked you on a charter, rather than regular, flight to Cusco.

Transportation from the airport to downtown Cusco (20 min.) is by taxi or private hotel car. Most hotels, even less expensive *hostales,* prearrange airport pickup. Taxi fare is officially S/15 to S/20 from the airport to the center.

By Bus   Buses to Cusco arrive from Lima, Arequipa, Puno/Juliaca, and Puerto Maldonado in the Amazon basin. The journey from Lima to Cusco takes 20 to 26 hours by land; from Puno, 7 to 10 hours; and from Arequipa, 12 hours. There is no single, central bus terminal in Cusco. Most buses arrive at the **Terminal Terrestre,** Av. Vellejos Santoni, Cdra. 2, Santiago (✆ **084/224-471**), several kilometers from the city center on the way to the airport. Buses to and from the Sacred Valley (Urubamba buses, which go through either Pisac or Chinchero) use small, makeshift terminals on Calle Puputi s/n, Cdra. 2, and Av. Grau s/n, Cdra. 1. For service from Lima, contact the major companies, including **Ormeño** (www.grupo-ormeno.com.pe/ormeno.php; ✆ **01/472-5000**), **Cruz del Sur** (www.cruzdelsur.com.pe; ✆ **01/311-5050**), **Oltursa** (www.oltursa.com.pe; ✆ **01/708-5000**), and **Transportes Civa** (www.civa.com.pe; ✆ **01/418-1111**). From Puno, **Cruz del Sur** (see above) and **Inka Express** (www.inkaexpress.com; ✆ **084/247-887**) offer daily service to Cusco. From Arequipa, your best bests are **Civa** and **Cruz del Sur.**

By Train   Cusco has two main PeruRail train stations. Trains from Puno arrive at **Estación de Huanchaq** (also spelled Wanchaq), Av. Pachacútec s/n (www.perurail.com; ✆ **084/238-722**), at the southeast end of Avenida El Sol. Trains from Ollantaytambo and Machu Picchu arrive at **Estación Poroy** (✆ **084/581-414**) on the outskirts of Cusco. Visitors should be particularly cautious at train stations, where thieves have been known to prey on distracted passengers. Sadly, trains no longer depart from the historic main station in Cusco.

Visitor Information

As the top tourist destination in Peru, Cusco is well equipped with informa-tion outlets. There's a small, occasionally unoccupied branch of the **Oficina de Información Turística** (✆ **084/237-364**) at the Velasco Astete Airport in the arrivals terminal; it's open daily from 6am to 5pm. The principal **Oficina**

de Información Turística is located at Portal de Harinas 177, on the Plaza de Armas (© **084/252-974**). It's open Monday through Sunday from 8am to 8pm. It sells the essential *boleto turístico* (tourist ticket; see "Cusco's *Boleto Turístico*" on p. 125).

South American Explorers has an office and club in Cusco at Av. Pardo 847 (www.saexplorers.org; © **084/245-484**). The office stores luggage, maintains lists of trail reports for members, and has a library of useful information for trekking and mountaineering. If you're traveling extensively, and independently, through Peru, it's worth becoming a member of this helpful group.

TOURS

Pretty much every Cusco travel agency offers half-day city tours that take in the cathedral and other major sights (as little as $15–$20 per person). Agencies also promote tours of the Inca ruins circuit on the outskirts of town. **WOWCusco!** (www.hop-on-hop-off-cusco.weebly.com; © **084/682-720**) is a hop-on, hop-off tour of the city on a bus that runs from Monday to Saturday, from 9am to 5pm. It visits mostly archeological sites outside of the city, such as Sacsayhuamán, Kenko, and the Cristo Blanco lookout point, stopping and ending at Plaza San Francisco, for S/35 per person. **Cusco Bus Panoramico** (www.cuscobuspanoramico.com; © **084/635-001**) offers five daily open-top bus tours, lasting 1½ hours each, for $10 per person, stopping at 15 sites, including Sacsayhuamán.

CITY LAYOUT

The Incas designed their capital in the shape of a puma, with the head at the north end, at Sacsayhuamán (whose zigzagged walls are said to have represented the animal's teeth). This is pretty difficult to appreciate today; even though much of the original layout of the city remains, it has been engulfed by growth. Still, most of Cusco can be seen easily on foot, and walking is certainly the best way to take in this historic mountain city that is equal parts Inca capital, post-Conquest colonial city, and modern tourist magnet. For outlying attractions, such as the handful of Inca ruins that lie just beyond the center of town, taxis or tour buses are the best option.

The old center of the city is organized around the stunning and busy Plaza de Armas, the focal point of life in Cusco. The streets that radiate out from the square—Plateros, Mantas, Loreto, Triunfo, Procuradores, and others—are loaded with travel agencies, shops, restaurants, bars, and hotels. The major avenue leading from the plaza southeast to the modern section of the city is Avenida El Sol, where most banks are located. The district of San Blas is perhaps Cusco's most picturesque barrio; the labyrinthine neighborhood spills onto cobblestone streets off Cuesta San Blas, which leads to crooked alleys and streets and viewing points high above the city.

Much of what interests most visitors is within easy walking distance of the Plaza de Armas. The major Inca ruins are within walking distance for energetic sorts who enjoy a good uphill hike.

Cradled by the southeastern Andes Mountains that were so fundamental to the Inca belief system, Cusco sits at a daunting altitude of 3,400m (11,000 ft.). The air is noticeably thinner here than almost any city in South America, and the city, best explored on foot, demands arduous hiking up precipitous stone steps—leaving even the fittest of travelers gasping for breath and saddled with headaches and nausea. It usually takes a couple of days to get acclimatized. You'll need to take it easy for the first few hours or even couple of days in Cusco. Pounding headaches and shortness of breath are the most common ailments, though some travelers are afflicted with severe nausea (others may little feel the effects of the altitude except when walking up Cusco's steep hills). Drink lots of water, avoid heavy meals, and do as the locals do: Drink *mate de coca*, or coca-leaf tea. (Don't worry, you won't get high or arrested, but you will adjust a little more smoothly to the thin air.) If that doesn't cure you, ask whether your hotel has an oxygen tank you can use for a few moments of assisted breathing. If you're really suffering, look for an over-the-counter medication in the pharmacy called "Soroche Pills." And if that doesn't do the trick, it may be time to seek medical assistance; see "Fast Facts" below. Increasingly, travelers are basing themselves in one of the lower-altitude villages of the Sacred Valley, but there is so much to see and do in Cusco that an overnight stay (at a minimum) is pretty much required of anyone who hasn't previously spent time in the area.

NEIGHBORHOODS IN BRIEF

The only neighborhoods most visitors are likely to see are the **Centro Histórico** (radiating outward from the Plaza de Armas), home to most restaurants, hotels, bars, and tourist services, as well as the main historic sights; artsy **Barrio de San Blas,** which climbs into the hills just north from the Plaza de Armas, stretching to the Sacsayhuamán ruins overlooking the city and home to many boutique hotels, restaurants, art galleries, and shops; and **modern Cusco,** the extension of the city along Avenida de la Cultura and Avenida El Sol on the way to the airport, which is the location of a few hotels, banks, and offices.

Getting Around Cusco

Getting around Cusco is straightforward and relatively simple, especially because so many of the city sights are within walking distance of the Plaza de Armas in the historic center. You will mostly depend on leg power and omnipresent, inexpensive taxis to make your way around town.

By Foot   Most of Cusco is best navigated by foot, although because of the city's 3,400m (11,000-ft.) elevation and steep climbs, walking is demanding. Allow extra time to get around, and carry a bottle of water. You can walk to the major ruins just beyond the city—Sacsayhuamán and Q'enko—but you should be rather fit to do so. It's also best to undertake those walks in a small group and not alone.

By Taxi   Cusco is crawling with taxis. Unlike in Lima, taxis are regulated and charge standard rates (although they do not have meters). Taxis are inexpensive (S/3 for any trip within the historic core during the day, S/5–S/6 at night) and are a good way to get around, especially at night. Hailing a cab in Cusco is considerably less daunting than in Lima, but you should still have your hotel call a registered taxi when traveling to train or bus stations or the airport, and when returning to your hotel late at night (there have been reports of muggings tied to rogue taxis). Taxis can be hired for return trips to nearby ruins or for a half- or full day. To the airport, taxis charge S/15 to S/20 from the city center; to distant Terminal Terrestre (bus station), they charge S/10.

By Bus   Most buses—called variously *colectivos, micros,* and *combis*—cost S/1.50, slightly more after midnight, on Sunday, and on holidays. You aren't likely to need buses often, or ever, within the city, though the *colectivos* that run up and down Avenida El Sol are also a useful option for some hotels, travel agencies, and shopping markets (taxis are much easier and not much more expensive). A bus departs from Plaza San Francisco to the airport, but it isn't very convenient. Buses and *combis* are most frequently used to travel from Cusco to towns in the Sacred Valley, such as Pisac, Calca, Ollantaytambo, and Urubamba. Those buses depart from small terminals on Calle Puputi s/n, Cdra. 2 (via Pisac), and Av. Grau s/n, Cdra. 1 (via Chinchero).

By Train   The most popular means to visit Machu Picchu and the Sacred Valley sights is by train. PeruRail trains from Cusco to Ollantaytambo and Machu Picchu Pueblo (also called Aguas Calientes) leave from **Estación Poroy,** a 15-minute cab ride from downtown. Reservations for these trains, especially in high season (May–Sept), should be made several days or weeks in advance. Make reservations online at www.perurail.com or www.incarail.com; also see p. 200 in Chapter 8 for more information, including trains that travel between Machu Picchu and the Sacred Valley only.

By Car   Renting a car in the Cusco region—more than likely to visit the beautiful Sacred Valley mountain villages—is a more practical idea than in most parts of Peru. Rental agencies include **Hertz,** at the airport (www.hertz.

A New Airport in Chinchero

Cusco's Aeropuerto Internacional Velasco Astete was never prepared for the surging number of travelers who have begun flocking to the city in the past decade. The airport is unable to handle large planes, and flights are frequently canceled because of weather. Thankfully, a new airport is planned near Chinchero, on the way to Urubamba, 35km (22 miles) from Cusco. It is expected to be completed by the year 2020, capable of handling international flights from the U.S. and Europe, bypassing the need to fly to Lima and transfer. Not everyone is thrilled, though. Some feel placing a major airport here comes with enormous social and environmental risks, harming the centuries-old framework of this traditional village and stunning landscape.

com; ℭ **01/445-5716**) and **Europcar,** Calle Saphy 639 (www.europcar.com; ℭ **084/262-655**). Rates range from $45 per day for a standard four-door to $95 or more per day for a Toyota Hilux four-wheel-drive.

[FastFACTS] CUSCO

ATMs/Banks Most banks with ATMs are located along Avenida El Sol. Banks include **Banco Santander Central Hispano,** Av. El Sol 459; **Banco de Crédito,** Av. El Sol 189; and **Banco Continental,** Av. El Sol 366. The external ATMs nearest the Plaza de Armas are at **Banco de la Nacion,** Av. El Sol 226; **Banco del Sur,** Av. El Sol 457; and **Banco Latino,** Av. El Sol 395. A few ATMs are also located at the entrances to stores and restaurants on the Plaza de Armas and Plaza Regocijo.

Doctors & Hospitals English-speaking personnel are available at **Hospital EsSalud,** Av. Anselmo Álvarez s/n (ℭ **084/237-341**); **Clínica Pardo,** Av. de la Cultura 710 (ℭ **084/624-186**); **Clinica San Jose,** Av. Los Incas 1408 (www.sanjose.com.pe; ℭ **084/232-295**); **MacSalud,** Av. de la Cultura 1410 (www.macsalud.com; ℭ **084/582-060**); **Hospital Regional,** Av. de la Cultura s/n (ℭ **084/223-691**); and **Clínica Paredes,** Lechugal 405 (ℭ **084/225-265**). For **yellow-fever** vaccinations, go to Hospital Antonio Loren on Tuesday or Hospital Regional on Saturday from 9am to 1pm.

Embassies & Consulates The **U.S. consulate** is located at Av.

Pardo 845 (CoresES@state.gov; ℭ **084/231-474**). The **honorary U.K. consulate** is at Manu Expeditions, Urbanización Magisterial, G-5 Segunda Etapa (bwalker@terra.com.pe; ℭ **084/239-974**).

Emergencies For general emergencies and **police,** call ℭ **105.** For **tourist police,** call ℭ **084/249-654.** For **fire,** call ℭ **103.** In a medical emergency, go to **Hospital EsSalud,** Av. Anselmo Álvarez s/n (ℭ **084/223-030**), or contact **Tourist Medical Assistance** (ℭ **084/260-101**).

Internet Access Internet *cabinas* are everywhere in the old section of Cusco, and many permit cheap overseas Internet-based calls for as little as S/1 per minute. Rates are generally S/2 per hour. Among the cabinas: **Explora,** Arequipa 251; and **Speed X,** Procuradores 50 and Tecsecocha 400.

Language Schools For intensive Spanish courses, try **Academia Latinoamericana de Español,** Av. El Sol 580 (www.latinoschools.com; ℭ **084/243-364**); **Amauta,** Suecia 480 (www.amautaspanish.com; ℭ **084/262-345**); **Amigos,** Zaguan del Cielo B-23 (www.spanishcusco.com; ℭ **084/242-292**); or **San Blas Spanish School,** Tandapata 688 (ℭ **084/247-898**).

Mail Cusco's main post office, Serpost, is at Av. El Sol 800 (ℭ **084/224-212**). A **DHL/Western Union** office is at Av. El Sol 627-A (ℭ **084/244-167**).

Massage The in-house masseurs at fancy hotel spas, such as the Palacio del Inka, Monasterio, and the **Inca Spa,** within the Hotel Eco Inn, Av. El Sol 1010 (www.incaspa.com.pe; ℭ **084/581-280**), are usually your best option for a full-body massage and a clean setting. Among the independent options, the most highly recommended is **Ying Yang Massage,** Av. El Sol 106 (Galerías La Merced) (yinyang_masajes@hotmail.com; ℭ **084/243-592** or cell **084/984-939717**), where the rooms are nice and a 1-hour full-body massage is S/75; hotel visits are also possible for a small supplement. Young women advertising "massage, massage" for as little as $7 (sometimes of dubious quality or intent) are on virtually every street in the old town.

Pharmacies Find **Inka-Farma** locations at Av. El Sol 210 and Ayacucho 175; **Botica Fasa** locations at Ayacucho 220 and Av. El Sol 130.

Police The **Policía Nacional de Turismo,** or National Tourism Police (Saphy 510; ℭ **084/249-654**) has an English-speaking staff trained to handle the needs of foreign visitors. Or contact **iPerú/INDECOPI** (Servicio de Protección al Turista, or Tourist Protection Bureau), Portal Carrizos 250, Plaza de Armas (📞 084/252-974).

Safety Cusco on the surface certainly seems to be an easygoing, if increasingly congested, Andean city, and I've never found it to be anything to the contrary. In Cusco, as in all of Peru, you're much more likely to find locals warm and welcoming than threatening. Yet over the years there have been isolated reports of violent muggings (some using the "chokehold" method) on empty streets,

as well as reports of rapes, attempted rapes, and other sexual assaults. While I have never had a problem in the city and never met anyone who has, it's advisable to take some precautions and remain vigilant at all times. Incidents of drink-spiking at nightclubs have been reported; be aware of your drinking companions in bars and don't allow strangers to buy you drinks. Do not walk alone late at night (young women should travel in groups larger than two); have restaurants and bars call registered taxis to transfer you to your hotel. Young people staying in inexpensive hostels should be

particularly cautious of hotel visitors and belongings. It's a good idea to be at your most vigilant, especially in the neighborhoods of San Blas, in the side streets leading off the Plaza de Armas, near the Central Market, and at bus and train hubs; still, robberies and attacks have occurred at the ruins at Sacsayhuamán on the outskirts of the city and even along the Inca Trail.

Telephone Cusco's area code is **084.** The principal **Telefónica del Perú** office, where you can make long-distance and international calls, is at Av. El Sol 382–6 (📞 084/241-114). It's open Mon–Sat 8am–10pm.

EXPLORING CUSCO

The stately **Plaza de Armas ★★★**, lined by arcades and carved wooden balconies and framed by the Andes, is the focal point of Cusco and the heart of the *centro histórico*. Lively but still loaded with colonial character, it is one of the most familiar sights in Peru. You will cross it, relax on benches in its center, and pass under porticoes that line the square with shops, restaurants, travel agencies, and bars innumerable times during your stay in Cusco. It's the best people-watching spot in the city. The plaza—which was twice its present size in Inca days—is bordered by two of Cusco's most important churches and the remains of original Inca walls on the northwest side of the square, thought to be the foundation of the Inca Pachacútec's palace. Most of Cusco's main attractions are easy walking distance from the Plaza.

Many principal sights both within the historic quarter of Cusco and beyond the city are included in the *boleto turístico* (see the box below), but a few very worthwhile places of interest, such as the cathedral, Templo del Qoricancha (Temple of the Sun), Museo Machu Picchu, and Museo de Arte Precolombino (MAP), are not included.

Around the Plaza de Armas

La Catedral ★★★ RELIGIOUS SITE   Built on the site of the palace of the Inca Viracocha, Cusco's cathedral, which dominates the Plaza de Armas, is a beautiful religious and artistic monument. Completed in 1669 in the Renaissance style and now handsomely restored, the cathedral possesses some 400 canvasses of the distinguished Escuela Cusqueña that were painted

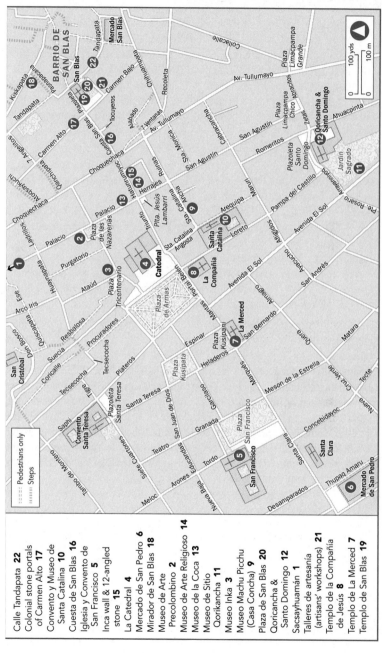

Calle Tandapata **22**
Colonial stone portals
of Carmen Alto **17**
Convento y Museo de
Santa Catalina **10**
Cuesta de San Blas **16**
Iglesia y Convento de
San Francisco **5**
Inca wall & 12-angled
stone **15**
La Catedral **4**
Mercado de San Pedro **6**
Mirador de San Blas **18**
Museo de Arte
Precolombino **2**
Museo de Arte Religioso **14**
Museo de la Coca **13**
Museo de Sitio
Qorikancha **11**
Museo Inka **3**
Museo Machu Picchu
(Casa Concha) **9**
Plaza de San Blas **20**
Qoricancha &
Santo Domingo **12**
Sacsayhuamán **1**
Talleres de artesanía
(artisans' workshops) **21**
Templo de la Compañía
de Jesús **8**
Templo de La Merced **7**
Templo de San Blas **19**

123

from the 16th to 18th centuries. There are also amazing woodcarvings, including the spectacular cedar choir stalls. The main altar—which weighs more than 401kg (884 lb.) and is fashioned from silver mined in Potosí, Bolivia—features the patron saint of Cusco. To the right of the altar is a particularly Peruvian painting of the Last Supper, with the apostles drinking *chicha* (fermented maize beer) and eating *cuy* (guinea pig). The **Capilla del Triunfo** (the first Christian church in Cusco) is next door, to the right of the main church. It holds a painting by Alonso Cortés de Monroy of the devastating earthquake of 1650. To the right of the entrance to the Capilla (the right nave, next to the choir stalls) is an altar adorned by the locally famous "El Negrito" (see box).

Plaza de Armas (north side). No phone. Admission not included in *boleto turístico*; S/25 adults, S/12.50 students. Mon–Sat 10am–6pm, Sun 2–6pm.

Museo Inka ★ MUSEUM Housed in one of Cusco's finest colonial mansions, the 17th-century Palace of the Admiral, this museum is a superb introduction to the Inca culture. Through ceramics, textiles, mummies, jewelry, and reportedly the world's largest collection of wooden drinking vessels (*qeros*), the exhibits walk visitors through Incan history from pre-Inca civilizations to post-conquest life. Also on display are temporary exhibitions of ceramics, musical instruments, carved mate gourds, and textiles—female weavers can often be seen in the courtyard. Because admission is not included in the *boleto turístico,* this institution is often overlooked. Allow up to 2 hours for a complete walk-through.

Cuesta del Almirante 103 (corner of Ataúd and Tucumán). http://museoinka.unsaac. edu.pe. ⓒ **084/224-051.** Admission not included in *boleto turístico*; S/10 adults, S/5 students. Mon–Fri 8am–6pm, Sat 9am–6pm.

Templo de la Compañía de Jesús ★ RELIGIOUS SITE Cater-cornered to the cathedral is this Jesuit church, which rivals the former in grandeur and prominence on the square (an intentional move by the Jesuits, and one that had church diplomats running back and forth to the Vatican). Begun in the late 16th century, it was almost entirely demolished by the quake of 1650, rebuilt, and finally finished 18 years later. Like the cathedral, it was also built on the site of an important palace, that of the Inca Huayna Cápac (said to be

---

El Negrito

A famous local figure is "El Negrito" (also known as "El Señor de los Temblores," or Lord of the Earthquakes), a brown-skinned figure of Christ on the cross known as the protector of Cusco. Found in La Catedral, at an altar to the right of the entrance to the Capilla (in the right nave, next to the choir stalls), the figure was originally paraded around the city by frightened residents during the 1650 earthquake. When the earthquake finally ceased, locals attributed it to a miracle and transformed El Negrito into an object of devotion (locals still deliver fresh flowers in his honor daily). The figure's crown was stolen a couple of years ago and not recovered; the one now adorning his head is gold, a gift of a parishioner.

CUSCO'S *boleto* TURÍSTICO

The city's *boleto turístico* includes admission to 16 places of interest in and around Cusco and the Sacred Valley. Though it is no longer much of a bargain, the *boleto* is the only way to get into a number of churches, museums, and ruins (however, not all are indispensable). Arguably the city's top two sights, La Catedral and Qoricancha, are not included and charge separate admissions. The full ticket costs S/130 for adults and S/70 students with ID and children, and is valid for 10 days; it is available at the tourism office at Mantas 117-A ((C) **084/263-176**), which is open Monday to Friday 8am to 6:30pm and Saturday 8am to 2pm. In addition to the main tourist office, the *boleto* can be purchased at OFEC, Av. El Sol 103, office 101 (Galerías Turísticas; (C) **084/227-037**), Monday to Saturday 8am to 6pm, and Casa Garcilaso, at the corner of Garcilaso y Heladeros s/n ((C) **084/226-919**), Monday to Friday 8am to 5pm and Saturday 8am to 4pm.

You can also buy a partial ticket for S/70 that only covers either attractions in the city or ruins and sites outside of Cusco. Make sure you carry the ticket with you when you're planning to make visits (especially on day trips outside the city), as guards will demand to see it so they can punch a hole alongside the corresponding picture. Students must also carry their International Student Identification Card (ISIC), as guards often demand to see it. For more information, visit www.cosituc.gob.pe.

The full *boleto* allows admission to the following sights: in Cusco, Convento de Santa Catalina, Museo Municipal de Arte Contemporáneo, Museo Histórico Regional, Museo de Sitio Qoricancha, Museo de Arte Popular, Centro Qosqo de Arte Nativo, and Monumento al Inka Pachacuteq; the nearby Inca ruins of Sacsayhuamán, Q'enko, Pukapukara, Tambomachay, Pikillacta, and Tipón; and the Valle Sagrado attractions of Moray, Pisac, Ollantaytambo, and Chinchero.

the most beautiful of all the Inca rulers' palaces). Inside, it's rather gloomy, but the gilded altar is stunning, especially when illuminated. The church possesses several important works of art, including a picture of Saint Ignatius de Loyola by the local painter Marcos Zapata, and the Cristo de Burgos crucifixion at the main altar. Also of note are the paintings to either side of the entrance, which depict the marriages of Saint Ignatius' nephews; one is the very symbol of Peru's *mestizo* character, as the granddaughter of Manco Inca weds the man who captured the last Inca, Tupac Amaru, the leader of an Indian uprising.

Plaza de Armas (southeast side). Admission not included in *boleto turístico*; S/10 adults, S/5 students. Mon–Sat 11am–noon and 3–4pm.

San Blas & East of the Plaza de Armas

Barrio de San Blas ★★ NEIGHBORHOOD   Cusco's most atmospheric and picturesque neighborhood, San Blas, a short but increasingly steep walk from the Plaza de Armas, is lined with artists' studios and artisans' workshops, and stuffed with tourist haunts—many of the best bars and restaurants and a surfeit of hostels. It's a great area to wander around—many streets are

THE CUSCO school OF ART

The colonial-era **Escuela Cusqueña,** or Cusco School of art, that originated in the ancient Inca capital was a synthesis of traditional Spanish painting with local, *mestizo* elements—not surprising, perhaps, because its practitioners were themselves of mixed blood. Popular in the 17th and 18th centuries, the style spread from Cusco as far as Ecuador and Argentina. The most famous members of the school were Diego Quispe Tito, Juan Espinosa de los Monteros, and Antonio Sinchi Roca, even though the authors of a large majority of works associated with the school are anonymous. Most paintings were devotional in nature, with richly decorative surfaces. Artists incorporated recognizable Andean elements into their oil paintings, such as local flora and fauna, customs, and traditions—one depiction of the Last Supper has the apostles feasting on guinea pig and drinking maize beer—and representations of Jesus looking downward, like the Indians who were forbidden to look Spaniards in the eye. Original Escuela Cusqueña works are found in La Catedral, the Convent of Santa Catalina, the Museum of Religious Art, and a handful of other churches in Cusco. Reproductions of original paintings, ranging from excellent in quality to laughable, are available across Cusco, particularly in the galleries and shops of San Blas.

pedestrian-only—though exercise caution with your belongings, especially at night. The neighborhood affords some of the most spectacular panoramic vistas in the city. In the small plaza at the top and to the right of Cuesta San Blas is the little white **Templo de San Blas,** said to be the oldest parish church in Cusco (no phone; admission S/15 adults, S/7.50 students; Mon–Sat 2–5:30pm). Although it's a simple adobe structure, it has a marvelously carved *churrigueresque* cedar pulpit. Some have gone as far as proclaiming it the finest example of woodcarving in the world; carved from a single tree trunk, it is certainly impressive. The pulpit comes with an odd story, and it's difficult to determine whether it's fact or folklore: It is said that the carpenter who created it was rewarded by having his skull placed within his masterwork (at the top, beneath the feet of St. Paul) upon his death. Also worth a look is the baroque gold-leaf main altar.

Begins roughly at Calle Choquechaca, as the neighborhood climbs into the hills.

Museo de Arte Precolombino (MAP) ★ MUSEUM   An extension of the renowned Museo Larco in Lima, from where this vast collection is on loan, this museum of pre-Columbian artwork is sophisticated and beautifully designed. The space is layered in history. It began as an Inca ceremonial court, which was followed by the Santa Clara convent, and later became the mansion Casa Cabrera of the conquistador Alonso Díaz. Arranged by material—gold, silver, ceramic—the 450 pieces display the rich artistic expressions of Peruvian cultures like the Incas, Moche, Chimú, and Chancay. The pieces date from 1250 B.C. to A.D. 1532. An hour or two will be sufficient to explore the entire site, which also includes a room of Cusqueña School religious paintings. Within the courtyard is an unusual-looking, modern glass box, which is home to the MAP Café, one of Cusco's top restaurants (see p. 138).

Casa Cabrera, Plaza de las Nazarenas s/n. http://map.museolarco.org. © **084/237-380.** Admission not included in *boleto turístico*; S/22 adults, S/11 students & children. Daily 9am–10pm.

Museo de Arte Religioso (Palacio Arzobispal) ★ MUSEUM   Housed in a handsome colonial palace that previously belonged to the archbishop of Cusco—and before that it was the site of the palace of Inca Roca and then the home of a Spanish marquis—this museum is often overlooked in a city full of great museums. Don't be so quick to rule this one out, though; inside the extravagant old house is a nice collection of colonial religious paintings, an impressive portal and Moorish-style doors, a balcony, carved-cedar ceilings, stunning stained-glass windows, and a small chapel. Even if you don't go in, you'll likely walk past it, as it's on the corner of Hatunrumiyoc, a pedestrian alleyway lined with magnificent Inca stonemasonry.

Corner of Hatunrumiyoc and Palacio. © **084/225-211.** Admission not included in *boleto turístico*; S/10 adults, S/5 students. Mon–Fri 8am–12:30pm and 3–6pm.

Museo de la Coca ★ MUSEUM   Though calling this a museum might be a stretch, if you have 30 minutes to kill or it's raining out, it's worth popping in. It's really tiny, just a couple of small rooms with models and diagrams detailing the cultural role and science behind coca and coca leaves and how it's been used by locals throughout history in the Andes (including its more polemical present). A store with coca products like coca candies, tea, and beer takes up most of the space.

Calle Palacio 122. © **084/501-020.** Admission S/10 adults, S/5 students, free for children. Daily 9am–8pm.

Qoricancha & South of the Plaza de Armas

Convento y Museo de Santa Catalina ★★ RELIGIOUS SITE   A small convent a couple of blocks west of the Plaza de Armas, Santa Catalina was built between 1601 and 1610 on top of the Acllahuasi, where the Inca emperor sequestered his chosen Virgins of the Sun. The convent contains a museum of colonial and religious art. The collection includes an excellent selection of Escuela Cusqueña paintings, featuring some of the greatest works of Amerindian art—a combination of indigenous and typically Spanish styles—in Cusco. The collection also includes four paintings of the Lord of the Earthquakes (El Señor de los Temblores) painted by Amerindians. The interior of the monastery is quite beautiful, with painted arches and an interesting chapel with baroque frescoes of Inca vegetation. Other items of interest include macabre statues of Jesus and an extraordinary trunk that, when opened, displays the life of Christ in three-dimensional figurines. (It was employed by the Catholic Church's "traveling salesmen," who were used to convert the natives in far-flung regions of Peru.)

Santa Catalina Angosta s/n. © **084/226-032.** Admission not included in *boleto turístico*; S/8 adults, S/5 students. Daily 8am–5:30pm.

THE magic OF INCA STONES: A WALKING TOUR ★★

Dominating the ancient streets of Cusco are dramatic **Inca walls,** constructed of mammoth granite blocks so exquisitely carved that they fit together without mortar, like jigsaw-puzzle pieces. The Spaniards razed many Inca constructions but built others right on top of the original foundations. (Even hell-bent on destruction, they recognized the value of good engineering.) In many cases, colonial architecture has not stood up nearly as well as the Incas' bold structures, which were designed to withstand the immensity of seismic shifts common in this part of Peru.

Apart from the main attractions detailed in this section, a brief walking tour will take you past some of the finest Inca constructions that remain in the city. East of the Plaza de Armas, **Calle Loreto,** originally called Intikkijllu, is the oldest surviving Inca wall in Cusco and one of the most distinguished. The massive wall on one side, composed of meticulously cut rectangular stones, once formed part of the Acclahuasi, or the "House of the Chosen Maidens," the Inca emperor's Virgins of the Sun. East of the Plaza de Armas, off Calle Palacio, is **Hatunrumiyoc,** a cobblestone street lined with impressive walls of polygonal stones. Past the Archbishop's Palace on the right side is the famed **12-angled stone** (appropriated as the symbol of Cuzqueña beer),

which is magnificently fitted into the wall. Originally, this wall belonged to the palace of the Inca Roca. This large stone is impressively cut; the Incas almost routinely fitted many-cornered stones (with as many as 32, as seen at Machu Picchu, or even 44 angles) into structures. From Hatunrumiyoc, make your first right down another pedestrian alleyway, Inca Roca; about halfway down on the right side is a series of stones said to form the shape of a **puma,** including the head, large paws, and tail. It's not all that obvious, so if you see someone else studying the wall, ask him to point out the figure. **Siete Culebras (Seven Snakes),** the alleyway connecting Plaza Nazarenas to Choquechaca, contains Inca stones that form the foundation of the chapel within Hotel Monasterio. Other streets with notable Inca foundations are **Herrajes, Pasaje Arequipa,** and **Santa Catalina Angosta.** Only a couple of genuine Inca **portals** remain. One is at Choquechaca 339 (the doorway to a *hostal*), and another is at Romeritos 402, near Qoricancha.

Not every impressive stone wall in Cusco is Incan in origin, however. Many are transitional period (post-Conquest) constructions, built by local masons in the service of Spanish bosses. Peter Frost's "Exploring Cusco" (available in local bookstores) has a good explanation of what to look for to distinguish an original.

Museo de Sitio Qorikancha ★ MUSEUM   Don't confuse this subterranean museum along Avenida El Sol with the actual Qorikancha on the hill above—the latter is not included in the *boleto turístico* pass. There are just three small rooms here, displaying Inca and pre-Inca ceramics, metalwork, and textile weavings. Most interesting are the photos of the excavation of Qorikancha. You won't need a ton of time here, but it's worth popping in.

Av. El Sol s/n (across the esplanade from Qoricancha). Admission by *boleto turístico.* Mon–Sat 9:30am–5:30pm.

Museo Machu Picchu (Casa Concha) ★★ MUSEUM Opened in 2011, this well-curated museum just off the plaza displays the long-awaited artifacts that Hiram Bingham unearthed in 1911 when discovering Machu Picchu. Bingham brought 360 pieces back to Yale, where they were subject to an international dispute between Peru and the university. They are now housed in a carefully restored colonial mansion, where a priceless 18th-century mural has been uncovered. On display are skeletal remains, as well as ceramics and stone objects. Perhaps more intriguing are the photos of Bingham and of excavations of the site. A video of notable researchers such as Richard Burger explaining the archaeological significance of the site is worth the time. You'll spend 1 hour here maximum.

Santa Catalina Ancha, 320. www.museomachupicchu.com. ℂ **084/255-535.** Admission not included in *boleto turístico;* S/20 adults, S/10 students. Mon–Sat 9am–5pm.

Qoricancha & Santo Domingo ★★★ HISTORIC SITE Qoricancha and Santo Domingo together form perhaps the most vivid illustration in Cusco of the Andean culture's collision with western Europe. Like the Great Mosque in Córdoba, Spain—where Christians dared to build a massive church within the perfect Muslim shrine—the temple of one culture sits atop and encloses the other. The extraordinarily crafted Temple of the Sun was the most sumptuous temple in the Inca Empire and the apogee of the Incas' naturalistic belief system. Some 4,000 of the highest-ranking priests and their attendants were housed here. Dedicated to the worship of the sun, it was apparently a glittering palace straight out of El Dorado legend: *Qoricancha* means "golden courtyard" in Quechua, and in addition to hundreds of gold panels lining its walls, there were life-size gold figures, solid-gold altars, and a huge golden sun disc. The sun disc reflected the sun and bathed the temple in light. During the summer solstice, the sun still shines directly into a niche where only the Inca chieftain was permitted to sit. Other temples and shrines existed for the worship of lesser natural gods: the moon, Venus, thunder, lightning, and rainbows. Qoricancha was the main astronomical observatory for the Incas.

Hang a Right at Donkey Lips

Cusco is littered with difficult-to-pronounce, wildly spelled street names that date to Inca times. In the bohemian neighborhood of San Blas, though, they're particularly colorful. Here's a primer of atmospheric street names and their literal meanings:
Atoqsayk'uchi Where the fox got tired
Tandapata Place of taking turns
Asnoqchutun Donkey lips

Siete Diablitos Seven little devils
Siete Angelitos Seven little angels
Usphacalle Place of sterility/place of ashes
Saqracalle Where the demons dwell
Pumaphaqcha Puma's tail
Cajonpata Place shaped like a box
Rayanpata Place of myrtle flowers
P'asñapakana Where the young women are hidden
P'aqlachapata Place of bald men

After the Spaniards ransacked the temple and emptied it of gold (which they melted down, of course), the exquisite polished stone walls were employed as the foundations of the Convent of Santo Domingo, constructed in the 17th century. The baroque church pales next to the fine stonemasonry of the Incas—and that's to say nothing about the original glory of the Sun Temple. Today all that remains is Inca stonework. Thankfully, a large section of the cloister has been removed, revealing four original chambers of the temple, all smoothly tapered examples of Inca trapezoidal architecture. Stand on the small platform in the first chamber and see the perfect symmetry of openings in the stone chambers. A series of Inca stones displayed reveals the fascinating concept of male and female blocks and how they fit together. The 6m (20-ft.) curved wall beneath the west end of the church, visible from the street, remains undamaged by repeated earthquakes and is perhaps the greatest extant example of Inca stonework. The curvature and fit of the massive dark stones is astounding.

Once the Spaniards took Cusco, Francisco Pizarro's brother Juan was given the eviscerated Temple of the Sun. He died soon afterward, though, at the battle at Sacsayhuamán, and he left the temple to the Dominicans, in whose hands it remains.

Plazoleta Santo Domingo. *℗ 084/222-071.* Admission not included in *boleto turístico;* S/10 adults, S/5 students & children. Mon–Sat 8:30am–6:30pm, Sun 2–5pm.

West of the Plaza de Armas

Iglesia y Convento de San Francisco ★ RELIGIOUS SITE   This
large and austere 17th-century convent church, thoughtfully restored, extends the length of the square of the same name. It is best known for its collection of colonial artworks, including paintings by Marcos Zapata and Diego Quispe Tito, both of considerable local renown. A monumental canvas (12 × 9m/39 × 30 ft.) that details the genealogy of the Franciscan family (almost 700 individuals) is by Juan Espinoza de los Monteros. The Franciscans also decorated the convent with ceiling frescoes and a number of morbid displays of skulls and bones. The church is worth a visit mainly for those with extra time in Cusco.

Plaza de San Francisco s/n. *℗ 084/221-361.* Admission S/5 adults, S/3 students. Mon–Sat 9am–4pm.

Mercado de San Pedro ★★ PUBLIC MARKET   Though it's just a few
blocks from the main plaza, Cusco's central market is missed by many tourists. It is an amazing place to tap into the city at its most quotidian and traditional, a place where tourists are no more than an afterthought. There are aisles of native potatoes, including freeze-dried varieties like *chuño.* There are heavy blocks of cheese from dairy farms in the region. Juice bars squeeze jungle fruits. The range of produce, meats, household items, and oddities (such as medicinal plants from the rainforest) is daunting. For most, it's an experience not to be missed. It's generally a secure place that regularly sees tourists with expensive cameras, though as with any busy market, keep a hand on your belongings.

Calle Santa Clara, s/n. No tel. Admission free. Daily 7am–4pm.

Plaza Regocijo ★ PUBLIC SQUARE/MUSEUMS   This is Cusco's other main plaza, but actually, during Inca times, this pleasant, leafy square was merged with the Plaza de Armas, though a row of colonial buildings now divides the two. Today, Plaza Regocijo is full of shops and restaurants, as well as notable historic mansions, but is slightly less feverish than the main square. There is a pair of oft-overlooked museums here, too: the **Museo Histórico Regional,** a regional history museum with archaeological and colonial artifacts, including furnishings and Escuela Cusqueña art, is housed in the mansion where Garcilaso de la Vega, an important Peruvian writer and chronicler of Inca history and culture, once lived (he was himself a descendant of Incas); and within the Palacio Municipal, the small **Museo de Arte Contemporáneo,** which features contemporary works of local artists.

Calles Garcilaso at Heladeros. Museo Histórico Regional and Museo de Arte Contemporáneo: daily 9am–5pm; admission by *boleto turístico*.

Templo de la Merced ★ RELIGIOUS SITE   Erected in 1536 and rebuilt after the great earthquake in the 17th century, La Merced ranks just below the cathedral and the La Compañía church in importance. It has a beautiful facade and lovely cloisters with a mural depicting the life of the Merced Order's founder. The sacristy contains a small museum of religious art, including a fantastic solid-gold monstrance swathed in precious stones. In the vaults of the church are the remains of two famous conquistadors, Diego de Almagro and Gonzalo Pizarro.

Calle Mantas s/n. ✆ **084/231-831.** Admission S/5, S/3 students. Mon–Sat 8:30am–noon and 2–5pm.

Inca Ruins Near Cusco ★★★

The easiest way to see the following set of Inca ruins just outside Cusco is as part of a half-day tour. The hardy might want to approach it as an athletic archaeological expedition: If you've got 15km (9⅓ miles) of walking and climbing at high altitude in you, it's a beautiful trek. Otherwise, you can walk to Sacsayhuamán and nearby Q'enko (the climb from the Plaza de Armas is strenuous and takes 30–45 min.), and take a *colectivo* or taxi to the other sites. Alternatively, you can take a Pisac/Urubamba minibus (leaving from the bus station at Calle Intiqhawarina, off Avenida Tullumayo, or Huáscar 128) and tell the driver you want to get off at Tambomachay, the ruins farthest from Cusco, and work your way back on foot. Some even make the rounds by bike

---

Those Fabulously "Sexy" Ruins

The pronunciation of Sacsayhuamán, like many Quechua words, proves difficult for most foreigners to wrap their tongues around, so locals and tour guides have several jokes that point to its similarity to the words "sexy woman" in English. You haven't really experienced Cusco until you've heard the joke with that punch line a dozen times—from old men, guides, and even little kids.

or horseback. You can easily and cheaply contract a horse at Sacsayhuamán, but don't expect to ride freely in the countryside—you'll walk rather slowly to all the sites alongside a guide.

Visitors with less time in Cusco or less interest in taxing themselves might want to join a guided tour, probably the most popular and easiest way to see the sites. Virtually any of the scads of travel agencies and tour operators in the old center of Cusco offer them. Some well-rated traditional agencies with a variety of programs include **Milla Turismo,** Av. Pardo 689 (www.milla turismo.com; ℐ **084/231-710**), and **SAS Travel,** Garcilaso 270, Plaza San Francisco (www.sastravelperu.com; ℐ **084/249-194**).

Admission to the following sites is by *boleto turístico,* and they are all open daily from 7am to 6pm. Guides, official and unofficial, hover around the ruins; negotiate a price or decide upon a proper tip. There are a handful of other Inca ruins on the outskirts of Cusco, but the ones discussed below are the most interesting.

These sites are generally safe, but at certain times of day—usually dawn and dusk before and after tour groups' visits—several ruins are said to be favored by thieves. It's best to be alert and, if possible, go accompanied.

Note that new finds are continually being uncovered here, even as close to Cusco as the vicinity around Sacsayhuamán. Archaeologists most recently discovered an ancient, pre-Inca temple, irrigation canals, and a series of rooms that held mummies and idols. The temple is believed to have been built by the Killke culture, which occupied the region around present-day Cusco from A.D. 900 to 1200.

Sacsayhuamán ★★★

The greatest and nearest to Cusco of the Inca ruins, Sacsayhuamán reveals some of the Incas' most extraordinary architecture and monumental stonework. Usually referred to as a garrison or fortress—because it was constructed with forbidding, castle-like walls—it was more likely a religious temple, although most experts believe it also had military significance. The Inca emperor Pachacútec began the site's construction in the mid–15th century, although it took nearly 100 years and many thousands of men to complete it. Massive blocks of limestone and other types of stone were brought from as far as 32km (20 miles) away.

The ruins, a steep 30-minute (or longer) walk from the center, cover a huge area, but they constitute perhaps one-quarter of the original complex, which could easily house more than 10,000 men. Today, what survive are the astounding outer walls, constructed in a zigzag formation of three tiers. (In the puma-shaped layout of the Inca capital, Sacsayhuamán is said to form the animal's head, and the zigzag of the defense walls forms the teeth.) Many of the base stones employed are almost unimaginably massive; some are 3.5m (11 ft.) tall, and one is said to weigh 300 tons. Like all Inca constructions, the stones fit together perfectly without the aid of mortar. It's easy to see how hard it would have been to attack these ramparts with 22 distinct zigzags; the design would automatically expose the flanks of an opponent.

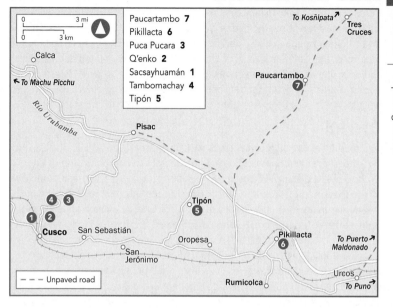

Paucartambo **7**	
Pikillacta **6**	
Puca Pucara **3**	
Q'enko **2**	
Sacsayhuamán **1**	
Tambomachay **4**	
Tipón **5**	

Above the walls are the circular foundations of three towers that once stood here; they were used for storage of provisions and water. The complex suffered such extensive destruction that the primary function of Sacsayhuamán continues to be debated. What is known is that it was the site of one of the bloodiest battles between the Spaniards and native Cusqueños. More than 2 years after the Spaniards had initially marched on Cusco and installed a puppet government, the anointed Inca (Manco Inca) led a seditious campaign that took back Sacsayhuamán and nearly defeated the Spaniards in a siege of the Inca capital. Juan Pizarro and his vastly outnumbered but superior armed forces stormed Sacsayhuamán in a horrific battle in 1536 that left thousands dead. Legend speaks of their remains as carrion for giant condors in the open fields here. After the defeat of the Inca troops and the definitive Spanish occupation of Cusco, the Spaniards made off with the more manageably sized stone blocks from Sacsayhuamán to build houses and other structures in the city below.

The **Inti Raymi** festival is celebrated here annually, and it is truly a great spectacle—one of the finest in Peru (see "Cusco's Spectacular Celebrations" on p. 136). A flat, grassy esplanade (where the main ceremony of the festival is celebrated) separates the defense walls from a small hill where you'll find the "Inca's Throne" and large rocks with well-worn grooves, used by children and often adults as slides. Nearby is a series of claustrophobia-inducing tunnels—pass through them if you dare.

Walking directions: A couple of paths lead to the ruins from downtown Cusco. You can take Almirante, Suecia, or Plateros. Head northwest from the Plaza de Armas. Take Palacio (behind the cathedral) until you reach stairs and signs to the ruins; or at the end of Suecia, climb either Huaynapata or Resbalosa (the latter name means "slippery") until you come to a curve and the old Inca road. Past the San Cristóbal church at the top, beyond a plaza with food and juice stands, is the main entrance to the ruins. Plan about an hour here for a brief run-through, and up to 3 hours if you're a photography buff or if you have kids who want to play on the slides and in the tunnels.

Q'enko ★

The road from Sacsayhuamán leads past fields where, on weekends, Cusqueños play soccer and have cookouts, to the temple and amphitheater of Q'enko (*Kehn*-koh), a distance of about a kilometer (½ mile). The ruins are due east of the giant white statue of Christ crowning the hill next to Sacsayhuamán; follow the main road and you'll see signs for Q'enko, which appears on the right. A great limestone outcrop was hollowed out by the Incas, and, in the void, they constructed a cave-like altar. (Some have claimed that the smooth stone table inside was used for animal sacrifices.) Visitors can duck into the caves and tunnels beneath the rock. You can also climb on the rock and see the many channels cut into the rock, where it is thought that either *chicha* or, more salaciously, sacrificial blood coursed during ceremonies. (Q'enko might have been a site of ritual ceremonies performed in fertility rites and solstice and equinox celebrations.) Allow a half-hour to tour the site, not including travel time.

Puca Pucara

A small fortress (the name means "red fort") just off the main Cusco–Pisac road, this might have been some sort of storage facility or lodge, or perhaps a guard post on the road from Cusco to the villages of the Sacred Valley. It is probably the least impressive of the area sites, although it has nice views of the surrounding countryside. From Q'enko, Puca Pucara is a 90-minute to 2-hour walk along the main road; allow a half-hour for your visit.

Tambomachay

On the road to Pisac (and a short, signposted walk off the main road), this site is also known as Los Baños del Inca (Inca Baths). Located near a spring just

---

Cusco = Cuzco = Q'osqo

Spanish and English spellings derived from the Quechua language are a little haphazard in Cusco, especially because there has been a linguistic movement to try to recuperate and value indigenous culture. Thus, you might see Inca written as Inka; Cusco as Cuzco, Qosqo, or Q'osqo; Qoricancha as Coricancha or Koricancha; Huanchaq as Huanchac or Wanchac; Sacsayhuamán as Sacsaywaman; and Q'enko as Qenko, Kenko, or Qenqo. You're likely to stumble across others, with similar alphabetical prestidigitation, all used interchangeably.

The Peruvian authorities are notorious for messing with ancient Inca ruins, trying to rebuild them rather than let them be what they are: ruins. You'll notice at Sacsayhuamán and other Inca sites that unnecessary and misleading restoration has been undertaken. The grotesque result is that small gaps where original stones are missing have been filled in with obviously new and misplaced garden rocks—a disgrace to the perfection pursued and achieved by Inca stonemasons.

a short walk beyond Puca Pucara, the ruins consist of three tiers of stone platforms. Water still flows across a sophisticated system of aqueducts and canals in the small complex of terraces and a pool, yet another testament to Inca engineering. These were not baths as we know them, however; most likely this was instead a place of water ceremonies and worship. The exquisite stonework indicates that the *baños* were used by high priests and nobility only. Plan on spending an hour here.

ESPECIALLY FOR KIDS

Cusco is a blast to walk around, so entertaining the kids and finding suitable restaurants and things to do shouldn't be a problem for most families. Kids old enough to appreciate a bit of history might enjoy the exceptionally laid-out **Museo de Arte Precolombino (MAP),** as well as the **Museo Inka,** both of which will give them a good grounding in pre-Columbian civilizations and Inca culture. Beside ceramics and textiles, the Museo Inka displays cool mummies and tiny hand-painted Inca drinking vessels. You'll find Andean women weaving traditional textiles in the courtyard.

Cusco resonates with remnants of the ancient capital; a walking tour with the kids will take you past **Inca walls** with giant granite blocks that look like the pieces of a giant jigsaw puzzle. Have the kids count the hand-cut angles in the **12-angled stone** and find the outlines of the **puma figure** (see "The Magic of Inca Stones: A Walking Tour" on p. 128). Observing the walls will give you a chance to impress your family with your knowledge of Andean history. Explain that the Incas built these massive walls without mortar or cement of any kind and with no knowledge of the wheel or horses, and that they constructed one of the world's greatest empires, reaching from one end of South America to another, without a written language and with runners who relayed messages to rulers.

Another good activity for artistically inclined children is to pop into **artists' studios** in the funky neighborhood of San Blas. Then walk—if you have the energy—up to the ruins of **Sacsayhuamán.** There you'll find more massive stones and gorgeous views of the city and surrounding mountains, but kids will really dig the huge rocks with slick grooves that make fantastic slides. There are also some cool tunnels cut into stones nearby, which kids might enjoy much more than their parents.

CUSCO'S spectacular **CELEBRATIONS**

Cusco explodes with joyous celebration of both its Amerindian roots and Christian influences during festivals, which are crowded but splendid times to be in the city if you can find accommodations. It's worth planning a trip around one of the following fiestas.

Inti Raymi ★★★, the fiesta of the winter solstice (June 24, but lasting for days before and after), is the star attraction. It's an eruption of Inca folk dances, exuberant costumes, and grand pageants and parades, including a massive one that takes place at the stately Sacsayhuamán ruins overlooking the city. Inti Raymi is one of the finest expressions of local popular culture on the continent, a faithful reenactment of the traditional Inca Festival of the Sun. It culminates in high priests sacrificing two llamas, one black and one white, to predict the fortunes of the coming year. Cusco's **Carnaval week,** with lots of music, dance, and processions, is part of the buildup for Inti Raymi.

Semana Santa, or Easter week (late Mar or Apr), is an exciting traditional expression of religious faith, with stately processions through the streets of Cusco, including a great procession led by El Señor de los Temblores (Lord of the Earthquakes) on Easter Monday. On Good Friday, booths selling traditional Easter dishes are set up on the streets.

In early May, the **Fiesta de las Cruces (Festival of the Crosses),** a celebration popular throughout the highlands, is marked by communities decorating large crosses that are then delivered to churches. Crucifix vigils are held on all hilltops that are crowned by crosses. Festivities, as always accompanied by lively dancing, give thanks for bountiful harvests. Early June's **Corpus Christi** festival is another momentous occasion, with colorful religious parades featuring 15 effigies of saints through the city and events at the Plaza de Armas and the cathedral (where the effigies are displayed for a week).

On December 24, Cusco celebrates the **Santuranticuy Festival,** one of the largest arts-and-crafts fairs in Peru. Hundreds of artisans lay out blankets in the Plaza de Armas and sell carved Nativity figures and saints' images, in addition to ceramics and *retablos* (altars). The tradition was begun by the Bethlehemite Order and Franciscan Friars.

A hugely popular Andean festival that attracts droves from Cusco and the entire region is the **Virgen del Carmen,** celebrated principally in Paucartambo (see "Side Trips from Cusco," p. 165) and with only a slightly lesser degree of exuberance in Pisac and smaller highland villages.

And, of course, the biggest family attraction of all lies beyond Cusco: Few are the kids who aren't fascinated by the ruins of **Machu Picchu.** The easygoing towns of the **Sacred Valley** are also great spots for families; see Chapters 7 and 8 for more information.

WHERE TO EAT

Visitors to Cusco have a huge array of restaurants and cafes at their disposal; eateries have sprouted up even faster than *hostales* and bars, and most are clustered around the main drags leading from Plaza de Armas. The dining scene has changed drastically in the past decade. Many of the city's most popular restaurants used to be large tourist joints with Andean music shows and mediocre food, though there has been a shift toward the upscale, more ingredient-driven restaurants with good wine and cocktail lists. Still around are the many economical, informal places favored by backpackers and adventure travelers—some offer midday three-course meals (*menus del día*) for as little as S/10. However, Cusco has also seen an influx of fast-food chains, such as KFC, Starbucks, and McDonald's, which have all touched down on the plaza. (Come on people, you've come all this way to Peru, live a little.) Prices, too, have crept steadily upward at the top end of the scale. Though you can still eat very inexpensively, Cusco is now also a place to reward yourself with a good meal if you've been trekking in the jungle or the mountains.

Cheap eateries line the narrow length of Calle Procuradores, which leads off the Plaza de Armas across from the Compañía de Jesús church and is sometimes referred to as "Gringo Alley." Many are pizzerias, as Cusco has become known for its wood-fired, crispy-crust pizzas. Lurking on Procuradores and Plaza de Armas are hawkers armed with menus, hoping to lure you inside restaurants. Most represent decent, upstanding restaurants (though some occasionally offer drugs and other services), but if you know where you want to dine, a polite "no, gracias" is usually all it takes to get them off your trail.

Several cool bars, such as the Museo de Pisco, also double as (often quite good) restaurants, primarily for their young and hip clients who'd prefer to get their food the same place as their cocktails. Baco, owned by the folks who operate one of the best restaurants in Cusco, Cicciolina, is as much chic restaurant as wine bar, and serves great gourmet pizzas (closed on Sundays); see p. 140.

Not all restaurants in Cusco accept credit cards; many of those that do, especially the cheaper places, will levy a 10 percent surcharge to use plastic, so you're better off carrying cash (either *soles* or dollars). Top-flight restaurants often charge both a 10 percent service charge and an 18 percent sales tax, neither of which is included in the prices listed below.

For restaurants in San Blas, see the "Where to Eat in Central Cusco" map on p. 139.

Very Expensive

Fallen Angel ★ NOVO ANDINO/STEAK   You come to Fallen Angel more for the experience than the food. This wildly eccentric, artistically designed funhouse is beloved for continually breaking the norms in terms of typical Cusco restaurant decor. There are bathtub tables filled with fish and floating cherubs with tears in their eyes. There are splashes of clouds and color everywhere you look. When it's busy, there are few places as fun. When you are the only ones there, it's just awkward. The menu, overpriced for some items, is full of ups and downs. Standard beef and pasta dishes are usually a safe bet, while the seafood and fusion dishes aren't worth your attention.

Plazoleta Nazarenas 221. www.fallenangelincusco.com. © **084/258-184.** Reservations recommended. Main courses S/40–S/58. Mon–Fri 11am–11pm, Sat–Sun 2–11pm.

Le Soleil ★★ CLASSIC FRENCH   Polyglot French-Polish chef Arthur Marcinkiewicz is easily the most classically trained cook in the Cusco region and visiting his restaurant is a special treat. The elegant, formal eatery in a beautifully converted *casona* focuses on classical French dishes with preparations that stay mostly true to form, a miracle in Cusco where many ingredients are near impossible to get. While Le Soleil is by far more expensive than anything else in Cusco right now, for the quality it's still a reasonable deal for the five- or seven-course tasting menus or the dishes like duck à l'orange or lamb shank that's cooked for 16 hours with smoked lentils and pear purée with lavender. The wine list is entirely French.

San Agustín 275. www.restaurantelesoleilcusco.com. ⓒ **084/240-543.** Reservations recommended. Main courses S/41–S/98; prix-fixe dinner menus (5–7 courses) S/145–S/186. Mon–Tues and Thurs–Sun 12:30–3pm and 7–10:30pm.

MAP Café ★ NOVO ANDINO   Clashing brilliantly against the surrounding colonial building, this modern, minimalist glass-and-steel box in the middle of a cobblestone patio holds one of the city's most fashionable restaurants. The New Andean dishes served here are not as avant-garde as the glass-walled setting inside the Museo de Arte Precolombino. Instead, MAP Café emphasizes elegant preparations of classic regional dishes, or international preparations of local ingredients. This might be the only restaurant in the world where *sara lawa,* a traditional creamed corn soup, can be seen on the same menu as confit guinea pig legs. By the way, the museum (see p. 126) stays open late, making it possible to step in before or after dinner.

Casa Cabrera (in courtyard of Museo de Arte Precolombino), Plaza Nazarenas 231. www.cuscorestaurants.com. ⓒ **084/242-476.** Reservations recommended. Main courses S/28–S/55. Daily 11am–3pm and 6–10pm.

Expensive

Baco ★ WINE BAR/PIZZA   This spinoff from the always great Cicciolina (see below) is all about the wine. The cellar here is one of the more extensive in Cusco, with mostly Chilean, Argentine, and Spanish wines that pair with a largely international menu of hearty pastas and meats. I'm personally a fan of the oven-baked pork belly with a spicy apple sauce. The atmosphere is warm and convivial with fresh flowers and modern art on the walls. Like Cicciolina, the experience isn't limited to a formal dinner; it has some bar space where you can stop in for a glass of wine and small plates.

Calle Ruinas 465. www.cicciolinacuzco.com/english/baco_home.html. ⓒ **084/242-808.** Main courses S/22–S/48. Mon–Sat 3:30–10:30pm.

Calle del Medio ★ PERUVIAN   The part-bar, part-restaurant establishment holds down a prominent second-level corner right above the Plaza de Armas, with a handful of colonial balcony windows with primo views. The contemporary Peruvian menu is smaller than at ChiCha (below), but otherwise it's quite comparable in price and quality. Standouts include glazed pancetta with figs, *aji panca* over quinoa, and rocoto peppers stuffed with shrimp. The bar and lounge side picks up in the evenings, while the dining room, with its ornate wallpaper and golden mirrors, stays relative busy for

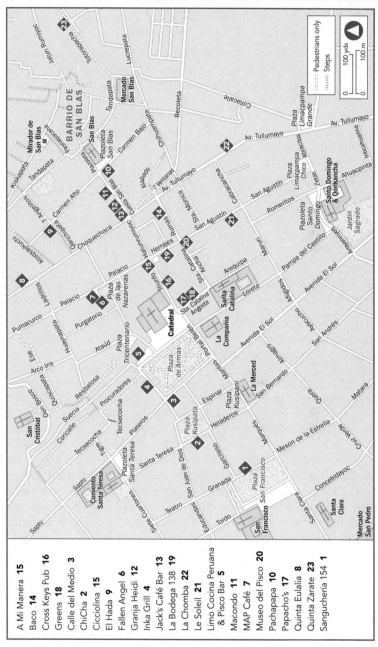

A Mi Manera **15**
Baco **14**
Cross Keys Pub **16**
Greens **18**
Calle del Medio **3**
ChiCha **2**
Cicciolina **15**
El Hada **9**
Fallen Angel **6**
Granja Heidi **12**
Inka Grill **4**
Jack's Café Bar **13**
La Bodega 138 **19**
La Chomba **22**
Le Soleil **21**
Limo Cocina Peruana & Pisco Bar **5**
Macondo **11**
MAP Café **7**
Museo del Pisco **20**
Pachapapa **10**
Papacho's **17**
Quinta Eulalia **8**
Quinta Zarate **23**
Sangucheria 154 **1**

both lunch and dinner. The signature pisco infusions, which make for endless combinations of pisco sours and *chilcanos,* are lined up behind the bar.

Calle del Medio 113, near the Plaza de Armas. www.calledelmediorestaurante.com. ✆ **084/248-340.** Main courses S/28–S/42. Daily 11am–3am.

ChiCha ★★ NOVO ANDINO   It's hard to imagine that Peruvian megastar chef Gastón Acurio would open restaurants in Madrid and San Francisco before he made the short hop from Lima to Cusco. He's here now, though, and like most of his other restaurants, ChiCha is consistent, high in quality, and a great value. It's hard to go wrong in this two-room space, flanked on each side by the open kitchen and the bar. The menu pays tribute to regional cuisine, albeit gussied up in the way that only Acurio knows. There are regional classics, like *adobo de cerdo,* where chunks of pork are cooked in a rich sauce of *chicha, ají* peppers, and spices. There's ceviche made with trout and *tarwi,* a super-nutritious bean-like seed. There are even international dishes touched with local ingredients, like pizza with alpaca carpaccio, cooked in a wood-fired oven. Another standout is pita stuffed with lamb, served with a *muña* (a type of Andean mint) cucumber sauce and *uchucuta,* the local chile blend. Like Acurio's other restaurants, ChiCha has a long list of original cocktails, mostly involving pisco.

Plaza Regocijo 261, 2nd floor. www.chicha.com.pe. ✆ **084/240-520.** Reservations recommended. Main courses S/16–S/40. Mon–Sun noon–10:30pm.

Cicciolina ★★★ MEDITERRANEAN/NOVO ANDINO   Unless you were looking for Cicciolina, you wouldn't know it was here. Diners have to go through a courtyard and then walk upstairs to enter what looks like a Tuscan farmhouse, where bushels of garlic and peppers hang from the wood-beamed ceilings. You'll first see the long wooden bar and a few high bistro tables, where you can order cheese or Peruvian-Mediterranean tapas to pair with wines by the glass. Take a few steps further and you'll find a high-ceilinged dining room, with tall chairs, deep-red walls, and antique mirrors. Though the menu occasionally changes, the food here is some of the most consistent in Cusco. You can count on house-made pastas—you'll see them hanging in the open kitchen—and soulful plates like veal ossobuco. There are small nods to Peru as well, with alpaca filets and *causa,* a layered yellow potato casserole. What many don't realize is that Cicciolina also serves breakfast from the ground-floor bakery, with hot croissants and poached eggs that blow most hotel buffets out of the water.

Triunfo 393, 2nd floor. www.cicciolinacuzco.com. ✆ **084/239-510.** Reservations recommended. Main courses S/23–S/48. Daily 8–11am, noon–3pm and 6–10pm.

Greens ★ VEGETARIAN/HEALTH FOOD   Now right off the main plaza, instead of in its original San Blas home, Greens is the most health-conscious spot in Cusco's exploding restaurant scene. The setting, with its oversized prints of herbs and vegetables and recycled plastic bottle lampshades, fits the part. Much of the menu is sourced from the restaurant's organic farm in the Sacred Valley and other local producers. Healthy food is the main emphasis.

While many dishes are vegetarian (quinoa soup, beet and sweet potato ravioli), there are also some excellent meat dishes, like grilled alpaca with ratatouille. A full range of juices from Peruvian fruits is available, too.

Santa Catalina Angosta 135, 2nd floor. www.cuscorestaurants.com. ✆ **084/243-379.** Reservations recommended. Main courses S/28–S/45. Daily 11am–11pm.

Inka Grill ★ PERUVIAN/NOVO ANDINO   While Inka Grill isn't as revolutionary as it was when it opened in 1998, back when Cusco had no nice restaurants whatsoever, it remains a dependable option. The two-level space, right on the plaza, is filled with antiques and candle sculptures, which have spent a decade piling up one on top of the other. Few dishes are overly exotic, as the menu tries to present Andean ingredients in familiar ways. Quinoa is served as a risotto, with chunks of chicken breast spiced with *ají panca*. A traditional *ayaviri* lamb stew comes with mashed potatoes. There are also pizzas, sandwiches, pastas, and salads, all with just the slightest touch of the Andes.

Portal de Panes 115. www.cuscorestaurants.com. ✆ **084/262-992.** Reservations recommended. S/23–S/55. Mon–Sat 8am–midnight.

Limo Cocina Peruana & Pisco Bar ★★ PERUVIAN/SUSHI   Part of the new wave of high-end restaurants that have opened in Cusco recently, Limo, on the second level of a colonial building on the plaza, looks like it will be sticking around for the long haul. Part of the local restaurant group headed by chef Coque Ossio that also includes Greens and the MAP Café, Limo's elegant decor makes for a unique dining experience. White chairs and splashes of red paint play off the original high-beamed ceilings and stone walls. It's hard to pin down the menu, as it bounces around from contemporary Peruvian to Japanese, often blending the two in unusual ways. There are plenty of standouts, like crunchy *causa* rolls with smoked trout and avocado, or alpaca steak served with a mushroom and *ají amarillo* quinotto.

Portal de Carnes 236, 2nd floor. www.cuscorestaurants.com. ✆ **084/240-668.** Reservations recommended. Main courses S/20–S/40. Daily noon–11pm.

Moderate

A Mi Manera ★ PERUVIAN   This quaint little upstairs restaurant, 1 block from the main plaza, has grown a following for its straightforward Peruvian dishes. There isn't any fusion or funky names, just nice ingredients prepared classically with very few twists aside from a few specialties like quinoa gnocchi. Try the *adobo* (chicken made with *chicha* and yucca). Call in advance and you can sample the house's oven-baked *cuy* (guinea pig) with stuffed pepper and potatoes. Also with advanced notice you can get cooking classes for $30 per person, which include two dishes and a pisco sour.

Triunfo 393, 2nd floor. www.amimaneraperu.com. ✆ **084/222-219.** Reservations recommended. Main courses S/30–S/50. Daily 8am–11pm.

Cross Keys Pub ★ BRITISH   The Cross Keys is Cusco's only authentic English-style pub and it is regularly filled with a mix of expats and tourists. With its leather stools and long wooden bar, it looks the part even better than it did when it was on a second floor overlooking the plaza. The English owner also owns Manu Expeditions and serves as the British Consul in Cusco. There's a standard menu of pub grub, such as fish and chips and wings. A full English breakfast is served all day. Two daily happy hours—6:30 to 7:30pm and 9 to 9:30pm—offer discounted wine, beer, and cocktails.

Calle Triunfo 350, 2nd floor. ℰ **084/229-227.** Main courses S/15–S/28. Daily 8am–midnight.

La Bodega 138 ★★ PIZZA/ITALIAN Most first-time visitors are shocked to learn that Cusco is a pizza town. The prevalence of wood-burning ovens made the transition to pies easy when foreign tourists began to arrive in town decades ago. Today it is hard to find a really bad pizza in Cusco, though finding a great one is more difficult. Some of the best can be found at La Bodega, in part because the restaurant uses higher-quality ingredients than most of the places near the plaza. Aside from typical pizzas, there are interesting combinations like bacon and *sauco* (elderberry), which you definitely won't find anywhere else. The pastas can be hit or miss. The kicker here is the well-chosen wine list and a few hard-to-find Peruvian craft beers.

Herrajes 138. ℰ **084/260-272.** Reservations not accepted. Main courses S/20–S/40. Mon–Sat 1–11pm.

Macondo ★ NOVO ANDINO/INTERNATIONAL With a name that nods to the town that is the setting for Colombian magical realist author Gabriel García Márquez's *One Hundred Years of Solitude,* you can expect a place that is anything but ordinary. The cafe and bar, full of vivid colors and artwork, feels like a gallery space or a head shop, with a soundtrack that tends to be weird and dreamy. The cooking tries to explore Peruvain cuisine in fun new ways. Some dishes work and some do not. Do order the chicken juane, seafood risotto, or alpaca mignon with bacon in mushroom and white-wine sauce. Skip the curried trout. The cocktail list is varied, though they can be made well one day and poorly the next.

Cuesta San Blas 571, San Blas. ℰ **084/227-887.** Reservations not accepted. Main courses S/21–S/36. Daily 8:30am–10:45pm.

Museo del Pisco ★★ TAPAS/BAR The Museo del Pisco has the widest selection of artisanal piscos anywhere in Peru. Many are quite specific, from renowned Peruvian producers like Cholo Matías or Cepas del Loro, and are best served straight or in flights where you can compare the variations of a single grape or region. There's an extensive cocktail list, too, though many don't realize the rambling three-level space with pisco diagrams on the walls also has a kitchen, serving a short but well-curated list of dishes like duck prosciutto, alpaca burgers, and *aji de gallina*–filled *tequeños.*

Santa Catalina Ancha 398. www.museodelpisco.org. ℰ **084/262-709.** Main courses S/22–S/40. Daily 11am–1am.

Pachapapa ★ ANDEAN/PIZZA This upscale remake of a traditional Cuzqueña *quinta,* a simple restaurant serving local dishes, is a pleasant choice for exploring the regional cuisine. It's really more of a pseudo *quinta,* owned by the prestigious Cusco Restaurants group. The place is set inside a rustic whitewashed building across from the San Blas church, with an open court-yard filled with potted plants. Most of the food comes from a wood-burning oven. The high heat produces excellent pizzas and calzones, as well as more typical dishes that are baked in clay pots like *aji de gallina* (shredded chicken in a spicy sauce) and *seco de cordero* (lamb stewed with beer and spices). House specialties like *cuy* (guinea pig served with Huacatay mint) and *pacha-manca* (a potluck of meat and tubers) can be arranged for large groups with advanced notice.

Plazoleta San Blas 120. www.cuscorestaurants.com. ℂ **084/241-318.** Main courses S/22–S/40. Daily 11:30am–11pm.

Papacho's ★ BURGERS   You almost don't want to like this gourmet burger joint from Gastón Acurio, opening right on the plaza, his second Cusco restaurant after ChiCha just one plaza away. But this one is good. Sure, it's pub grub, but there are lots of Peruvian touches like using Amazonian chiles to spice the wings and huacatay sauce on some burgers. The space is very loud and rock 'n' roll, with a long bar that serves original pisco cocktails and punches and craft beers. Considering there are a handful of international fast-food chains within a 1-minute walk, you could do much worse and won't have nearly as much fun.

Portal de Belén 115, 2do nivel, Plaza de Armas. www.papachos.com. ℂ **084/245-359.** Main courses S/24–S/32. Daily noon–midnight.

Inexpensive

Granja Heidi ★ VEGETARIAN/CAFE   A staple on the Cusco scene for years, this second-floor restaurant's name translates to almost exactly what it is: food from Heidi's farm. Owned by a German woman who stocks her pantry with ingredients that come straight from her land outside Cusco, the restaurant is all-around enjoyable and an excellent value. The interior is airy and cheery, with large windows that open to the street. Blond wood and ceiling beams contribute to a clean, rustic feel. Diners will find breakfast fare like quiches and yogurt, as well as a varied menu of dishes based on what's in season or fresh, like squash soup or lamb stir-fry. Desserts are a specialty, highlighted by cheesecakes and crepes.

Cuesta San Blas 525, San Blas. ℂ **084/238-383.** Reservations not accepted. Main courses S/14–S/32. No credit cards. Daily 11am–9:30pm.

Jack's Café Bar ★ CAFE/INTERNATIONAL   Whether you've landed in Cusco at an hour way too early in the morning, before your hotel room is ready, and you want somewhere comfortable to relax, or you've just returned from a grueling trip in the mountains and want some sustenance, laid-back Jack's is where you will likely end up. Owned by the same guy who owns Paddy's Irish Pub (see p. 152), this is a favorite gringo hangout, with a dozen or so wood tables, a rack of English-language magazines, and a menu of international comfort foods. Breakfast, served all day, is the best option, with

When the day warms up under a huge blue sky in Cusco, you'll want to be outside. Cusco doesn't have many sidewalk cafes, but it does have a trio of *quintas*, traditional open-air restaurants that are most popular with locals on weekends. These are places to get large portions of good-quality Peruvian cooking at pretty reasonable prices. Among the dishes they all offer are *tamales, cuy chactado* (fried guinea pig with potatoes), *chicharrón* (deep-fried pork, usually served with mint, onions, and corn), alpaca steak, *lechón* (suckling pig), and *costillas* (ribs). You can also get classics such as *rocoto relleno* (stuffed hot peppers) and *papa rellena* (potatoes stuffed with meat or vegetables). Vegetarian options include *sopa de quinoa* (grain soup), fried *yuca*, and *torta de papa* (potato omelets). *Quintas* are open only for lunch (noon–5 or 6pm), and most people make a visit their main meal of the day. Main courses cost between S/15 and S/45.

La Chomba ★★ Chowhounds looking for a divey restaurant with good food that only locals seem to know about will be more than satisfied with this rustic *picantería* a 10-minute walk from the Plaza de Armas. The clunky wood tables are worn from decades of use and Christmas decorations stay up all year-round, making this as authentic an experience as they come. The food is cheap and hearty. Specialties include *chicharrón, malaya frita* (fried, extra-fatty steak), and *cuy*. Order a giant glass of *frutillada*, a type of *chicha de jora* (low-alcohol, fermented-maize beer), which La Chomba flavors with strawberries. The portions are absolutely huge and most will feed two. If you are searching for authenticity, look no further. Calle Tullomayo 339. © **084/221-644.**

Quinta Eulalia ★ Eulalia has been around since 1941, making it Cusco's oldest *quinta*. From a lovely colonial courtyard (only a 5-min. walk from the Plaza de Armas), there are views of the San Cristóbal district to the surrounding hills from the upper eating area. It's a great place to dine on a sunny day, and the Andean specialties are reasonably priced. Choquechaca 384. © **084/224-951.**

Quinta Zarate ★ Located at the eastern end of town, this relaxed place has a lovely, spacious garden area with great views of the Cusco Valley. Portions are very large, and the trout is a standout; try the ceviche de trucha (trout marinated in lime and spices). This *quinta* isn't difficult to find, though it's a decent hike from the square in San Blas. Totora Paccha 763, at the end of Calle Tandapata. © **084/245-114.**

caramelized banana pancakes, huevos rancheros, and oversized toasted sandwiches. At night there are burgers and Thai curries. If you just want an actual brewed coffee or hot chocolate, they have that, too.

Choquechaca 509 (corner of Cuesta San Blas). www.jackscafecusco.com. © **084/254-606.** Reservations not accepted. Main courses S/12–S/24. No credit cards. Daily 7:30am–11pm.

Sanguchería 154 ★ SANDWICHES Opened in late 2015, this cozy, artisanal sandwich shop with exposed brick and stone walls comes from the owners of popular pizzeria La Bodega 138. All the sandwiches, using primo ingredients, are made to order. There's a mix of classic sandos, both Peruvian and international, like the *lechón, asado,* meatball, and Philly cheesesteak. Wash it down with their fresh-made juices or a local craft beer.

Granada 154, Plaza San Francisco. ℰ **084/592-424.** Sandwiches S/15–S/25. Mon–Sat noon–9pm.

SHOPPING

The Cusco region is Peru's center of handicraft production, especially hand-woven textiles, and along with Lima is the country's premier shopping destination. Many Cusqueño artisans still employ ancient weaving techniques, and they produce some of the finest textiles in South America. Cusco overflows with tiny shops stuffed with colorful wares and large markets crammed with dozens of stalls. Sadly, many of the handicrafts are now mass-produced outside of the region, though authentic textiles and crafts can still be found if you look in the right places.

Items to look for (you won't have to look too hard because shopping opportunities are pretty much everywhere you turn) include alpaca-wool sweaters, shawls, gloves, hats, scarves, blankets, ponchos, and *chullos,* the distinctive Andean knit caps with ear coverings; silver jewelry; antique blankets and textiles; woodcarvings, especially nicely carved picture frames; ceramics; and Escuela Cusqueña reproduction paintings.

The barrio of **San Blas,** the streets right around the **Plaza de Armas** (particularly calles Plateros and Triunfo), and **Plaza Regocijo** are the best and most convenient haunts for shopping outings. Many merchants sell similar merchandise, so some price comparison is always helpful. If sellers think you've just arrived in Peru and don't know the real value of items, your price is guaranteed to be higher. Although bargaining is acceptable and almost expected, merchants in the center of Cusco are confident of a steady stream of buyers, and, as a result, they are often less willing to negotiate than their counterparts in markets and more out-of-the-way places in Peru. Most visitors will find prices delightfully affordable, though, and haggling beyond what you know is a fair price, when the disparity of wealth is so great, is generally viewed as bad form. The best shops are the ones, like **Centro de Textiles Tradicionales del Cusco,** that guarantee that a high percentage of the sale price goes directly to the artisan.

Helados Artesanales

For the best artisanal ice creams and gelatos in Cusco, or maybe the best outside Italy, drop into **El Hada,** Arequipa 167 (ℰ **084/253-744**), a sweet little joint scooping up coffee, cacao, passion fruit, and other organic ice creams made on a daily basis with the best local ingredients, as well as homemade cakes. Most unexpected is the Italian-made Rocket espresso machine, cranking out excellent coffee drinks using the best small-batch Peruvian coffees from the Amazon, Puno, and other regions.

Alpaca & Andean Fashions

It's difficult to walk 10 paces in Cusco without running into an alpaca goods shop. Almost everyone in Cusco will try to sell you what they claim to be 100 percent alpaca scarves and sweaters, but many sold on the street and in tourist stalls are of inferior quality (and might even be mixed with man-made materials such as fiberglass). What is described as "baby alpaca" might be anything but. To get better-quality examples, not to mention more stylish and original, you need to visit a store that specializes in upscale alpaca fashions or buys direct from artisans; they are more expensive, but compared to international alpaca prices, still a true bargain. If you are looking for vicuña, which is more luxurious and pricier than alpaca, buy only from a reputable store. Besides the shops below, see "Art & Handicrafts" and "Designer Apparel" below for less traditional takes on alpaca goods.

Some of the best alpaca-goods shops are **Kuna** ★★, Plaza Recocijo 202 and Portal de Panes 127/Plaza de Armas (kuna.com.pe; ⓒ **084/243-233**), which features some of the finest, most modern alpaca and wool fashions for men and women, including great shawls, overcoats, and deconstructed and reversible, two-color jackets; and **Sol Alpaca** ★, San Juan de Dios 214 (www. solalpaca.com; ⓒ **084/232-687**), another of Cusco's most stylish and contemporary alpaca goods shops, with delicate sweaters, scarves, and shawls in great colors, nubby jackets, and the bonus of an excellent Indigo *artesanía* shop inside. Other boutiques worth a look, whose names let you know what you'll find inside, include **Alpaca's Best** ★, Plaza Nazarenas 197–199/Portal Confituria 221 (ⓒ **084/245-331**); **Alpaca 3,** Ruinas 472 (ⓒ **084/226-101**); and **Alpaca Treasures,** Heladeros 172 (ⓒ **084/438-557**).

Many shops in Cusco feature sheep's wool or alpaca *chompas,* or jackets, with Andean designs (often lifted directly from old blankets and weavings). A different take on Peruvian fashions, sure to appeal to more stylish backpackers, is available at **Mundo Hemp,** Qanchipata 596, San Blas (ⓒ **084/258-411**), where you'll find 100 percent natural hemp clothes and housewares, as well as a funky little cafe.

Antiques

Most of the best antiques dealers are found in San Blas. **Antigüedades Arcangel,** Cuesta de San Blas 591 (ⓒ **084/633-754**), has a nice mix of religious and other antiques from the Cusco region and across Peru, including some accessibly priced gift items. **Galería de Arte Cusqueño Antigüedades,** at Plazoleta San Blas 114 (ⓒ **084/237-857**), stocks a range of antiques, from textiles to art and furniture.

Art & Handicrafts (Artesanía)

Especially noteworthy is the **Centro de Textiles Tradicionales del Cusco** ★★★, Av. El Sol 603 (www.textilescusco.org; ⓒ **084/228-117**), an organization dedicated to fair-trade practices. It ensures that 70 percent of the sale price of the very fine textiles on display goes directly to the nine communities and individual artisans it works with. On-site is an ongoing demonstration of weaving and a very good, informative textiles museum. Prices are a bit higher than what you may find in generic shops around town, though the textiles are also higher quality, and much more of your money will go to the women who work for days on individual pieces. Also try **Inkakunaq Ruwaynin,** in the courtyard of Tullumayo 274 (www.tejidosandinos.com; ✆ **084/260-942**), a weaving cooperative with ancestral designs sourced from isolated communities from throughout the region.

There are several large markets targeting the tourist trade in *artesanía.* For antique textiles, there's a good little stall at the end of the corridor (on the right side as you enter) within the **Feria Artesanal** at Plateros 334. The stalls aren't numbered, and you might have to ask the owner to pull his older, more valuable pieces from a trunk he keeps them in, but he has some of the finest quality ceremonial textiles in Cusco. **Centro Artesanal Cusco,** at the end of Avenida El Sol, across from the large painted waterfall fountain, is the largest indoor market of handicrafts stalls in Cusco, and many goods are slightly cheaper here than they are closer to the plaza.

More specialized shops congregate in the Centro Histórico. **Casa Ecológica Cusco,** Triunfo 393 (✆ **084/255-427**), has a good selection of high-quality, handmade textiles from highland communities (in addition to natural medicines and organic food products). Equal parts contemporary art gallery and shop dedicated to nicely selected, handmade *artesanía* (such as *tablas de Sarhua*) and jewelry, **Apacheta ★,** San Juan de Dios 250 (interior) (www. apachetaperu.com; ✆ **084/238-210**), makes for good one-stop shopping. **Indigo Arte y Artesanía ★,** Plazoleta de Limacpampa Chico 473 (✆ **084/240-145**), off Avenida El Sol across from the Hotel Eco Inn, is similar, though more traditional and loaded with good gift ideas from across Peru. **La Casa de la Llama ★,** Palacio 121 (✆ **084/240-813**), features very nice quality and distinctive alpaca designs and leather goods, including embroidered reversible belts, baby alpaca stoles, and adorable and very colorful kids' sweaters.

San Blas is swimming with art galleries, artisan workshops, and ceramics shops. You'll stumble upon many small shops dealing in reproduction Escuela Cusqueña religious paintings and many workshops where you can watch artisans in action. Several of the best ceramics outlets are also here, and a small handicrafts market usually takes over the plaza on Saturday afternoon. Several artists in the San Blas area open their studios as commercial ventures, although the opportunity to watch a painter work can be fairly expensive. Look for flyers in cafes and restaurants in San Blas advertising such workshops.

Arte Aller ★, Cuesta de San Blas 580 (✆ **084/241-171**), is a small and crowded shop crammed with great folk and religious art, including those uniquely Peruvian handmade Christmas ornaments. Marked by a sign that says ETHNIC PERUVIAN ART, **Aqlla ★,** Cuesta de San Blas 565 (✆ **084/249-018**), has great silver jewelry, folk and religious art, and fine alpaca items. For a general selection of *artesanía,* check out **Artesanías Mendivil ★★,** known internationally for its singular saint figures with elongated necks, but also featuring a nice selection of mirrors, carved wood frames, Cusco School reproductions, and other ceramics. It has locations at Plazoleta San Blas 619 (☎ 084/233-247), Hatunrumíyoc 486 (☎ 084/233-234), and Plazoleta San Blas 634 (☎ 084/240-527). **Artesanías Olave** ★★, the outlets of a high-quality crafts shop that does big business with tourists, are located at Triunfo 342 (☎ 084/252-935), Plazoleta San Blas 100 (☎ 084/246-300), and Plazoleta San Blas 651 (☎ 084/231-835). **Juan Garboza Taller** (workshop), Tandapata 676, Plazoleta San Blas (☎ 084/248-039), specializes in pre-Inca-style ceramics. **Tater Camilo Vera,** at Calle Soytuqhatu 705 (☎ 084/506-228), is a master ceramicist with stunning glazed wares that fuse colonial, Incan, and pre-Incan designs with modern techniques.

Designer Apparel

The most unique designer in Cusco, or pretty much anywhere in Peru, for that matter, is a woman from Northern Ireland, Eibhlin Cassidy, who sells her original clothing designs for women at her shop, **Hilo** ★★★, Carmen Alto 260, San Blas (www.hilocusco.com; ☎ 084/254-536). Eibhlin has a keen eye for patterns and sometimes startling combinations of fabrics and color and adornments, like buttons; her whimsical but beautiful tops and jackets may not be for everyone, but to me it's wearable art. **L'Atelier by Grid,** at Carmen Alto 227A in San Blas (www.latelierbygrid.com; ☎ 084/248-333), sells unique items from Peruvian designers like Millo or Cocoliso, including modern jewelery and handbags, alongside vintage clothing. **Tawa Concept,** at Limacpampa Chico 400 (www.tawaconcept.com; ☎ 084/437-654), is a contemporary shop and art gallery with a pop and graphic design sensibility, selling artwork, photo prints, and T-shirts designed by young Peruvian artists.

Cusco finally has a flashy mall like the ones in Lima, **Centro Comercial Real Plaza,** at Av. Collasuyo 2964 (www.realplaza.pe), with all sorts of designer brands and shops, many of them Peruvian, like menswear designer M.bö and chocolate shop La Iberica. There's also a movie theater, food court, restuarants, and modern supermarket.

Foodstuffs & Mercado Central

Cusco's famous, frenzied **Mercado Central** (Central Market, also referred to as Mercado San Pedro) ★★ near the San Pedro rail station is shopping of a much different kind—almost more of a top visitors' attraction than a shopping destination. Its array of products for sale—mostly produce, food, and household items—is dazzling; even if you don't come to shop, this rich tapestry of modern and yet highly traditional Cusco still shouldn't be missed. If you're an adventurous type who doesn't mind eating at street stalls (which are generally pretty clean), you can get a ridiculously cheap lunch for about $1. Don't take valuables (or even your camera), though, and be on guard because the market is frequented by pickpockets targeting tourists. The market is open daily from 8am to 4pm or so.

A great selection of chocolate in many forms, including dark chocolate bars with high cacao percentages, chocolates flavored with Peruvian fruits and spices, chocolate liquors, cacao tea, and countless other chocolate snacks and gifts can be found at the **ChocoMuseo,** at Calle Garcilaso 210 on Plaza Regocijo (www.chocomuseo.com; ℭ **084/244-765**), which has branches in Pisac and Ollantaytambo. There is a small museum in the back of the shop and they also give truffle-making and bean-to-bar chocolate-making workshops. **The Coca Shop,** Carmen Alto 115, San Blas (ℭ **084/260-774**), features all things derived from coca leaves (save the obvious), including coca- and *lúcuma*-infused chocolates and teas, as well as quinoa and kiwicha from farming cooperatives in the region. For Cusco's best artisanal ice cream and gelato, homemade cakes, as well as terrific Peruvian small-batch coffees from an Italian-made Rocket machine, drop into the adorable **El Hada** ★★, Arequipa 167 (ℭ **084/254-102**).

Jewelry & Silver

Ilaria ★★★, one of the finest jewelry stores in Peru (www.ilariainternational.com), deals in fine silver and unique Andean-style pieces, and has several branches in Cusco: at Hotel Monasterio, Palacios 136 (ℭ **084/221-192**); at the Casa Andina Private Collection, Plazoleta de Limacpampa Chico 473 (p. 158); at Hotel Libertador, Plazoleta Santo Domingo 259 (ℭ **084/223-192**); and at the principal location at Portal Carrizos 258 on the Plaza de Armas (ℭ **084/246-253**), as well as at the airport. Many items, although not inexpensive, are an excellent value for handmade silver. Luxury Brazilian brand **H. Stern** (www.hstern.net) also has stores inside the JW Marriott Hotel (Calle Ruinas 432) and Hotel Monasterio (ℭ **084/252-030;** Calle Palacio 136).

Another nice shop with silver items is **Joyeria Cachi,** at Triunfo 392 (www.joyeriacachi.com; ℭ **084/701-022**), with elegant, intricate earrings, necklaces, brooches, and art. **Chimú Art & Gifts,** Carmen Alto 187-B, San Blas (ℭ **084/801-968**), is a funky shop featuring cool contemporary designs in silver, many based on interpretations of Chimú culture art. Rocío Pérez shows her original designs (packaged in handmade bags) at her little shop, **Jewelry Esma,** at Triunfo 393.

Outdoor Gear

As the gateway to outdoor highlands and Sacred Valley activities, including mountain climbing, trekking, and cycling, Cusco is well-stocked with outdoor gear shops for those who aren't adequately equipped for their adventures. In the last few years, the selection of international, high-end name brands has increased while prices have come down to pretty standard international levels. **Tatoo Adventure Gear** ★★, Portal Espinar 144 (https://tatoo.ws/pe; ℭ **084/236-703**), has probably the best selection of camping, trekking, and mountain climbing shoes, backpacks, and equipment. International outdoor brand **The North Face** has set up in Cusco on the Plaza de Armas, at Portal Comercio 195 (www.thenorthface.com.pe; ℭ **084/227-789**), with a good selection of high-quality jackets, pants, and apparel for hiking and climbing. Prices tend to be considerably higher than what you will find in North America.

Woodwork

Lots of shops have hand-carved woodwork and frames. However, the best spots for handmade baroque frames (perfect for your Cusco School reproduction or religious shrine) are **La Casa del Altar,** Mesa Redonda Lote A, near the Plaza de Armas (© **084/244-712**), which makes *retablos* (altarpieces) and altars in addition to frames.

ENTERTAINMENT & NIGHTLIFE

Most first-time visitors to Cusco are surprised to find that this Andean city with such a pervasive, gentle indigenous influence and colonial atmosphere also has such a rollicking nightlife. It's not as diverse (or sophisticated) as Lima's, but the scene, tightly contained around the Plaza de Armas, is predominantly young and rowdy, a perfect diversion from the rigors of trekking and immersion in Inca and colonial history. Some older visitors might find the late-night, spring-break party atmosphere a little jarring in such a historic, stately place. No doubt that's what motivated the mayor's office to move to shut down several of the rowdiest late-night clubs in the historic center in recent years.

Even though the city is inundated with foreigners during many months of the year, bars and discos happily aren't just gringolandia outposts. Locals (as well as Peruvians from other cities, principally Lima, and other South Americans) usually make up a pretty healthy percentage of the clientele. Clubs are in such close range of each other—in the streets just off the Plaza de Armas and in San Blas (where the city's artsier bars and cafes proliferate)—that virtually everyone seems to adopt a pub-crawl attitude, bopping from one bar or disco to the next, often reconvening with friends in the plaza before picking up a free drink ticket and free admission card from one of the many girls on the square handing them out.

For those who are saving their energy for the Inca Trail and other treks, there are less rowdy options, such as Andean music shows in restaurants and more sedate bars.

Bars & Pubs

In high season, bars are often filled to the rafters with gringos hoisting cheap drinks and trading information on the Inca Trail or their latest jungle or rafting adventure (or just trying to pick up Peruvians or each other). Most bars are open from 11am or noon until 1 or 2am. Many have elastic happy hours offering half-price drinks, making it absurdly cheap to tie one on. (Travelers still adjusting to Cusco's altitude, though, should take it easy on alcohol in their first days in the city. You've never had a hangover until you've had one above 3,000 meters.)

A handful of restaurants are excellent places to drop into for a cocktail or glass of wine. The mixologists at **Limo** (p. 141) can hold their own with any bartenders in the city, and the list of pisco cocktails, most with exotic fruit juices and other ingredients, is superb—a great place to begin or end the evening. **Baco** (p. 138) is an oenophile's hangout, a good place to sample Chilean, Argentine, and Spanish wines in quiet, romantic environs. Its sister restaurant **Cicciolina** (p. 140) also has a very appealing wine and cocktail bar right up front, with tons of ambience. Gastón Acurio's two eateries, **Papa-cho's** (p. 143) and **ChiCha** (p. 140), each have a great bar program with a long list of original and classic pisco cocktails, plus craft beers, as does **Calle del Medio** (p. 138).

The best cocktail bar in Cusco, however, is the **Museo de Pisco** (p. 137), which isn't a museum at all. The three-level bar specializes in Peruvian piscos, offering up a dizzying number of different bottles from some of Peru's cult producers that you won't find outside the country. Sip on them straight or as a flight, which allows you to notice the subtle differences in the grapes or regions where the pisco was produced. There's also a long list of classic and original pisco cocktails, and there's live music on some nights. A close runner-up is **Huaringas** ★, Plazoleta Nazarenas 167 (www.huaringas.com; ℂ **084/240-235**), the Cusco offshoot of this iconic Lima bar. The crisp, clean cocktail joint with contemporary Andean decor and a long white bar specializes in variations of the pisco sour and *chilcano,* flavored with dozens of different infusions of native fruits and herbs.

Los Perros ★, Tecsecocha 436 (ℂ **084/241-447**), is a laid-back but trendy lounge bar owned by an Australian–Peruvian couple. "The Dogs" has comfy sofas, good food and cocktails (including hot wine), and a hip soundtrack. The bar attracts an international crowd that takes advantage of the book exchange and magazines, and plenty of folks quickly become regulars, making it their spot for dining as well as just hanging out and drinking. The sedate and good-looking restaurant and cocktail lounge **Marcelo Batata,** Palacios 121 (ℂ **084/224-424**), has a coveted rooftop terrace with amazing rooftop and star views.

One of the oldest pubs in town is the **Cross Keys** ★, Triunfo 350 (ℂ **084/229-227**), owned by the English honorary consul and especially popular with Brits who come to play darts or catch up on European soccer on satellite, and knock back pints of ale; it's stuffed to the gills late at night. Pub grub is available, if you can manage to get an order in. American-owned **Norton Rat's Tavern,** Santa Catalina Angosta 116 (ℂ **084/246-204**), next door to the La Compañía church, is a rough-and-tumble bar, the type of biker-friendly place that you might find in any American Midwestern city. Nice balconies

Raw Fish: A Cure for What Ails You

If you hang out so much and so late in Cusco that you wind up with a wicked hangover—which is even more of a problem at an altitude of 3,300m (11,000 ft.)—adopt the tried-and-true Andean method of reviving yourself. For once, the solution is not coca-leaf tea—

it's ceviche that seems to do the trick. Something about raw fish marinated in lime and chili makes for a nice slap in the face. Late Sunday mornings at the *cevichería* are often part of the weekly routine for pale-faced folks hiding behind sunglasses.

overlook the action below on the plaza. **Paddy's Irish Pub,** Triunfo 124, Plaza de Armas (www.paddysirishbarcusco.com; ✆ **084/247-719**), claiming to be the world's highest authentic Irish pub, is cozy, relaxed, and often crowded, with expats catching up on *fútbol* (soccer, of course) and rugby and downing Guinness on draft. **El Duende Lounge Bar,** Tecsecocha 429 (✆ **084/437-519**), is a good place for drinks and meeting Peruvian young people.

Dance Clubs

Several late-night dance clubs have come and gone in the last few years, but a few of the old warhorses remain popular. A pretty young crowd, both backpackers and young Peruvians, is lured to the discos by all the free drink cards handed out on the Plaza de Armas. **Mama Africa ★★**, Portal de Panes 109, 3rd Floor (✆ **084/246-544**), boasts sweaty charm and features occasional live music and DJs who spin an international dance mix of Latin, reggae, rock, and techno music for a mix of locals and gringos (each often looking to hook up). Its loungier sister bar, **Mushrooms,** is one floor down. There are several other nightclubs on or within a few blocks of the plaza, though most have a very thrown-together feel and only last for a year or two before the next thing takes their place.

Live Music Clubs

Live music is a nearly constant feature of the Cusco nightlife scene, and it's less about itinerant bands of *altiplano* musicians in colorful vests and sandals playing woodwind instruments than live Latin rock, pop, and salsa. Live music tends to begin around 11pm in most clubs, and happy hours are generally from 8 to 9 or 10pm.

The coolest place in Cusco for nightly live music has long been **Ukuku's ★★**, Plateros 316, second floor (www.ukukusbar.com; ✆ **084/254-911**). It was recently closed down by the mayor for its loud, wee-hours antics, but locals hope to see it reopen. Check to see if it has, and if so, expect again to see a range of acts that extends from bar rock to Afro-Peruvian, and a crowd that comes to get a groove on, jamming the dance floor. Bar-lounge **Song Thé,** which shares a colonial patio with Hotel Arqueólogo and Divina Comedia restaurant (Calle Pumacurco 406; www.jazzbarcusco.sitew.com), has regular jazz and opera performances with no cover fee.

In San Blas, **Km. 0 ★**, Tandapata 100 (✆ **084/254-240**), is a Spanish-owned joint with a rocker's heart, a tiny ramshackle place with live rock, Latin, and blues music nightly; "happy hours all night"; and a variety of tapas.

For a traditional folklore music-and-dance show with panpipes and costumes—well, ponchos, alpaca hats, and sandals, at a minimum—you'll need to check out one of the tourist-oriented restaurants featuring nightly entertainment. In addition to the longtime show restaurants **El Truco** (Plaza Regocijo 261; ✆ **084/232-441**) and **La Retama** (Portal de Panes 123, 2nd Floor; ✆ **084/226-372**), **Tunupa,** Portal Confiturías 233, 2nd Floor (✆ **084/252-936**), offers a good traditional music-and-dance show, as well as a panoramic view of the Plaza de Armas. Plenty of first-time visitors and groups get a kick out of them at least once, though I'm not a fan.

CAFE society

If you really just want to chill out and have a coffee, a beer, or some dessert, drop into one of the city's comfortable cafes. The following are all good places for a light meal during the day, but at night they tend to take on some of that smoky Euro-cafe sheen, and travelers get all metaphysical about their treks through the Andes. **El Hada ★★**, Arequipa 167 (✆ **084/254-102**), is the closest thing to a hipster coffee shop, with small-batch beans sourced from around the region, plus fancy coffee drinks and artisanal ice creams. **Café Ayllu ★**, Almagro 133 (✆ **084/232-357**), is a busy little place, a traditional Cusco cafe that draws as many

locals as gringos. It's known for its *ponche de leche* (a milky beverage, often served with a shot of pisco) and *lenguas* (a flaky pastry with manjar blanco crème in the middle). It also offers good breakfasts, sandwiches, and the mainstay, coffee.

Café Perla ★, 304 Plazoleta Santa Catalina (✆ **084/239-590**), is one of the few places in Cusco that roasts its own coffee. You can also find fresh juices and snacks. Also try the **Museo del Café,** Calle Espaderos 136 (www.museodelcafecusco. com; ✆ **084/263-264**), which also roasts coffee and is more refined, sourcing beans direct from small farmers in Cusco's La Convención province.

Theater & Dance

For music and folkloric dance performances, **Teatro Municipal,** Mesón de la Estrella 149 (✆ **084/221-847**), and particularly the long-running **Centro Q'osqo de Arte Nativo ★**, Av. El Sol 684 (✆ **084/227-901**), feature good Peruvian music and folkloric dance performances. Check with the tourist office for a schedule of events.

WHERE TO STAY

As the top tourist destination in Peru, where virtually every visitor seems to pass and stay at least a night or two, Cusco has developed a remarkable cornucopia of lodgings, with hundreds of hotels, inns, and *hostales* of all stripes and prices. More continue to sprout, and few seem to close. Although the sheer number of offerings, at every budget level, means that you can pretty confidently land in Cusco without a reservation (outside of popular festivals like Inti Raymi and Fiestas Patrias at the end of June and July) and find a decent place to stay, many of the better and more popular hotels at all levels fill up throughout high season and even in shoulder months. It's best to firm up a reservation as soon as you know your dates of stay in Cusco unless you're willing to wing it and aren't that picky.

Most of the city's most desirable accommodations are very central, in the Centro Histórico and within walking distance of the Plaza de Armas. The artsy San Blas neighborhood is also within walking distance, although many hotels and *hostales* in that district involve steep climbs up the hillside. (The upside is that guests are rewarded with some of the finest views in the city.) Some visitors may want to avoid hotels and inns too close to the Plaza de

Most Cusco hotels have annoyingly early checkout times—often 9 or 9:30am—due to the deluge of early-morning flight arrivals to the city. At least in high season, hotels are very serious about your need to rise and shine (and many travelers are up and out very early anyway, on their way to Machu Picchu or trekking excursions), but you can always store your bags until later.

Armas; that zone's crowded bars and nightclubs, many of which are open until sunrise, tend to produce throngs of rambunctious and usually inebriated young people who stumble downstairs and howl at the moon or bellow at the people who just rejected them inside.

Hotels have really mushroomed in the last few years in Cusco, but the high-end boutique category in particular has exploded. There used to be just the Monasterio and the Libertador on the higher end; now there are a dozen upscale properties with full-service spas, oxygen-enriched air, and gourmet restaurants. Though the style quotient has risen—and along with it, prices—Cusco remains a backpackers' delight, with a glut of inns of all stripes at the moderate and budget levels. Many *hostales* have more atmosphere and are likely to provide a better overall experience than more expensive—and more institutional—hotels. Prices listed below are rack rates for travel in high season and include taxes. During the low season (Nov–Apr), prices often drop precipitously, even at mid-range inns and backpacker hostels—sometimes as much as 50 percent—as hotels fight for a much-reduced number of visitors.

At the lower end, hot water can be an issue at many hotels—even those that swear they offer 24-hour hot showers.

Many hotels and inns will arrange free airport transfers if you communicate your arrival information to them in advance.

Near the Plaza de Armas
VERY EXPENSIVE

Hotel Monasterio ★★★   While the competition has heated up in recent years—like that from Belmond's newer, more luxurious sister hotel Palacio Nazarenas next door (see below)—the Monasterio remains one of the most magical places to stay in Cusco, if not all of South America. Set within the San Antonio Abad monastery, built in 1592 on the foundations of Inca Amaru Qhala's palace, this national historic landmark was transformed into a hotel in 1965. Inside these stone walls, which surround a beautiful cloistered courtyard with a fountain and a 300-year-old cedar tree, lies an immaculate collection of Peruvian history: an 18th-century Escuela Cusqueña art collection, a Baroque-style gilded chapel, and entrance stones bearing the Spanish coat of arms and the image of Bishop Monsignor Juan Serricolea y Olea. The Monasterio is as much a museum as it is a hotel. Rooms, which can be enriched with oxygen (an extra $30 per night in deluxe rooms; already included in

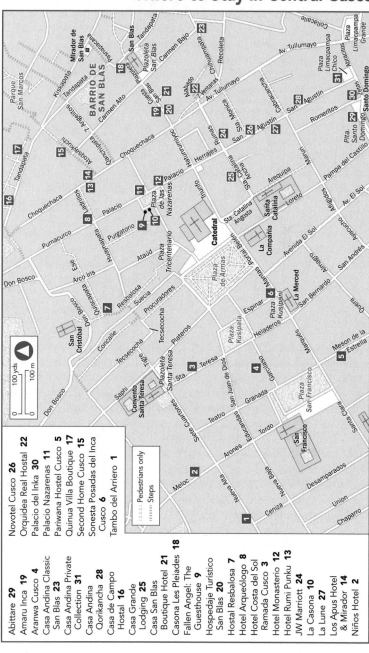

Abittare **29**
Amaru Inca **19**
Aranwa Cusco **4**
Casa Andina Classic San Blas **23**
Casa Andina Private Collection **31**
Casa Andina Qorikancha **28**
Casa de Campo Hostal **16**
Casa Grande Lodging **25**
Casa San Blas Boutique Hotel **21**
Casona Les Pleiades **18**
Fallen Angel: The Guesthouse **9**
Hospedaje Turístico San Blas **20**
Hotel Resbalosa **7**
Hotel Arqueólogo **8**
Hotel Costa del Sol Ramada Cusco **3**
Hotel Monasterio **12**
Hotel Rumi Punku **13**
JW Marriott **24**
La Casona **10**
La Lune **27**
Los Apus Hotel & Mirador **14**
Niños Hotel **2**

Novotel Cusco **26**
Orquidea Real Hostal **22**
Palacio del Inka **30**
Palacio Nazarenas **11**
Pariwana Hostel Cusco **5**
Quinua Villa Boutique **17**
Second Home Cusco **15**
Sonesta Posadas del Inca Cusco **6**
Tambo del Arriero **1**

Pedestrians only
Steps

suites) to combat *soroche* (altitude sickness), feature rich wood furnishings and historic artwork. Some suites have private terraces, while others are two levels. Its signature Peruvian-Mediterranean restaurant Illary has courtyard seating when the weather is nice. The more relaxed El Tupay restaurant features a couple of local opera singers 3 nights a week.

Palacios 136, Plaza Nazarenas. www.monasteriohotel.com. © **084/241-777.** 126 units. $385–$470 deluxe doubles; $595–$1,340 suites. Rates include breakfast buffet. **Amenities:** 2 restaurants; cafe; bar; concierge; oxygen on demand ($30 surcharge); Wi-Fi.

JW Marriott El Convento Cusco ★★ The first thing you see when you walk into this hotel, which is situated right around the corner from the Plaza de Armas, is a stunning piece of artwork behind the reception desk made of 6,000 pieces of Swarovski crystals, an homage to the Incan sun god Inti. The 16th-century convent, constructed over an Inca foundation, is a virtual museum where Inca walls are exposed under glass, as well as pre-Inca artifacts found during the excavation of the site. Most rooms overlook a stone courtyard, with some suites having private patios or looking onto centuries-old stone walls. The modern decor gives subtle nods to the Inca and colonial past, while the marble bathrooms have both tubs and rain showers. Oxygen can be pumped into the room to help with altitude sickness for an additional fee. A huge basement spa features an indoor pool, plus a full range of signature treatments.

Calle Ruinas 432, Cusco. www.marriott.com. © **084/582-200.** 153 units. $313–$403 doubles; $466–$1,059 suites. Rates include breakfast buffet. **Amenities:** 2 restaurants; bar; indoor pool; spa; business center; fireplace lounge; Wi-Fi.

La Casona ★★★ Opened in 2009 across from the storied Monasterio, this might be the most understated hotel in Cusco. Its beautifully restored 16th-century colonial manor house doesn't have a sign out front, and there's not even a lobby or rooms with numbers. With just 11 suites, it's much smaller than the Monasterio, therefore your experience will be more intimate. Staying at La Casona is like staying at a private home where everyone knows your name. The service is superb, and the personal concierges take care of guests' every need, from dinner reservations to booking private guided trips to the Maras salt mines. Rooms, which surround a stone courtyard, are huge, have heated wood floors, and are decorated with actual Cusco School paintings. The hotel is part of the eco-friendly Peruvian chain Inkaterra and a member of the luxe Relais & Châteaux family.

Plazoleta Nazarenas 167, Plaza Nazarenas. www.inkaterra.com. © **800/442-5042** in U.S. and Canada, 01/610-0400 for reservations. 11 units. $539–$649 suites. Rates include breakfast buffet. **Amenities:** Restaurant; concierge; Wi-Fi (free).

La Lune ★★★ Above the very elegant and very elegant French Le Soleil (see p. 137), which has the same owner, is this very elegant and very French hotel. There is just a single suite carved out of the second floor of this 18th-century *casona*. It's more of an apartment than hotel, with two bedrooms and a separate living area with French accents and a gas fireplace. The bathroom is more spa-like, with stone walls, fresh flowers, and Jacuzzi tubs. The suite is beyond comfortable and ideal for a well-heeled family or a pair of couples traveling together. The suite is divided into two separate entrances if there are multiple parties that want to rent seperately. Additionally, all meals are included at Le Soleil. Service is personalized and staff goes out of its way to make sure guests have absolutely everything they could ever need.

San Agustín 275, Cusco. www.onesuitehotelcusco.com. ℂ **084/240-543.** $550 suite; $1,000 2-bedroom apartment. Rates include 3 meals and massages. **Amenities:** Restaurant; Wi-Fi (free).

Palacio del Inka ★★ Palacio del Inka reopened in 2013 after a multi-year renovation that completely overhauled the accommodations and turned the place into an elite Luxury Collection hotel. One of Cusco's original five stars, it is once again one of the city's best. Built on the foundations of the "Acllahuasi," where the Inca chieftain kept maidens, the colonial-era residence was also home to conquistador Francisco Pizarro. Recent renovations have done a fine job of modernizing the historic structure without losing its essence. Remaining are the stone archways, the magnificent colonial courtyard, coffered wood ceilings, and terra-cotta tiles. Joining them are signature Luxury Collection beds and state-of-the-art technology like LED TVs and docking stations. The space is just a bit swankier than it once was. The handsome Rumi bar and Inti Raymi restaurant occupy the ground floor, and there's a full spa with the same thermal circuit found in Libertador's Paracas and Sacred Valley hotels.

Plazoleta Santo Domingo 259 (across from Qorikancha). www.palaciodelinkahotel.com. ℂ **01/518-6510.** 203 units. $275–$295 deluxe doubles; $330–$425 suites. **Amenities:** Restaurant; coffee shop; concierge; fitness center; sauna; Wi-Fi.

Palacio Nazarenas ★★★ Few thought that Belmond would ever be able to out-luxe its hotel next door, the Monasterio, long considered one of the continent's top accommodations. The luxe hotel chain pulled it off, though, with this 55 oxygen-enriched-suites stunner. The structure is a 16th-century convent, built over Inca foundations, with an astounding five interior courtyards. That's on top of two chapels, and let's not forget the secret passageways once used by the nuns. Service here is top-notch, with your personal butler making your acquaintance by e-mail even before you arrive, and then coming to your room to shake you a pisco sour from your complimentary bar, or to cut off a brick of herbal soap made on-site. With the many years it took to restore the property, Belmond made sure to not miss a single detail, from the heated wooden floors, to soaking tubs equipped with bath salts from the mines at Maras, to marble bathrooms with Prija bath products. The resort-like pool and spa has glass floors so you can admire the Inca stonework below. Next to it is the restaurant Senzo, which serves elegant *novo andino* food using many herbs grown in the courtyards (which are also used in the spa).

Plazoleta Nazarenas 144. www.palacionazarenas.com. ℂ **084/458-2222.** 55 units. $595–$1,925 suites. Rates include breakfast, complimentary minibar. **Amenities:** Restaurant; bar; concierge, pool, spa; Wi-Fi.

EXPENSIVE

Aranwa Cusco ★★ Opened in 2010, the second hotel from the quietly expanding Peruvian chain Aranwa is hidden away in a 16th-century colonial mansion beyond Plaza Regocijo. The stone walls, heavy wood bed frames, incredible collection of antique furniture, and oil paintings from the Cusco School are reminiscent of better-known pads but without the elevated price tag. The in-room highlights are without a doubt the marble bathrooms, which are some of the best around, with heated floors, Scottish showers, and deep soaking tubs. (Classic rooms miss out on the soaking tubs, but are otherwise just as comfortable.) An intelligent oxygen system pumps in 30 percent more air than normal to the rooms. Note that the layout of the historical mansion results in some rooms being smallish or having odd angles.

255 San Juan de Dios, near Plaza Regocijo. www.aranwahotels.com. © **855/384-6625** when calling from the U.S. 43 units. $230–$264 doubles; $281–$298 suites. Rates include breakfast buffet. **Amenities:** Restaurant; bar; concierge; Wi-Fi.

Casa Andina Private Collection ★★ The only real downside of this nicely refurbished 18th-century mansion is that it is a bit removed from the heart of the old city. It could be worse, though. It's on a small square and only about a 10- or 15-minute walk to the plaza. Aside of that, the setup is nearly as good as the pricier colonial-style hotels. There are four beautiful patios, and rooms fall into two categories: colonial-style with stone walls and reproduced furniture or modern and minimalist. They are all spacious and have all of the standard amenities. A lovely deep-red lounge area with a roaring fireplace and gourmet restaurant provide plenty of warmth and comfort on a chilly Andean night.

Plazoleta de Limacpampa Chico 473, Cusco. www.casa-andina.com. © **866/220-4434** toll-free in the U.S., 08/082-343-805 in the U.K., or 01/213-9739. 93 units. $162 doubles; $193 suites. Rates include breakfast buffet. **Amenities:** Restaurant; bar; babysitting; concierge; Wi-Fi (free).

Fallen Angel: The Guesthouse ★ From the whimsical mind of Andrés Zuniga, who also created the fantasyland restaurant Fallen Angel downstairs, this eccentric, distinctive guesthouse on Plaza Nazarenas is without a doubt Cusco's most unique place to stay. Imagine Prince decorating a colonial-style building and you'll have a hint of what the five oversized rooms here look like. The funky, eclectic vibe might be too much for some to handle, but those with an open mind will appreciate the break from the norm, especially those who want to shower in a room with Inca walls, or sleep in a bed fit for royalty in outer space. You'll find the same amenities as the top luxury hotels in town. Breakfast is taken at Fallen Angel.

Plazoleta Nazarenas 221. www.fallenangelincusco.com. © **084/258-184.** 5 units. $209–$275 suites. Rates include breakfast, airport transfer, and massage. **Amenities:** Restaurant; bar; Wi-Fi.

Hotel Costa del Sol Ramada Cusco ★ Now part of the Wyndham brand, this hotel is conveniently priced a step below the luxe brands while retaining much of the same atmosphere. The 17th-century mansion, built by a Spanish nobleman, the marquis of Picoaga, and much of the stonework remains, including archways and patios, as do original murals. Rooms are divided between colonial and contemporary wings. The colonial rooms are a much better choice with their high ceilings, replica wood furniture, and floral prints. The contemporary rooms feel more like standard rooms in any other mid-range hotel.

Santa Teresa 344, Cusco. www.costadelsolperu.com/cusco. ℂ **01/711-332-0000.** 90 units. $129–$149 doubles. Rates include breakfast buffet. **Amenities:** 2 restaurants; fireplace cocktail bar; concierge; Wi-Fi.

MODERATE

Abittare ★ Opposite Qorikancha, this true boutique hotel that opened in 2015 has found a happy balance of Scandinavian minimalism and Andean architecture without being tacky. Surrounding a central courtyard, the rooms are small and feature wood floors, area rugs, and woven baskets filled with plants. Cloud-like beds are backed by reclaimed wood headboards, while retro metal lamps hang from the ceiling. There is little in the way of extra amenities, but if you are spending most of your time exploring the city and all you need is a comfortable room with a good location and a reasonable price, this is for you.

Plazoleta Santo Domingo 263, Cusco. www.abittare-hotels.com. ℂ **084/241-739.** 44 units. $86–$104 doubles; $120–$156 suites. Rates include breakfast. **Amenities:** Business center; lounge; Wi-Fi (free).

Casa Andina Qorikancha ★ Though Peruvian chain Casa Andina's collection of mid-range hotels in Cusco doesn't stand out as much as it once did, this is still an overall decent value if all you are looking for is a good location and the standard set of amenities you'd find at any average American hotel. The Qorikancha location, 3 blocks from the Plaza de Armas, is less claustrophobic than the two hotels near the plaza. Simple rooms with blood-red walls, green woodwork, and comfy beds surround two laid-back courtyards. It's not quite as nice or new as Casa Andina's San Blas hotel or the pricier Private Collection hotel, and the tired faux-Andean decor could certainly use a face-lift, but you'll sleep well here. The water will be hot, the Wi-Fi will work, and the breakfast buffet has everything you could want.

San Agustín 371. www.casa-andina.com. ℂ **084/252-633;** for reservations in the U.S. 866/220-4434, Lima 01/446-8848. 57 units. $79–$91 doubles. Rates include breakfast buffet. **Amenities:** Concierge; Wi-Fi.

Hotel Arqueólogo ★ A 5-minute walk from the main square, in the flat San Cristobal neighborhood, this quirky late-19th-century house has its pluses and minuses. The good: There's a pleasant interior courtyard and sunny garden, and some rooms have high beamed ceilings and hardwood floors that are full of character. There's also a decent restaurant and bar/lounge with some of the best live music in Cusco. The bad: Some rooms are rather cramped, the decor (like the pillowcases that say "Buenas Noches") can seem weird, essentials like Wi-Fi and hot water can be spotty at times, and the rooms have no phone. If some of the faults don't bother you, the value is quite good.

Pumacurco 408, Cusco. www.hotelarqueologo.com. ℂ **084/232-522** or 877/289-5148 in the U.S. 20 units. $99–$149 doubles. Rates include breakfast buffet and a free airport transfer. **Amenities:** Restaurant; Wi-Fi (free).

Hotel Rumi Punku ★ The name of this midsize, family-run hotel translates to "stone door" (one of three belonging to private houses in Cusco), after the Inca-built trapezoidal entrance to the 16th-century house. The building is a timeline of Cusco history with additional walls dating to the Incas and three flower-filled courtyards with stone fountains, carved wood balconies, and a chapel dating to the colonial period. The clean bedrooms are spacious, with hardwood floors, Norwegian thermal blankets, and paintings from local artists. Additional features include a top-floor dining room, where breakfast is served, that has panoramic views of the city, as well as a spa with a "Finnish" sauna and Jacuzzi tub ($15 extra).

Choquechaca 339, Cusco. www.rumipunku.com. ℂ **084/221-102.** 40 units. $95–$130 doubles; $200 suites. Rates include breakfast buffet and airport pickup. **Amenities:** Restaurant; spa; gym; Jacuzzi; fireplace lounge; Wi-Fi.

Novotel Cusco ★ This fairly large complex from the French Novotel chain, set within a 16th-century colonial building, won't knock your socks off, but it won't let you down, either. The location isn't right on the plaza, but the few blocks' walk isn't at a steep incline. The rooms are fairly standard and what you might expect from a big international chain. The 16 superior rooms in the converted colonial section of the hotel maintain an atmosphere found at posher hotels like the Monasterio and are worth the extra cost. In the heated patio is a cozy French restaurant, plus a warm bar with a fireplace.

San Agustín 239, at the corner of Pasaje Santa Mónica. www.novotel.com. ℂ **084/581-033.** 99 units. $104–$156 doubles. Rates include breakfast. **Amenities:** Restaurant; bar; babysitting; concierge; sauna; Wi-Fi.

Sonesta Posadas del Inca Cusco ★ Here's the deal with Sonesta's original Cusco property: It's an above-average hotel with a friendly staff that sits on flat ground, just off the Plaza de Armas. While the top hotels on Plaza Nazarenas in hilly San Blas are fine and dandy, for older travelers or those already winded from *soroche,* climbing those steep streets isn't always the best option. The main entrance of the building faces Plaza Regocijo, though views of the main plaza and neighboring cathedrals can be had from the relatively spacious rooms. Interiors feature earth-toned color schemes and modern bathrooms. Sonesta has opened a newer, much larger, and more modern hotel down Avenida El Sol, which has similar rates, though the key here is location.

Portal Espinar 108. www.sonesta.com. ℂ **084/227-061.** 22 units. $113–$136 doubles. Rates include breakfast buffet. **Amenities:** Restaurant; business center; luggage storage; Wi-Fi.

Tambo del Arriero ★ This 17th-century building was designed as an inn when it was first built, attracting passing muleteers. The family-owned property, about 5 blocks from the plaza in a quiet residential neighborhood, weaves around two sunny courtyards wrapped in wooden balconies. The rooms feature wood floors and period furnishings, though they have surprisingly modern amenities like marble tubs and iPod docks. The best room in the house is No. 108, an expansive suite with its own private patio. There's no sense of this being a corporate hotel; rather, it's warm and authentic, a uniquely Cusco hotel.

Nueva Alta 484, Cusco. www.tambodelarriero.com. ✆ **084/260-709.** 18 units. $120 doubles; $150–$230 suites. Rates include breakfast buffet and free airport pickup/drop-off. **Amenities:** Coffee bar; Wi-Fi (free).

INEXPENSIVE

Casa Grande Lodging ★   Those looking for something super-cheap and clean and right near the plaza need look no further than Casa Grande, built atop the Palace of Inca Yupanqui. Housed in a 19th-century colonial house with original stonework, this is one of the last remaining family-run hostels near the plaza. Rooms surround a sunny cobblestone courtyard lined with wooden balconies. The accommodations are simple: The floors creak, the carpets are tired, and the only hot water you get is from electric shower heads, but the quirky space and friendly service is more than enough for many. Downstairs rooms don't get much light and can be dungeon-like, so be sure to reserve those on the second floor.

Santa Catalina Ancha 353, near the Plaza de Armas. ✆ **084/224-907.** 21 units. $44 doubles. Rate includes continental breakfast. **Amenities:** Museum; laundry; Wi-Fi (free).

Hostal Resbalosa ★   Up a steep cobblestone pedestrian-only street in San Cristobal, this backpacker haunt is quite basic yet still a step up from most youth hostels. The rooms are a good size and have hardwood floors, big windows with views of the city from some, and dependable hot-water showers. The best feature is the large rooftop terrace with 180-degree views, ideal for hanging out and reading your guidebook.

Resbalosa 494, Cusco. www.hostalresbalosa.com. ✆ **084/224-839.** 20 units. $16 doubles with shared bathroom; $22 doubles with private bathroom. No credit cards.

Niños Hotel ★★   When Dutch-born Jolanda van den Berg moved to Cusco in 1996, she took in 12 Peruvian street children. Soon after, she opened two homes for girls through her foundation Niños Unidos Peruanos. Her message of goodwill has not slowed one bit since then, and today the foundation cares for 600 disadvantaged children with the assistance of 80 helpers. Funding comes from the five restaurants she runs, plus this lovely hotel in a restored colonial building about 10 minutes from the Plaza de Armas. Each of the large rooms, which surround a pleasant courtyard, feature hardwood floors, beamed ceilings, comfy beds, and original artwork. The hotel has been so successful—reservations are a must as it sometimes fills up 6 months out—that another 20-room sister hotel has been added 2 blocks away. There's also an annex with a set of apartments for longer stays. The valley retreat Niños Hotel Hacienda (rates start at $55) is located in the town of Huasao, just 30 minutes from Cusco, where few tourists ever venture. It's a nice option for those wanting to get a little bit off the tourist trail.

Meloc 442, near the Plaza de Armas. www.ninoshotel.com. © **084/231-424.** 20 units. $53 doubles with private bathroom; $50 doubles with shared bathroom; apartments $44 double or $388 per month. No credit cards. **Amenities:** Restaurant; cafe.

Pariwana Hostel Cusco ★   One of just a few good youth hostels in Cusco, the Pariwana is favored by students, volunteers, and young backpackers. The setting isn't exactly some no-frills craphole; rather, it's a beautiful 16th-century colonial manor house built around a beautiful courtyard just 2 blocks from the Plaza de Armas. The rooms are split between double rooms with bathrooms to standard dorm rooms of several sizes (overall capacity is for 220 people), including dorm rooms for women only. There's a full bar and restaurant on-site, plus Ping-Pong, pool tables, and all sorts of nightly group activities and excursions. Oh yeah, and breakfast is served until 1pm.

Mesón de la Estrella 136, Cusco. www.pariwana-hostel.com. © **084/233-751.** 60 units. S/175–S/225 doubles with private bathroom; S/145 doubles with shared bathroom; S/32–S/49 per person in dorm room with shared bathroom. Rates include breakfast. No credit cards. **Amenities:** Restaurant; bar; lockers; Ping-Pong; billiards; Wi-Fi (free).

San Blas
MODERATE
Casa Andina Classic San Blas ★   This is my favorite of the Casa Andina classic hotels in Cusco, of which there are four. It's up a side street, a little bit removed from the action, on a San Blas slope, though it has some of the most unique views of the city anywhere. The colonial structure is built around an interior two-tiered grass and stone courtyard, giving it the feel of a rural mountain inn. The decorations and service are standard Casa Andina: a blend of colonial and Andean touches, hot showers, working Wi-Fi, nothing over the top. Tower rooms are the best choice and have open-air lounges overlooking the courtyard.

Chihuampata 278. www.casa-andina.com. © **866/220-4434** toll-free in the U.S., 08/082-343-805 in the U.K., or 01/213-9739. 38 units. $79–$99 doubles; $91–$107 superior doubles. Rates include breakfast buffet. **Amenities:** Restaurant (lunch & dinner on request); concierge; Wi-Fi (free).

Casa San Blas Boutique Hotel ★   Down a dead-end pedestrian-only alleyway, Cuesta San Blas halfway up San Blas, this is one of the better-located mid-range hotels in Cusco. Set in a restored 18th-century *casona*, the hotel's panoramic-view terrace is its most redeeming quality. The standard rooms are smallish and rather plain, with just a hint of colonial decor. The two-level junior suites on the top floor, with kitchenettes and wood-beamed ceilings, are a much better value, can easily fit a family of five, and offer spectacular views of the city below.

Tocuyeros 566. www.casasanblas.com. © **084/254-852.** 18 units. $136 doubles; $198–$240 suites. Rates include airport transfer and breakfast. **Amenities:** Restaurant; piano bar; massage room; room service; Wi-Fi (free).

Los Apus Hotel & Mirador ★   With a little bit of a mountain chalet feel—you can thank the Swiss owners for that—this often overlooked small hotel on a quiet street at the top of San Blas has plenty of perks. The rooftop terrace, great for trading travel tales, has superb views, while the large glass-covered atrium over the central courtyard helps bring about a communal air usually found in hostels. The price is a bit high for the location and the no-frills decor, though the high-ceilinged first-floor rooms and higher-floor rooms with private balconies make up for it. Prices drop considerably during the low season.

Atocsaycuchi 515, corner of Choquechaca. www.losapushotel.com. ✆ **084/264-243.** 20 units. $108 doubles. Rates include breakfast. **Amenities:** Restaurant; Wi-Fi (free).

Orquidea Real Hostal ★   This unassuming inn on a San Blas hill is pure old-school Cusco. This is how budget travelers used to stay here before youth hostels and backpacker dives. The colonial building has original Inca walls and exposed wood beams, but its most authentic feature is the brick fireplace in every room (though you'll more likely just use the standing electric heaters). The furnishings and decorations in the wood-floor rooms are very basic, though the hot water is actually hot for 24 hours a day, and the views of the city are spectacular. Made-to-order eggs for breakfast will round out an all-around pleasant stay.

Alabado 520, San Blas, Cusco. www.cusco-hotel.net. ✆ **084/221-662;** for reservations in the U.S. ✆ 888/671-2852. 11 units. $58 doubles; $85 suites. Rates include continental breakfast and airport pickup. **Amenities:** Cafeteria; Wi-Fi (in public areas).

Quinua Villa Boutique ★★   These five independent apartments, hidden away up a flight of San Blas stairs, are some of the most unique accommodations in the city. The mini-compound, owned by an Italian man named Cristiano, is layered on top with three levels of terracing, surrounding a pleasant courtyard. Most of the units have two stories, and all include kitchens and wood-burning fireplaces, plus hand-carved wooden balconies and wrought-iron grills. Each has a theme based around a time period, from a pre-Inca perspective to a contemporary look at Peruvian pop culture. Eighty percent of the beautiful furnishings and carvings found in the apartments and around the complex were designed by local artisans. Breakfast is served in your room.

Pasaje Santa Rosa A-8 (Mirador T'oqokachi), San Blas, Cusco. www.quinua.com.pe. ✆ **084/242-646.** 5 units. $98–$165 doubles. Rates include breakfast and airport pickup. **Amenities:** Museum; Wi-Fi (free).

Second Home Cusco ★   High in San Blas, at the end of Carmen Alto, this is the second charming boutique property (the other is in Lima's Barranco district) run by the children of Peruvian artist Victor Delfín. This one is tiny. With just three rooms, it's like crashing at a friend's house—if your friend has great taste in contemporary artwork, that is. There are high ceilings throughout, and rooms feature modern bathrooms and fine bedding and linens. The art is what will probably make the biggest impression, like the chimney in the entryway that's shaped like a puma's head. Discounts are available for longer stays.

Atocsaycuchi 616. www.secondhomecusco.com. ✆ **084/235-873.** 3 units. $120 doubles. Rates include breakfast and airport transfers. **Amenities:** Wi-Fi (free).

INEXPENSIVE

Amaru Inca ★   This cheery yellow republican house in San Blas, hugging a large garden patio with stellar city views, has some of the best value accommodations in Cusco. Regular renovations and improvements mean it isn't as inexpensive as it once was, but it still attracts backpackers looking for something more than just a dormitory-style bed and unwilling to break the bank. The decor, with its handicraft market paintings of Andean life, borders on kitschy. There is natural light aplenty, plus some interesting wood and stonework. Rooms come in a range of sizes. Overall, Amaru is a friendly and relaxed spot that gets a lot of return visitors. If the hostel is full, the same owners have a couple of simpler properties elsewhere in and around San Blas, like Amaru Colonial and Hostal Mallqui, a youth hostal.

Cuesta San Blas 541. 16 units. www.amaruhostal.com. ✆ **084/225-933.** $60–$85 doubles. Rates include continental breakfast. **Amenities:** Coffee shop; Wi-Fi (free).

Casa de Campo Hostal ★   At a midpoint between the Plaza de Armas and Sacsayhuamán, high up on a San Blas hillside, Casa de Campo has a vibe more reminiscent of a more rural Sacred Valley hotel. The chalet-style rooms are rustic and small, with wool blankets and wood beams. They're spread out on three levels. Vegetation grows everywhere and covers everything on the property, from the terraced gardens to the facade. The major challenge is the location and the walk there (then walking up stairs to the rooms), though the trade-off is its phenomenal views of the city.

Tandapata 298, San Blas, Cusco. www.hotelcasadecampo.com. ✆ **084/244-404.** 49 units. $70 doubles; $100–$120 suites. Rates include breakfast buffet. **Amenities:** Restaurant.

Casona Les Pleiades ★   This clean, functional B&B with French owners won't wow you, but it has a lot going for it. The rooms are bright and cheery and there's usually a towel elephant or towel swan on the bed to make you smile. Rooms open up onto an interior patio, though lovelier is the sunny terrace with excellent views of Cusco below. The downside is that it's on a pedestrian-only street in San Blas, a steep walk with heavy luggage.

Tandapata 116, San Blas, Cusco. www.casona-pleiades.com. ✆ **084/506-430.** 7 units. $77–$82 doubles. Rates include breakfast. **Amenities:** Lounge; Wi-Fi (free).

Hospedaje Turístico San Blas ★   This airy colonial house is right on San Blas's main drag, only about halfway up so the climb there isn't too strenuous. The rooms are basic and most lack natural light, so when not sleeping you will likely migrate to the glassed-in courtyard with standing heaters and couches, or the sun terrace with good views. It's a good place to meet up with fellow travelers.

Cuesta San Blas 526, San Blas, Cusco. www.sanblashostal.com. ✆ **084/244-481.** 20 units. $44–$54 doubles. Rates include continental breakfast and airport pickup. No credit cards. **Amenities:** Coffee shop; Wi-Fi (free).

SIDE TRIPS FROM CUSCO

Many visitors "do" Machu Picchu in a single day, taking a morning train out and a late-afternoon train back to Cusco. For possibly the most impressive creation of humanity you might ever see, that's just not enough time there, in my opinion. Still, that's all many people have time for. The Sacred Valley villages and famed markets (especially Pisac and Chinchero) also constitute day trips for loads of travelers. Again, though, the area is so rich and offers so much for travelers with time to do more than whiz through it, that the area—including Pisac, Urubamba, Ollantaytambo, Chinchero, and Moray—is treated separately in Chapter 7, as is the great Inca ruins of Machu Picchu in Chapter 8.

A Cusco-area **ruins hike,** either on foot or on horseback, of the Inca sites within walking distance of the capital—Sacsayhuamán, Q'enko, Puca Pucara, and Tambomachay—makes for a splendid day-long excursion (or half-day, if you make at least some use of public transportation or a taxi). For more information on the individual sites, see "Inca Ruins near Cusco," earlier in this chapter.

Adventure travelers might want to concentrate on other **outdoor sports** that can be done around Cusco, including treks, biking excursions, and whitewater rafting. See the "Extreme Sacred Valley: Outdoor Adventure Sports" box in Chapter 7.

Paucartambo ★★

110km (68 miles) NE of Cusco

Most visitors who venture to very remote Paucartambo (and there aren't many of them) do so for the annual mid-July **Fiesta de la Virgen del Carmen ★★★**, one of Peru's most outrageously celebrated festivals (it lasts several days, and most attendees, be they villagers or foreigners, camp out because there is nowhere else to stay); see the "Cusco's Spectacular Celebrations" box on p. 136 for more details. Yet the beautiful, small, and otherwise quiet mountain village might certainly be visited during the dry season (May–Oct) if you've got the patience to venture way off the beaten track. A few travelers stop en route to jungle destinations like Puerto Maldonado and the Manu Biosphere Reserve.

The peaceful colonial town, once a mining colony, has cobblestone streets and a lovely Plaza de Armas with white structures and blue balconies, but not a whole lot else—that is, until it is inundated by revelers donning wildly elaborate and frequently frightening masks, and drinking as if Paucartambo were the last surviving town on the planet. The colorful processions and traditional dances are spectacular, and a general sense of abandonment of inhibitions (senses?) reigns. Mamacha Carmen, as she's known locally, is the patron saint of the *mestizo* population. During the festival, there's a small office of tourist information on the south side of the plaza. More information on the celebrations is available from the main tourist office in Cusco (p. 117).

AND THEN THERE WERE 12: THE inca EMPERORS

The Inca Empire, one of the greatest the Americas have ever known, had 12 rulers over its lifetime from the late 12th century to the mid–16th century. The emperors, or chieftains, were called Incas; the legendary founder of the dynasty was Manco Cápac. The foundations of the palaces of the sixth and eighth leaders, Inca Roca and Viracocha Inca, respectively, are still visible in Cusco. Pachacútec was a huge military figure, the Inca responsible for creating a great, expansive empire. He was also an unparalleled urban planner. He made Cusco the capital of his kingdom, and, under his reign, the Incas built Qoricancha, the fortresses at Pisac and Ollantaytambo in the Sacred Valley, and mighty Machu Picchu. Huayna Cápac, who ruled in the early 16th century, was the last Inca to oversee a united empire. He divided the Inca territory, which, by that time,

stretched north to Ecuador and south to Bolivia and Chile, between his sons, Huáscar and Atahualpa, which resulted in a disastrous civil war. Atahualpa eventually defeated his brother but was captured by Francisco Pizarro in Cajamarca and killed by the Spaniards in 1533, which led to the ultimate downfall of the Incas. The 12 Incas, in order, are as follows:

1. Manco Cápac
2. Sinchi Roca
3. Lloque Yupanqui
4. Mayta Cápac
5. Cápac Yupanqui
6. Inca Roca
7. Yahuar Huácac
8. Viracocha Inca
9. Pachacútec
10. Tupac Inca
11. Huayna Cápac
12. Atahualpa

Depending on when you visit, you might be able to get a simple bed at one of several small and very basic inexpensive inns in town, like the **Hostal Quinta Rosa Marina** and the **Albergue Municipal,** neither of which has a phone.

Another 45km (28 miles) beyond Paucartambo is **Tres Cruces (Three Crosses)** ★, sacred to the nature-worshiping Incas and still legendary for its mystical sunrises in the winter months (May–July are the best). Tres Cruces occupies a mountain ridge at the edge of the Andes, before the drop-off to the jungle. From a rocky outcropping at nearly 4,000m (13,100 ft.) above sea level, hardy travelers congratulate themselves for having gotten there, as much as for the sight they've come to witness, as they gaze into the distance out over the dense, green Amazon cloud forest. The sunrise is full of intense colors and trippy optical effects (including multiple suns). Even for those lucky enough to have experienced the sunrise at another sacred Inca spot, Machu Picchu, it is truly a hypnotic sight.

Getting There   Gallinas de Rocas minibuses leave daily for Paucartambo from Cusco's Avenida Huáscar, near Garcilaso (departure times vary; the journey takes 4–6 hr.). For the Virgen del Carmen festival (July 15–17), some small agencies organize 2- and 3-day visits, with transportation, food, and camping gear (or arrangements for use of a villager's bed or floor) included. Look for posters in the days preceding the festival. To get to Tres Cruces, see whether any Cusco travel agencies are arranging trips; otherwise, you'll either have to hire a taxi from Cusco or hitchhike from Paucartambo. (Ask around; some villagers will be able to hook you up with a ride.) Make sure you leave in the middle of the night to arrive in time for the sunrise.

Tipón ★

23km (14 miles) SE of Cusco

Rarely visited by tourists, who are in more of a hurry to see the villages and Inca ruins of the Sacred Valley north of Cusco, the extensive complex of Tipón is nearly the equal of the more celebrated ruins found in Pisac, Ollantaytambo, and Chinchero. For fans of Inca stonemasonry and building technique, Tipón's well-preserved agricultural terracing is among the best created by the Incas and makes for a rewarding, if not easily accessible, visit. Peter Frost writes in "Exploring Cusco" (Nuevas Imágenes, 1999) that the terracing is so elaborately constructed that it might have been instrumental in testing complex crops rather than used for routine farming. Others have theorized that it may have been used as a park for Inca nobility. There are also baths, a temple complex, and irrigation canals and aqueducts that further reveal the engineering prowess of the Incas. The ruins are a healthy hour's climb (or more, depending on your physical condition) up a steep, beautiful path, or by car up a dirt road. The uncluttered distant views are tremendous. The truly adventurous and fit can continue above the first set of ruins to others perched even higher (probably another 2 hr. of climbing). During the rainy season (Nov–Mar), it's virtually impossible to visit Tipón.

Getting There *Combis* for "Urcos" leave from Avenida Huáscar in Cusco; request that the driver drop you off near Tipón, which is between the villages of Saylla and Oropesa. The site is 4km (2½ miles) from the highway; it's open daily from 7am to 5:30pm. Admission is by Cusco's *boleto turístico.*

Pikillacta & Rumicolca

38km (24 miles) SE of Cusco

These pre-Inca and Inca ruins might go unnoticed by most, were it not for their inclusion on the Cusco tourist ticket. Although the Cusco region is synonymous with the Incas, the Huari, and other cultures preceded them. **Pikillacta** is the only pre-Inca site of importance near Cusco. The Huari culture occupied the complex, a huge ceremonial center, from about A.D. 700 to 1100 before suddenly abandoning it. The two-story adobe buildings, of rather rudimentary masonry, aren't in particularly good shape, although they are surrounded by a defensive wall. Many small turquoise idols, today exhibited in the Museo Inka in Cusco, were discovered at Pikillacta.

Less than a kilometer from Pikillacta, across the main road, is **Rumicolca,** an Inca portal—a gateway to the Valle Sagrado—constructed atop the foundations of an ancient aqueduct that dates to the Huari. The difference in construction techniques is readily apparent. The site was a travel checkpoint controlling entry to the Cusco Valley under the Incas.

Getting There *Combis* for "Urcos" leave from Avenida Huáscar in Cusco and drop passengers for Pikillacta near the entrance. Both sites are open daily from 7am to 5:30pm. Admission is by Cusco's *boleto turístico.*

THE SACRED VALLEY

The Urubamba Valley was sacred to the Incas, and it's not hard to understand why. Better known as the Sacred Valley, it's a serene and incomparably lovely stretch of small villages and ancient ruins spread across a broad plain, split by the Urubamba River and framed by magnificent Andes peaks and a massive sky. The Incas built several of the empire's greatest estates, temples, and royal palaces between the sacred centers of Cusco and Machu Picchu, positioned like great bookends at the south and north ends of the valley. Many visitors use the valley as a base for visiting the region, as it's about 300m (1,000 ft.) lower than Cusco, making it a better introduction for visitors prone to altitude-related health problems.

History   The entire valley is suffused by the great, if brief, presence of the Incas. From extraordinary temples to fortresses, no region in Peru is more marked by the continent-spanning civilization. Today, Quechua-speaking residents work fields with primitive tools and harvest salt using methods unchanged since the days of the Incas.

Sightseeing   The Valle Sagrado has taken off as a destination on its own, rather than just a blitzkrieg-style coach trip. There are superb ruins, traditional markets and villages, and cultural attractions of every sort. Several highlights, such as the ruins of Pisac and Ollantaytambo, as well as the market town of Chinchero, are visited as part of Cusco's *boleto turístico*.

Nature   Through the verdant valley rolls the revered Río Urubamba, a pivotal religious element of the Incas' cosmology (counterpart to the Milky Way). The fertile valley was a major center of agricultural production for native crops such as white corn, coca, and potatoes along terraced mountain slopes. And of course, the valley is surrounded on all sides by the stunningly beautiful Andes.

Where to Stay & Eat   Home to some of Peru's finest country lodges, the valley is perfect for either a relaxing pace or nonstop activity. The kings of swank and serenity are the Tambo del Inka and Inkaterra Hacienda Urubamba, but there are affordable alternatives like the Green House. Dining focuses on the produce and pseudo-grains that made the region the Incas' breadbasket.

Active Pursuits   The Sacred Valley region is one of the best in Peru for hiking, white-water rafting, mountain biking, and horseback riding. The classic treks to Machu Picchu steal much of the spotlight, but there are better trails here for adventurers seeking solitude and authenticity.

THE BEST TRAVEL EXPERIENCES IN THE SACRED VALLEY

o **Climbing to Pisac's ruins:** Leave the busy artisans' market behind and hike the trail up the mountainside to the Inca fortress ruins. At the top are spectacular views of the valley's agricultural terracing, mountain vistas, and Pisac laid out beneath your feet. See p. 173.

o **Appreciating Ollanta's genius:** In the shadow of imposing ruins is a superb example of Inca engineering: Ollantaytambo's 15th-century grid of *canchas,* a masterful urban plan of cobblestone streets, courtyards, and canals that still carry water rushing down from the mountains. See p. 192.

o **Instagramming Maras and Moray:** One site contains circular terraces carved out of the earth with a purpose that remains a mystery, while the other features pre-Inca salt ponds that hang off a steep mountainside. Get your camera ready, because these sites are as photogenic as Machu Picchu. See p. 179.

o **Kicking back at a luxe hotel:** Revel in the lower altitude and greater serenity of the Urubamba Valley by relaxing at a country hotel, complete with spa, stunning views, and all the activities you could want—or not. See p. 185.

o **Strolling in the valley:** The pretty and rural Urubamba Valley is perfect for gentle walks. Choose between a steep walk up from Pisac town to the ruins or a leisurely hike amid Andean meadows in the Chicón Valley, among others. See p. 172.

PISAC ★★

32km (20 miles) NE of Cusco

The pretty Andean village of Pisac lies at the eastern end of the valley. Although prized principally for its hugely popular Sunday artisan market, an obligatory stop on most Sacred Valley tours, Pisac deserves to be more widely recognized for its splendid Inca ruins, which rival Ollantaytambo. Perched high on a cliff is the largest fortress complex built by the Incas, with commanding, distant views from atop the mountain, over a luxuriously long valley of green patchwork fields.

Essentials

Getting There   A *combi* or *colectivo* (S/4) from Cusco (Calle Puputi s/n, Cdra. 2; no phone) to Pisac takes 45 minutes to an hour, dropping passengers just across the river at the edge of town, a 3-block walk uphill from the main

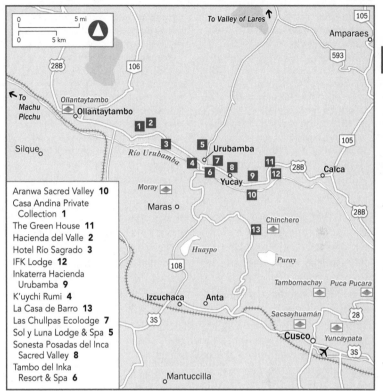

Aranwa Sacred Valley **10**
Casa Andina Private Collection **1**
The Green House **11**
Hacienda del Valle **2**
Hotel Río Sagrado **3**
IFK Lodge **12**
Inkaterra Hacienda Urubamba **9**
K'uychi Rumi **4**
La Casa de Barro **13**
Las Chullpas Ecolodge **7**
Sol y Luna Lodge & Spa **5**
Sonesta Posadas del Inca Sacred Valley **8**
Tambo del Inka Resort & Spa **6**

square (and market). From Pisac, buses return to Cusco and depart for other parts of the valley—Yucay, Urubamba (both a half-hour journey), and Ollantaytambo (1 hr.)—from the same spot. Although a taxi to Pisac on your own costs about S/35 to S/40, it is often possible to go by hastily arranged private car for as little as S/10 per person. Private cars congregate near the bus terminal and leave when they have three or four passengers; just get in and ask the price (everyone pays the same fare).

Visitor Information   You're best off getting information on Pisac and the entire Sacred Valley before leaving Cusco at the **Tourist Information Office,** Mantas 117-A, a block from the Plaza de Armas (✆ **084/263-176**) or the **iPéru office,** Av. El Sol 103, Of. 102 (✆ **084/252-974**). Cusco's **South American Explorers Club,** Av. Pardo 847 (www.saexplorers.org; ✆ **084/245-484**) is also an excellent source of information, particularly on the Inca Trail and alternative treks, mountaineering, and white-water rafting in the valley. Inquire there about current conditions and updated transportation alternatives. Beyond that, the best sources of information are hotels.

Local buses (usually small *combis* or *colectivos*) are the easiest and cheapest way to get to and around the Sacred Valley. They are often full of local color, if not much comfort. (Tall people forced to stand will not find them much fun.) Buses to towns and villages in the Sacred Valley—primarily to Pisac, Urubamba, and Chinchero—use small, makeshift terminals on Calle Puputi s/n, Cdra. 2, and Av. Grau s/n, Cdra. 1, in Cusco. They leave regularly throughout the day, departing when full; no advance reservations are required. Fares are S/4.

You can also hire a taxi from Cusco to get to any of the valley towns or for a day-long tour of the Sacred Valley—expect to pay about S/90 to S/120. Shared private cars (*autos*) to Urubamba leave from Calle Pavitos 567, with four passengers per car (they're generally station wagons with room for luggage in back and take just 50 min.).

Tours   Pretty much every Cusco travel agency offers a good-value, 1-day Sacred Valley tour (as little as $25 per person for a full-day guided tour), and most provide English-speaking guides. The tours generally include Pisac, Ollantaytambo, and Chinchero. It's not enough time to explore the ruins, though a quickie tour gives at least a taste of the valley's charms. The first Sacred Valley visit on most itineraries is Pisac. Although you will travel comfortably by chartered, air-conditioned bus and will not have to worry about connections, you won't be able to manage your time at each place (indeed, you'll have precious little time in each place—only enough for a quick look around and a visit to ruins or the local market).

Fast Facts   There's an **ATM** on the main square, but it's probably wise to exchange much of the money you'll need before leaving Cusco, especially if coming on Sunday to the crowded market. There's a **post office** on the corner of Comercio and Intihuatana.

Exploring Pisac

Pisac (also spelled Pisaq) has few items of interest to most visitors, but two are biggies: the market and the hilltop ruins. You could manage a superficial visit to both in just a couple of hours, but an in-depth visit, especially if hiking to the ruins, requires a full morning or afternoon. The Jardín Botanico, on the other hand, is unknown to most tourists who pass through, though if you have the time, it's worth a quick visit.

JARDÍN BOTÁNICO FELIPE MARÍN MORENO ★

Set within an interior courtyard just 1 block from Pisac's main plaza, it's a wonder why more tourists don't notice this pleasant botanical garden (© **084/635-563**). Created in 1917 by Felipe Marín Moreno, a Peruvian botanist and explorer, the garden is where he could experiment with native plants and seeds, as well as those he collected from various institutions and botanists around the world. Of particular interest are the more than 100 types of cactus and 200 types of potatoes in the garden, which is now managed by Marín's son. The entrance is at Calle Grau 485. Admission is S/6. The garden is open daily from 9am to 4pm, though there's not always someone at the entrance, so you might need to ring the bell or wait around for a little while until someone can let you in.

PISAC MARKET ★★

Pisac's extremely popular *mercado,* or artisan market, draws many hundreds of shoppers on Sunday morning in high season, when it is without a doubt one of the liveliest in Peru. (There are slightly less popular markets the rest of the week as well.) Hundreds of stalls crowd the central square—marked by a small church, San Pedro el Apóstolo, and massive *pisonay* trees—and spill down side streets. Traditionally, sellers came from many different villages, many of them remote populations high in the Andes, and wore the dress typical of their village, though this is becoming less the norm as products are increasingly mass-produced and stalls are set up every day of the week. Dignitaries from the local villages usually lead processions after Mass (said in Quechua), dressed in their versions of Sunday finery. The market is much like Cusco: touristy but endearing, and an essential experience in Peru. If you've never been to a Peruvian market, this is the place to start, though the market at Chinchero (p. 182) strikes me as considerably more authentic.

The goods at the market—largely sweaters and ponchos, tapestries and rugs, musical instruments, and carved gourds—are familiar to anyone who's spent a day in Cusco, but prices are occasionally lower on selected goods such as ceramics. While tourists shop for colorful weavings and other souvenirs, locals are busy buying and selling produce on small streets leading off the plaza. The market begins at around 9am and lasts until mid-afternoon. It is so well-worn on the Cusco tourist circuit that choruses of *"¿Foto? Propinita"* (photograph for a small tip) ring out among the mothers and would-be mothers here to show off their children, dressed up in adorable local outfits.

PISAC RUINS ★★

The Pisac ruins are some of the finest and largest in the entire valley. Despite the excellent condition of many of the structures, little is conclusively known about the site's actual purpose. It appears to have been part city, part ceremonial center, and part military complex. It might have been a royal estate of the Inca emperor Pachacútec. It was certainly a religious temple, and although it

Boleto Turístico in the Valle Sagrado

The Cusco *boleto turístico* (tourist pass) is essential for visiting the Sacred Valley, in particular the ruins of Pisac and Ollantaytambo, as well as the market and town of Chinchero. You can purchase it at any of those places if you haven't already bought it in Cusco before traveling to the valley. You can also purchase the partial ticket that just covers the Sacred Valley sites if you aren't planning to make use of the full ticket in Cusco. See p. 125 in Chapter 6 for more information.

was reinforced with the ramparts of a massive citadel, the Incas never retreated here to defend their empire against the Spaniards (and Pisac was, unlike Machu Picchu, known to Spanish forces).

The best but most time-consuming way to see the ruins is to climb the hillside, following an extraordinary path that is itself a slice of local life. Trudging along steep mountain paths is still the way most Quechua descendants from remote villages get around these parts; many people you see at the Pisac market will have walked a couple of hours or more through the mountains to get there. To get to the ruins on foot (about 5km/3 miles, or 60 min.), you'll need to be pretty fit and/or willing to take it very slowly. Begin the ascent at the back of Pisac's main square, to the left of the church. (If you haven't already purchased a *boleto turístico,* required for entrance, you can do so at the small guard's office at the beginning of the path as you climb out of town.) The path bends to the right through agricultural terraces. There appear to be several competing paths; all of them lead up the mountain to the ruins. When you come to a section that rises straight up, choose the extremely steep stairs to the right. (The path to the left is overgrown and poorly defined.) If an arduous trek is more than you've bargained for, you can hire a taxi in Pisac (easier done on market days) to take you around the back way. (The paved road is some 9.5km/6 miles long.) If you arrive by car or *colectivo* rather than by your own power, the ruins will be laid out the opposite way to that described below.

From a semicircular terrace and fortified section at the top, called the **Qorihuayrachina,** the views south and west of the gorge and valley below and agricultural terraces creeping up the mountain slopes are stunning. Deeper into the nucleus, the delicately cut stones are some of the best found at any Inca site. The most important component of the complex, on a plateau on the upper section of the ruins, is the **Templo del Sol (Temple of the Sun),** one of the Incas' most impressive examples of masonry. The temple was an astronomical observatory. The **Intihuatana,** the so-called "hitching post of the sun," resembles a sundial but actually was an instrument that helped the Incas to determine the arrival of important growing seasons rather than to tell the time of day. Nearby (just paces to the west) is another temple, thought to be the **Templo de la Luna (Temple of the Moon),** and beyond that is a ritual bathing complex, fed by water canals. Continuing north from this section, you

---

The Virgen del Carmen Festival

Pisac celebrates the Virgen del Carmen festival (July 16–18) with nearly as much enthusiasm as the more remote and more famous festival in Paucartambo (p.194). It's well worth visiting Pisac during the festival if you are in the area.

---

can either ascend a staircase path uphill, which forks, or pass along the eastern (right) edge of the cliff. If you do the latter, you'll arrive at a tunnel that leads to a summit lookout at 3,400m (11,200 ft.). A series of paths leads from here to defensive ramparts **(K'alla Q'asa),** a ruins sector called **Qanchisracay,** and the area where taxis wait to take passengers back to Pisac.

In the hillside across the Quitamayo gorge, at the back side (north end) of the ruins, are hundreds of dug-out holes where *huaqueros* (grave robbers) have ransacked a cemetery that was among the largest known Inca burial sites.

The ruins are open daily from 7am to 5:30pm; admission is by Cusco's *boleto turístico* (p. 125). Note that to explore the ruins thoroughly by foot, including the climb from Pisac, you'll need 3 to 4 hours, though about half that if you stick to the main area by the road. Most people visit Pisac as part of a whirlwind day tour through the valley, which doesn't allow enough time either at the market or to visit the ruins. Taxis leave from the road near the bridge and charge around S/15 to S/20 to take you up to the ruins.

Where to Eat in Pisac

For eats in Pisac, there are several good restaurants right on the plaza, most with similar menus. Check out funky little corner cafe **Blue Llama ★** (℗ **084/203-135**), decorated like a children's book, with excellent breakfasts like fluffy waffles or French toast, plus juices and sandwiches. **Ulrike's Café ★**, Plaza de Armas 828 (℗ **084/203-195**), run by a German expat, has breakfast to hearty lunches and vegetarian options, such as homemade lasagna, omelets, salads, and great desserts (like Ulrike's famous strudel or any number of cheesecakes). **Mullu Café ★** (www.mullu.pe; ℗ **084/203-073**) is the most interesting, serving local ingredients like Ayaviri lamb, alpaca, and quinoa with a touch of Asian fusion. For a snack or lunch on the run, check out the excellent *hornos coloniales* (colonial bakeries), which use traditional, wood-fired ovens; one, called **Horno Colonial Santa Lucía,** is near the southwest corner of the main square next to Hotel Pisaq, while another (unnamed) is on Mariscal Castilla 372, a short walk from the plaza. Both serve excellent empanadas and breads, and are especially popular on market days (often selling out of empanadas by 2pm). Another good lunch or dinner option is **Ayahuasca,** Bolognesi s/n (℗ **084/797-625**), a cute little cafe a couple of blocks from the plaza, on the way to the bus stops. You can get a simply prepared but very good-value menu (*lomo saltado* [beef and potato stir-fry] and other classic Peruvian highlander dishes) for just S/10. Pick up chocolate at the **Choco Museo** (www.chocomuseo.com; ℗ **084/203-020**), as well as chocolate drinks or cakes. Inquire within about chocolate-making workshops.

Where to Stay in Pisac

If either of the two places below is full or beyond your budget, check out these inexpensive basic inns in town: **Hospedaje Chaska Pisac,** Av. Amazonas 124 (www.pisachotel.com; ℗ **084/903-086**), centrally located at the entrance to town on the river, with a nice garden and communal kitchen, offering private rooms and shared backpacker dorms; or **Hostal Varayoq,** Mariscal Castilla 380 (℗ **084/620-803**), a basic inn with good Wi-Fi and free breakfast near the plaza.

MODERATE

Paz y Luz ★   This hotel and healing center, owned by New Yorker Diane Dunn, author of the book "Cusco: Gateway to Inner Wisdom," is set 1km (.6 mile)

EXTREME sacred VALLEY: OUTDOOR ADVENTURE SPORTS

Peru is a star on South America's burgeoning adventure and extreme sports circuit, a far cry from when just traveling to Peru was adventure enough. These days, many gringos in Peru have Gore-Tex boots on their feet and adrenaline rushes on their minds.

The Cusco–Sacred Valley region is one of the best in Peru—and all of South America—for white-water rafting, mountain biking, trekking, and horseback riding. Many tour operators in Cusco organize adventure trips, some lasting a single day and some lasting multiple days, with a focus on one or more extreme sports. Participants range from novices to hard-core veteran adventure junkies; no experience is required for many trips, but make sure you sign up for a program appropriate for your level of interest and ability. I suggest that you thoroughly check out potential agencies and speak directly to the guides, if possible. Booking a tour in Cusco rather than your home country may lead to a large discount. Trips booked in advance may be changed if there are not enough participants, or farmed out to another subcontracting agency.

Bungee Jumping & Zipline Action Valley Cusco Adventure Park, Calle Santa Teresa 325 (Plazoleta Regocijo), Cusco (www.actionvalley.com; ℂ 084/240-835), is an adventure park

11km (7 miles) from Cusco, with not just bungee jumping but paintball and other suspended-line activities, such as "swing" and "slingshot." **Cola de Mono Canopy** (www.canopyperu.com; ℂ 084/509-742) claims to operate one of the highest ziplines in South America; zip among the lush treetops of Santa Teresa, 15km (9 miles) from Machu Picchu, at speeds of up to 48 kmph (30 mph).

Horseback Riding Perol Chico, Carretera Urubamba-Ollantaytambo Km 77, Urubamba (www.perolchico.com; ℂ 01/950-314-065 or 01/950-314-066) is a ranch in the Sacred Valley and one of the top horseback-riding agencies in Peru. It offers full riding vacations, with Peruvian Paso horses and stays at the ranch (in rustic cottages), as well as from 1-day to up to 11-day rides.

Mountain Biking Mountain biking is catching on in Peru, and tour operators are rapidly expanding their services and equipment. Cusco's nearby ruins and the towns, villages, and gorgeous scenery of the Sacred Valley (and the Manu jungle, for more adventurous excursions) are the best areas. **Peru Discovery** (www.perudiscovery.com; ℂ 054/274-541) and **Gravity Peru** (www.gravityperu.com; ℂ 084/228-032) are two of the top specialists, with a half-dozen bike trips that include hard-core excursions. **Amazonas**

away from town on the road to Pisac's ruins. It began as a few rooms in Dunn's house, but has grown to almost two dozen, along with a restaurant, healing rooms, and conference space. As the name Peace and Light suggests, there's a new-age spin to this hotel, which offers Andean healing workshops, meditation, and sacred-plant ceremonies. Rooms are quite simple with wood floors, Andean artwork, and splendid views of the Pisac ruins and surrounding valley.

Carretera Pisac Ruinas s/n. www.pazyluzperu.com. ℂ 084/216-293. 25 units. S/220 doubles; S/260 suites (weekly and monthly rates available). Rates include continental

Explorer, **Apumayo Expediciones, Eric Adventures** (for contact information, see "White-Water Rafting," below), and **Manu Adventures** (www.manu adventures.com; © **084/261-640** or 213/283-6987 in the U.S. or Canada), offer 1- to 5-day organized mountain-biking excursions ranging from easy to rigorous. For a locally based group, including mountain bike rentals and extended as well as shorter cyclotourism rides around Urubamba, contact Omar Zarzar at **Eco Montana** (www.ecomon-tana.com). A popular day's ride is from Moray to Salineras de Maras.

Paragliding Now that you can no longer hop a helicopter to Machu Picchu, there are other less intrusive ways to get aerial views of the Sacred Valley. **Flying Expedition** (www.flyingexpedition.org; © **084/239-476**) runs tandem paragliding trips from Cerro Sacro near Chinchero with licensed pilots. **Parapente Cusco** (www.parapentecusco.com; © **084/670-144**) runs tandem trips from Mauq'a Taray near Pisac, including transfer from your hotel in Cusco.

Trekking In addition to the groups listed in "Inca Trail Agencies" (p. 216) and "The Road Less (or More Comfortably) Traveled: Alternatives to the Inca Trail" (p. 220), which organize Inca Trail and other regional treks, these companies handle a variety of trekking excursions: **Andina Travel** (www.andinatravel.

com; © **084/251-892**); **Aventours** (www.aventours.com; © **084/224-050**); **Enigma** (www.enigmaperu.com; © **084/222-155**); **Manu Expeditions** (www.manuexpeditions.com; © **084/225-990**); **Mountain Lodges of Peru** (www.mountainlodgesofperu.com; © **084/262-640**); **Andean Treks** ★★ (www.andeantreks.com; © **800/683-8148** or 617/924-1974); and **Peru for Less** ★★ (www.peruforless.com; © **817/230-4971**). **Peru Discovery** (see "Mountain Biking," above) also organizes excellent trekking expeditions.

White-Water Rafting There are some terrific Andean river runs near Cusco, ranging from mild Class II to moderate and world-Class IV and V, including 1-day Urubamba River trips (Huambutío–Pisac and Ollantaytambo–Chillca), multi-day trips to the more difficult Apurímac River, and, for hard-core rafters, the Tambopata (10 days or more) in the Amazon jungle. Recommended agencies include **Amazonas Explorer** ★★ (www.amazonas-explorer.com; © **084/252-846**); **Apumayo Expediciones** (www.apumayo.com; © **084/246-018**); **Eric Adventures** (www.ericadventures.com; © **084/272-862**); **Loreto Tours** (www.loretotours.com; © **084/228-264**); **Mayuc** (www.mayuc.com; © **084/242-824**); and **Swissraft Peru** ★ (www.swissraft-peru.com; © **084/264-124**).

breakfast. **Amenities:** Restaurant, 2 healing rooms; workshops and sacred-plant ceremonies; Wi-Fi.

Pisaq Inn ★★ Right on Pisac's main plaza overlooking the market stalls, this charming inn is run by a friendly Peruvian–American couple who also operate a tour company, and is the best option in town. The colorful rooms have hardwood floors and are decorated with Andean textiles and handcrafted furnishings. The hotel's restaurant, Cuchara de Palo, has a wood-burning oven and serves dishes with produce from a local organic farm. A small spa with reasonably priced massages and a flower-filled courtyard round out the amenities.

Plaza Constitución 333. www.pisacinn.com. © **084/203-062.** 11 units. S/183–S/237 doubles. Rates include breakfast. **Amenities:** Restaurant; bar; sauna; computer room; Wi-Fi.

URUBAMBA & ENVIRONS ★★

78km (48 miles) NW of Cusco

Centrally located Urubamba, the transportation hub of the valley, is also its busiest and best equipped to handle visitors. The town itself doesn't have a whole lot more than a handsome main plaza and a few restaurants to offer, but the surrounding region is lovely, and several of the best hotels in the region are located within a radius of a few miles, either just south near Yucay, an attractive colonial village, or north on the road toward Ollantaytambo. The area as a whole makes a fine base from which to explore the Sacred Valley.

Essentials
GETTING THERE
By Bus   To Urubamba (1½–2 hr. from Cusco), you can go either via Pisac or via Chinchero (a slightly more direct route). Buses, or *combis* (S/6), depart from Av. Grau s/n, Cdra. 1, in Cusco and arrive at **Terminal Terrestre** (no phone), the main bus terminal, about a kilometer from town on the main road to Ollantaytambo. Buses from the Urubamba terminal depart for Cusco and Chinchero (1 hr.), as well as Ollantaytambo (30 min.). *Combis* for other points in the Sacred Valley depart from the intersection of the main road at Avenida Castilla, for S/1 to S/3. To continue on to Yucay, just a couple of kilometers down the road, catch a *mototaxi* or a regular taxi in Urubamba or a *colectivo* along the highway (headed east, the opposite direction of the bus terminal from town).

By Taxi   From Cusco, you can catch a cab to Urubamba for about S/60 to S/70. Shared cars in Cusco leave from Calle Pavitos 567 for Urubamba; they charge just S/10 per person and take about an hour. If you're headed directly to the valley upon arrival in Cusco, have your hotel arrange for pickup at the airport. You can easily negotiate for the driver to take you to Pisac or Chinchero to visit the markets for a brief stopover along the way. For taxi or mini-van trips around the valley, try **Cusco Taxi** (www.officialcuscotaxi.com; © **084/652-880**).

VISITOR INFORMATION
You should pick up information on the Sacred Valley before leaving Cusco, at the main **Tourist Information Office,** Mantas 117-A, a block from the Plaza de Armas (© **084/263-176**); at **iPerú,** Av. El Sol 103, Of. 102 (© **084/252-974**), or from Cusco's **South American Explorers Club,** Av. Pardo 847 (www.saexplorers.org; © **084/245-484**). In Urubamba, you might be able to

scare up some limited assistance at Av. Cabo Conchatupa s/n; in Yucay, try the office of **Turismo Participativo,** Plaza Manco II 103 (© **084/201-099**).

FAST FACTS

If you need cash, you'll find ATMs on either side of the main road to Yucay from Urubamba. For medical assistance, go to **Centro de Salud,** Av. Cabo Conchatupa s/n (© **084/201-334**), or **Hospital del Instituto Peruano de Seguridad Social,** Av. 9 de Noviembre s/n (© **084/201-032**). If you need a post office in Urubamba, you'll find one on the Plaza de Armas.

Exploring Urubamba

The main square of Urubamba, the **Plaza de Armas,** is attractively framed by a twin-towered colonial church and pisonay trees. Dozens of *mototaxis,* a funky form of local transportation not seen in other places in the valley (and widely seen in only a few other places in Peru), buzz around the plaza in search of passengers. The most activity is around the **market,** at the corner of Jirón Comercio and Jirón Sucre, a sprawling produce market that spills into the surrounding streets. With few tourists exploring this maze of unique tubers and seasonal fruits, it's one of the more authentic markets in the Sacred Valley.

Worth visiting in town is the beautiful home workshop of **Pablo Seminario ★**, a ceramicist whose whimsical work features pre-Columbian motifs and is sold throughout Peru. Visitors either love or hate the style, which was once sold by Pier 1 Imports in the U.S. The grounds of the house, located at Berriozábal 405 (www.ceramicaseminario.com; © **084/201-002**), feature a mini-zoo, with llamas, parrots, nocturnal monkeys, falcons, rabbits, and more. The workshop is open daily from 8am to 7pm.

Yucay, just south of Urubamba, is a pleasant and quiet little village with extraordinary views of the surrounding countryside. The Spaniards "bequeathed" the land to their puppet Inca chieftain, Sayri Túpac, who built a palace here. Inca foundations are found around the attractive **main plaza,** and some of the best agricultural terracing in the valley occupies the slopes of mountains around the village. However, the most interesting sights are all beyond Urubamba: the ancient salt pans of Maras, the Inca site at Moray, and Chinchero, a historic market town.

The **Museo Inkariy ★** (www.museoinkariy.com; © **084/792-819**) opened in 2014, after more than a decade of planning by a group of artists and archaeologists, outside of town at Km 53, near Calca on the road to Pisac. The museum is very family-friendly and makes a good general introduction to the major civilizations that formed in Peru, each one with a two-room house filled with artifacts, colorful graphics, and various easy-to-understand displays.

SALINERAS DE MARAS ★★

10km (6 miles) NW of Urubamba

Near Urubamba (in the middle of the Sacred Valley between Urubamba and Ollantayambo) is the amazing sight of the **Salineras de Maras,** thousands of

Chicha Here, Get Your Warm Chicha

Throughout the valley, you'll see modest homes marked by long poles topped by red or white flags (or balloons). These *chicha* flags indicate that home-brewed fermented maize beer, or *chicha*, is for sale inside. What you'll usually find is a small, barren room with a handful of locals quietly drinking huge tumblers of pale yellow liquid. Tepid *chicha*, which costs next to nothing, is definitely an acquired taste.

individual ancient salt mines that form unique terraces in a hillside. The mines, small pools thickly coated with crystallized salt like dirty snow, have existed in the same spot since Inca days and are still operable. The salt has become a gourmet item in top restaurants around Peru. Families pass them down like deeds and continue the backbreaking and poorly remunerated tradition of salt extraction (crystallizing salt from subterranean spring water). Although the site as a whole is extraordinary and photogenic—from afar it looks like a patchwork quilt spread over a ravine, or a sprawling, multilevel cake with white and caramel-colored icing—it's surreal to watch workers standing ankle-deep and mining salt from one of nearly 6,000 pools cascading down the hillside. If you have a good sense of balance, you can walk among salt-encrusted paths to get close-up photographs. A small fee (S/5) is collected at the entrance, where a collection of small shops sells nicely packaged salts, salt carvings, and other gifts touched with Maras salt in some way. Opening hours are from dawn to dusk.

Getting There   To get to Maras, take a taxi from the Maras/Moray turnoff on the road from Chinchero to Urubamba (S/30 round-trip), where there are usually taxis waiting. Most visitors will combine a visit to Maras with a trip to Moray (S/70–S/80 round-trip from the turnoff, or around S/90 from Urubamba). Even better is the walk (5km/3 miles) along a path (a little over an hour) from the village of Maras, a route taken by some of the salt-mine workers (as if their work weren't grueling enough). Still more extreme and rewarding is the trek to the salt mines from the Inca ruins at Moray. It is one of the most stunningly beautiful walks in the region, a feast of blue-green cacti, deep red-brown earth, snowcapped mountains, plantings of corn and purple flowering potatoes, and small children tending to sheep. It's only for those who are in good shape, however; allow about 4 hours to cover the entire 14km (7½ miles), all the way out to the main Urubamba–Ollantaytambo road.

MORAY ★★
9km (5½ miles) NW of Maras

Among the wilder and more enigmatic Inca sites in Peru are the concentric ring terraces found in Moray. Unique in the Inca oeuvre, the site is not the ruins of a palace or fortress or typical temple, but what almost appears to be a large-scale environmental art installation. Three main sets of rings, like bowls, are set deep into the earth, forming strange sculpted terraces. The largest of the three has 15 levels. From above, they're intriguing, but it's even cooler to go down into them and contemplate their ancient functions. Many spiritually inclined travelers who come to the Sacred Valley for its special energy find that Moray possesses a very strong and unique vibe. The site may have had ritualistic purposes, but it was likely an agricultural development station where masterful and relentlessly curious farmers among the Incas tested experimental crops and conditions. The depressions in the earth (caused by erosion) produced intense microclimates, with remarkable differences in temperature from top to bottom, that the Incas were evidently studying. Moray is at its most spectacular after the end of the rainy season, when the terraces are a magnificent emerald green. Entrance to Moray is by Cusco *boleto turístico,* but you can also pay S/10 at the entrance if you don't have one.

Cusco Restaurants, which runs several of the top restaurants in Cusco, operates **El Parador de Moray** (www.cuscorestaurants.com; ✆ **084/254-753**) in a colonial house overlooking one of the terraces, offering a lunch buffet with advance notice.

Getting There   Moray is usually visited on a combined trip with Maras (see above), though from the Maras/Moray turnoff round-trip taxi fare is around S/40. Moray is removed from the main road that travels from Urubamba to Chinchero, so there is no public transportation of any kind. Increasingly, Sacred Valley tours are beginning to include the site on their itineraries.

CHINCHERO ★★
28km (17 miles) NW of Cusco

Popular among tour groups for its bustling Sunday market that begins promptly at 8am, Chinchero is spectacularly sited and much higher than the rest of the valley and even Cusco; at 3,800m (12,500 ft.) and far removed from the river, technically Chinchero doesn't belong to the Urubamba Valley. The sleepy village has gorgeous views of the snowy peak of Salcantay and the Vilcabamba and Urubamba mountain ranges in the distance. Sunset turns the fields next to the church—where child shepherds herd their flocks and grown men play soccer without goal posts—gold against the deepening blue sky.

It might once have been a great Inca city, but except on the main market day, Chinchero remains a graceful, traditional Andean Indian village. Its 15,000 inhabitants represent as many as 12 different indigenous communities. The town's main points of interest, in addition to the fine market, are the expansive main square, with a handsome colonial church made of adobe and built on Inca foundations, and some Inca ruins, mostly terraces that aren't quite as awe-inspiring today as their counterparts in Ollantaytambo and Pisac.

In the main plaza is a formidable and famous Inca wall composed of huge stones and 10 trapezoidal niches. The foundations once formed the palace of the late-15th-century Inca Tupac Yupanqui. The early-17th-century *iglesia* (church) ★ has some very interesting, if faded, frescoes outside under the porticoes and mural paintings that cover the entire ceiling. The church is open

Monday through Saturday from 9am to 5pm and Sunday from 9am to 6pm. Across the plaza is the **Museo de Sitio** (no phone), a rather spare municipal museum that holds a few Inca ceramics and instruments; it's open Tuesday through Sunday from 8am to 5pm, and admission is free.

The market comprises two marketplaces: one focusing on handicrafts; the other, mainly produce. The **Chinchero market ★★** is one of the best places in the entire valley for Andean textiles and common goods such as hats, gloves, and shawls. Even on Sunday, it is more authentic than the one at Pisac (although some visitors might find Pisac more lively and fun). Chinchero's sellers of *artesanía*—who are more often than not also the craftspeople, unlike the mere agents you'll find in Pisac and other places—dress in traditional garb, and even the kids seem less manipulative in pleading for your attention and *soles*. Midweek (especially Tues and Thurs), there are usually fewer sellers who set their wares on blankets around the main square, and you'll have a better chance of bargaining then. There are several small textile shops center in town with good quality items, too.

Through the terraces to the left of the church is a path leading toward a stream and to some finely sculpted Inca masonry, including stone steps, water canals, and huge stones with animal figures.

Nearly everyone visits Chinchero on a half-day visit from either Cusco or Urubamba; there's not much else in the way of infrastructure to detain you, although there are a handful of small shops and inexpensive restaurants in town or on the main road where the bus drops you off. One serving pretty good Andean specialties is **Merienda,** Calle Albergue s/n (www.restaurante-merienda.com; © **98/375-0516**), owned by a young couple that trained in some of Cusco's top restaurants. It's open daily from 8:30am to 8:30pm.

There are just a couple of spots in and around town to spend the night, the best of which is the charming adobe lodge **La Casa de Barro,** Calle Miraflores 147, beside the municipality (www.lacasadebarro.com; © **084/306-031;** $80 doubles), with a restaurant and 11 cheery rooms with wood floors.

Getting There *Colectivos* leave every half-hour or so from Tullumayo in Cusco for Chinchero (a 90-min. journey). Buses also leave every 20 minutes or so from the Terminal Terrestre in Urubamba (a 50-min. trip). Entrance to Chinchero—officially to just the market and church, but, in practice, to the whole town, it seems—is by *boleto turístico* (see p. 125). If you try to visit the church and main square without a *boleto,* you will be asked to purchase one (you can purchase the partial version that covers only Sacred Valley sites if you wish, rather than the entire Cusco ticket).

Where to Eat in Urubamba

Because so many hotels are scattered about the Urubamba region, and somewhat isolated, many guests, especially at the upscale accommodations, dine at their hotels; the major ones listed below (Tambo del Inka, Inkaterra, Casa Andina, Río Sagrado, and Sol y Luna) have good—but pricey for the area—restaurants. Perhaps best for drop-ins is the fine restaurant of IFK Lodge

(p. 187). Its restaurant, **Nunay** ★★★, overlooks the Urubamba River from a shaded terrace. Many of the ingredients are foraged for or sourced from local farmers within a few miles of the property and turned into *novo andino* specialties. Despite the relaxed setting, the food is rather progressive and beautifully plated. Call for reservations because the restaurant is often full with hotel guests.

The best and coolest restaurant directly in the town of Urubamba is **El Huacatay** ★★★, Jr. Arica 620 (www.elhuacatay.com; ℂ **084/201-790**), popular with wealthier Peruvians and visiting gringos. A few blocks from the main square, this surprising gourmet restaurant, in an old home built around a garden set back from a nondescript Urubamba street, is the perfect place for a long, relaxing lunch on the patio under bamboo shade or a more elegant dinner in the warm, intimate dining room (which has only five tables) or brightly colored lounge area. Run by a Peruvian chef Pío and his German wife Iris, the restaurant's chef-driven menu is a bit of a rarity in these parts, and it focuses on Andean specialties, such as quinoa soup, alpaca lasagna, and coca-infused gnocchi. Portions are large and attractively presented, and although fairly priced for the setting, service, and quality, the restaurant is more upscale than most in the area. The restaurant accepts only cash and Visa cards; reservations on weekends and evenings are recommended.

Another very good restaurant, also right in town, is **PaCa PaCa** ★, Av. Mariscal Castilla 640 (tel] **084/201-181**), a quirky, brightly painted eatery and shop located through a small colonial courtyard and up some stairs. The food is casual and eclectic, with a handful of pizzas (evenings only) and pastas, plus curry and a fun cocktail list. Downstairs in the same building is a great little sweets shop, **Las Marias** ★, with cakes, cookies, and coffee. **Tres Keros** ★, Avenida Sr. de Torrechayoc (main road Urubamba–Ollantaytambo), second floor (tel] **084/201-701**), is the work of a very hands-on chef and owner, Ricardo Behar (either unfailingly charming or a blowhard, depending on your disposition). He prepares surprisingly creative Peruvian cuisine, with great local ingredients and fish that comes in from the capital, at this cozy upstairs spot with a high, pitched bamboo ceiling and corner fireplace. The fresh salads, *lomo saltado* (made with beef tenderloin), and alpaca steak are particularly good, as is the small selection of wines. Lunch and dinner are served Monday through Saturday. A good spot for a simple breakfast or lunch of sandwiches, soups, and salads (you can also get lunch to go if you're off on a hike), is **Café Plaza,** Bolivar 440 (no phone). The wildly colorful little cafe also serves more sophisticated dishes, such as river trout and alpaca steak in pepper sauce, though you are better off sticking with something simple, like the *butifarra* and other sandwiches.

A unique valley restaurant for fine dining is **Huayoccari Hacienda Restaurant** ★★, Carretera Cusco–Urubamba, Km 64 (ℂ **084/962-2224** or 984/620-621 in Cusco), several miles southeast of Urubamba near the Inkaterra hotel. The restaurant, in an exceedingly elegant farmhouse high in the hills above the Sacred Valley, is tough to make reservations at and hard to find.

(It works almost exclusively with tour agencies, though most hotel receptions can also arrange lunches and dinners.) The $50 (cash only) prix-fixe menu starts with a pisco sour in the antique-filled common room or out among the gardens. Then diners, who feel as though they belong to an exclusive club, are admitted to the wood-paneled dining room—which has large picture windows framing views of the Andes—for a simple but well-prepared meal of local vegetables, soups (such as *crema de maiz*), and fresh river trout. The place is rather emphatically designed to feel like one is a guest in the home of a local agricultural patron. (And in fact, the home and restaurant belong to the Lambarri-Orihuela family, one of the valley's most distinguished and oldest families.)

Several restaurants are scattered about the main valley highway and cater to bus tours and groups that storm through the Sacred Valley three times a week on market day. **Tunupa,** Km 77, Carretera Pisaq–Ollantaytambo (on the left side of the road on the way to Ollanta; ✆ **084/963-0206**), owned by the same folks who own the restaurant of the same name in Cusco, is one of the most popular. In a massive, purpose-built hacienda with long corridors that form dining halls overlooking the Urubamba River, it's something akin to a Peruvian bier hall. Even though it can get crowded on market days at lunchtime, it's a fair value for an all-you-can-eat buffet for $20, including a pisco sour. Better is **Hacienda Alhambra** ★, Ctra. Urubamba–Ollantaytambo s/n (near Hotel Sol y Luna; ✆ **084/201-200**), a similar restaurant targeting bus tours, but in a more relaxed and intimate manner. The dining rooms are smaller, and there are tables outdoors under a thatched roof, with lovely garden and mountain views. Its buffets are daily from 10am to 3:30pm. On the main road to Ollantay, **Wayra,** Fundo Huincho Lote A-5 (www.hotelsolyluna.com/wayra; ✆ **084/201-620**), is an indoor/outdoor facility with wood-fired cooking run by the same owners as Sol y Luna Lodge. Besides the family-style lunch, there is a horse show.

Shopping

Aside from the famous valley handicrafts markets in **Pisac** and **Chinchero** and renowned ceramicist **Pablo Seminario** (see p. 179), Urubamba has just a few small shops that may be of interest to travelers. **PaCa PaCa,** Av. Mariscal Castilla 640 (tel] **084/201-181**), began as a shop at a different location, but today coexists with a small restaurant. It sells funky, colorful knit items like handbags and scarves. **Ecofería Tanpu,** on the second block of Calle Berriozabal, is a flea market that runs the first and third Sunday or every month, from 9am to 4pm. On sale are artisanal food products, handmade jewelry, clothes, and all sorts of original items.

Entertainment & Nightlife

Urubamba is a pretty sleepy town at night, and most guests stick close to their hotels, especially if they have early-morning plans. Best bets for a drink are the top-echelon hotel bars: **Chichi Wasi** (Sol y Luna Lodge & Spa); **El Bar del Huerto** (Hotel Río Sagrado), a lounge with views of the Urubamba River and a well-heeled rustic look; and **Kiri Bar** ★★ (Tambo del Inka), which has a super-chic cocktail bar just off the swank lobby, with high ceilings and a cool backlit onyx photography mural over the bar, as well as superb cocktails. See the section that follows for addresses of each. Additionally, there are a few small bars on Av. Mariscal Castilla frequented by the local community, though they never seem to last very long.

Where to Stay in Urubamba

This section of the Sacred Valley continues to attract hoteliers and developers, who all seem intent on adding new-country luxury resort hotels—a sure sign of the region's growing importance and affluence, at least in terms of foreign travelers. A simpler, in-town alternative to the more upscale hotels reviewed below is the pleasant and good-value **Posada Las Tres Marías,** Jr. Zavala 307, Urubamba (www.posadatresmarias.com; ✆ **084/201-006**), a modern house in the center of town with gardens and seven large rooms ($50 doubles).

VERY EXPENSIVE

Hotel Río Sagrado ★★   This stylish Belmond property beside the Urubamba River is built of natural materials, giving it the look of an Andean village from afar. As you get closer you notice the heated infinity pool and the chic guests drinking pisco sours on lounge chairs, then the spa and the two-story riverfront villas. The rooms are spacious, decorated in colorful Andean textiles, and all have a large private terrace, with suites adding a garden and double the square footage. Yoga classes, shaman ceremonies, and numerous outdoor activities can be booked directly from the hotel.

Km. 75.8, Carretera Cusco–Urubamba, Urubamba. www.belmond.com. ✆ **01/610-8300** for reservations or **084/201-631.** 21 units. $475 doubles; $525 suite; $1,025 villa. Rates include breakfast. **Amenities:** Restaurant; bar; concierge; exercise room; indoor/outdoor pool; spa; Wi-Fi.

Inkaterra Hacienda Urubamba ★★★   Upon opening in 2015, after eco-conscious hotelier Inkaterra had already had been working on a reforestation project in the surrounding mountains, locals began to notice that many of the native animals were showing up in greater numbers. Of all of the hotels in the Sacred Valley, Hacienda Urubamba, on a quiet hillside isolated from other hotels, is the most connected to the landscape. The included excursions differ from the standard Sacred Valley experiences and include exploring its sustainable farm, bird-watching, and a short hike in the mountains. Activity centers on the stunning main lodge, with a restaurant and lounge with a fireplace, designed of stone and large glass windows, resembling a colonial hacienda. Some of the posh rooms are there, though most are spread out around the property in standalone villas reached by golf cart. Every little extra you could imagine are inside, like heated towel racks, iPads, and complimentary minibars.

Km. 62, Carretera Cusco–Urubamba, Urubamba. www.inkaterra.com. ✆ **51/610-0400** for reservations. 32 units. $355–$405 doubles. Rates include breakfast and afternoon tea, plus some excursions. **Amenities:** Restaurant; bar; concierge; Wi-Fi.

Sol y Luna Lodge & Spa ★★ One of the oldest hotels in the Sacred Valley remains one of the best. Now part of the luxe Relais & Chateaux label, this chic country retreat has maintained its quality despite the growing numbers of better-known luxury brands that have become its competition. The property is set back from the road to Ollantaytambo, surrounded by beautiful gardens filled with wildflowers and hummingbirds. Decorated with Andean folk art, the *casitas,* topped with clay tiles, are designed from natural materials like stones, adobe bricks, and wood beams. The facilities here are the most comprehensive in the valley, beginning with the region's original spa with signature treatments and yoga classes, not to mention a farm-to-table restaurant and its own tour program.

Ctra. Urubamba–Ollantaytambo s/n, Huicho (2km/1¼ miles west of Urubamba). www.hotelsolyluna.com. ℭ **084/201-620.** 33 units. $350 doubles; $525 family bungalow. Rates include breakfast buffet. **Amenities:** Restaurant; pub; spa; room service; tour agency; Wi-Fi.

Tambo del Inka Resort & Spa ★★★ In terms of sheer luxury in the Sacred Valley, this Starwood Luxury Collection property designed by the celebrated Lima architect Bernardo Fort-Brescia is at the top. What's perhaps the hotel's biggest achievement is that it's not some out-of-place, modernist monstrosity, but that it only subtly stands out along the Urubamba riverfront in the middle of town. With nods to Inca design motifs and soaring two-story windows in common areas that take in the sacred *apus,* the contemporary interiors manage to be sumptuous and culturally aware. The rooms feature earthy tones and every top-of-the-line amenity you can think of. Aside from the hotel's own train station for service direct to Machu Picchu, the hotel's best features are a dramatic indoor/outdoor lap pool and one of the region's top spas with an extensive, impressive water circuit.

Avenida Ferrocarril s/n, Urubamba. www.starwoodhotels.com. ℭ **800/325-3589** in the U.S. and Canada or 01/581-777. 128 units. $276 and up doubles; $380–$525 suites. Rates include breakfast buffet. **Amenities:** Restaurant; bar; concierge; exercise room; indoor/outdoor pool; spa and water circuit; Wi-Fi.

EXPENSIVE

Aranwa Sacred Valley ★ The Sacred Valley location is the first and best property of the small Peruvian hotel group Aranwa. The sprawling, beautifully landscaped grounds are built around a 17th-century hacienda along the river, with numerous trails and a lake, not to mention a plethora of weird yet welcome extras like a movie theater, colonial chapel, art gallery, and top-notch spa with original treatments with Andean themes. Opt for the more interesting colonial rooms with antique furnishings in the original buildings if you want atmosphere, instead of the comfy but modern rooms that could be found anywhere. The enormous suites are some of the best in the Sacred Valley, set along the river or on the lake, adding kitchenettes and Jacuzzis.

Antigua Hacienda Yaravilca, Huayllabamba. www.aranwahotels.com. ℭ **01/434-1452** for reservations, or 084/205-080. 115 units. $200–$220 doubles; $710 and up suites. Rates include breakfast buffet. **Amenities:** 3 restaurants; bar; concierge; exercise room; outdoor pool; spa; theater; Wi-Fi.

Hacienda del Valle ★   Isolated, closer to Ollantaytambo than Urubamba, this quaint colonial-style inn feels far from the tourist herds elsewhere in the valley. The village-like property criss-crosses with streams, and from its hillside perch, there are fantastic views of the surrounding mountains. The rooms are spread out in clusters of stucco buildings with clay tile roofs. With their wood floors, clunky furnishings, and tile, rooms have a lived-in feel, though are still relatively well-kept. Getting in and out of the property can be problematic without private transportation or taxis, so be sure to add those expenses when factoring in the rate.

Quinto paradero, Yanahuara (sector Pucará). www.hhp.com.pe. ℂ **084/201-408.** 28 units. $180 doubles; $250 suites. Rates include breakfast buffet. **Amenities:** Restaurant; lounge; room service; Wi-Fi.

MODERATE

Casa Andina Private Collection ★   Peruvian hospitality group Casa Andina has gone downhill in recent years, though its properties, including this mountain-chalet type hotel that is part of its elite private collection group, are still a great value and in a nice setting. With so many other hotels moving into the area, this great but not spectacular hotel was forced to lower its prices and give its high-ceilinged rooms a face-lift in the first half of 2016, bringing the decor and amenities up to speed. The range of amenities includes an Andean-styled spa and a planetarium, a wonderful addition for the area's clear skies.

Quinto paradero, Yanahuara. www.casa-andina.com. ℂ **01/213-9718.** 96 units. $143 doubles; $177 suites. Rates include breakfast buffet. **Amenities:** Restaurant; concierge; exercise room; room service; spa; Wi-Fi.

IFK Lodge ★★   This relaxed, reasonably priced lodge on the banks of the Urubamba River is a total find. Decorated with rough-hewn, hand-carved furnishings, the rooms feature earthy tones with splashes of bright Andean textiles. Rooms and common areas have phenomenal views of the surrounding mountains, while strategically placed plants and flowers, both inside and out, bring plenty of life to the rustic setting. The lodge's restaurant, Nunay, with a fireplace and terrace overlooking the river, is driven by the region's incredible ingredients, which are collected wild and bought from nearby farmers. The lodge occasionally sets up *pachamanca,* traditional Andean feasts, in the garden.

Km. 57.2 Carretera Calca-Urubamba Huarán. www.ifk.pe. ℂ **01/974-791-456** for reservations. 20 units. $100 doubles; $140–$150 suites; $260 family apartment. Rates include breakfast. **Amenities:** Restaurant; bar; tour desk; Wi-Fi.

K'uychi Rumi ★   Self-catering travelers and families will appreciate this alternative lodging option. Submerged in the trees, this rustic resort is comprised of a handful of two-story, two-bedroom adobe houses that can sleep up to six people and are built from eco-friendly materials. The units are connected by walkways, and each features a spacious living room with a fireplace, kitchenette, dining room, and balcony. Every unit is individually decorated with locally made wood furnishings and textiles. Aside from an octagonal building with a TV that's used for communal activities, there are little other property amenities to speak of.

Carretera Urubamba–Ollantaytambo s/n, Urubamba. www.urubamba.com. ℂ **084/201-169.** 7 units. $140 doubles; $230 family bungalow (four people). Rates include breakfast. **Amenities:** Wi-Fi.

Sonesta Posadas del Inca Sacred Valley ★ Built as a monastery in the late 1700s, then later used as a private hacienda, this atmospheric colonial-village-like complex is one of the most reliable properties in the Sacred Valley. While newer hotels have got it beat in luxury, the history of the property and many original details like stone fountains and worn wooden beams are not something that can be re-created. The rooms are weirdly decorated with red brick or wood floors and faux-stone walls, while the bathrooms can be somewhat cramped. The grounds are more impressive, with a chapel brought in whole from a provincial town, a maze of gardens, and a good restaurant with one of the area's best lunch buffets.

Plaza Manco II de Yucay 123, Yucay. www.sonesta.com. ℂ **084/201-107,** or 01/222-4777 for reservations (800/SONESTA [766-3782] in the U.S. and Canada). 88 units. $138–$160 doubles. Rates includes breakfast buffet. **Amenities:** Restaurant; bar; lounge; spa; Wi-Fi.

INEXPENSIVE

Las Chullpas Ecolodge ★ With so many hotels feeling increasingly corporate, this quirky, self-described "ecological guesthouse" is a nice change of pace. The rustic rooms have a very DIY atmosphere, with hand-painted tiles, mismatching wood beams, and brick chimineas. Each has a unique layout, and some rooms sleep up to four. The owner prepares decent organic and vegetarian meals in the fireplace-warmed dining room. The staff can help set up tours in the region, including multi-day hikes into the mountains.

Querocancha s/n, Urubamba (up a long dirt road 3km/2 miles from Urubamba). www.chullpas.pe. ℂ **084/201-568.** 9 units. $60 doubles; $80 suites. Rates include breakfast buffet. **Amenities:** Restaurant; bar/lounge; Wi-Fi (free).

The Green House ★★ In Huarán, at the edge of the Sacred Valley, a bit more off the beaten track than most hotels listed here, this laid-back inn is one of the best options in its price range. Sustainability and the connection to nature is a theme that runs throughout the property, from the adobe walls, natural dye paints, and solar water heater to the views of the *apus* from the soaring, wall-of-glass living area with a fireplace. The friendly American owner and her mother (who live on the grounds) have uniquely decorated each of the airy, rustic rooms and offer an array of healing services. Three-course dinners are available for an additional S/70.

Carretera, Km 60, Pisac–Ollantaytambo, Calca (11km/7 miles from Urubamba). www.thegreenhouseperu.com. ℂ **01/941-299-944.** 4 units. $100 doubles. Rates include breakfast. **Amenities:** Restaurant; video lounge; Wi-Fi.

OLLANTAYTAMBO ★★★

97km (60 miles) NW of Cusco; 21km (13 miles) W of Urubamba

A tongue twister of a town—the last settlement before Aguas Calientes and Machu Picchu—this historic and lovely little place at the northwestern end of the Sacred Valley is affectionately called Ollanta (Oh-*yahn*-tah) by locals. Plenty of outsiders who can't pronounce it fall in love with the town, too, and the town, which was oh-so-quiet just a few years ago, is now firmly on the tourist trail, fast on its way to becoming a tiny version of Cusco. New cafes, restaurants, and *hostales* now ring the main square and line the street that connects the old town to the ruins, but Ollanta is trying to negotiate its newfound popularity and is doing its best to avoid being overrun with shoddy tourist establishments, as happened in Aguas Calientes. Despite its quick transformation, though, Ollantaytambo remains one of the most enjoyable places in the Sacred Valley, the one place (other than Machu Picchu, of course) not to be missed. The scenery surrounding Ollantaytambo is stunning: The snowcapped mountains that embrace the town frame a much narrower valley here than at Urubamba or Pisac, and both sides of the gorge are lined with Inca stone *andenes,* or agricultural terraces. Most extraordinary are the precipitous terraced ruins of a massive temple-fortress built by the Inca Pachacútec. Below the ruins, Ollantaytambo's old town is a splendid grid of streets dating to Inca times and lined with immaculately carved stone walls, blooming bougainvillea, and perfect canals, still carrying rushing water down from the mountains. Though during much of the day tour buses deposit large groups at the foot of the fortress (where a handicrafts market habitually breaks out to welcome them) and tourists overrun the main square, the old town remains pretty quiet, a traditional and thoroughly charming Valle Sagrado village.

Ollantaytambo is one of the best spots to spend the night in the Sacred Valley—although accommodations are limited to mostly small inns and simple hotels—especially if you want to be able to wander around the ruins alone in the early morning or late afternoon, before or after the groups overtake them. With the town's expanding roster of traveler services, it's now a good place to hang out for several days, not just an overnight on the way to or back from Machu Picchu.

Essentials

GETTING THERE

By Train Ollantaytambo lies midway on the Cusco–Machu Picchu train route. Trains traveling to Aguas Calientes (Machu Picchu) from Cusco or Urubamba stop first at Ollantaytambo, though many other services start the journey from here. PeruRail trains depart Cusco from **Estación Poroy** (© **084/221-352**), a 15-minute taxi ride from Cusco, and arrive in Ollantaytambo 90 minutes later. The train station in Ollantaytambo is a long 10-minute walk from the main square. For additional details, see "Getting There" in Chapter 8.

By Bus The cheapest way to Ollantaytambo is to catch a *combi* or *colectivo* from Cusco to Urubamba (S/6) and transfer at the terminal there to a frequent *combi* (S/3) for Ollanta (30 min.). Buses drop passengers at the Plaza de Armas in the old town, about a kilometer from the ruins.

By Taxi Taxis between Ollantaytambo and Cusco generally charge about S/80 to S/90 each way. Shared taxis (for about S/10 per person) to Urubamba are frequently available; a private taxi from the bus station in Urubamba to Ollanta will run another S/15 to S/20.

VISITOR INFORMATION

You're better off getting information on the Sacred Valley before leaving Cusco, either at the main **Tourist Information Office** (© 084/263-176), Av. El Sol 103, or at Cusco's branch of the **South American Explorers Club** (© 084/245-484). Your best bet for exchanging cash in Ollantaytambo is in small shops. If you need medical assistance, go to **Centro de Salud,** Calle Principal (© 084/204-090). The **post office** is on the Plaza de Armas.

Exploring Ollantaytambo

FORTRESS RUINS ★★★

The Inca elite adopted Ollantaytambo, building irrigation systems and a crowning temple designed for worship and astronomical observation. Rising above the valley and an ancient square (Plaza Mañaraki) are dozens of rows of stunningly steep stone terraces carved into the hillside. The temple ruins, which appear both forbidding and admirably perfect, represent one of the Inca Empire's most formidable feats of architecture. The Incas successfully defended the site against the Spanish in 1537, protecting the rebel Manco Inca after his retreat here from defeat at Sacsayhuamán. In all probability, the complex was more a temple than a citadel to the Incas.

The upper section—reached after you've climbed 200 steps—contains typically masterful masonry of the kind that adorned great Inca temples. A massive and supremely elegant door jamb—site of many a photo—indicates the principal entry to the temple; next to it is the **Temple of Ten Niches.** On the next level are six huge pink granite blocks, amazingly cut, polished, and fitted together; they appear to be part of rooms never completed. This **Temple of the Sun** is one of the great stonemasonry achievements of the Incas. On the stones, you can still make out faint, ancient symbolic markings in relief. Across the valley is the quarry that provided the stones for the structure; a great ramp descending from the hilltop ruins was the means by which the massive stones were transported—thousands of workers essentially dragged them around the river—from several kilometers away.

A footpath wends up the hill behind an outer wall of the ruins to a clearing and a wall with niches that have led some to believe prisoners were tied up here—a theory that is unfounded. Regardless of the purpose, the views south over the Urubamba Valley and of the snowcapped peak of Verónica are outstanding.

The ruins are open daily from 7am to 5:30pm; admission is by *boleto turístico* only (see p. 125). To experience the ruins in peace before the tour

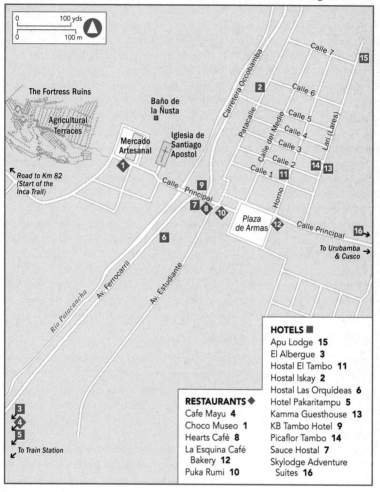

0 100 yds
0 100 m

The Fortress Ruins

Agricultural Terraces

Baño de la Ñusta

Mercado Artesanal **1**

Iglesia de Santiago Apostol

← Road to Km 82 (Start of the Inca Trail)

Carretera Occobamba

Patacalle

Calle 7 **15**

2 Calle 6

Calle 5

Calle del Medio

Calle 4

Calle 3

Calle 2

Lari (Lares)

14 **13**

Calle 1 **11**

Calle Principal **9**

7 **8** **10**

Horno

Plaza de Armas

12 Calle Principal **16** →

To Urubamba & Cusco

6

Av. Ferrocarril

Río Patacancha

Av. Estudiante

3
4
5
↙ To Train Station

RESTAURANTS ◆
Cafe Mayu **4**
Choco Museo **1**
Hearts Café **8**
La Esquina Café Bakery **12**
Puka Rumi **10**

HOTELS ■
Apu Lodge **15**
El Albergue **3**
Hostal El Tambo **11**
Hostal Iskay **2**
Hostal Las Orquídeas **6**
Hotel Pakaritampu **5**
Kamma Guesthouse **13**
KB Tambo Hotel **9**
Picaflor Tambo **14**
Sauce Hostal **7**
Skylodge Adventure Suites **16**

buses arrive, plan on getting to them before 11am. Early morning is best of all, when the sun rises over mountains to the east and then quickly bathes the entire valley in light.

At the bottom of the terraces, next to the Patacancha River, are the **Baños de la Ñusta (Princess Baths),** a place of ceremonial bathing. Wedged into the mountains facing the baths are granaries built by the Incas (not prisons, as some have supposed). Locals like to point out the face of the Inca carved into the cliff high above the valley. (If you can't make it out, ask the guard at the entrance to the ruins for a little help.)

OLD TOWN ★★★

Below (or south of) the ruins and across the Río Patacancha is the finest extant example of the Incas' masterful urban planning. Many original residential *canchas,* or blocks, each inhabited by several families during the 15th century, are still present; each *cancha* had a single entrance opening onto a main courtyard. The finest streets of this stone village are directly behind the main square. Get a good glimpse of community life within a *cancha* by peeking in at **Calle del Medio** (Chautik'ikllu St.), where a couple of neighboring houses have a small shop in the courtyard and their ancestors' skulls are displayed as shrines on the walls of their living quarters. The entire village retains a solid Quechua air to it, unperturbed by the crowds of gringos who wander through, snapping photos of children and old women. It's a starkly traditional place, largely populated by locals in colorful native dress and women who pace the streets or fields, absent-mindedly spinning the ancient spools used to make handwoven textiles.

Ollantaytambo is an excellent spot in the valley for gentle or more energetic walks around the valley and into the mountains. One of the more accessible walks is the climb up to **Pinkuylluna** ★★ and the hills overlooking the old town; take the stairs off Calle Lares K'ikllu, northeast of the Plaza de Armas and with the widest rushing canals in town. A sign reads To PINKUYLLUNA. Though the climb is initially very steep, you can clamber over the entire hilltop and explore old Inca granaries. The views of Ollantaytambo, across town to the ruins and of the surrounding valley, are stupendous.

Where to Eat in Ollantaytambo

Every year, more small, tourist-oriented cafes and restaurants pop up in Ollantaytambo to cater to the crowds that hang out in the day and increasingly spend the night here. If you're staying in Ollanta and don't mind a drive, you might also consider catching a taxi to one of the fine restaurants along the main road from Urubamba to Ollantaytambo; see "Where to Eat in Urubamba," earlier in this chapter.

One of my favorite spots in Ollantaytambo is **Cafe Mayu** ★★, Estación de Tren Ollantaytambo (www.elalbergue.com; ℂ **084/204-014**), part of the El Albergue *hostal* (see below). The attractive cafe, which looks like it's been around much longer than it has, features homemade pastas (such as fettuccine with three Andean cheeses), quinoa and other salads, and tasty sandwiches. It also serves excellent breakfasts and great coffee and a locally famous brownie with vanilla ice cream. The chefs can set up a *pachamanca* lunch at its farm on the terraces on the other side of the tracks with advance notice. Additionally, it runs a cafeteria and a small stand on the train platform (after entering through the gate) where you can have craft beer from Cervecería del Valle or locally roasted coffee, or pick up a boxed lunch that you can take with you to Machu Picchu (and it will be better than anything else you can pick up along the way). It opens at 5am to service the first train passengers.

Another good choice, although simple and unadorned, is **Hearts Café** ★, in a new location on Av. Ventiderio s/n (ℂ **084/436-726**), begun by a British

WE CALL IT *CHOCLO:* foods OF THE INCAS

Wondering what the Incas cultivated on all those amazing, steeply terraced fields that so elegantly grace the hillsides? Sure, they grew *papas* (potatoes) and *coca* (coca leaves), but corn was perhaps the Incas' most revered crop. Although corn was important throughout the Americas in pre-Columbian times, the Inca Empire raised it to the level of a sacred state crop. Corn was a symbol of power, and the Incas saved their very best lands for its cultivation. The *choclo* of Cusco and the Sacred Valley was considered the finest of the empire. It is still an uncommon delight: Huge, puffy, white kernels with a milky, sweet taste, it's best enjoyed in classic corn-on-the-cob style, boiled and served with a hunk of salty Andean cheese.

Pachamanca is a classic *sierra* dish, an indigenous barbecue of sorts, perfected by the Incas. The word is derived from *Pachamama* or "Mother Earth" in Quechua. A *pachamanca* is distinguished by its underground preparation. Several types of meat, along with potatoes, chopped *ají* (chile pepper), herbs, and cheese, are baked in a hole in the earth over hot stones. Banana leaves are placed between the layers of food. The act of cooking underground was symbolic for the Incas; they worshiped the earth, and to eat directly from it was a way of honoring Pachamama and giving thanks for her fertility. Peruvians still love to cook *pachamancas* in the countryside.

Quinoa, which comes from the word that means "moon" in Quechua (another central element in the Inca cosmology), was the favored grain of the Incas. The grain, which expands to four times its original volume when cooked and contains a greater quantity of protein than any other grain, remains central to the Andean diet. Most often seen in *sopa a la criolla,* it is often substituted for rice and incorporated into soups, salads, and puddings.

woman, Sonia Newhouse, who operates an NGO that works with highland community women and children—to which all profits of this restaurant are donated. Besides feeling good about spending your *soles* here, it's a cozy little spot for breakfast (served all day), sandwiches, empanadas, fruit juices, and full, good-value dinners. On the plaza, **La Esquina Café Bakery** ★ (*©* 084/204-078) is a lively spot run by a husband and wife team with local coffees, craft beer, and hearty breakfasts and lunch specials. They have a great veggie burger and house-baked sweets like cakes and cinnamon rolls.

Puka Rumi, Av. Beniterio s/n (*©* 084/204-091), is a little bar/cafe run by a friendly woman named Rufina, serving everything from eggs to *churrasco* (steaks) and chicken; it's especially good for a cold beer on the tiny terrace. **Tawachaki,** Plaza Araccama s/n (*©* 084/204-114), is a cozy restaurant with above-average Andean classics like *cuy chactado* (roasted guinea pig) and *rocot relleno* (stuffed peppers). There's an all-day happy hour with pisco sours and *chilcanos,* making it a fine stop after a tour of the ruins.

Shopping

While most shoppers make a beeline for the market directly in front of the entrance to the ruins, those in search of higher-quality, handwoven alpaca

Sacred Valley Festivals

The traditional Andean villages of the Sacred Valley are some of the finest spots in Peru to witness vibrant local festivals celebrated with music, dance, and processions. Among the highlights are Christmas; **Día de los Reyes Magos (Three Kings Day,** Jan 6); **Ollanta-Raymi** (celebrated in Ollantaytambo the week after its big brother, Cusco's Inti Raymi, during the last week of June); and Chinchero's **Virgen Natividad** (Sept 8), the most important annual fiesta in that village. The **Fiesta de las Cruces (Festival of the Crosses,** May 2–3) is celebrated across the highlands with enthusiastic dancing and decoration of large crosses. Pisac celebrates a particularly lively version of the **Virgen del Carmen** festival held in Paucartambo (July 16).

fiber textiles (with all-natural dyes and fibers), produced by artisans from Quechua mountain communities, should visit **Awamaki ★**, Calle Principal (✆ **084/792-529**), the retail outlet of an NGO that runs a weaving project and ensures that profits make it back to the women of the Patacancha Valley. The organization also organizes excellent trips ★★ to the Patacancha communities for weaving demonstrations and visits with local families and artisans.

Entertainment & Nightlife

A spot for decent cocktails, as well as fruit juices and milkshakes, is **Blue Puppy Lounge & Restaurant,** Calle Horno s/n (✆ **084/630-464**), a combination restaurant and upstairs lounge-bar. Tables at one end have views of the main square.

Outside of town on the road to Urubamba in Pachar, **Cerveceria del Valle,** also known as the Sacred Valley Brewing Co. (www.sacredvalleybrewing company.com; ✆ **984/553-892**), has a taproom selling unique Andean-inspired ales and lagers that are made with glacial spring water. It's open Friday to Sunday from 2 to 7pm.

Where to Stay

In addition to the hotels below, budget travelers gravitate toward the first inexpensive options (which, for the most part, don't offer hot water) they come across: **KB Tambo Hotel** (www.kbperu.com; ✆ **084/204-091**), owned by a mountain-biking American and with nice rooms constructed a few years ago ($15–$20 per person); **Hostal Las Orquídeas,** Av. Ferrocarril s/n (www.lasorquideasollantaytambo.com; ✆ **084/204-032**), a relaxed B&B with clean and simple rooms around a courtyard for $45; and **Kamma Guesthouse,** Calle Lari 659 (✆ **084/436-821**), a clean and friendly place on a cobblestone street with good views from a rooftop lounge and small and simple rooms ($35 for a double). Tucked into the Old Town on a quiet street, simple and comfortable **Hostal El Tambo,** Calle Horno s/n (✆ **084/204-003**), is built around an attractive, verdant patio. Rates are $30 for doubles, or $10 per person in dorms.

VERY EXPENSIVE

Skylodge Adventure Suites ★   This hotel does things a little bit differently. Rather than walking to your four-walled room, you either climb or ride a zipline to the side of a mountain, suspended on a rock face 400m (1,312 ft.) above the ground, where the glass pod that holds your bed for the night is waiting. The owners claim it's the world's first hanging lodge and a million star hotel. Regardless of the clichés, the experience of sleeping comfortably on the side of a mountain with spectacular 300-degree views is one you probably won't forget. It's not exactly roughing it. The pods are equipped with solar power and have simple yet private bathrooms. Each pod holds up to four guests.

Km 200, Ctra. Urubamba–Ollantaytambo, Pachar. www.naturavive.com. ℗ **084/793-019.** 3 units. $290 per person. Rates include *via ferrata*, ziplines, dinner, breakfast, and transportation to/from Cusco. **Amenities:** Restaurant; lounge; room service.

EXPENSIVE

Hotel Pakaritampu ★   Despite being overpriced, there's little else in Ollantaytambo at this price range, or at least not within walking distance to the train station. The highs include well-manicured gardens full of flowers and hummingbirds, great views of the ruins and surrounding mountains, and a fireplace lounge for chilly nights. The rooms have a cookie-cutter feel, though they have amenities that are hard to come by here, like cable TV and reliable Wi-Fi. A decent restaurant on the grounds can pack you a lunch for Machu Picchu.

Av. Ferrocarril s/n, Ollantaytambo. www.pakaritampu.com. ℗ **084/204-020.** 39 units. $191 doubles; $397 suites. Rates include breakfast. **Amenities:** Restaurant; bar; TV lounge; Wi-Fi.

MODERATE

El Albergue ★★   A classic Peruvian inn if there ever was one. Right on the train platform, the property originally opened in 1925 under the name Santa Rosa, though it is now owned by a longtime American resident of Ollantaytambo who doesn't seem to miss a beat. The tight space is packed with extras, like lush gardens and a eucalyptus-fired sauna, plus one of the better restaurants in town and even a cafe and waiting room for train passengers. The rooms, all with private bathrooms, have a timeless quality to them, featuring handcrafted wood furnishings and contemporary artwork above the beds.

Av. Estación s/n (next to the railway station platform), Ollantaytambo. www.elalbergue. com. ℗ **084/204-014.** 16 units. $99–$109 doubles; $179–$199 superiors. Rates include continental breakfast. **Amenities:** Restaurant; cafe; sauna; Wi-Fi (free).

Sauce Hostal ★   This intimate inn is in the middle of Ollantaytambo, right between the main square of the village, the road to the ruins, and the road to the train station. The rooms are quite plain, though well-equipped. Half of the rooms have incredible views of the ruins. Its breakfasts source unique Andean produce like *sauco, aguaymanto, sachatomate,* and tiny papayas, as well as fresh milk and honey, from its own farm on the outskirts of town.

Ventiderio 248, Ollantaytambo. www.hostalsauce.com.pe. ℗ **084/204-044.** 6 units. $110 doubles. Rates include breakfast. **Amenities:** Restaurant; bar; laundry; Wi-Fi.

HIKING TRAILS IN THE sacred VALLEY

Energetic travelers with a fierce desire to get outdoors and exercise their legs in the Sacred Valley can do much more than the standard ruins treks and even the Inca Trail, although the latter is certainly the best-known trek in Peru. Other trails are considerably less populated, so if you're looking for isolation in the Andes, give some of these treks a try. The entire valley is virtually tailor-made for treks, but Ollantaytambo and Yucay are particularly excellent bases for treks into the lovely, gentle hillsides framing the Urubamba Valley. The Cusco office of **South American Explorers** (*C* **084/245-484**) is very helpful, with trip and trail reports for members.

o **Km 82 of the Inca Trail:** Whether or not you're planning to do the Inca Trail, hiking the section from Km 82 to Km 88 is a nice addition to the classic or mini route. By staying to the north (or railroad) side of the Río Urubamba, you'll pass several good ruins sites, including Salapunku and Pinchanuyoq, finally reaching the Inca bridge at Km 88.

o **Pumamarca ruins:** You can reach the small but well-preserved Inca ruins of Pumamarca by a pretty trek along the banks of the Río Patacancha, which takes you through tiny villages. The walk

from Ollantaytambo takes about 5 hours round-trip. To get there, take the road that leads north out of Ollanta along the Patacancha. After it crosses the river, it turns into a footpath and passes the village of Munaypata. Veer left toward the valley and terracing, and then turn sharply to the right (northeast), toward the agricultural terraces straight ahead.

o **Pinkuylluna:** The mountain looming above Ollantaytambo makes for an enjoyable (though initially very steep) couple-hour trek up, past Inca terracing and old granaries. However, the trail isn't very clearly marked in sections, so it might be worthwhile to ask around town for a guide.

o **Huayoccari:** Adventurous trekkers in search of solitude should enjoy the 2-day hike (one-way) from Yucay to the small village of Huayoccari, which passes some of the valley's loveliest scenery, from the Inca terraces along the San Juan River ravine to Sakrachayoc and ancient rock paintings overlooking caves. After camping overnight, trekkers continue to the Tuqsana pass (4,000m/13,100 ft.) and descend to Yanacocha Lake before arriving at Huayoccari.

INEXPENSIVE

Apu Lodge ★ On the outskirts of town, the highlight of this colorful, family-run inn is its elevated setting with superb views over the stone streets and clay tile roofs to the ruins. The rooms feature adobe walls and wood floors. They're decorated with pieces of local artwork, though are otherwise rather simplistic. Each does have a modern bathroom with 24-hour hot water, though.

Calle Lares s/n, Ollantaytambo. www.apulodge.com. *C* **084/797-162.** 9 units. $75 doubles; $140 family suite. Rates include breakfast. **Amenities:** Library; book exchange; shaman ceremonies; Wi-Fi (in public areas).

Hostal Iskay ★ Set amid Inca terraces and lush gardens, this cool spot with killer views of the ruins run by a Catalan guy is one of the better bargains here. Though clean and well-kept, the standard rooms are somewhat cramped. For not a lot more, the superior rooms, which have a terrace or are separated from the others, are a better option.

Patacalle s/n, Ollantaytambo. www.hostaliskay.com. © **084/204-004.** 7 units. $45 doubles; $57–$67 superiors. Rates include breakfast. **Amenities:** Wi-Fi.

Picaflor Tambo ★ In a lovingly restored traditional Ollanta house with stone walls and immaculately carved wood doors and window frames, this is one of the most authentic guesthouses in town. The rooms, surrounding an interior courtyard, are bright and airy, especially the four on the second floor. Each has a modern bathroom with 24-hour hot water. The views of the ruins from the terrace are to be enjoyed at every change in the light.

Calle Lari 444, Ollantaytambo. www.picaflortambo.com. © **084/436-758.** 6 units. $60 doubles; $75–$85 suites. Rates include breakfast. **Amenities:** Wi-Fi.

MACHU PICCHU & THE INCA TRAIL

8

The stunning and immaculately sited Machu Picchu, the fabled "lost city of the Incas," is South America's greatest attraction, drawing ever-increasing numbers of visitors from across the globe. The Incas hid Machu Picchu so high in the clouds that it escaped destruction by the empire-raiding Spaniards, who never found it. It is no longer lost, of course—you can zip there by high-speed train or trek there along a 2- or arduous 4-day trail—but Machu Picchu retains its perhaps unequaled aura of mystery and magic. From below it remains totally hidden from view, although no longer overgrown with brush, as it was when it was rediscovered in 1911 by the Yale archaeologist and historian Hiram Bingham with the aid of a local farmer who knew of its existence. The majestic setting the Incas chose for it, nestled in almost brooding Andes Mountains and frequently swathed in mist, also remains unchanged. When the early-morning sun rises over the peaks and methodically illuminates the ruins' row by row of granite stones, Machu Picchu leaves visitors as awe-struck as ever.

History   There is plenty of mystery surrounding the construction of Machu Picchu, as the Incas left no written records. It is believed to have been constructed at the orders of the 9th Inca emperor, Pachacútec (also called Pachacuti Inca Yupanqui), sometime in the mid-1400s. While the official purpose of the city isn't clear, it wasn't inhabited for very long. When the Spanish arrived in the 1500s, Machu Picchu was abandoned, leaving the jungle to overtake the stones for the next several centuries, until American explorer Hiram Bingham stumbled upon it, thinking it was the lost city of Vilcabamba.

Sightseeing   Machu Picchu's popularity continues to grow by leaps and bounds, straining both its infrastructure and the fragile surrounding ecosystem, forcing state officials to limit the number of visitors in high season. The great majority of visitors to Machu

Picchu still visit it as a day trip from Cusco, but many people feel that a few hurried hours at the ruins during peak hours, amid throngs of people following guided tours, simply do not suffice. By staying at least 1 night, either at the one upscale hotel just outside the grounds of Machu Picchu or down below in the town of Aguas Calientes (also officially called Machu Picchu Pueblo), you can remain at the ruins later in the afternoon after most of the tour groups have gone home, or get there for sunrise—a dramatic, unforgettable sight. Many visitors find that even a full single day at the ruins does not do them justice.

Nature   Many visitors are surprised when arriving to Machu Picchu how lush and vibrant the greenery is around them. They are expecting the altitude of Cusco, but instead find tropical forests and mountainsides blanketed in orchids. The Machu Picchu Sanctuary is more than just ruins, but part of a larger reserve rich in biodiversity. More than a dozen hummingbirds are found here, and rare species like the cock-of-the-rock or golden-headed quetzal can be spotted with the right guide. Even Andean spectacled bears, the same as Paddington, can be seen on the mountain across from the Inkaterra Hotel.

Where to Stay & Eat   The base for most visitors, Aguas Calientes is a small, ramshackle tourist-trade village with the feel of a frontier town, dominated by sellers of cheap *artesanía* and souvenirs and weary backpackers resting up and celebrating their treks along the Inca Trail over cheap eats and cheaper beers. The Peruvian government has been doing its level best to spruce up the town, lest its ramshackle look turn off visitors to Peru's greatest spectacle. It has fixed up the Plaza de Armas, built a nicely paved *malecón* riverfront area, and added new bridges over and new streets along the river. Attempts to give it a makeover have long been complicated by flooding and mudslides, the most recent in 2010 (when five people died and some 2,000 tourists were stranded at Machu Picchu, eventually evacuated by helicopter). Although Aguas Calientes does look considerably better than it once did, and despite its spectacular setting—surrounded by cloud forest vegetation and Andes peaks on all sides—it's still probably not a place you want to hang out for long.

Active Pursuits   Most visitors come here for one thing: to visit Machu Picchu. Aside from climbing to Huayna Picchu, the steep mountain overlooking Machu Picchu, those who stay a while can take several short hikes in the area. Of course, there's the Inca Trail, the iconic 4- or 2-day hike to the ruins that is on everyone's bucket list.

THE BEST TRAVEL EXPERIENCES AROUND MACHU PICCHU

o **Hiking the Inca Trail:** Simply put, this is one of the world's great hikes. Crossing from alpine tundra into cloud forest, over mountain passes and Inca ruins, opt between the rugged classic 4-day trek or a shortened 2-day walk. See p. 212.

- **Climbing to Huayna Picchu:** That towering mountain backdrop featured in every postcard of Machu Picchu? You can climb that. This steep hike along narrow paths gives you a viewpoint of the citadel unlike any other. See p. 209.
- **Strolling in the Mandor Valley:** Following the railroad tracks along the Vilcanota River from Aguas Calientes brings you to a world of green ferns and secluded waterfalls. Rich bird life awaits, too, so bring your binoculars. See p. 224.
- **Taking the train from Ollantaytambo:** Wending your way through the valley's lush green fields, on the banks of the rushing Urubamba River and far below the towering Andes, is reward enough, but the sense of anticipation makes most people positively giddy. See p. 201.
- **Spying orchids and bears at the Inkaterra Machu Picchu Pueblo Hotel:** Staying at this upscale ecolodge gets you easy access to the hotel's 372 different native species of orchids, the world's largest collection. The spectacled bear rehabilitation project is one of the few places you can get up close to this rare species. See p. 227.

MACHU PICCHU

120km (75 miles) NW of Cusco

Machu Picchu is situated on a mountaintop, 2,430m (7,970 ft.) above sea level, amidst a tropical mountain forest surrounded by *apus,* the sacred peaks of Inca mythology. No matter how many tourists crowd the site each day, there is no denying just how enchanting this marvel of human invention truly is.

Visiting the majestic site requires some advanced planning. Outside of a series of switchbacks from the town of Aguas Calientes below Machu Picchu, there are no roads there. Visitors arrive either by a few hours on a train or a few days on foot via the Inca Trail. While some will make the long, arduous trip here from Cusco and back in the same day, a good percentage of visitors will spend the night in an Aguas Calientes hotel, opting to visit the site during off-peak hours to avoid the crowds and have time to soak up some of the cloud forest.

Essentials
GETTING THERE
By Train Most people travel to Machu Picchu by train (indeed, the only other way to get there is by foot). You can go to Aguas Calientes, at the base of the ruins, from either Cusco or two points in the Sacred Valley (Ollantaytambo and Urubamba). The 112km (70-mile) trip from Cusco is a truly spectacular train journey. It zigzags through lush valleys hugging the Río Urubamba, with views of snowcapped Andes peaks in the distance. From Cusco, **PeruRail** (www.perurail.com; © **01/612-6700** in Lima, **084/581-414** in Cusco) operates three tourist trains from **Estación Poroy,** a 25-minute taxi ride from Cusco, all arriving in under 4 hours: the **Expedition,** the slowest and least expensive ($85 one-way); the **Vistadome,** the faster middle-class service ($98); and the top-of-the-line and pricey luxury line **Hiram Bingham,** named

after the discoverer of Machu Picchu ($475 one-way, including meals, cocktails, and a guided tour at the ruins). Scheduled times, the number of services, and the number of cars on the train and seats available vary by the season, though Expedition and Vistadome classes usually offer several departure times each day, leaving from Poroy as early as 6:20am and returning as late as 7pm. Make your train reservations as early as possible; tickets can be purchased online or at PeruRail offices in Ollantaytambo or Cusco, which are open Monday through Friday from 8:30am to 5:30pm, Saturday and Sunday from 8:30am to 12:30pm. Most hotels or tour operators can also book your train tickets for a small fee. *Note:* During the rainy season, from January through April, PeruRail trains operate out of Pachar station in the Sacred Valley instead of Poroy. Passengers take a 90-minute bus transfer from Wanchaq station in Cusco to Pachar.

Travelers already based in the Urubamba Valley have additional options to travel by train to Machu Picchu. **PeruRail** travels to Machu Picchu from a private train station on the grounds of **Tambo del Inka Resort & Spa** (see p. 186) in Urubamba. Vistadome trains make the 2½-hour journey.

From the station in Ollantaytambo to Machu Picchu, the journey takes under 2 hours. **Inca Rail,** Portal de Panes 105/Plaza de Armas in Cusco (www.incarail.com; *℟* **084/233-030** in Cusco), operates tourist, executive, and first-class trains, with fares ranging from $49 to $65 for adults. Trains (five per day) begin running at 6:40am, with the last return at 7pm. PeruRail's Expedition and Vistadome services also originate in Ollantaytambo, leaving several times a day, from 5:10am to 9pm. Fares range from $58 to $89 each way. Both train companies permit online booking and ticketing, with major credit cards accepted.

Tip: For the best views on the way to Machu Picchu, sit on the left side of the train.

Estación Machu Picchu Pueblo, the train station in Aguas Calientes, is along the river side of the tracks, just beyond the market stalls of Avenida Imperio de los Incas. Porters from several hotels greet the trains upon arrival each morning.

Train Schedules to Machu Picchu

Train schedules have changed with alarming frequency in the past few years, according to season and, it seems, the whims of some scheduler—and that's likely to be especially true now that there are two companies handling service (rather than just one), all employing the same tracks. It's wise to make your reservation at least several weeks (or more) in advance, especially in high season. For PeruRail's high-end Hiram Bingham service, reservations several weeks or more in advance are recommended. It's also smart to verify hours and fares at your hotel (if you're staying in one of the better ones with good service and informed personnel), the Tourist Information Office in Cusco (p. 117), or via PeruRail (www.perurail. com; *℟* **084/238-722**) or Inca Rail (www.incarail.com; *℟* **084/233-030**).

endangered MACHU PICCHU

Machu Picchu survived the Spanish onslaught against the Inca Empire, but in the last few decades it has suffered more threats to its architectural integrity and pristine Andean environment than it did in nearly 500 previous years of existence. In the past, UNESCO has threatened to add Machu Picchu to its roster of endangered World Heritage Sites and not to withdraw that status unless stringent measures were taken by the Peruvian government to protect the landmark ruins.

Clearly, the preservation of Machu Picchu continues to face significant challenges. In the past few years, the ruins have again been named on another notorious list, the 2010 World Monuments Watch, which details the 100 most endangered sites in the world. (In 2002, in recognition of the Peruvian government's adoption of tougher regulations on the Inca Trail and the suspension of a proposed cable-car plan, Machu Picchu was removed from the list.)

Uncontrolled development and environmental mismanagement in Aguas Calientes paired with tourism at Machu Picchu increasing from 9,000 visitors in all of 1992 to close to 5,000 on a single busy day (the site receives more than 1 million visitors annually) has meant that Peru has significant environmental and conservation issues to face.

The Peruvian government has only slowly responded to pressure from UNESCO, foreign governments, and watchdog groups, introducing measures to clean up and restrict access to the historic Inca Trail. One unique measure adopted was a debt-swap initiative, in which the government of Finland traded 25 percent of Peru's then-outstanding debt (more than $6 million) for conservation programs targeting Machu Picchu. Government officials have taken positive steps to regulate the number of visitors and the traffic flow. Closures of the site for repairs and a new entrance will also help alleviate the wear and tear of the thousands of feet that walk over the ancient stones every day. Yet clearly much more needs to be done to protect these singular ruins, Peru's most acclaimed treasure.

By Bus   You can't travel from Cusco to Machu Picchu by bus until the final leg of the journey, when buses wend their way up the mountain, performing exaggerated switchbacks for 15 minutes before depositing passengers at the entrance to the ruins. The cost is $12 each way. There's no need to reserve in advance; just purchase your ticket at the little booth in front of the lineup of buses, at the bottom of the market stalls. Buses begin running at 5:30am and come down all day, the last one descending at 5:30pm. Some people choose to purchase a one-way ticket and walk down (30–45 min.) to Aguas Calientes, which can be dangerous given the lack of clear walking paths.

By Foot   The celebrated **Inca Trail (Camino del Inca)** is almost as famous as the ruins themselves, and the trek is rightly viewed as an attraction in itself rather than merely a means of getting to Machu Picchu under your own power. There are two principal treks: one that takes 4 days (43km/27 miles) and another shorter and less demanding route that lasts just 2 days. The trails begin outside Ollantaytambo (at Km 82 of the Cusco–Machu Picchu railroad track); you can return to Cusco or Ollantaytambo by train. See "Hiking the

Historic Sanctuary of Machu Picchu

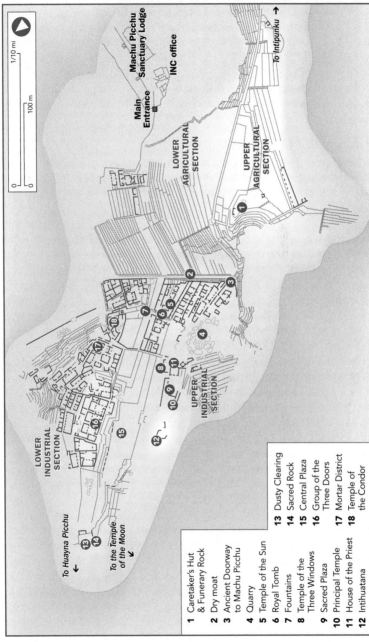

1 Caretaker's Hut & Funerary Rock
2 Dry moat
3 Ancient Doorway to Machu Picchu
4 Quarry
5 Temple of the Sun
6 Royal Tomb
7 Fountains
8 Temple of the Three Windows
9 Sacred Plaza
10 Principal Temple
11 House of the Priest
12 Intihuatana
13 Dusty Clearing
14 Sacred Rock
15 Central Plaza
16 Group of the Three Doors
17 Mortar District
18 Temple of the Condor

To Intipunku →

Machu Picchu Sanctuary Lodge

INC office

Main Entrance

LOWER AGRICULTURAL SECTION

UPPER AGRICULTURAL SECTION

UPPER INDUSTRIAL SECTION

LOWER INDUSTRIAL SECTION

To Huayna Picchu →

To the Temple of the Moon ↓

Inca Trail," later in this chapter, for more details; many new regulations have been introduced in the past few years.

For those who take the train to Aguas Calientes but still want a small dose of what it's like to walk to Machu Picchu, it's straightforward (if a little difficult) to walk up to the ruins from town up a steep path that cuts across the switchback road. It takes a little over an hour to make it up and about 45 minutes to descend. Because you'll probably want to save your energy for exploring Machu Picchu, if you are fit and want to walk at least one-way, I recommend walking down from the ruins (which is still pretty strenuous on one's knees).

Appreciating Machu Picchu

Since its rediscovery in 1911 and initial exploration by an American team of archaeologists from Yale during the following 4 years, the ruins of Machu Picchu have resonated far beyond the status of mere archaeological site. Reputed to be the legendary "lost city of the Incas," it is steeped in mystery and folklore. The unearthed complex, the only significant Inca site to escape the ravenous appetites of the Spanish conquistadors in the 16th century, ranks as the top attraction in Peru, arguably the greatest in South America and, for my money, one of the world's most stunning sights. Countless glossy photographs of the stone ruins, bridging the gap between two massive Andean peaks and swathed in cottony clouds, just can't do it justice. It is dreamlike and remains so, even though it's a mandatory visit for virtually everyone who travels to Peru.

Invisible from the Urubamba Valley below, Machu Picchu lay dormant for more than 4 centuries, nestled 2,430m (7,970 ft.) above sea level under thick jungle and known only to a handful of Amerindian peasants. Never mentioned in the Spanish chronicles, it was seemingly lost in the collective memory of the Incas and their descendants. The ruins' unearthing, though, raised more questions than it answered, and experts still argue about the place Machu Picchu occupied in the Inca Empire. Was it a citadel? An agricultural site? An astronomical observatory? A ceremonial city or sacred retreat for the Inca emperor? Or some combination of all of these? Adding to the mystery, this complex city of exceedingly fine architecture and masonry was constructed, inhabited, and deliberately abandoned all in less than a century—a mere flash in the 4,000-year history of Andean Peru. Machu Picchu was very probably abandoned even before the arrival of the Spanish, perhaps as a result of the Incas' civil war. Or perhaps it was drought that drove the Incas elsewhere.

Bingham mistook Machu Picchu for the lost city of Vilcabamba, the last refuge of the rebellious Inca Manco Cápac (see "Bingham, the 'Discoverer' of Machu Picchu" on p. 210). Machu Picchu, though, is not that lost city (which was discovered deeper in the jungle at Espíritu Pampa). Most historians believe that the 9th Inca emperor, Pachacútec (also called Pachacuti Inca Yupanqui)—who founded the Inca Empire, established many of the hallmarks of its society, and built most of the greatest and most recognizable of Inca

Not a Woman's World

For years, the world thought Machu Picchu had been almost entirely populated by the Inca's chosen "Virgins of the Sun." Bingham and his associates originally reported that more than three-quarters of the human remains found at the site were female. Those findings have been disproved, however; the sexual makeup of the inhabitants of Machu Picchu was no different than anywhere else in society: pretty much 50/50.

monuments—had the complex constructed sometime in the mid-1400s, probably after the defeat of the Chancas, a rival group, in 1438. Machu Picchu appears to have been both a ceremonial and agricultural center. Half its buildings were sacred in nature, but the latest research findings indicate that it was a royal retreat for Inca leaders rather than a sacred city, per se. Never looted by the Spaniards, many of its architectural features remain in excellent condition—even if they ultimately do little to advance our understanding of the exact nature of Machu Picchu.

One thing is certain: Machu Picchu is one of the world's great examples of landscape art. The Incas revered nature, worshiping celestial bodies and more earthly streams and stones. The spectacular setting of Machu Picchu reveals just how much they reveled in their environment. Steep terraces, gardens, and granite and limestone temples, staircases, and aqueducts seem to be carved directly out of the hillside. Forms echo the very shape of the surrounding mountains, and windows and instruments appear to have been constructed to track the sun during the June and December solstices. Machu Picchu lies 300m (1,000 ft.) lower than Cusco, but you'd imagine the exact opposite, so nestled are the ruins among mountaintops and clouds. The ruins are cradled at the center of a radius of Andean peaks, like the pistil at the center of a flower.

Appreciating Machu Picchu for its aesthetic qualities is no slight to its significance. The Incas obviously chose the site for the immense power of its natural beauty. They, like we, must have been in awe of the snowcapped peaks to the east; the rugged panorama of towering, forested mountains and the sacred cliff of Putukusi to the west; and the city sitting gracefully like a proud saddle between two huge *cerros,* or peaks. It remains one of the most thrilling sights in the world. At daybreak, when the sun's rays creep silently over the jagged silhouette, sometimes turning the distant snowy peaks fiery orange, and then slowly, with great drama, cast brilliant light on the ruins building by building and row by row, it's enough to move some observers to tears and others to squeals of delight.

VISITING THE RUINS

Named a UNESCO World Heritage Site in 1983 and declared one of the "New Seven Wonders of the World," Machu Picchu's image around the world continues to grow, as does the number of people who want to visit the ruins. Until recently, as many as 5,000 visitors a day visited Machu Picchu during high

8

MACHU PICCHU & THE INCA TRAIL

Machu Picchu

Package Visits to Machu Picchu

Machu Picchu packages that include round-trip train fare between Cusco and Aguas Calientes, shuttle bus and admission to the ruins, a guided visit, and sometimes lunch at Machu Picchu Sanctuary Lodge for same-day visits can be purchased from travel agencies in Cusco. Package deals generally start at around $200; it's worth shopping around for the best deal. Try **SAS Travel**, Calle Garcilaso 270, Plaza San Francisco (www.sastravelperu.com; ✆ **084/249-194**) or **Chaska Tours,** Garcilaso 265, second floor (www.chaskatours.com; ✆ **084/240-424**)—or any of the tour agencies listed later in this chapter (see the "Inca Trail Agencies" section) that organize Inca Trail treks. Packages that include overnight accommodations at the ruins or in Aguas Calientes can also be arranged.

season, but the number of visitors permitted on a daily basis has now been capped at 2,500—making reservations in advance of your visit pivotal. I'd recommend purchasing tickets online at least 1 week in advance (but if you're traveling in high season, from May to October, make them as early as possible to avoid a crushing disappointment). Even with the new regulations, you've got to arrive very early in the morning or stay past 3pm for a bit of splendid Inca isolation. Still, the place is large enough to escape most tour-group bottlenecks. Perhaps the worst times to visit are from July 28 to August 10, when Peruvian national holidays land untold groups of schoolchildren and families at Machu Picchu, or solstice days (June 21 and Dec 21), when everyone descends on the ruins for a glimpse of the dazzling effects of the sun's rays. During the rainy season (Nov–Mar), you are very likely to get rain for (often) brief periods during the day, and Machu Picchu is usually obscured by clouds in the morning.

For information on the shuttle buses to the ruins, see "Getting There," earlier in the chapter.

The ruins are open daily from dawn to dusk. The first visitors, usually those staying at the hotel, arriving from the Inca Trail, or boarding the very first buses that leave at 5:30am, enter at 6am. Everyone is ushered out by 6pm. Tickets no longer can be purchased at the entrance: They may be reserved, purchased **online** (Visa only), and printed (www.machupicchu.gob.pe; ✆ **084/582-030**). Tickets can also be purchased in Aguas Calientes at the **Centro Cultural Machu Picchu,** Av. Pachacútec s/n (✆ **084/211-196**), near the main plaza (cash only, *soles*). In Cusco, tickets may be purchased (cash or Visa only) at the **Dirección Regional de Cultura,** Av. de la Cultura 238 (✆ **084/236-061**); **Dircetur** offices, Portal de Mantas 117-A (✆ **084/246-074**); **PeruRail,** Av. Pachacútec s/n; **IncaRail,** Portal de Panes, 105/Plaza de Armas; or **Hotel Monasterio,** Calle Palacios, 136/Plazoleta Nazarenas. The entrance fee is S/128 adults (S/65 students with an ISIC card; free for children under 8). Tickets are valid for 3 days from date of purchase, but are good for a single day's entrance only. Note that another new regulation is that advance tickets are required for additional access to **Huayna Picchu,** the steep trail to the mountaintop overlooking Machu Picchu, and **Templo de la Luna** (see p. 208). Access for these components frequently sells out weeks in advance. Capacity is limited to two groups of 200 people each, with the first entry from 7 to 8am and the second from 10 to 11am. The combination ticket (Machu Picchu–Huayna Picchu–Templo de la Luna) is S/152 adults, S/77 students.

Along with your entrance ticket, you will be given an official Institute of National Culture map of the ruins, which gives the names of the individual sections, but no detailed explanations. The numbers indicated in brackets below follow our own map, "Historic Sanctuary of Machu Picchu," on p. 203. English-speaking guides can be independently arranged on-site; most charge around $30 to $40 for a private 2-hour tour. Individuals can sometimes hook up with an established group for little more than $5 per person.

EXPLORING MACHU PICCHU

After passing through the entrance, you can either head left and straight up the hill, or go down to the right. The path up to the left takes you to the spot above the ruins, near the **Caretaker's Hut** and **Funerary Rock** [1] that affords the classic postcard overview of Machu Picchu. If you are here early enough for sunrise (6:30–7:30am), by all means do this first. The hut overlooks rows and rows of steep agricultural terraces (generally with a few llamas grazing nearby). In the morning, you might see exhausted groups of trekkers arriving from several days and nights on the Inca Trail. (Most arrive at the crack of dawn for their reward, a celebratory sunrise.)

From this vantage point, you can see clearly the full layout of Machu Picchu, which had defined agricultural and urban zones; a long **dry moat** [2] separates the two sectors. Perhaps a population of 1,000 lived here at the high point of Machu Picchu.

Head down into the main section of the ruins, past a series of burial grounds and dwellings and the **main entrance to the city** [3]. A section of stones, likely a **quarry** [4], sits atop a clearing with occasionally great views of the snowcapped peaks (Cordillera Vilcabamba) in the distance (looking southwest).

Down a steep series of stairs is one of the most famous Inca constructions, the **Temple of the Sun ★★★** [5] (also called the Torreón). The rounded, tapering tower has extraordinary stonework, the finest in Machu Picchu: Its

Beware: Bogus Machu Picchu Entrance Tickets

With the increased interest in Machu Picchu (and higher prices associated with a visit), perhaps it's inevitable that counterfeit entrance tickets have become a reality. The Peruvian Ministry of Culture warns tourists not to purchase tickets to Machu Picchu or any other archaeological site in the Cusco region from anyone other than official outlets (see above). The falsified tickets are frequently offered in the Plaza de Armas in Cusco, and fake websites even pop up from time to time (make sure you purchase from www.machu picchu.gob.pe).

large stones fit together seamlessly. From the ledge above the temple, you can appreciate the window perfectly aligned for the June winter solstice, when the sun's rays come streaming through at dawn and illuminate the stone at the center of the temple. The temple is cordoned off, and entry is not permitted. Below the temple, in a cave carved from the rock, is a section traditionally called the **Royal Tomb** [6], even though no human remains have been found there. Inside is a meticulously carved altar and series of niches that produce intricate morning shadows. To the north, just down the stairs that divide this section from a series of dwellings called the **Royal Sector,** is a still-functioning water canal and series of interconnected **fountains** [7]. The main fountain is distinguished by both its size and excellent stonework.

Back up the stairs to the high section of the ruins (north of the quarry) is the main ceremonial area. The **Temple of the Three Windows ★★** [8], each trapezoid extraordinarily cut with views of the bold Andes in the distance across the Urubamba gorge, is likely to be one of your lasting images of Machu Picchu. It fronts one side of the **Sacred Plaza** [9]. To the left, if you're facing the Temple of the Three Windows, is the **Principal Temple** [10], which has masterful stonework in its three high walls. Directly opposite is the **House of the Priest** [11]. Just behind the Principal Temple is a small cell, termed the **Sacristy,** renowned for its exquisite masonry. It's a good place to examine how amazingly these many-angled stones (one to the left of the door jamb has 32 distinct angles) were fitted together by Inca stonemasons.

Up a short flight of stairs is the **Intihuatana ★** [12], popularly called the "hitching post of the sun." It looks to be a ritualistic carved rock or a sort of sundial, and its shape echoes that of the sacred peak Huayna Picchu beyond the ruins. The stone almost certainly functioned as an astronomical and agricultural calendar (useful in judging the alignment of constellations and solar events and, thus, the seasons). It does appear to be powerfully connected to mountains in all directions. The Incas built similar monuments elsewhere across the empire, but most were destroyed by the Spaniards (who surely thought them to be instruments of pagan worship). The one at Machu Picchu survived in perfect form for nearly 5 centuries until 2001, when a camera crew sneaked in a 1,000-pound crane, which fell over and chipped off the top section of the Intihuatana.

Huayna Picchu: Advance Reservations Required

Advance tickets are now required for additional access to **Huayna Picchu,** the steep climb to the mountaintop overlooking Machu Picchu, and **Templo de la Luna** (see p. 209). Access frequently sells out weeks in advance, as capacity is limited to two groups of 200 people each, with the first entry from 7 to 8am and the second from 10 to 11am. The combination ticket (Machu Picchu–Huayna Picchu–Templo de la Luna) is S/152 adults, S/77 students. Climbing to the top of Huayna Picchu for those physically able is one of the highlights of visiting Machu Picchu, making advance planning more necessary than ever.

Follow a trail down through terraces and past a small plaza to a **dusty clearing** [13] with covered stone benches on either side. Fronting the square is a massive, sculpted **Sacred Rock** [14], whose shape mimics that of Putukusi, the sacred peak that looms due east across the valley. This area likely served as a communal area for meetings and perhaps performances. Many locals (as well as visitors) believe that the Sacred Rock transmits a palpable force of energy; place your palms on it to see if you can tap into it.

To the left of the Sacred Rock, down a path, is the gateway to **Huayna Picchu ★★★**, the huge outcrop that serves as a dramatic backdrop to Machu Picchu. Although it looks forbidding and is very steep, anyone in reasonable physical shape can climb it. The steep path up takes most visitors an hour or more, although some athletic sorts ascend the peak in less than 25 minutes. Note that only 400 people per day (admitted in two groups: 7–8am and 10–11am) are permitted to make the climb, and there is an additional cost associated with it. If you are keen on ascending Huayna Picchu for the views and exercise, make your reservations as far in advance as possible (for more information, see the box above). At the top, you'll reach a platform of sorts, which is as far as many get, directly overlooking the ruins. Most who've come this far and are committed to reaching the apex continue on for a few more minutes, up through a tight tunnel carved out of the stone to a rocky perch with 360-degree views. There's room for only a handful of hikers, and the views are so astounding that many are tempted to hang out as long as they can—so new arrivals might need to be patient to win their place on the rock. The views of Machu Picchu and the panorama of forested mountains are quite literally breathtaking.

Ascending Huayna Picchu is highly recommended for energetic sorts of any age, but young children are not allowed. In wet weather, you might want to reconsider, though, because the stone steps can get slippery and become very dangerous.

Returning back down the same path (frighteningly steep at a couple of points) is a turnoff to the **Temple of the Moon,** usually visited only by Machu Picchu completists. The trail dips down into the cloud forest and then climbs again, and is usually deserted. Cleaved into the rock at a point midway down the peak and perched above the Río Urubamba, it almost surely was not a lunar observatory, however. It is a strangely forlorn and mysterious place of caverns, niches, and enigmatic portals, with some terrific stonework, including carved thrones and an altar. Despite its modern name, the temple was likely used for worship of the Huayna Picchu mountain spirit. The path takes about 1 to 1½ hours round-trip from the detour.

Passing the guard post (where you'll need to sign out), continue back into the main Machu Picchu complex and enter the lower section of the ruins, separated from the spiritually oriented upper section by a **Central Plaza** [15]. The lower section was more prosaic in function, mostly residential and industrial. Eventually, you'll come to a series of cells and quarters, called the **Group of the Three Doors** [16] and the **Mortar District** or Industrial Sector

bingham, THE "DISCOVERER" OF MACHU PICCHU

Hiram Bingham is credited with the "scientific discovery" of Machu Picchu, but in fact, when he stumbled upon the ruins with the aid of a local *campesino*, he didn't know what he'd found. Bingham, an archaeologist and historian at Yale University (and later governor of Connecticut), had come to Peru to satisfy his curiosity about a fabled lost Inca city. He led an archaeological expedition to Peru in 1911, sponsored by Yale University and the National Geographical Society. Bingham was in search of Vilcabamba the Old, the final refuge of seditious Inca Manco Cápac and his sons, who retreated there after the siege of Cusco in 1537.

From Cusco, Bingham and his team set out for the jungle through the Urubamba Valley. The group came upon a major Inca site, which they named Patallacta (Llaqtapata), ruins near the start of the Inca Trail. A week into the expedition, at Mandorpampa, near today's Aguas Calientes, Bingham met Melchor Arteaga, a local farmer, who told Bingham of mysterious ruins high in

the mountains on the other side of the river and offered to guide the expedition to them. In the rain, the two climbed the steep mountain. Despite his grandiose claims, the ruins were not totally overgrown; a small number of *campesinos* were farming among them.

In "The Lost City of the Incas," Bingham writes: "I soon found myself before the ruined walls of buildings built with some of the finest stonework of the Incas. It was difficult to see them as they were partially covered over by trees and moss, the growth of centuries; but in the dense shadow, hiding in bamboo thickets and toggled vines, could be seen here and there walls of white granite ashlars most carefully cut and exquisitely fitted together . . . I was left truly breathless."

Bingham was convinced that he'd uncovered the rebel Inca's stronghold, Vilcabamba. Yet Vilcabamba was known to have been hastily built—and Machu Picchu clearly was anything but—and most accounts had it lying much deeper in the jungle. Moreover, the Spaniards

[17]. By far the most interesting part of this lower section is the **Temple of the Condor** [18]. Said to be a carving of a giant condor, the dark rock above symbolizes the great bird's wings and the pale rock below quite clearly represents its head. You can actually crawl through the cave at the base of the rock and emerge on the other side.

Apart from the main complex, west of Machu Picchu, is the **Inca Bridge,** built upon stacked stones and overlooking a sheer, 600m (nearly 2,000 ft.) drop. Critical to the citadel's defense, the bridge can be reached in an easy half-hour from a clearly marked narrow trail.

For those who haven't yet had their fill of Machu Picchu, the climb up to **Intipunku (Sun Gate)** is well worth it. The path just below the **Caretaker's Hut** leads to the final pass of the route Inca Trail hikers use to enter the ruins. The views from the gateway, with Huayna Picchu looming in the background, are spectacular. Two stone gates here correspond to the all-important winter and summer solstices; on those dates, the sun's rays illuminate the gates like

were known to have ransacked Vilca-bamba, and there is no evidence of Machu Picchu having suffered an attack. Despite these contradictions, Bingham's pronouncement was accepted for more than 50 years. The very name should have been a dead giveaway: Vilcabamba means "Sacred Plain" in Quechua, hardly a description one would attach to Machu Picchu, nestled high in the mountains.

In 1964, the U.S. explorer Gene Savoy discovered what are now accepted as the true ruins of Vilcabamba, at Espíritu Pampa, a several-day trek into the jungle. Strangely enough, it seems certain that Hiram Bingham had once come across a small section of Vilcabamba, but he dismissed the ruins as minor.

The Machu Picchu ruins were excavated by a Bingham team in 1915. A railway from Cusco to Aguas Calientes, begun 2 years earlier, was finally completed in 1928. The road up the hillside to the ruins, inaugurated by Bingham himself, was completed in 1948. Bingham died still believing Machu Picchu was Vilcabamba, even though he'd

actually uncovered something much greater—and more mysterious.

Bingham took some 11,000 pictures of Machu Picchu on his second visit in 1912 and eventually removed more than 45,000 artifacts for study in the U.S. (with the permission of the Peruvian government under the agreement that they would be returned to Peru when there was a suitable place for their storage and continued study). Peru claims the agreement was for 18 months, but the objects remained at Yale University's Peabody Museum in New Haven, Connecticut, for nearly a century. After years of negotiations and threats of lawsuits, Yale and the Peruvian government finally came to an agreement that recognizes that Peru holds title to the artifacts. Some 40,000 museum-quality Bingham artifacts have, at long last, been returned to Peru, a selection of which are on display at the **Museo Machu Picchu** (Casa Concha) in Cusco (see p. 129), which was inaugurated to celebrate the centennial of Bingham's 1911 discovery of Machu Picchu.

a laser. Following a similar path as the Sun Gate, the often overlooked trail up **Montaña,** also called Machu Picchu Mountain, offers a rarely seen yet spectacular view of Machu Picchu. It is believed that Inca priests performed rituals on the summit. Look for the signs near the Caretaker's Hut that signal the trail head. From there you will take a 20-minute walk to a guard post where you'll show your passport and entrance ticket. (*Note:* Like Huayna Picchu, you need to make a reservation when purchasing your ticket and pay an additional fee. The combination entrance to Machu Picchu and Montaña is S/142, and there is a limit of 400 people who can enter each day.) From here it takes about 90 minutes to reach the summit. You need to enter before 11am and be at the top no later than 12:30pm.

For a more detailed guide of the ruins and Machu Picchu's history, look for Peter Frost's "Exploring Cusco" (Nuevas Imágenes, 1999) or Ruth M. Wright and Dr. Alfredo Valanecia Zegarra's "The Machu Picchu Guidebook" (3D Press, 2011), both available in Cusco bookstores.

HIKING THE INCA TRAIL ★★★

At its most basic, the Inca Trail (Camino del Inca) was a footpath through the Andes leading directly to the gates of Machu Picchu. Contrary to its image as a lone, lost, remote city, Machu Picchu was not isolated in the clouds. It was the crown of an entire Inca province, as ruins all along the Inca Trail attest. Machu Picchu was an administrative center in addition to its other putative purposes. That larger purpose is comprehensible only to those who hike the ancient royal route and visit the other ruins scattered along the way to the sacred city.

More than that, though, the Incas conceived of Machu Picchu and the great trail leading to it in grand artistic and spiritual terms. Hiking the Inca Trail—the ancient royal highway—is, hands down, the most authentic and scenic way to visit Machu Picchu and get a clear grasp of the Incas' overarching architectural concept and supreme regard for nature. As impressive as Machu Picchu itself, the trail traverses a 325-sq.-km (125-sq.-mile) national park designated as the Machu Picchu Historical Sanctuary. The entire zone is replete with extraordinary natural and man-made sights: Inca ruins, exotic vegetation and animals, and dazzling mountain and cloud-forest vistas.

Today the Inca Trail—which, as part of the Machu Picchu Historical Sanctuary, has been designated a natural and cultural World Heritage Site—is the most important and most popular hiking trail in South America, followed by many thousands of ecotourists and modern-day pilgrims in the past 3 decades. Its extreme popularity in recent years—more than 75,000 people a year hike the famous trail—has led to concerns among environmentalists and historians that the trail is suffering potentially irreparable degradation. The National Institute of Culture (INC) and the Ministry of Industry, Tourism, Integration, and International Trade (MITINCI), reacting to pressure from groups such as UNESCO (which threatened to rescind Machu Picchu's World Heritage Site status), instituted far-reaching changes in practices designed to limit the number of visitors and damage to Machu Picchu and the Inca Trail, though these alone may not be enough to forestall the trail's damage; see the "Inca Trail Regulations" box on p. 219.

There are two principal ways to walk to Machu Picchu: either along the traditional, fairly arduous 4-day/3-night path with three serious mountain passes, or as part of a more accessible 2-day/1-night trail (there's also an even shorter 1-day trek that covers just the last part of the trail, which is suitable for inexperienced walkers). You can hire porters to haul your packs or suck it up and do it the hard way. Independent trekking on the Inca Trail without an official guide has been prohibited since 2001. **You must go as part of an organized group arranged by an officially sanctioned tour agency.** (At the end of 2011, 188 agencies, both in Cusco and beyond, were allowed to sell Inca Trail packages.) A couple or a small number of people can organize their own group if they are willing to pay higher prices for the luxury of not having to join an ad hoc group.

The Inca Trail

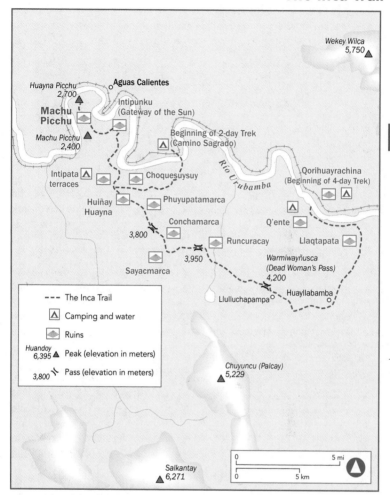

Wekey Wilca
5,750 ▲

Huayna Picchu
2,700 ▲   o **Aguas Calientes**

Machu Picchu 🏛️   Intipunku
(Gateway of the Sun)

Machu Picchu
2,400 ▲   Beginning of 2-day Trek
                          (Camino Sagrado)
                          △

Intipata △   🏛️ Choquesuysuy   Qorihuayrachina
terraces   🏛️   Río Urubamba   (Beginning of 4-day Trek)
                                                            🏛️

   Huiñay 🏛️   🏛️ Phuyupatamarca   △
   Huayna   Q'ente 🏛️
              Conchamarca   Llaqtapata
        3,800   🏛️   🏛️ Runcuracay   🏛️
                             3,950 ↯   Warmiwayñusca
          🏛️   (Dead Woman's Pass)
     Sayacmarca   4,200
                                                 ↯   Huayllabamba
                           o Llulluchapampa o

--- The Inca Trail

△ Camping and water

🏛️ Ruins

Huandoy
6,395 ▲ Peak (elevation in meters)

3,800 ↯ Pass (elevation in meters)

Chuyuncu (Palcay)
5,229 ▲

Salkantay
▲ 6,271

0 _____ 5 mi
0 _____ 5 km

8

MACHU PICCHU & THE INCA TRAIL | Hiking the Inca Trail

Sadly, even with the new regulations, hiking the Inca Trail, beautiful and mystical as it remains for most, is not a silent, solitary walk in the clouds. At least in high season, you will contend with groups walking the trail both in front of and behind you, and some will invariably be noisy student groups.

PREPARING FOR THE INCA TRAIL

The classic **4-day route** is along hand-hewn stone stairs and trails through sumptuous mountain scenery and amazing cloud forest, past rushing rivers and dozens of Inca ruins. The zone is inhabited by rare orchids, 419 species of birds, and even the indigenous spectacled bear. The trek begins at

213

ON THE TRAIL OF "NEW" INCA CITIES: THE discovery CONTINUES

Ever since the demise of the Inca Empire, rumors, clues, and fabulous tales of a fabled lost Inca city stuffed with gold and silver have rippled across Peru. The tales prompted searches, discoveries, and, often, reevaluations. Machu Picchu wasn't the lost and last city Hiram Bingham thought it was—Vilcabamba the Old was the last refuge of the Incas. The search continues, though, and incredibly, new discoveries continue to occur in the Andes. First, it was Choquequirao in the early 1990s. More recently, other teams have announced the discoveries of other lost Inca cities.

The discovery of **Qorihuayrachina** (also called **Cerro Victoria,** the name of the peak it rests on), 35km (22 miles) southwest of Machu Picchu in the Andes, was announced by the National Geographic Society in March 2002. Led by Peter Frost, a group of explorers uncovered the ruins of a large settlement that might have been occupied by the Incas long before they'd built a continent-spanning empire. Among the ruins are tombs and platforms, suggestive of an important burial site and sacred rites, although there are also indications that the site was an entire city. The ruins cover 6 sq. km (2⅓ sq. miles) and occupy a spectacular mountaintop location with panoramic views of the Vilcabamba range's snowcapped peaks, which were considered sacred by the Incas. Archaeologists, claiming that Qorihuayrachina is one of the most important sites found in the Vilcabamba region since it was abandoned by the Incas nearly 500 years ago, have high hopes that the ruins will help them

piece together the Inca Empire from beginning to end.

Frost claimed the site was the largest of its kind found since 1964. Comprising 100 structures, including circular homes, storehouses, cemeteries, funeral towers, roadways, waterworks, farming terraces, a dam, and a pyramid, the city might have been occupied by the Incas who fled Cusco after the Spanish conquest. The ruins are secluded in cloud forest in the remote Vilcabamba region.

Just months after the discovery of Qorihuayrachina in 2002, the British Royal Geographic Society, led by Hugh Thompson and Gary Ziegler, announced the finding of a major new Inca site, **Cota Coca,** only a few kilometers away but across a deep canyon from Choquequirao (a road might have connected the two). Wholly unknown to the outside world until its discovery, Cota Coca—97km (60 miles) west of Cusco—appears to have been an administrative and storage center.

Llaqtapata was rediscovered by a U.S. and British team using remote (aerial) infrared technology and (re)surfaced in November 2003. Just 3km (1¾ miles) from Machu Picchu, it, too, had been visited by Bingham and by several explorers in the 1980s, so it's open to interpretation how new its "discovery" in fact is.

How long these discoveries might go on is anyone's guess. According to Hugh Thompson, "The physical geography of southeast Peru is so wild, with its deep canyons and dense vegetation, that it is possible that there are even more ruins waiting to be discovered. The fact that we have found two in 2 years means there could be many more out there."

Qorihuayrachina near Ollantaytambo—more easily described as Km 88 of the railway from Cusco to Aguas Calientes. The 43km (26-mile) route passes three formidable mountain passes, including the punishing "Dead Woman's Pass," to a maximum altitude of 4,200m (13,800 ft.). Most groups enter the ruins of

Machu Picchu at sunrise on the fourth day, although others, whose members are less keen on rising at 3:30am to do it, trickle in throughout the morning.

The **2-day version** of the trail is being promoted by authorities as the Camino Sagrado del Inca, or "Sacred Trail," although it might also be called the Camino "Lite." It is a reasonable alternative to the classic trail if time or fitness is lacking. The path rises only to an elevation of about 2,750m (9,020 ft.) and is a relatively easy climb to Huiñay Huayna and then down to Machu Picchu. The minitrail begins only 14km (8¾ miles) away from Machu Picchu, at Km 104, and it circumvents much of the finest mountain scenery and ruins. Groups spend the night near the ruins of Huiñay Huayna before arriving at Machu Picchu for sunrise on the second day. More and more people of all ages and athletic abilities are tackling the Inca Trail; the Peruvian government, in addition to adopting more stringent regulations governing its use, placed flush toilets in campsites several years ago in an attempt to make the trail cleaner and more user-friendly.

Either way you go, it is advisable to give yourself a couple of days in Cusco or a spot in the Sacred Valley to acclimatize to the high elevation. Cold- and wet-weather technical gear, a solid backpack, and comfortable, sturdy, broken-in (and waterproof) hiking boots are musts (also needed: sleeping bag, flashlight/headlamp, and sunblock). Above all, respect the ancient trail and its environment. Whatever you pack in, you must also pack out. You should also choose your dates carefully. The dry season (June–Oct) is the most crowded time on the trail, but it's excellent in terms of weather. Shoulder seasons can be best of all, even with the threat of a bit of rain; May is perhaps best, with good weather and slightly lower numbers of trekkers. Other months—especially December through March—are simply too wet for all but the hardest-core trail vets. **The entire trail is closed for maintenance and conservation during the month of February**—which is one of the rainiest and least appealing months for trekking to Machu Picchu anyway. For the most popular months (May–Sept), early booking (at least 3 months in advance) is essential.

The Peruvian government has sought to not only limit the number of trekkers on the Inca Trail (now capped at 200 trekkers and 300 trek staff, or 500 total per day), but also to maximize revenue from one of its foremost attractions. Thus, the cost of hiking the trail has steadily climbed—it now costs at least three times what it did just a few years ago. Standard-class 4-day treks, the most common and economical service, start at around $500 per person, including entrance fees ($93 adults, $47 students) and return by tourist rail. Independent trekkers generally join a mixed group of travelers; groups tend to be between 12 and 16 people, with guaranteed daily departures. The cost includes a bus to Km 88 to begin the trek, an English-speaking guide, tents, mattresses, three daily meals, and porters who carry all common equipment. Tips for porters or guides are extra (and considered mandatory). Personal porters, to carry your personal items, can be hired for about $150 for the 4 days. Premium-class services generally operate smaller group sizes (a maximum of 10 trekkers), and you generally get an upgrade on the return train. Prices for premium group treks, organized for small private groups, range from $750 to as high as $1,500 per person. Note that entrance fees to the Inca Trail and Machu Picchu should always be included in your package price.

Prices vary for trail packages based on services and the quality and experience of the agency. For the most part, you get what you pay for. Rock-bottom prices (anything below $500, generally) will probably get you an inexperienced guide who speaks little English, food that is barely edible, camping equipment on its last legs, and a large, rowdy group (usually 16 young trekkers). Especially important is the ability of an agency to guarantee departure even if its desired target number of travelers is not filled. Students with ISIC identification can expect about a $40 discount.

Be wary of hidden costs; never purchase Inca Trail (or, for that matter, any tour) packages from anyone other than officially licensed agencies, and be careful to make payments (and get official receipts) at the physical offices of the agencies. If you have questions about whether an agency is legitimate or is authorized to sell Inca Trail packages, ask for assistance at the main tourism information office in Cusco (see p. 117).

To guarantee a spot with an agency (which must request a trek permit for each trekker), it is imperative that you make a reservation and pay for your entrance fee a minimum of 15 days in advance (though in practice you'd be wise to do this at least 4–6 months or more in advance if you plan to go during the peak months of May–Oct). Reservations can be made as much as a year in advance. Gone are the days when trekkers could simply show up in Cusco and organize a trek on the fly. Changing dates once you have a reservation is difficult, if not impossible. If spots remain on agency rosters, they are offered on a first-come, first-served basis.

The entrance ticket for the 2-day Camino Sagrado, purchased in Cusco, is $51 for adults and $44 for students. Basic pooled service (maximum 16 trekkers) costs about $200 to $250 per person (including the entrance fee).

INCA TRAIL AGENCIES

Only officially sanctioned travel agencies are permitted to organize group treks along the Inca Trail; an overwhelming number, nearly 190 tour operators (!)—both Peruvian and international—have been granted government licenses to

---

Howling at the Moon

For a truly spectacular experience on the Inca Trail, plan your trip to coincide with a full moon (ideally, departing 2 or 3 days beforehand). Locals say the weather's best then, and having your nights illuminated by a full or near-full moon, especially for the early rise and push into Machu Picchu on the last day, is unforgettable.

MACHU PICCHU & THE INCA TRAIL | Hiking the Inca Trail

sell and operate Inca Trail treks. With the higher-end agencies, it is usually possible to assemble your own private group, with as few as two hikers. Budget trekkers will join an established group. In addition to cost, hikers should ask about group size (12 or fewer is best; 16 is the most allowed), the quality of the guides and their English-speaking abilities, the quality of food preparation, and porters and equipment. You should also make certain that the agency guarantees daily departures so that you're not stuck waiting in Cusco for a group to be assembled.

Recommended agencies that score high on those criteria follow. Some of the larger international adventure-tour operators, including several listed in Chapter 9, "Planning Your Trip to Lima, Cusco & Machu Picchu," also handle the Inca Trail and alternative treks in Cusco and the Sacred Valley.

o **Andean Life** (www.andeanlifeperu.com; ℰ **866/356-5524** in the U.S. and Canada): A reputable mid-range company offering both pooled basic and premium private treks with good guides.

o **Andean Treks** ★★ (www.andeantreks.com; ℰ **800/683-8148** in the U.S. and Canada, or 617/924-1974): A longtime (since 1980), well-thought-of outdoors operator based in Watertown, Massachusetts, running 5-day treks along the Inca Trail as well as numerous other programs in Latin America.

o **Andina Travel** ★ (www.andinatravel.com; ℰ **084/251-892** in Cusco): A progressive company interested in sustainable development, owned by a Cusco native and his North American business partner, offering classic Inca Trail and alternative treks.

o **Apumayo Expediciones** ★ (www.apumayo.com; ℰ **084/246-018**): A veteran of adventure tourism in the region with fixed departures for hikes.

o **Big Foot Cusco** (www.bigfootcusco.com; ℰ **084/233-836**): A popular and dependable budget agency.

o **Chaska Tours** ★ (www.chaskatours.com; ℰ **084/240-424**): A very capable mid-range company, run by a Dutch and Peruvian team, praised for its private and group treks to Machu Picchu as well as Choquequirao.

o **Enigma Adventure Tours** ★ (www.enigmaperu.com; ℰ **084/222-155**): An upscale adventure travel operator with a good reputation and specialized and alternative hiking and trekking options, good for small-group and private treks.

o **Explorandes** ★★ (www.explorandes.com; ℰ **084/506-758**): One of the top high-end agencies and among the most experienced in treks and mountaineering across Peru. Especially good for forming very small private groups.

o **InkaNatura** ★ (www.inkanatura.com; ℰ **01/203-5000**): A long-running agency offering well-planned and comfortable Inca Trail treks.

o **Mayuc** ★ (www.mayuc.com; ℰ **888/493-2109** in the U.S. and Canada or 084/242-824 in Cusco): Especially good for pampered Inca Trail expeditions (porters carry all packs). It aims to be low impact, and hosts smaller groups.

- **SAS Travel** ★ (www.sastravelperu.com; ☎ **084/249-194**): Large, long-established agency serving budget-oriented trekkers. Very popular, responsible, and well organized.
- **United Mice** ★ (www.unitedmice.com; ☎ **084/221-139**): Started by one of the trail's most respected guides, this is another of the top trekking specialists organizing affordable mid-range treks.

DAY-BY-DAY: THE CLASSIC INCA TRAIL TREK

The following is typical of the group-organized 4-day/3-night schedule along the Inca Trail.

Day 1   Trekkers arrive from Cusco, either by train, getting off at the midway stop, Ollantaytambo, or Km 88; or by bus, at Km 82, the preferred method of transport for many groups. (Starting at Km 82 doesn't add an appreciable distance to the trail.) After crossing the Río Urubamba (Vilcanota), the first gentle ascent of the trail looms to Inca ruins at **Llaqtapata** (also called **Patallacta,** where Bingham and his team first camped on the way to Machu Picchu). The path then crosses the Río Cusichaca, tracing the line of the river until it begins to climb and reaches the small village (the only one still inhabited along the trail) of **Huayllabamba**—a 2- to 3-hour climb. Most groups spend their first night at campsites here. Total distance: 10 to 11km (6¼–6¾ miles).

Day 2   Day 2 is the hardest of the trek. The next ruins are at **Llullucharoc** (3,800m/12,460 ft.), about an hour's steep climb from Huayllabamba. **Llulluchapampa,** an isolated village that lies in a flat meadow, is a strenuous 90-minute to 2-hour climb through cloud forest. There are extraordinary valley views from here. Next up is the dreaded Abra de Huarmihuañusqa, or **Dead Woman's Pass,** the highest point on the trail and infamous among veterans of the Inca Trail. (The origin of the name—or who the poor victim was—is anybody's guess.) The air is thin, and the 4,200m (13,780-ft.) pass is a killer for most: a punishing 2½-hour climb in the hot sun, which is replaced by cold winds at the top. It's not uncommon for freezing rain or even snow to meet trekkers atop the pass. After a deserved rest at the summit, the path descends sharply on complicated stone steps to **Pacamayo** (3,600m/11,810 ft.), where groups camp for the night. Total distance: 11km (6¾ miles).

About Tipping

At the end of the Inca Trail, guides, cooks, and especially porters expect—and fully deserve—to be tipped for their services. They get comparatively little of the sum hikers pay to form part of the group, and they depend on tips for most of their salary, much like waitstaff in American restaurants. Tip to the extent that you are able (for guides and porters that should probably be about $5–$10 per day, in *soles*). Tipping a relatively huge amount relative to what they earn—I've heard stories of trekkers tipping a couple of hundred dollars—is going way overboard.

INCA TRAIL regulations

For decades, individuals trekked the Inca Trail on their own, but hundreds of thousands of visitors—more than 75,000 a year—left behind so much detritus that not only was the experience compromised for most future trekkers, but the very environment was also placed at risk. The entire zone has suffered grave deforestation and erosion. The Peruvian government, under pressure from international organizations, has finally instituted changes and restrictions designed to lessen the human impact on the trail and on Machu Picchu itself: In the first couple of years, regulations were poorly enforced, but in 2003, the government announced its intentions to fully and strictly enforce them.

All trekkers are now required to go accompanied by a guide and a group. In addition, the overall number of trekkers permitted on the trail was significantly reduced, to 200 per day (with an additional 300 trek staff, for a total daily number admitted of 500); the maximum number of trekkers per group outing is capped at 16; only professionally qualified and licensed guides are allowed to lead groups on the Inca Trail; the maximum loads porters can carry has been limited to 20kg (44 lb.); and all companies must pay porters the minimum wage (about $15 per day).

These changes have cut the number of trekkers on the trail in half and have made reservations essential. Guarantee your space on the trail by making a reservation at least a month in advance of your trip (but 4–6 months or more in advance for high season May–Oct; reservations can be made as much as a year in advance). Travelers willing to wing it stand an outside chance of still finding available spots a week or a few days before embarking on the trail, perhaps even at discounted rates, but waiting until you arrive in Cusco is a ridiculous risk if you're really counting on doing the Inca Trail.

The key changes for travelers are that it is no longer possible to go on the trail independently and no longer dirt-cheap to walk 4 days to Machu Picchu. The good news is that the trail is more organized and that hope for its preservation is greater. But if you're looking for solitude and a more spiritual experience, you might consider one of the "alternative ruins treks"; see the box on p. 220 for more details.

Day 3   By the third day, most of the remaining footpath is the original work of the Incas. (In previous sections, the government "restored" the stonework with a heavy hand.) En route to the next mountain pass (1 hr.), trekkers encounter the ruins of **Runcuracay.** The circular structure (the name means "basket shaped") is unique among those found along the trail. From here, a steep 45-minute to 1-hour climb leads to the second pass, **Abra de Runcuracay** (3,900m/12,790 ft.), and the location of an official campsite just over the summit. There are great views of the Vilcabamba mountain range. After passing through a naturally formed tunnel, the path leads past a lake and a stunning staircase to **Sayacmarca** (3,500m/11,480 ft.), named for its nearly inaccessible setting surrounded by dizzying cliffs. Among the ruins are ritual baths and a terrace viewpoint overlooking the Aobamba Valley, suggesting that the site was not inhabited but instead served as a resting point for travelers and as a control station.

THE road LESS (OR MORE COMFORTABLY) TRAVELED: ALTERNATIVES TO THE INCA TRAIL

The legendary Inca Trail was once very much off the beaten path and at the cutting edge of adventure travel—for hardcore trekkers only. Although the Peruvian government adopted new measures to restrict the numbers of trekkers along the trail, it has become so popular and well-worn that in high season it's tough to find the solitude and quiet contemplation such a sacred path deserves. Trekkers and travelers looking for more privacy, greater authenticity, or bragging rights are seeking out alternatives, and many adventure-travel companies are catering to them by offering less accessible trails to keep one step ahead of the masses. Several international operators now offer custom-designed alternatives to the traditional Inca Trail, and many Peru cognoscenti believe this is the future of trekking in Cusco and the Sacred Valley. Some of the challenging treks terminate in visits to Machu Picchu, while others explore stunning but much less-visited Inca ruins like Choquequirao. **Adventure Life ★** (www.adventurelife. com; ✆ **800/344-6118**) promotes a 10-day Cachiccata trek and 11-day Ausangate trip alternative; **Andean Treks ★★** (www.andeantreks.com; ✆ **800/683-8148**) offers a 4-day "Moonstone to Machu Picchu" trek, as well as others to Choquequirao and Ausangate; **Mountain Travel Sobek ★★** (www. mtsobek.com; ✆ **888/831-7526**) offers a 9-day (7 days hiking) "Discovering the Lares Region"; **Peru for Less ★★** (www.peruforless.com; ✆ **877/2609-0309**), originally based in the U.S., recently launched a series of small-group alternative treks in the Vilcabamba region, with trips to Choquequirao, Ausangate, and Espíritu Pampa; and **Wilderness Travel ★★** (www.wildernesstravel. com; ✆ **800/368-2794**) has a 17-day (13 days hiking) "Choquequirao to Machu Picchu Hidden Inca Trail" tour. Most treks range from about $600 to $4,000 per person. **Note:** Keep in mind that these tour groups may change the names and details of their available treks at any time; call or review their websites for what's available at the time of your trip.

The trend toward luxury, or soft, adventure has gained traction in the Peruvian Andes, and companies offering treks to Machu Picchu and other highland destinations are targeting more affluent and creature comfort–oriented travelers who want the adventure experience without roughing it too much. **Mountain Lodges of Peru ★★★** (www.mountain lodgesofperu.com; ✆ **877/491-5261** in

The trail backtracks a bit on the way to **Conchamarca,** another rest stop. Here, the well-preserved Inca footpath drops into jungle thick with exotic vegetation, such as lichens, hanging moss, bromeliads, and orchids, and some of the zone's unique bird species. After passing through another Inca tunnel, the path climbs gently for 2 hours along a stone road, toward the trail's third major pass, **Phuyupatamarca** (3,800m/12,460 ft.); the final climb is considerably easier than the two that came before it. This is a spectacular section of the trail, with great views of the Urubamba Valley. Some of the region's highest snowcapped peaks (all over 5,500m/18,040 ft.), including Salcantay, are

the U.S. and Canada), a Peruvian adventure travel company, has constructed several lodges on private lands in the Vilcabamba mountain range west of the Sacred Valley and also in the Lares Valley. The inns are stunning, not only for their high-altitude locations but also their sophisticated architecture and amenities—which include whirlpools, hot showers, fireplaces, and sleek dining rooms. Mountain Lodges offers its own 7-day treks to Salkantay (beginning at $3,240 per person), culminating in a visit to Machu Picchu, as well as 5- or 7-day treks in the Lares Valley (beginning at $2,250 per person). The company has also contracted with international trekking and adventure companies, including **Backroads** (www.backroads.com; (**C**) **800/462-2848**), **Wilderness Travel,** and **Mountain Travel Sobek** (see above), which have booked the lodges for their own 9-day (5 days trekking) "Machu Picchu Lodge to Lodge" or "Inn to Inn" packages. Prices for full trips, including stays in Cusco, run to $4,995 per person. **Andean Lodges**

★ (www.andeanlodges.com; (**C**) **305/434-7167** in the U.S. and Canada, or 084/224-613), a rare joint initiative between the Cusco tour group Auqui Mountain Spirit and local Quechua shepherding communities, operates four simple and ecofriendly mountain lodges, which it claims are the highest altitude lodges in the world (at 4,000–4,500m/13,000–15,000 ft.), along the Camino del Apu Ausangate (in the Vilcanota range). Trek prices start at $870 per person.

If the notion of soft or luxury adventure travel doesn't excite your inner hard-core adventurer, consider one of the spectacularly scenic (and arduous) 4- to 11-day treks that have gained wider traction in the last few years: **Salcantay, Vilcabamba, Espíritu Pampa,** and **Choquequirao,** the last two "lost" Inca cities only truly unearthed in the past decade. All are increasingly offered by local trek tour agencies in Cusco and some of the most established international trekking and Peruvian travel companies (see above). Much as I hate to disparage the legendary Camino Inca, it has become too popular and laden with restrictions and hassles for many adventure travelers to enjoy it the way it was intended. By going off the standard trekking grid, not only can you be sure that when you get back to Cusco not everyone in the coffeehouse will have the same bragging rights, but also you are likely to have a more authentic, peaceful, and exhilarating outdoors and cultural experience.

clearly visible, and the end of the trail is in sight. The tourist town of Aguas Calientes lies below, and trekkers can see the backside of Machu Picchu (the peak, not the ruins).

From the peak, trekkers reach the beautiful, restored Inca **ruins of Phuyupatamarca.** The ancient village is another one aptly named: It translates as "Town above the clouds." The remains of six ceremonial baths are clearly visible, as are retaining-wall terraces. A stone staircase of 2,250 steps plummets into the cloud forest, taking about 90 minutes to descend. The path forks, with the footpath on the left leading to the fan-shaped **Intipata terraces.**

On the right, the trail pushes on to the extraordinary ruins of **Huiñay Huayna ★★**, which are actually about a 10-minute walk from the trail. Back at the main footpath, there's a campsite and ramshackle trekkers' hostel offering hot showers, food, and drink. The grounds are a major gathering place for trekkers before the final push to Machu Picchu, and for some, they're a bit too boisterous and unkempt, an unpleasant intrusion after all the pristine beauty up to this point on the trail. Although closest to Machu Picchu, the Huiñay Huayna ruins, nearly the equal of Machu Picchu, were only discovered in 1941. Their name, which means "Forever Young," refers not to their relatively recent discovery, but to the perpetually flowering orchid of the same name that is found in abundance nearby. The stop was evidently an important one along the trail; on the slopes around the site are dozens of stone agricultural terraces, and 10 ritual baths, which still have running water, awaited travelers. Total distance: 15km (9⅓ miles).

Day 4   From Huiñay Huayna, trekkers have but one goal remaining: reaching Intipunku (the Sun Gate) and descending to Machu Picchu, preferably in time to witness the dramatic sunrise over the ruins. Most groups depart camp at 4am or earlier to reach the pass at Machu Picchu and arrive in time for daybreak, around 6:30am. Awaiting them first, though, is a good 60- to 90-minute trek along narrow Inca stone paths, and then a final killer: a 50-step, nearly vertical climb. The descent from Intipunku to Machu Picchu takes about 45 minutes.

Having reached the ruins, trekkers have to exit the site and deposit their backpacks at the entrance gate near the hotel. There, they also get their entrance passes to Machu Picchu stamped; the pass is good for 1 day only. Total distance: 7km (4⅓ miles).

AGUAS CALIENTES (MACHU PICCHU PUEBLO)

Renamed Machu Picchu Pueblo by the Peruvian government—a name adopted by few—Aguas Calientes is quite literally the end of the line. It's a gringo outpost of *mochileros* (backpackers) outfitted in the latest alpaca and indigenous weave fashions: hats, gloves, sweaters—they are walking (if unshaved) advertisements for Peruvian artisanship. Making it Peru's own little Katmandu, the trekkers hang out for a few days after their great journey to Machu Picchu, sharing beers and tales, and scoring a final woven hat or scarf, or at least celebratory T-shirt, to wear as a trophy back home.

To be honest, there's not much else to do in Aguas Calientes, which might as well be called Aires Calientes, given its sweltering heat and humidity for much of the year. A purpose-built jumble of cheap construction and a blur of pizza joints, souvenir stalls, and *hostales,* it's a place tourism officials would probably like a do-over on. But if you squint hard enough, and your legs are tired enough, you might just find a little ramshackle charm in it.

Aguas Calientes (Machu Picchu Pueblo)

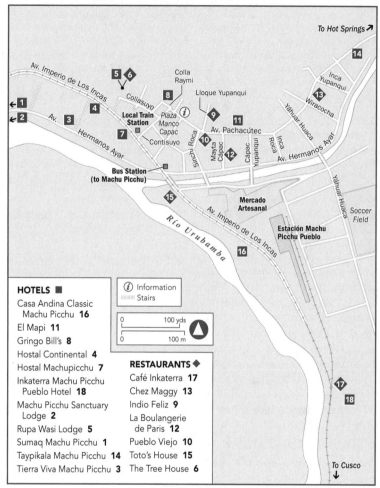

To Hot Springs ↗

Av. Imperio de Los Incas

Colla Raymi

Inca Yupanqui

Collasuyo

Lloque Yupanqui

Wiracocha

Yáhuar Huaca

1

2

Av.

3

Hermanos Ayar

5 **6**

8

4

Local Train Station

Plaza Manco Cápac

i

9

11

Av. Pachacútec

Contisuyo

7

Sinchi Roca

Mayta Cápac

Cápac Yupanqui

Inca Roca

Av. Hermanos Ayar

10

12

13

14

Bus Station (to Machu Picchu)

15

Av. Imperio de Los Incas

Mercado Artesanal

Estación Machu Picchu Pueblo

Yáhuar Huaca

Soccer Field

Río Urubamba

16

17

18

To Cusco ↓

HOTELS ■

Casa Andina Classic Machu Picchu **16**

El Mapi **11**

Gringo Bill's **8**

Hostal Continental **4**

Hostal Machupicchu **7**

Inkaterra Machu Picchu Pueblo Hotel **18**

Machu Picchu Sanctuary Lodge **2**

Rupa Wasi Lodge **5**

Sumaq Machu Picchu **1**

Taypikala Machu Picchu **14**

Tierra Viva Machu Picchu **3**

i Information

Stairs

0   100 yds
0   100 m

RESTAURANTS ◆

Café Inkaterra **17**

Chez Maggy **13**

Indio Feliz **9**

La Boulangerie de Paris **12**

Pueblo Viejo **10**

Toto's House **15**

The Tree House **6**

Exploring Aguas Calientes

Aguas Calientes has a river rushing through its middle and *baños termales,* or outdoor **hot springs**—the source of the town's name—at the far end of Avenida Pachacútec. Many visitors find springs to be hygienically challenged, but they're popular with folks who've completed the Inca Trail and are in desperate need of muscular relaxation (not to mention a bath). The one pool with freezing mountain water can be tremendously restorative if you've just finished a long day at the ruins, but the smell of iron is overpowering. The springs are open from 5am to 9pm; admission is S/15. Just be sure to leave your valuables locked up at the hotel.

The most recent mudslide at Machu Picchu occurred in January 2010, when five people (including two on the Inca Trail) were killed and 2,000 tourists stranded, requiring airlift evacuations by helicopter. Officials said the rains that swelled the Urubamba River were the heaviest in 15 years, and floods affected 80,000 people living in or near Aguas Calientes, leaving many homeless. Train service to Machu Picchu was not restored for more than a month. It was the latest in a series of catastrophic rain-related events near the ancient ruins. In October 2005, an avalanche destroyed part of the train track leading from Cusco to Machu Picchu, stranding 1,400 travelers, and before that, in April 2004, two massive mudslides at the tail end of the rainy season hit Aguas Calientes, killing six local people and stranding as many as 1,500 tourists for the duration of Easter weekend.

Such destructive rains may not be the norm, but they highlight both the dangers of traveling in the highlands during the wet season as well as the precarious infrastructure of Aguas Calientes and its ill-preparedness to handle the explosive growth of tourism in recent years.

Adventurous sorts not yet exhausted from climbing might want to climb the sacred mountain **Putukusi ★★**, which commands extraordinary distant views across the river to the ruins of Machu Picchu. Look for the trail head on the right side of the railroad just out of town. (A signpost reads Km 111.) Veer to the right up stone steps until you reach a clearing and a series of stone-carved switchbacks. At the summit, the view of Machu Picchu, nestled like an architectural model between its two famous peaks, is incredible. In good condition, the trek up takes about 75 minutes; the descent takes 45 minutes.

Another good trail, particularly for bird-watchers, is the short trail to **Mandor Valley ★** and a waterfall found there. From the railroad tracks, walk downstream (beyond the old train station) until you come to the ravine (about 3km/1¾ miles). A short climb takes you to the waterfall.

VISITOR INFORMATION

Aguas Calientes has an **iPerú** office, Av. Pachacútec, Cdra. 1 s/n (© **084/211-104**), about one-third of the way up the main drag in town. It has photocopies of town maps and some basic hotel and Machu Picchu information.

FAST FACTS

The main bank in Aguas Calientes is **Banco de Crédito,** Av. Imperio de los Incas s/n, though there are several ATMs around town. Shops and restaurants along the two main streets, Avenida Imperio de los Incas and Avenida Pachacútec, also buy dollars from travelers in need at standard exchange rates.

You'll find the **police** on Avenida Imperio de los Incas, down from the railway station (© **084/211-178**).

There are Internet *cabinas* at a couple of places on the Plaza de Armas, though almost every hotel should have a computer or Wi-Fi available. There's a **post office** at Colla Raymi 101. A *posta de salud* (health clinic) is located at Av. Imperio de los Incas, s/n.

Where to Eat

Scores of small and friendly restaurants line the two main drags (okay, the only two real streets) in Aguas Calientes, Avenida Imperio de los Incas and Avenida Pachacútec. There's a proliferation of cheap pizzeria pit stops hugging the railroad tracks; if you're looking for an easy meal of wood-fired pizza, almost any spot in town can accommodate you. Menu hawkers, often the children of the cook or owner, will try to lure you in with very cheap menu deals.

For lunch during visits to the ruins, you have two main choices: the expensive buffet at Machu Picchu Sanctuary Lodge or a sack lunch. I recommend the latter, especially because lunch is when lots of tourists vacate the ruins; pick up a sack lunch at Rupa Wasi or Gringo Bill's (see below), or assemble one from the breakfast buffet of your hotel. *Note:* You cannot enter Machu Picchu with disposable plastic water bottles.

MODERATE

Café Inkaterra ★★ PERUVIAN/INTERNATIONAL   At the entrance to the Inkaterra Machu Picchu Pueblo Hotel on the riverfront, this is the classiest, most intimate dining space in town. Large windows, contemporary photography, and an Amazonian palm-thatched roof set the carefully curated atmosphere that the brand is known for. Service, as in the hotels, is impeccable. Prices are almost the same as other restaurants in town, yet the quality of the *novo andino* menu is quite good. Dishes jump between perfectly prepared Peruvian classics like *lomo saltado* (beef and potato stir-fry) and casual international staples like lasagna or burgers. Tea comes from the plantation on the property.

Av. Imperio de los Incas (Km 10, Línea Férrea Cusco-Quillabamba). www.inkaterra.com. ✆ **084/211-122.** Main courses S/35–S/65. Daily 11am–9pm.

Indio Feliz ★★ FRENCH   Indio Feliz is owned by a Peruvian woman and her French husband, who came to the area to cook for engineers building a hydroelectric plant and never left. Since it opened in 1995, it's become the restaurant of choice for many, and is regularly full. Every square inch of the lively, two-level space is filled with knickknacks, ranging from business cards to nautical memorabilia. The menu seamlessly fuses Andean ingredients into French classics, like garlic trout, or roasted chicken in a pisco-based sauce. There's a great prix-fixe menu (S/60, an excellent value) that comes with an appetizer, main course, and dessert. The funky Captain's Bar and Lounge is a nice place to pop in for a drink and catch up on travel gossip.

Capac Yupanqui 103, an alley to the left off Avenida Pachacútec. www.indiofeliz.com. ✆ **084/210-090.** Main courses S/28–S/55. Daily 11:30am–10pm.

Toto's House ★ PERUVIAN   Listen to the roar of the Vilcanota where it meets with the Aguas Calientes from this perfect corner perch, while sipping on a pisco sour and refueling after a long hike or busy day at the ruins. This is a simple, casual place with wood tables and floors. The huge menu serves the same international and Peruvian staples (*lomo saltado,* pizza) as everywhere else, though much of it is cooked in an open fire pit. Near the train station, the restaurant is often frequented by large tour groups on day trips from Cusco, who mostly stick to the popular lunch buffet (S/60).

Avenida Imperios de los Incas s/n. www.grupointi.com. ✆ **084/211-020.** Main courses S/25–S/40. Daily noon–10pm.

The Tree House ★★ PERUVIAN   Hidden away uphill at the Rupa Wasi hotel, most tourists don't even realize that this place exists. Among foodies in the know, though, there is little debate whether this is the top restaurant in Aguas Calientes. It is. In a town dominated by hotel restaurants and identical-menu mediocre backpacker fare, the Tree House makes pastas by hand and incorporates local ingredients into the dishes, like glazing pork ribs in an elderberry and tamarind sauce, or serving alpaca *anticuchos* (skewers) with *ají amarillo* (yellow chile pepper) fettuccine. The atmosphere here is pleasantly rustic. The interior is almost entirely made of wood, aside from a stone fireplace and a few blackboards that list the daily specials. Cooking lessons ($95) are offered twice per day, and are a good value, lasting 1 hour.

Calle Huanacaure 105 (2 blocks from the Plaza de Armas). www.rupawasi.net. ✆ **084/236-852.** Main courses S/30–S/55. Daily 10am–3pm and 6–10pm.

INEXPENSIVE

Chez Maggy ★ PIZZA/INTERNATIONAL   Right on restaurant row, this branch of the Cusco Chez Maggy, now a national chain, is the place to come for no-frills, reasonably priced, carb-loaded food that gets energy levels up. The menu is huge, taking in Mexican, pasta, and traditional Peruvian dishes. The wood-fired pizzas are some of the best in town. Although you won't be overly impressed with anything, you won't be disappointed, either. A few sidewalk tables offer great people-watching, while the dining room, illuminated by a skylight, is rather cluttered with the antiques of explorations past.

Av. Pachacútec 156. ✆ **084/211-006.** Main courses S/18–S/36. Daily 11am–10pm.

La Boulangerie de Paris ★ CAFE/BAKERY   Say what? A real French *boulangerie* in the town below Machu Picchu? Expats were particularly relieved when this actually decent bakery opened in mid-2012 near the bus stop for Machu Picchu. Fresh-baked croissants and baguettes, simple sandwiches and empanadas that can be taken to the ruins (saving mucho compared to the on-site snack bar), and pastries and sweets like coconut flan and tiramisu are available. The owners are socially conscious, too, training locals in the art of baking during 2-month courses, and often sending free bread to impoverished rural communities in the region. Note that it's cash only here.

Sinchi Roca. ✆ **084/797-798.** Main courses S/8–S/15. Daily 5am–9pm.

Pueblo Viejo ★★ ITALIAN   This lively spot just off the plaza is one of the few good non-hotel options in Aguas Calientes. With its pitched ceiling, couches and terrace for lounging, and a roaring fire, not to mention a craft beer list and original cocktails, sometimes it's the only restaurant full as the night wears on. The menu has gone through several phases in recent years, the latest being Italian, which seems like it might stick. There are more than a dozen wood-fired pizzas, house-made pastas, and a few fusion dishes like grilled alpaca tenderloin in a balsamic vinegar sauce.

Av. Pachacútec 108. © **084/211-193.** Reservations not accepted. Main courses S/24–S/48. Daily noon–midnight.

Shopping

Shopping may not be very exciting in Aguas Calientes—it's pretty much limited to mass-produced Machu Picchu souvenirs and touristy alpaca (or would-be alpaca) goods—but it's everywhere. The main **Mercado Artesanal** (*artesanía* and souvenir market) is a jumble of stalls clustered between the Río Aguas Calientes and the train station. You can't miss it. If you're going to pick up a T-shirt, cap, or other memento of your journey to Machu Picchu, this is the place.

Entertainment & Nightlife

Most gringos congregate at innumerable and largely indistinguishable bars along the train tracks and up Avenida Pachacútec. My vote for the best bar in town is **El Bar ★**, Av. Pachacútec 109 (© **084/211-011**), the house watering hole at **El MaPi,** the hipster hotel that took over a former government-run inn. The couches and terrace combined with the beer and cocktail list at **Pueblo Viejo** restaurant off the plaza make it a good option. In general, most tourists here have an early train or trip to the ruins planned, so most of the town is shut down by 10pm, with just a few random bars staying open late on the weekends.

Where to Stay

At the upper end, hotels in and around Machu Picchu Pueblo have suddenly gotten very expensive—more costly than anything comparable in all of Peru. And it's usually only the very fortunate—those who not only plan far ahead, but who also have very healthy bank accounts—who have the option of staying at the one upscale hotel next to the ruins. For the rest of us, below the ruins in Aguas Calientes, there are scores of *hostales* (inns) aimed at the grungy backpacker crowd, a couple of mid-range options, and a few self-styled ecolodges (some quite upscale, others more adventurous).

Although a few new hotels have popped up to take advantage of Machu Picchu's ever-expanding popularity, there are growing concerns about the environmental impact of new construction. Indeed, UNESCO, which named the whole Machu Picchu Historical Sanctuary a World Heritage Site, has threatened to withdraw the honor if Peru doesn't address growth and environmental concerns.

VERY EXPENSIVE

Inkaterra Machu Picchu Pueblo Hotel ★★★ Set on 5 hectares (12 acres) of cloud forest along the Vilcanota River, just a short walk from the train station, this is for many the preferred hotel in the area, even over the ruin-side Sanctuary Lodge. For naturalist-minded visitors, the Inkaterra's sprawling, carbon-neutral compound is on par with a trip to the Amazon because of the extraordinary diversity found here. There are 100 species of bird and 250 species of butterfly, a record-setting orchid collection, and an Andean bear rescue facility, all of which can be seen on guided excursions through the property. The large rooms are in Spanish-colonial tile-roofed *casitas* (bungalows) decorated with alpaca wool blankets, submerged in lush gardens with hummingbirds darting in every direction. Junior suites add fireplaces and small terraces. There's a spring-water pool and riverside restaurant that is as good as anything you will find in town, and it's all just a 10-minute walk past the train station.

Av. Imperio de los Incas, Km 10, Línea Férrea Cusco-Quillabamba. www.inkaterra.com. ✆ **800/442-5042** from U.S. and Canada, 084/211-122, 084/245-314 for reservations. 81 units. $548–$602 doubles; $655–$1,170 suites. Rates include breakfast buffet, a la carte dinner, and guided excursions on the property. **Amenities:** Restaurant; bar; spa; nature center; orchid garden; bear enclosure; Wi-Fi.

Machu Picchu Sanctuary Lodge ★★★ The Sanctuary Lodge is the most desired hotel in Aguas Calientes, if not all of Peru. Though it is a Belmond property with impeccable service, it's not nearly as memorable as the Monasterio in Cusco. The building that houses it is not overly luxurious and the rooms are smallish. The primary reason anyone will pay the excessive prices here is for the location, directly beside Machu Picchu, which is hard to compete with. The setting is among the most unique and most dramatic of any hotel in the world, making this a once-in-a-lifetime experience. Guests are able to access the ruins at sunrise, before the busloads of tourists from the valley below swarm the site. Many of the rooms have small terraces, opening to pleasant little gardens with extraordinary views of the ruins and the surrounding mountains. Some feel the hotel, originally designed to be temporary when it opened in the 1970s as a Peruvian government endeavor for attracting jet-setters and investors, should not be on the grounds of the already endangered site. Still, demand remains high year-round, and reservations at least 6 months in advance are recommended during high season. The buffet lunches ($40), which are somewhat mediocre, are open to everyone.

Machu Picchu (next to the ruins). www.belmond.com. ✆ **084/246-419.** 31 units. $975–$1,450 doubles; $1,750 suites. Rates include three meals daily. **Amenities:** 2 restaurants; bar; massage facilities; Wi-Fi.

Sumaq Machu Picchu ★★ Quite possibly the most modern hotel in Aguas Calientes, the Sumaq opened in 2007 near the Vilcanota River, about 5 minutes from the train station. With continual renovations, it keeps getting better. The once-plain downstairs sitting area now features a comfy bar and lounge area where you'll take your complimentary pisco sour on arrival or after a day at the ruins. The hotel has updated both towers, and the rooms face either the river or the mountains, some featuring small balconies. All have wood floors, gold trim, and subtle Inca touches, while the beds are as cozy as they come in the cloud forest, with hypoallergenic pillows and alpaca wool blankets. If you are treating yourself after a hike of the Inca Trail or an ascent of Huayna Picchu, you'll appreciate the full-service Aqlla spa, which offers a sauna, a hydrotherapy Jacuzzi, and massages with Andean stones. The above-average restaurant serves New Andean dishes and has beautiful views of the surrounding mountains, the perfect way to start the day while enjoying the included breakfast.

Av. Hermanos Ayar Mz 1 Lote 3. www.machupicchuhotels-sumaq.com. © **866/682-0645** in the U.S. and Canada, or 01/445-7828. 62 units. $482–$602 doubles; $745–$932 suites. Rates include breakfast. **Amenities:** Restaurant; bar; spa; business center; Wi-Fi.

EXPENSIVE

El Mapi ★★   El Mapi is the boutique sister property to Inkaterra's pricier Machu Picchu Pueblo Hotel. Rather than the brand's normally nature-centric themes, the decor here is sleeker and edgier, feeling more like an urban hotel with its central location. There's a trendy street-side restaurant and bar designed from wood and glass where guests can settle in with a welcome lemongrass lemonade. The rooms are functional and cozy, featuring 32-inch flatscreen TVs with satellite hookups. Most offer panoramic views of the Andes. Pricewise, it's the best value in town.

Av. Pachacutec. www.elmapihotel.com. © **511/422-6574.** 130 units. $220 doubles; $275 suites. Rates include breakfast buffet and dinner. **Amenities:** Restaurant; bar; business center; Wi-Fi.

MODERATE

Casa Andina Classic Machu Picchu ★   Immediately beside the train station, this mid-range hotel feels rather removed from the others, which are mostly on the other side of the river. This hotel is for those not wanting to waste a lot of time in town. It offers a good reliable room with cookie-cutter decor, a comfortable bed, clean modern bathroom, and LCD TV. It's a place where you can wake up with a hot shower, have a hearty breakfast and coffee, and enjoy a good view of the river.

Prolongación Imperio de los Incas Mz. 5. www.casa-andina.com. © **084/211-017.** 39 units. $95 doubles. Rates include breakfast. **Amenities:** Restaurant; bar; luggage storage; Wi-Fi.

Gringo Bill's ★★   No longer the backpacker haunt it was in 1979, when it was opened by an American expat and his Cuzqueña wife, Gringo Bill's is still one of the better-value accommodations in Aguas Calientes. Spread out over three floors and cutting into the hillside just off the Plaza de Armas, there are several patios and terraces, plus a lounge bar with a fireplace and a small restaurant. Plants are everywhere. The vibe is about as chilled out as you'll find. The rooms, ranging from doubles to five-person family suites, are pretty basic, but there are decent views of the mountains, all of the in-room amenities of the pricier hotels, and spaces that are kept clean. Staying for a few nights is usually good for a discount. English-language books and magazines are available.

Colla Raymi 104, Plaza de Armas. www.gringobills.com. © **084/211-046,** 084/241-545 for reservations. $98 doubles; $136–$250 suites. Rates include continental breakfast. **Amenities:** Restaurant; bar; spa; business center; Wi-Fi.

Taypikala Machu Picchu ★

For those willing to ignore a few negatives—it's quite a few blocks uphill, the Wi-Fi is spotty and doesn't reach to every room, and there isn't an elevator—this may be your best bet when most everything else is filled. While not nearly as interesting as its flagship hotel outside of Puno, this small Taypikala is quite pleasant, with wood flooring, bamboo furniture, and Andean ceramics and textiles layered throughout the hotel. Rooms have nearly floor-to-ceiling windows that face out at the green mountains. Those on the fourth floor have particularly nice views.

Avenida Pachucutec 808, Parque Wiñay Wayna. www.taypikala.com. © **084/211-060.** $120 doubles; $194 suites. Rates include breakfast buffet. **Amenities:** Restaurant; bar; business center; Wi-Fi.

Tierra Viva Machu Picchu ★

The growing Peruvian chain Tierra Viva has set up shop in Aguas Calientes at the site of the former Hatuchay Tower hotel on the banks of the Vilcanota River. The straightforward rooms are decorated with contemporary Andean art and open up to a five-floor lobby atrium centered by an elevator tower painted with colorful Andean city scenes. Overall, the sleek and modern property feels more like an urban boutique hotel than in a village with no roads leading out. Rack rates tend to be rather overpriced, though online rates can be as much as 25 percent off.

Av. Hermanos Ayar 401. www.tierravivahoteles.com. © **084/211-201.** 43 units. $150–$216 doubles; $316 suites. Rates include continental breakfast. **Amenities:** Restaurant; bar; business center; laundry; Wi-Fi (free).

INEXPENSIVE

Hostal Continental ★

Part of a mini-chain that includes the similar Hostal Machu Picchu and Hostal Presidente, the bland, no-frills Continental is a good option for those on a budget. Renovated in 2003, the rooms are smallish and basic, although they're also clean and cozy with hot water. The hotel is literally right beside the train tracks, so opt for the top floor on the riverside to avoid noise from early-morning trains. Breakfast is at the Presidente, a short walk away.

Av. Imperio de los Incas s/n. www.hostalcontinentalperu.com. © **084/211-065.** $77 doubles. Rates include taxes and continental breakfast. **Amenities:** Restaurant; bar; business center; laundry; Wi-Fi.

Hostal Machupicchu ★

Between the train tracks and the Vilcanota River, this is one of the better budget accommodations in Aguas Calientes. It's a sister hotel to the Continental. Don't expect the Ritz; it's a simple property with clean

airy rooms that open up motel-style to the outdoors. There's a free breakfast buffet and staff will store your luggage after checkout while you go to the ruins.

Av. Imperio de los Incas s/n. www.hostalmachupicchu.com. (✆) **888/790-5264** in the
U.S. or 084/211-065. 24 units. $65 doubles. Rates include continental breakfast. **Ameni-
ties:** Cafe; bar; Wi-Fi.

Rupa Wasi Lodge ★★   This friendly, eco-minded, cabin-like lodge sits
on a steep hill a few blocks above the Plaza de Armas. It's up a long flight of
stairs, which may deter some travelers, but rewards the more agile ones with
one of my favorite settings in town. Butting up against the natural areas of the
Machu Picchu Historic Sanctuary, visitors will see the occasional orchid or
hummingbird. The lodge, which has an alpine feel to it, is built from recycled
hardwoods and uses biodegradable products when possible. Skip the plain
downstairs rooms and upgrade to the three suites that take over the second and
third floors, featuring private patios with sweeping views of the Andes. The
on-site Tree House restaurant, with its farm-to-table menu, is one of the best
dining options in town and gives daily cooking classes. The restaurant will
also prepare a boxed lunch for a day at the ruins.

Calle Huanacaure 105 (2 blocks from the Plaza de Armas). www.rupawasi.net.
(✆) **084/211-101.** $60–$75 doubles; $110–$125 suites. Rates include continental breakfast. **Amenities:** Restaurant; bar; business center; laundry; Wi-Fi.

PLANNING YOUR TRIP TO LIMA, CUSCO & MACHU PICCHU

GETTING THERE

By Plane

All overseas flights from North America and Europe arrive at Lima's **Aeropuerto Internacional Jorge Chávez** (www.lap.com.pe; ℂ 01/517-3100; airport code LIM). Major international airlines from North and South America, Europe, and Asia all fly to Lima. Lima is a hub city for **LAN Airlines** (www.lan.com; ℂ 212/582-3250 in the U.S., or 01/213-8200), which has flights throughout South America as well as multiple destinations around North America and Europe. LAN flights also connect to Australia, New Zealand, and Tahiti through Chile. North American carriers have direct flights between Lima and cities including Atlanta, Chicago, Houston, Los Angeles, Miami, New York, Newark, Orlando, and Toronto. They include **American Airlines** (www.aa.com; ℂ 800/221-1212 in the U.S., or 01/211-9211), **Air Canada** (www.aircanada.com; ℂ 01/626-0900), **Avianca** (www.avianca.com; ℂ 01/213-6060), **Copa** (www.copaair.com; ℂ 01/709-2600), **Delta** (www.delta.com; ℂ 01/211-3250), **JetBlue** (www.jetblue.com; ℂ 01/517-2764), **Spirit** (www.spirit.com; ℂ 212/641-9131), and **United** (www.united.com; ℂ 01/712-9230).

Spanish carrier **Iberia** (www.iberia.com; ℂ 01/411-7801) offers flights between Lima and Madrid, sometimes with partners like British Airways or KLM that connect to Amsterdam, Paris, and London.

Within Peru, it's very important to reconfirm airline tickets in advance. For domestic flights, reconfirm 48 hours in advance; for international flights, reconfirm 72 hours before traveling (and be sure to arrive at the airport a minimum of 2 hr. in advance). Airport taxes are now included in the fares of tickets on both domestic flights and international flights. For domestic and international flight information, visit www.lap.com.pe or call 𝒞 **01/511-6055.** Connecting flights to other cities in Peru depart from the same terminal.

By Bus

You can travel over land to Peru through Ecuador, Bolivia, or Chile. Although the journey isn't short, Lima can be reached from major neighboring cities. If traveling from Quito or Guayaquil, you'll pass through the major northern coastal cities on the way to Lima. From Bolivia, there is frequent service from La Paz and Copacabana to Puno and then on to Cusco. From Chile, most buses travel from Arica to Tacna, making connections to either Arequipa or Lima.

The most common overland trip to Peru from a neighboring country is La Paz, Bolivia, to Puno (about 5 hr.), on the banks of Lake Titicaca (which is partly in Peru and partly in Bolivia). **Ormeño** (www.grupo-ormeno.com.pe/ ormeno.php; 𝒞 **01/472-5000**) travels to La Paz as well as Venezuela, Colombia, Ecuador, Chile, and Argentina.

By Cruise Ship

While cruises stopping in Peru are still quite few, the industry is growing. There are several ports along the Peruvian coasts where large cruise liners make stops, including the port of Callao in Lima and the port of San Martín at Paracas. Most cruises are part of extended trips that run along the Pacific coast of South America, including lengthy routes that round Cape Horn in southern Chile or cross the Panama Canal. Cruise lines include **Celebrity** (www.celebritycruises.com), **Holland America** (www.hollandamerica.com), **NCL** (www.ncl.com), **Princess** (www.princess.com), and **Silversea** (www. silversea.com).

SPECIAL-INTEREST TRIPS & TOURS

Study and volunteer programs, including Spanish-language programs, are often a great way to travel in and experience a country with greater depth than most independent and package travel allows. Cultural immersion and integration with locals are the aims of many such programs, leading to a richer experience for many travelers.

Volunteering, in particular, often leads to greater culture sensitivity and cross-cultural learning experiences. Especially in a developing, largely poor country such as Peru, volunteers see up close the realities of the lack of running water and electricity, the relative absence of luxuries, and simple, home-cooked foods—not to mention local customs and traditions. And at least for a short time, volunteers get the rewarding opportunity to lend their abilities and sweat toward addressing some of the challenges Peruvians face. Such aspects of Peruvian life might be considerably more difficult to apprehend if staying in nice hotels and dining at upscale restaurants.

Inca Trail Regulations

Trekkers once could embark on the Inca Trail on their own, but new regulations imposed by the Peruvian government to limit environmental degradation and damage to the trail itself now require all trekkers to go with officially sanctioned groups, guides, and porters.

Most volunteer organizations are not-for-profit entities that charge participants to go abroad (to cover administrative and other costs), so volunteering isn't usually a way to get a free vacation. If you're concerned, though, ask about the cost breakdown for costs and field expenses. Any established, reputable volunteer organization should be willing to do this. Then you could always compare those costs to what traveling on your own would amount to. See also "Volunteer & Working Trips," later in this chapter.

Because most travelers have limited time and resources, organized ecotourism or adventure travel packages, arranged by tour operators abroad or in Peru, are popular ways of combining cultural and outdoor activities. Birdwatching, horseback riding, rafting, and hiking can be teamed with visits to destinations such as Cusco, the Sacred Valley and Machu Picchu.

Traveling with a group has several advantages over traveling independently. Your accommodations and transportation are arranged, and most (if not all) of your meals are included in the cost of a package. If your tour operator has a reasonable amount of experience and a decent track record, you should proceed to each of your destinations quickly without the snags and long delays that you might face if you're traveling on your own. You'll also have the opportunity to meet like-minded travelers who are interested in nature and active sports. Some group trekking trips include *porteros* or *arrieros* (porters or muleteers) who carry extra equipment. On some luxury treks of the Inca Trail, porters will even carry your backpack, so all you have to do is hike your lazy self up and over the mountain passes.

In the best cases of organized outdoors travel, group size is kept small (10-15 people), and tours are escorted by knowledgeable guides who are either naturalists or biologists. Be sure to inquire about difficulty levels when you're choosing a tour. While most companies offer "soft adventure" packages that those in decent but not overly athletic shape can handle, others focus on more hard-core activities geared toward very fit and seasoned adventure travelers.

Academic Trips & Language Classes

Consider local language schools, located in Cusco, Lima, and Arequipa, which offer both short- and long-term study programs, often with home stays. **International Partners for Study Abroad** (www.studyabroadinternational. com/file/schools_Peru.html) lists a number of Spanish-study programs in Cusco. **Transitions Abroad** (www.transitionsabroad.com) occasionally lists Spanish-study programs of short duration in Peru and other South American countries; follow the "Study Abroad" tab on the website for options.

One standout school in Cusco is the **Amigos Spanish School,** Zaguan del Cielo B-23 (www.spanishcusco.com; © 084/242-292), a nonprofit school that assists disadvantaged children through its Amigos Foundation. In Lima, **El Sol Escuela de Español,** Grimaldo de Solar 469, Miraflores (www.elsol.idiomasperu.com; © 800/381-1806), marries language classes to cooking workshops, dance classes, and other activities. Also in Lima, **Instituto Cultural Peruano Norteamericano,** Angamos Oeste 160, Miraflores (www.icpna.edu.pe; © 01/241-1940) offers long-term classes, usually with daily 1-hour sessions from branches in Lima and Cusco.

Adventure Trips

These agencies and operators specialize in well-organized and coordinated tours that cover your entire stay. Many travelers prefer to have everything arranged and confirmed before arriving in Peru—a good idea for first-timers and during high season (especially for travel to Cusco and its immediate environs, including the Inca Trail). Many of these operators provide great service but are not cheap; 10-day tours generally cost upward of $2,500 or more per person, and do not include airfare to Peru.

Adventure Life (www.adventure-life.com; © 800/344-6118), based in Missoula, Montana, and specializing in Central and South America, has an interesting roster of rugged Peru trips, frequently with a community focus, including a 12-day multi-sport tour (mountain biking, hiking, rafting, jungle tour, and Machu Picchu), rainforest ecolodge tours, and a 10-day Cachiccata trek, as well as plenty of tour extensions. One Peru trip is specifically designed to raise money (40 percent of trip cost) for the organization's non-profit fund (which aims to give back to local communities).

Adventure Specialists (www.adventurespecialists.org; © 719/783-2086) specializes in treks, horse trips, and archaeology expeditions, as well as wildlife and birding adventures by dugout canoe in the Manu Biosphere Reserve. The founder is one of the archaeologists credited with the November 2003 rediscovery of Llactapata, a "lost" Inca city.

Andean Treks (www.andeantreks.com; © 617/924-1974) is a personalized, high-quality Latin American adventure-tour operator that focuses on trekking in the Andes and exploring the jungle throughout Peru. The Massachusetts-based group's roster of reasonably priced trips for all levels includes cloud-forest treks, llama trekking, and highlands treks that combine whitewater rafting or Amazon lodge stays. Trips range from easy to hard-core.

Backroads (www.backroads.com; © 800/462-2848) is a luxury-tour company that offers upscale, light-adventure trips around the globe, and it has several tours of Peru on its menu. It specializes in walking, hiking, and biking tours from Cusco to Machu Picchu, some of which incorporate stays at the **Mountain Lodges of Peru.** Service is personalized and the guides are top-notch.

Culture Explorers (www.cultureexplorers.com; © 215/870-3585) focuses on cultural immersion and creating a positive impact on the communities visited, which is why its award-winning tours consistently receive rave reviews. In Peru, its Culture Xplorers Weavers Awards, an annual awards celebration honoring the indigenous weavers of the Sacred Valley, brings together more than 500 weavers from nine participating communities to compete for pride and prizes, a unique event for any tourists to be a part of. The small-group programs are often timed to align with special events, such as rare Andean festivals that other operators do not have access to, and it runs excellent culinary tours as well. Accommodations are usually in 3- to 5-star hotels, and guides are top-quality.

Journeys International (www.journeys.travel; ✆ 800/255-8735), based in Ann Arbor, Michigan, offers small-group (4–12 people) natural history tours guided by naturalists. Trips include the 9-day "Amazon & Andes Odyssey," which includes the Tambopata National Reserve along with Cusco, Machu Picchu, and the Sacred Valley, as well as special Amazon and Inca trips for families.

Mountain Travel Sobek (www.mtsobek.com; ✆ **888/831-7526** or 0808/234-2243 in the U.K.) offers seven itineraries to Peru, including the 8-day "Andean Explorer," with day hikes and rafting. Options for mountaineers and committed trekkers include 13 days of strenuous trekking in Cordillera Blanca (mostly camping); a shorter 5-day (but still hard-core) trekking option in the same area; and a challenging 15-day rafting trip along the Tambopata River (half camping, half inns). A unique trip is the off-the-beaten path "Other Inca Trail"; the company also arranges luxury treks to Machu Picchu with stays at the cool inns owned and operated by **Mountain Lodges of Peru.** Trips are helpfully rated for difficulty.

Overseas Adventure Travel (www.oattravel.com; ✆ 800/955-1925) offers natural history and "soft adventure" itineraries, with optional add-on excursions. Tours are limited to 16 people and are guided by naturalists. All accommodations are in small hotels, lodges, or tent camps. The 11-day "Real Affordable Peru" includes rafting on the Urubamba and a *curandero* healing ceremony. The 16-day "Machu Picchu & Galápagos" tour features a good bit of walking.

Wilderness Travel (www.wildernesstravel.com; ✆ 800/368-2794) is a Berkeley-based outfitter specializing in cultural, wildlife, and hiking group tours that are arranged with tiered pricing (the trip cost varies according to group size). There are 13 different tours to Peru, including a 17-day Trekking in the Cordillera Huayhuash Blanca, Choquequirao trail to Machu Picchu, and a unique "Peru Festivals Trek." Wilderness Travel also offers soft luxury treks to Machu Picchu with stays at the cool inns owned and operated by **Mountain Lodges of Peru.** Trips are helpfully graded according to difficulty.

Wildland Adventures (www.wildland.com; ✆ 800/345-4453), based in Seattle, is one of the top international outdoor-tour companies with operations in Peru. It offers excellent special-interest trekking and rainforest expedition programs, with customizing options. There are lodge-based programs, primarily in the jungle; trekking expeditions, such as the Machu Picchu Mountain lodges trek; and special adventures focusing on photographing Peru's "Ancient Lands and Native Spirits." Wildland's programs are well designed, guides are very professional, and the organization is focused on authentic travel experiences.

Food & Wine Trips

Peru's sophisticated, diverse cuisine has attracted a great deal of worldwide attention in recent years, and gastronomic tourism is taking hold in Peru. Multiple companies offer food-centric vacations.

English-speaking Peruvian Ericka LaMadrid's **Delectable Peru** gourmet food tours (www.delectableperu.com; ✆ **239/244-2336** in the U.S.) are some of the most comprehensive food tours being offered in Lima. On the tours you can chat and take cooking classes with top Peruvian chefs, ask what ingredient(s) make a dish a delight, see where the magic happens in the kitchen, and learn about some of the many treats specific to Peru. Delectable Peru specializes in custom tours, many of them focusing on a specific dish or type of food, such as ceviche or Nikkei. Set tours are available as well.

Taste of Peru (www.taste-of-peru.com; ✆ **866/411-INCA**) is run by Magical Cusco Tours, a Peru/U.S.-based company in operation for more than 2 decades. Tours range from standard day trips and cooking classes at top Peruvian restaurants to multiday culinary tours with accommodations and transportation that combine an array of activities in different parts of the country, especially Lima and Cusco.

Aracari (www.aracari.com; ✆ **312/239-8726** in the U.S., or 020/3287-5262 in the U.K.), an upscale Peruvian agency that designs excellent custom tours, has a free Peru culinary guide on its website. On offer are a 12-day "Peru with Flavor" trip and personalized culinary tours with exclusive visits to private houses and haciendas for private luncheons and cocktails, as well as cooking classes, visits to food markets, and dining at some of the finest restaurants in Peru.

Guided Tours
BIKE TOURS

Mountain biking is still in its infancy in Peru, although fat-tire options are increasing. Several tour companies in those places rent bikes, and the quality of the equipment is continually being upgraded. If you plan to do a lot of biking and are very attached to your rig, bring your own.

Peru Bike (www.perubike.com; ✆ **01/260-8225**), based in Lima, has a great schedule of Andes Mountain–biking trips across Peru, including cool day trips around Lima and Pachacamac on GT bikes.

In Cusco, **Peru Discovery,** Triunfo (Sunturwasi) 392, Of. 113 (www.peru discovery.com/en; ✆ **054/274-541**), is the top specialist, with a half-dozen bike trips that include hard-core excursions. **Apumayo Expediciones** (www. apumayo.com; ✆ **084/246-018**) and **Eric Adventures** (www.ericadventures. com; ✆ **084/290-212**) offer 1- to 5-day organized mountain-biking excursions for novices and experienced single-trackers. In the Sacred Valley, **Ecomontana** (www.ecomontana.com), run by the mountain biker Omar Zarzar, rents good mountain bikes and organizes extended as well as shorter cyclotourism rides around Urubamba, with top equipment.

BIRD-WATCHING

Peru is one of the greatest countries on earth for birders. The bird population in Peru is, incredibly, about 10 percent of the world's total. With nearly 2,000 species of resident and migrant birds identified throughout Peru, great bird-watching sites abound. While many of the best birding destinations are in Amazonian regions not covered in this guide, the Cusco area, especially around Machu Picchu, as well as the Islas Ballestas, offer excellent bird-watching.

Birding Peru (www.birdingperu.com) is a Peru-based tour operator that links to birding trips offered by major outfitters to all regions of the country, including the highlands, coasts, and rainforest, and provides good general information on birding throughout Peru. The operator also has a portal with good information on birding in Peru featuring birding forums, information about specialized tour operators, and birding news.

Field Guides (www.fieldguides.com; ℂ **800/728-4953**) is an Austin, Texas–based specialty bird-watching travel operator with trips worldwide. It features six birding trips to Peru, including the Manu Biosphere Reserve, Tambopata, Machu Picchu and the eastern slope of the Andes, the Amazon, and a 24-day tour of the endemic-rich region of northern Peru. Group size is limited to 14 participants.

Kolibri Expeditions (www.kolibriexpeditions.com; ℂ **01/652-7689**), based in Lima, offers birding tours across Peru, including around Lima, the central coast, and condor-watching trips. Most are no-frills, budget camping trips, but the outfit also offers a few pampered, high-end trips.

WINGS (www.wingsbirds.com; ℂ **866/547-9868** from the U.S.) is a specialty bird-watching travel operator with 3 decades of experience in the field. It promotes three trips to Peru, including an 18-day trip to Machu Picchu and the Manu Biosphere Reserve and one to the north and Andes in search of the long-whiskered owlet. Group size is usually between 6 and 18 people.

HORSEBACK RIDING

Lovers of horseback riding will find several areas in Peru to pursue their interest, as well as hotels and operators that arrange everything from a couple hours in a saddle to 2-week trips on horseback.

For riding on the outskirts of Cusco, most local operators can arrange day-long trips, available for walking between the ruins (Sacsayhuamán, Q'enko, Puca Pucara, and Tambomachay) just beyond Cusco and in the countryside.

Perol Chico (www.perolchico.com; ℂ **01/9503-14065**), in Urubamba, operates a ranch and is one of the top horseback-riding agencies in Peru, offering full riding vacations with Peruvian Paso horses and stays at the ranch, as well as 1- and 2-day rides (and up to 12-day horseback adventures in the Sacred Valley).

Southwind Adventures (www.southwindadventures.com; ℂ **800/377-9463**) offers horse-packing among its roster of adventure trips in Peru.

SURFING

Though it remains somewhat under the general public's radar, Peru has recently become one of the world's top surfing destinations among surfing aficionados. It has 2,000km (1,200 miles) of Pacific coastline and huge possibilities for left and right reef breaks, point breaks, and monster waves, and boarders can hit the surf year-round. Northern beaches draw surfers to some of the best waves in South America, though there is also good surfing right in Lima and at the beaches to the south, but the water can be chilly. The north is better from October to March, while the surfing in the south is good April through December and tops in May.

Octopus Surf Tours (www.octopussurftours.com; ☎ **01/9940-05518**) is run by Peruvian surfer Marco Antonio Ravizza, aka Octopus, who has over 20 years' experience guiding surf tours throughout Peru. Bookings for its inexpensive small-group surfing tours in central and northern Peru are through **Wave Hunters** (www.wavehunters.com; ☎ **760/494-7391**), a California-based organization.

Volunteer & Working Trips

Below are several institutions and organizations that work on humanitarian and sustainable development projects in Peru. Some international relief organizations such as **Doctors Without Borders** (www.doctorswithoutborders. org) and **CARE** (www.care.org) accept volunteers to work crises and relief efforts. The devastating earthquakes in southern Peru in 2001 and 2007 brought hundreds of volunteers to Peru.

Cross-Cultural Solutions (www.crossculturalsolutions.org; ☎ **800/380-4777**), with offices in New Rochelle, New York, and Brighton, U.K., offers weeklong volunteer programs in Peru (in Lima's Villa El Salvador shantytown). The "Volunteer Abroad" section lists a number of opportunities for volunteering in Peru, including teaching and environmental research. **Projects Abroad** (www.projects-abroad.org; ☎ **888/839-3535**), with headquarters in New York and a local field office in Urubamba (in the Sacred Valley), organizes several unique volunteer and internship opportunities in Peru, including Inca restoration projects (such as the Sacsayhuamán ruins on the outskirts of Cusco), rainforest conservation, teaching, nursing, and dentistry. The **World Leadership School** (www.worldleadershipschool.com; ☎ **303/679-3412**) is a Colorado-based organization that operates 3- to 4-week programs concentrating on infrastructure and natural disaster prevention in El Carmen, on the desert coast; cultural preservation in Ollantaytambo, in the Sacred Valley; and climate change and ecosystem preservation in Puerto Maldonado, gateway to the southern Amazon. Lima-based **Mundo Azul** (www. mundoazul.org; ℂ **01/99410-4206**) takes volunteers on environmental conservation and sustainable development programs along the coast (marine biology research) and in the rainforest (threatened species). Trips off the coast south of Lima to view and photographically document the large population of playful dolphins may be the most fun you can have doing an environmentally conscious volunteer program.

Other volunteer programs include **Habitat for Humanity** (www.habitat. org; ℂ **800/422-4828**), with a base in Arequipa (ℂ **054/422-724**), and **Volunteers for Peace** (www.vfp.org; ℂ **802/259-2759**), based in Vermont.

Walking Tours

Peru is one of the world's great trekking and mountain-climbing destinations, and its mountains and gorgeous valleys, ideal for everything from hard-core climbs of 6,000m (19,700-ft.) peaks to gentle walks through green valleys, are one of the country's calling cards. The most celebrated trek, of course, is the Inca Trail to Machu Picchu—truly one of the world's most rewarding treks, provided that the crowds don't get you down in high season. Many agencies in Cusco offer guided treks to Machu Picchu; as do larger international operators, some of whom offer newer alternatives to the Inca Trail.

Trekking circuits of varying degrees of difficulty lace the valleys and mountain ridges of Peru's *sierra*. Yet only a few have become popular commercial trekking routes. Independent trekkers who like to blaze their own trail (metaphorically speaking—you should always stick to existing trails) have a surfeit of options in Peru for uncrowded treks.

The best months for climbing are during the dry season, between May and September (June-Aug is perhaps best).

Many tour companies based in the United States and elsewhere subcontract portions of their tours, particularly guided hikes and treks, to established Peruvian companies on the ground in Lima, Cusco, and across the country. Though it's often simpler to go with international tour companies, in some cases, independent travelers can benefit by organizing their tours directly with local agencies. Prices on the ground can be cheaper than contracting a tour from abroad, but there are risks of not getting what you want when you want it. Also, the world of subcontracting can be byzantine, and even Peruvian travel agencies hire out adventure and outdoor specialists.

One of the best independent resources for hiking and climbing information in Peru is the **South American Explorers** clubhouses in Lima and Cusco (www.saexplorers.org; ℂ **800/274-0568** in the U.S.). You have to become a member first ($60 per year) for full access to its trail reports and other information, but if you're serious about trails and climbs in Peru, it's money well spent. You can join via the website or on the spot at a clubhouse.

Class Adventure Travel (CAT) (www.cat-travel.com; ✆ **877/240-4770** in the U.S. and Canada, 0207/0906-1259 in the U.K.) is a fine all-purpose agency with offices in Lima and Cusco (it also has offices in Bolivia, Chile, and Argentina). In addition to professionally organizing virtually any kind of travel detail in Peru, its adventure offerings include rafting, trekking, and jungle tours.

Explorandes Peru (www.explorandes.com; ✆ **01/715-2323**) has been doing trekking and river expeditions in Peru for nearly 3 decades, and has regional offices in Lima, Cusco, Huaraz, and Puno. One of the top high-end agencies for treks and mountaineering in Peru, it's reasonably priced and especially good for forming very small private groups. It offers a number of soft adventure trips (with stays in hotels and full- and half-day river trips) and an even more impressive lineup of real adventure, including cool, unique trips such as llama trekking to Chavín, a festival trek, rafting on the Apurímac River, treks on southern peaks around Cusco, and hard-core trekking in the Cordillera Blanca and Huayhuash. Amazon extensions are available.

Mountain Lodges of Peru (www.mountainlodgesofperu.com; ✆ **01/421-7777**), a Peruvian trekking company, has built a series of small, spectacular lodges on private lands in the Vilcabamba mountain range west of the Sacred Valley. The sleek inns have whirlpools, fireplaces, and nice dining rooms. The company offers its own 6-day treks to Machu Picchu and also contracts with a handful of international adventure tour operators, including **Backroads, Mountain Travel Sobek,** and **Wilderness Travel.**

Peru for Less (www.peruforless.com; ✆ **817/230-4971**), which began in Texas and is now based in Lima, has added a whole roster of well-designed and personalized alternative trekking tours in the Cusco region, including small-group treks to Choquequirao and Vilcabamba, to its slate of more standard travel packages.

SAS Travel Peru (www.sastravelperu.com; ✆ **084/249-194**), based in Cusco, is one of the most popular agencies organizing outdoor travel for backpackers and budget-minded travelers. Its roster includes the Inca Trail, a number of short treks in the Cusco area, and a couple of longer, more challenging mountain treks lasting up to a week. Jungle treks are to Manu and Tambopata. SAS also offers white-water rafting, paragliding, climbing, mountain biking, and horseback riding.

GETTING AROUND

Because of its size and natural barriers, including difficult mountain terrain, long stretches of desert coast, and extensive rainforest, Peru is complicated to navigate. Train service is very limited, covering only a few principal tourist routes, and many bus trips take several days by land. Travel over land, though very inexpensive, can be extremely time-consuming and uncomfortable. Visitors with limited time tend to fly everywhere they can. However, for certain routes, inter-city buses are your only real option.

By Plane

Flying to major destinations within Peru, including Cusco, is the only practical way around the country if you want to see several places in a couple of weeks or less. Peru is deceptively large, and natural barriers make getting around difficult. Most major Peruvian cities can be reached by air, though not always directly. Flying to major destinations, such as Lima or Cusco, is simple and relatively inexpensive. One-way flights to most destinations are between $200 and $650. Prices fluctuate according to the season.

Peru's carriers, some of which are small airlines with limited flight schedules, include **LAN** (www.lan.com; ℰ **212/582-3250** in the U.S., or 01/213-8200 in Lima); **LC Peru** (www.lcperu.pe; ℰ **01/204-1313**); **Peruvian Airlines** (www.peruvian.pe; ℰ **01/716-6000**); **Star Perú** (www.starperu.com; ℰ **01/705-9000**); and **Avianca** (www.avianca.com; ℰ **01/511-8222**). All airlines fly in and out of Lima. LAN is the only domestic airline that flies to most major destinations in Peru (Arequipa, Cajamarca, Chiclayo, Cusco, Iquitos, Lima, Piura, Pucallpa, Puerto Maldonado, Tacna, Tarapoto, Trujillo, and Tumbes), while Peruvian Airlines, Star Perú, LC Busre, and Avianca all fly between Lima and Cusco, as well as a few other select routes.

Connections through Lima are often necessary, although a few destinations are accessible directly from Cusco, such as Arequipa, Juliaca, and Puerto Maldonado. Some routes might be limited to only certain days or are seasonal. Flight schedules and fares are apt to change frequently and without notice. One-way fares are generally half the round-trip fare. Flights should be booked several days or weeks in advance, especially in high season, and make sure that you get to the airport at least 1 hour in advance to avoid being bumped from a flight.

By Train

By far the most popular train routes in Peru connect Cusco, the Sacred Valley, and Machu Picchu. The train to Machu Picchu from Cusco is a truly spectacular journey. The two competing tourist train companies, **IncaRail** and **PeruRail,** also travel from the Sacred Valley (Ollantaytambo and Urubamba) to Machu Picchu. For prices and schedules of these and all Cusco and Sacred Valley trains, see Chapters 7 and 8. There are no train passes like you might find in Europe.

For additional information, contact **PeruRail** (www.perurail.com; ℰ **01/612-6700** in Lima, **084/581-414** in Cusco) or **IncaRail** (www.incarail.com; ℰ **084/233-030** in Cusco).

By Bus

Buses are the cheapest and most popular form of transportation in Peru—for many Peruvians, they are the only means of getting around—and they have by far the greatest reach. A complex network of private bus companies crisscrosses Peru, with many competing lines covering the most popular routes. Many companies operate their own bus stations, and their locations, dispersed across many cities, can be endlessly frustrating to travelers. Luggage theft is an issue on many economy-class buses; passengers should keep a watchful eye on carry-on items and pay close attention when bags are unloaded. Only a few long-distance companies have luxury buses comparable in comforts to European models (bathrooms, reclining seats, movies, Wi-Fi). These premium-class buses cost up to twice as much as regular-service buses, although for many travelers, the additional comfort and services are worth the difference in cost (which remains inexpensive).

For many short distances (such as Cusco to Pisac), *colectivos* (smaller buses without assigned seats) are the fastest and cheapest option.

Ormeño (www.grupo-ormeno.com.pe/ormeno.php; ✆ 01/472-5000), **Cruz del Sur** (www.cruzdelsur.com.pe; ✆ 01/311-5050), **Oltursa** (www.oltursa. com.pe; ✆ 01/708-5000), and **Transportes Civa** (www.civa.com.pe; ✆ 01/418-1111) are the bus companies with the best reputations for long-distance treks. Given the extremely confusing nature of bus companies, terminals, and destinations—which makes it impossible to even begin to list every possible option here—it is best to approach a local tourism information office or travel agency (most of which sell long-distance bus tickets) with a destination in mind and let the office direct you to the terminal for the best service (and, if possible, book the ticket for you).

By Car

Getting around Peru by rental car isn't the easiest or best option for the great majority of travelers. It is also far from the cheapest in most cases. Distances are long, the terrain is either difficult or unrelentingly boring for long stretches along the desert coast, roads are often not in very good condition, Peruvian drivers are aggressive, and accident rates are very high. The U.S. State Department warns against driving in Peru, particularly at night or alone on rural roads at any time of day. A four-wheel-drive vehicle is the best option in many places, but trucks and jeeps are exceedingly expensive for most travelers.

However, if you want maximum flexibility and independence for travels in a particular region (say, to get around the Sacred Valley outside of Cusco, or to visit the beaches and towns south of Lima along the coast) and you have several people to share the cost with you, a rental car could be a decent option. By no means should you plan to rent a car in Lima and head off for the major sights across the country; you'll spend all your time in the car. It is much more feasible to fly or take a bus to a given destination and rent a car there. The major international rental agencies are found in Lima, and a handful of international and local companies operate in other cities, such as Cusco. Costs average between $25 and $80 per day, plus 18 percent insurance, for an economy-size vehicle.

To rent a car, you need to be at least 25 years old and have a valid driver's license and passport. Deposit by credit card is usually required. Driving under the influence of alcohol or drugs is a criminal offense. Major rental companies in Peru include Alamo (www.alamo.com; ✆ 01/575-1111); **Avis** (www.avis. com; ✆ 01/444-0450); **Budget** (www.budgetperu.com; ✆ 01/517-1880);

combi OR carro? GETTING AROUND IN & OUT OF TOWN

Getting around Peru demands a mastery of terms that designate varied modes of transportation and a bewildering array of vehicles that aren't always easy to distinguish.

Within cities, travelers have several options. The most convenient and expensive are **taxis,** which function, for the most part, like taxis elsewhere in the world. However, taxis in Peru are wholly unregulated; in addition to registered, licensed taxis, you'll find "taxi" drivers who are merely folks with access to a two-bit car—usually rented for the purpose—and a taxi sticker to plunk inside the windshield. In Lima, this is overwhelmingly the case, and unregistered taxi drivers can be difficult to negotiate with for a fair price. There are no meters, meaning that you have to negotiate a price before (not after) accepting a ride. In other cities, such as Cusco, taxis conform to standard pricing (S/3–S/6 within town), so taking cabs outside of Lima is a considerably less daunting proposition for most travelers. An alternative in Lima is to download smartphone apps like Uber and Easy Taxi, which are safe, use GPS so they are rarely lost, and fix prices by distance, eliminating the need to haggle.

Combis are vans that function as private bus services. They often race from one end of town to another, with fare collectors hanging out the door barking the name of the route. Combis also cover routes between towns. These are being phased out in Lima. **Colectivos** are essentially indistinguishable from combis—they are vans that cover regular routes (such as between Cusco and Pisac), and they usually depart when they're full. Routes are often so popular, though, that colectivos leave regularly, as often as every 15 minutes, throughout the day.

For inter-city transport, there is a similar slate of options. **Micros** are small buses, often old and quite colorful, that travel between cities. Both colectivos and micros are crowded, have a reputation for pickpockets, and can be hailed at any place along the street without regard for bus stops. You pay a cobrador (money collector), who usually hangs out at the door barking destinations at would-be travelers, rather than the driver.

Autobuses (also called buses or omnibuses) are large coaches for long-distance travel on scheduled inter-city routes. Classes of buses are distinguished by price and comfort: Económico is a bare-bones bus with little more than a driver and an assigned seat; classes designated especial (or sometimes Inka) have reclining seats, videos, refreshments, and bathrooms.

As if that complex web of terms wasn't enough, there's an additional warning to heed: It's not uncommon to hear locals refer—loosely and confusingly—to buses as carros (which normally just means "car") and to colectivos as taxis.

Hertz (www.hertz.com.pe; ✆ **01/517-2402**); **National Car Rental** (www.nationalcar.com.pe; ✆ **01/578-7878**); and **Thrifty** (www.thriftyperu.com; ✆ **01/484-0749**). Taxes are included in the price. One U.S. gallon equals 3.8 liters or .85 imperial gallons.

For mechanical assistance, contact the **Touring Automóvil Club del Perú** (Touring Club of Peru) in Lima at www.touringperu.com.pe or ✆ **01/611-9999**.

TIPS ON HOTELS

A wide range of places to stay—including world-class luxury hotels in modern high-rise buildings and 16th-century monasteries and manor houses, affordable small hotels in colonial houses, rustic rural lodges, and inexpensive budget inns—can be found in Peru. Mid-range options have expanded in recent years, but the large majority of accommodations still court budget travelers and backpackers (outside Lima's hosting of international business travelers).

Those places go by many names in Peru. *Hotel* generally refers only to comfortable hotels with a range of services, but *hostal* (or *hostales*, plural) is used for a wide variety of smaller hotels, inns, and pensions. (Note that *hostal* is distinct from the English-language term "hostel.") At the lower end are mostly *hospedajes, pensiones,* and *residenciales.* However, these terms are often poor indicators—if they are indicators at all—of an establishment's quality or services. Required signs outside reflect these categories: H (hotel), HS (*hostal*), HR (*hotel residencial*), and P (*pensión*). As in most countries, the government's hotel-rating system means that establishments are awarded stars for the presence of certain criteria—a pool, restaurant, elevator, and so on—more than for standards of luxury. Thus, it is not always true that the hotel with the most stars is necessarily the most comfortable or elegant. Luxury hotels were once exceedingly rare outside Lima, Cusco, and Machu Picchu, but that is no longer the case; budget accommodations are plentiful across the country, and many of them are quite good for the price. Some represent amazing values at less than $60 a night for a double—with a dose of local character and breakfast, to boot.

The great majority of hotels in Peru are small and midsize independent inns; few international hotel chains operate in Peru. You'll find a handful of Marriott and Belmond hotels here and there, but by and large the chains you'll come into contact with are Peruvian. The most prominent, although they have only a handful of hotels each, are Casa Andina, Sonesta, Aranwa, and Libertador. Casa Andina and Sonesta hotels are comfortable, decorated similarly, and generally good values. Casa Andina also has an upscale line of Private Collection hotels in a few choice spots. The Libertador hotels are elegant four- and five-star establishments, largely in historic buildings, as are Aranwa.

In-room air-conditioning isn't as common, especially in lower-priced and moderately priced inns and hotels, as it is in many countries. In highland towns, such as Cusco, that's not usually a problem, as even in warmer months it gets pretty cool at night. In coastal towns it gets considerably warmer, though most hotels that don't offer air-conditioning units have ceiling or other fans. If you're concerned about having air-conditioning in your room in a warmer destination, it may be necessary to bump up to a more expensive hotel.

Advance reservations are strongly recommended during high season (June–Oct) and during national holidays and important festivals. This is especially

Breakfast

Most hotels in Peru include breakfast in their rates. Breakfast may range from a huge buffet breakfast (and not only at the largest and most luxurious hotels) to continental breakfasts or more austere, European-style breakfasts of bread, coffee, and jam.

true of hotels in the middle and upper categories in popular places such as Cusco and Machu Picchu. Many hotels quote their rates in U.S. dollars. If you pay in cash, the price will be converted into *soles* at the going rate. Note that at most budget and many mid-range hotels, credit cards are not accepted. Most published rates can be negotiated, and travelers can often get greatly reduced rates outside of peak season simply by asking.

Hotel taxes and service charges are an issue that has caused some confusion in recent years. Most upper-level hotels add a 19 percent general sales tax (IGV) and a 10 percent service charge to the bill. However, foreigners who can demonstrate they live outside of Peru are not charged the 19 percent tax (though they are responsible for the 10 percent service charge). In practice, hotels sometimes either mistakenly or purposely include the IGV on everyone's bill; presentation of a passport is sufficient to have the tax deducted from your tab. Many hotels—usually those at the midlevel and lower ranges—simplify matters by including the tax in their rates; at these establishments, you cannot expect to have the tax removed from your charges. At high-end hotels, be sure to review your bill and ask for an explanation of additional taxes and charges. Prices in this book do not include taxes and service charges unless otherwise noted. Breakfast and Wi-Fi is often included in the price, but check with the hotel before booking if either perk is important to you. The reviews in this book indicate when a hotel offers free Wi-Fi, but keep in mind that this is subject to change, as is the range of fees among hotels that charge for Wi-Fi access.

Safety can be an issue at some hotels, especially at the lower end, and extreme care should be taken with regard to personal belongings left in the hotel. Leaving valuables lying around is asking for trouble. Except for hotels at the lowest levels, most have safety deposit boxes. (Usually only luxury hotels have room safes.) Place your belongings in a carefully sealed envelope. If you arrive in a town without previously arranged accommodations, you should be minimally wary of taxi drivers and others who insist on showing you to a hotel. Occasionally, these provide excellent tips, but in general, they merely take you to a place where they are confident they can earn a commission.

A final precaution worth mentioning is the electric heater found on many showerheads. These can be dangerous, and touching them while functioning can prompt an unwelcome electric jolt.

SHOPPING IN PERU

Peru is one of the top shopping destinations in Latin America, with some of the finest and best-priced crafts anywhere. Its long traditions of textile weaving and colorful markets bursting with tourists have produced a dazzling display of alpaca-wool sweaters, blankets, ponchos, shawls, scarves, typical Peruvian hats, and other woven items. Peru's ancient indigenous civilizations had some of the world's greatest potters, and reproductions of Moche, Nasca, Paracas, and other ceramics are available. (Until recently, it was surprisingly easy to get your hands on the real thing, but that's no longer the case.) In some cities—especially Lima, Cusco, and Arequipa—antique textiles and ceramics are still available. Some dealers handle pieces that are 1,000 years old or more (and others simply claim their pieces are that old). However, exporting such pre-Columbian artifacts is illegal.

Lima and Cusco have the lion's share of tourist-oriented shops and markets—particularly in Lima, you can find items produced all over the country. You might find handcrafted *retablos* (altars) from Ayacucho, depicting weddings and other domestic scenes, that are famous throughout Peru, or excellent hand-painted textiles and decorative pottery that the Shipibo tribe of the northern Amazon produces. You'll also see items in the jungle made from endangered species—alligator skins, turtle shells, and the like. Purchasing these items is illegal, and it only encourages locals to further harm the natural environment and its inhabitants.

Baby alpaca and very rare vicuña are the finest woolens and are amazingly soft. Although many merchants are happy to claim that every woven wool item in their possession is alpaca or baby alpaca, much of what is sold in many tourist centers is anything but. Most, if not all, of the inexpensive, look-alike (S/15–S/60) sweaters, shawls, hats, and gloves you'll see in countless markets and stalls are made of acrylic or acrylic blends, and some are even blends of natural fibers and fiberglass. If your new "alpaca" sweater stinks when it gets wet, it's llama or sheep wool. If you want the real thing—which is not nearly as cheap but still much less expensive than what you'd pay for alpaca of such fine quality in other countries—visit one of the established chain stores in large cities (most have "alpaca" in the name). Cusco and Lima are also excellent places to shop for alpaca.

In Lima, Cusco, and most tourist centers, there are scores of general, look-alike *artesanía* shops, and prices might not be any higher than what you'd find at street markets. At stores and in open markets, bargaining—gentle, good-natured haggling over prices—is accepted and even expected. However, when it gets down to ridiculously small amounts of money, it's best to recognize that you are already getting a great deal on probably handmade goods and you should relinquish the fight over a few *soles*.

Many prices for goods include a 19 percent sales tax, which, unfortunately, is refundable only on purchases made at the international departure lounge of Jorge Chávez International Airport.

> ### Where Are You @?
>
> The @ symbol is hard to find on a Latin American keyboard. You must keep your finger on the "Alt" key and then press "6" and "4" on the number pad to the right. If you're still unsuccessful and at an Internet cafe, ask the assistant to help you type an *arroba*.

[FastFACTS] PERU

Addresses "Jr." doesn't mean "junior"; it is a designation meaning "Jirón," or street, just as "Av." (sometimes "Avda.") is an abbreviation for "Avenida," or avenue. "Ctra." is the abbreviation for *carretera*, or highway; cdra. means *cuadra*, or block; and "of." is used to designate office (*oficina*) number. Perhaps the most confusing element in Peruvian street addresses is "s/n," which frequently appears in place of a number after the name of the street; "s/n" means *sin número*, or no number. The house or building with such an address simply is unnumbered. At other times, a building number may appear with a dash, such as "102–105," meaning that the building in question simply contains both address numbers (though usually only one main entrance).

Business Hours Most stores are open from 9 or 10am to 12:30pm, and from 3 to 5 or 8pm. Banks are generally open Monday through Friday from 9:30am to 4pm, although some stay open until 6pm. In major cities, most banks are also open Saturday from 9:30am to 12:30pm. Offices are open from 8:30am to 12:30pm and 3 to 6pm, although many operate continuously from 9am to 5pm. Government offices are open Monday through Friday from 9:30am to 12:30pm and 3 to 5pm. Nightclubs in large cities often don't get going until after midnight, and many stay open until dawn.

Customs Exports of protected plant and endangered animal species—live or dead—are strictly prohibited by Peruvian law and should not be purchased. This includes headpieces and necklaces made with macaw feathers, unless authorized by the Natural Resources Institute (INRENA). Travelers have been detained and arrested by the Ecology Police for carrying such items. It is also illegal to take pre-Columbian archaeological items and antiques, including ceramics and textiles, and colonial-era art out of Peru. Reproductions of many such items are available, but even their export could cause difficulties at Customs or with overly cautious international courier services if you attempt to send them home. To be safe, look for the word "reproduction" or an artist's name stamped on reproduction ceramics, and keep business cards and receipts from shops where you have purchased them. Particularly fine items might require documentation from Peru's National Institute of Culture, or INC (www.cultura.gob. pe), verifying that the object is a reproduction and may be exported. You might be able to obtain a certificate of authorization from the INC kiosk at Lima's Jorge Chávez International Airport.

For information on what you're allowed to bring home, contact one of the following agencies:

U.S. citizens: U.S. Customs & Border Protection (CBP), 1300 Pennsylvania Ave., NW, Washington, DC 20229 (www.cbp.gov; ℂ **877/287-8667**).

Canadian citizens: Canada Border Services Agency (www.cbsa-asfc.gc.ca; ℂ **800/461-9999** in Canada, or 204/983-3500).

U.K. citizens: HM Customs & Excise (www.hmce.gov. uk; ℂ **0845/010-9000**, or from outside the U.K., 020/8929-0152).

Australian citizens: Australian Customs Service (www.border.gov.au; ℂ **1300/363-263**).

New Zealand citizens: New Zealand Customs, The Customhouse, 17–21 Whitmore St., Box 2218, Wellington (www.customs. govt.nz; ℂ **04/473-6099** or 0800/428-786).

Dentists The best dentists are found in Lima, and some offices specialize in foreign visitors looking for work done that is more inexpensive than their home countries and therefore have English-speaking staff. Try Peru Dental, at 355 Monterrey St., 4th Floor, Chacarilla (www.perudental. com; ℂ **01/202-2222**) or Smiles Peru, at Av. José

Prado 575, office 201 in Miraflores (www.smilesperu. com; ☎ 01/242-2152).

Disabled Travelers

Most disabilities shouldn't stop anyone from traveling. However, Peru is considerably less equipped for accessible travel than are most parts of North America and Europe. Comparatively few hotels are outfitted for travelers with disabilities, and only a few restaurants, museums, and means of public transportation make special accommodations for such patrons. There are few ramps, very few wheelchair-accessible bathrooms, and almost no telephones for the hearing-impaired. Though it continues to lag behind Europe and North America, Peru has been a perhaps unlikely leader in South America in terms of seeking to make its tourist infrastructure more accessible to people with disabilities. In 1998, Peru initiated a countrywide project targeting tourism establishments to improve facilities. Request a copy of "Tourism for the People with Disabilities: The First Evaluation of Accessibility to Peru's Tourist Infrastructure," available from the Peruvian embassy in your home country, before your visit to Peru. The 99-page report features evaluations of hotels, restaurants, museums, attractions, airports, and other services in Lima, Cusco, Aguas Calientes, and beyond.

A helpful website for accessible travel in Peru is **Access-Able Travel Source**

(www.access-able.com), which offers detailed destination articles on accessible travel in Peru and a wealth of specific information about Aguas Calientes, Cusco, Lima, and the Sacred Valley. Within individual reviews, you'll find information on ramps, door sizes, room sizes, bathrooms, and wheelchair availability.

Many travel agencies offer customized tours and itineraries for travelers with disabilities. **Apumayo Expediciones** (www. apumayo.com; ☎ 054/246-018) is way out in front in Peru, offering tours specifically designed for travelers with physical disabilities. **Accessible Journeys** (www.disabilitytravel.com; ☎ 800/846-4537 or 610/521-0339) caters specifically to slow walkers and wheelchair travelers and their families and friends. **InkaNatura Travel** (www. inkanatura.com) is also particularly well equipped to deal with travelers with disabilities: Beyond the website's specifics on Peru, it is an excellent resource with all kinds of general information and answers to frequently asked questions about traveling with disabilities.

Doctors

Skilled doctors and modern health-care facilities can be found primarily in Lima and other cities in Peru. In Lima, some of the major hospitals and clinics with English-speaking medical personnel and 24-hour emergency services include **Clínica**

Anglo-Americana, Alfredo Salazar, Block 3, San Isidro (☎ 01/712-3000); **Clínica San Borja,** Guardia Civil 337, San Borja (☎ 01/475-4000); and **Clínica Ricardo Palma,** Av. Javier Prado Este 1066, San Isidro (www.crp.com.pe; ☎ 01/224-2224).

In Cusco, you will find English-speaking personnel at **Hospital EsSalud,** Av. Anselmo Álvarez s/n (☎ 084/237-341); **Clínica Pardo,** Av. de la Cultura 710 (☎ 084/624-186); **Clínica San Jose,** Av. Los Incas 1408 (www.sanjose.com.pe; ☎ 084/232-295); and **Mac Salud,** Av. de la Cultura 1410 (www.macsalud.com; ☎ 084/582-060).

You can also inquire at the U.S. and British embassies (see "Embassies & Consulates," below) for lists of English-speaking doctors, dentists, and other health-care personnel in Lima.

If you need a non-emergency doctor, your hotel can recommend one, or contact your embassy or consulate. In any medical emergency, immediately call ☎ 105.

Drug & Drinking Laws

Until recently, Peru was the world's largest producer of coca leaves, the base product that is mostly shipped to Colombia for processing into cocaine. Cocaine and other illegal substances are perhaps not as ubiquitous in Peru as some might think, although in Lima and Cusco, they are sometimes offered to foreigners. (This is especially dangerous; many would-be dealers also operate as police informants, and some are said to be undercover narcotics officers themselves.) Penalties for the possession and use of or trafficking in illegal drugs in Peru are strict; convicted offenders can expect long jail sentences and substantial fines. Peruvian police routinely detain drug smugglers at Lima's international airport and land-border crossings. Since 1995, more than 40 U.S. citizens have been convicted of narcotics trafficking in Peru. If you are arrested on drug charges, you will face protracted pre-trial detention in poor prison conditions. Coca leaves, either chewed or brewed for tea, are not illegal in Peru, where they're not considered a narcotic. The use of coca leaves is an ancient tradition dating back to pre-Columbian civilizations in Peru. You might very well find that *mate de coca* (coca-leaf tea) is very helpful in battling altitude sickness. However, if you attempt to take coca leaves back to your home country from Peru, you should expect them to be confiscated, and you could even find yourself prosecuted. The hallucinogenic plants consumed in *ayahuasca* ceremonies are legal in Peru.

A legal drinking age is not strictly enforced in Peru, though officially it is 18. Anyone over the age of 16 is unlikely to have any problems ordering liquor in any bar or other establishment. Wine, beer, and alcohol are widely available—sold daily

at grocery stores, liquor stores, and in all cafes, bars, and restaurants—and consumed widely, especially in public during festivals. There appears to be very little taboo associated with public inebriation at festivals.

Electricity All outlets are 220 volts, 60 cycles AC (except in Arequipa, which operates on 50 cycles), with two-prong outlets that accept both flat and round prongs. Some large hotels also have 110-volt outlets.

Embassies & Consulates The following are all in Lima: **United States,** Avenida La Encalada, Block 17, Surco (☏ **01/434-3000**); **Australia,** Victor A. Belaúnde 147/ Vía Principal 155, Bldg. 3, Of. 1301, San Isidro (☏ **01/222-8281**); **Canada,** Calle Bolognesi 228, Miraflores (☏ **01/319-3200**); **United Kingdom** and **New Zealand,** Av. Jose Larco 1301, 22nd Floor, Miraflores (☏ **01/617-3000**).

The U.S. consulate is located at Av. Pardo 845 (CoresES@state.gov; ☏ **084/231-474**). The honorary U.K. consulate is at Manu Expeditions, Urbanización Magisterial, G-5 Segunda Etap (bwalker@terra.com.pe; ☏ **084/239-974**). Both are open daily from 9am to noon and 3 to 5pm.

Emergencies In case of an emergency, call the 24-hour **traveler's hotline** at ☏ **01/574-8000,** the general police emergency number at ☏ **105,** or the **tourist police** (POLTUR;

☏ **01/460-1060**). The **Tourist Protection Service** can assist in contacting police to report a crime; call ☏ **01/224-7888** in Lima, or **0800/4-2579** toll-free from any private phone (the toll-free number cannot be dialed from a public pay phone).

Family Travel Peruvians are extremely family-oriented, and children arouse friendly interest in locals. Although there aren't many established conventions, accommodations, or discounts for families traveling with children, Peru can be an excellent country in which to travel, as long as families remain flexible and are able to surmount difficulties in transportation, food, and accommodations. Few hotels automatically offer discounts for children or allow children to stay free with their parents. Negotiation with hotels is required. On buses, children have to pay full fare if they occupy a seat (which is why you'll see most kids sitting on their parent's or sibling's lap). Many museums and other attractions offer discounts for children 5 and under. Children's meals are rarely found at restaurants in Peru, but sometimes it's possible to specially order smaller portions. Peruvian food might be very foreign to many children—how many kids, or adults, for that matter, will be keen on tasting roasted guinea pig?—but familiar foods, such as fried chicken, pizza, and spaghetti, are easy to find in almost all Peruvian towns.

Health No vaccinations are officially required of travelers to Peru, but you are wise to take certain precautions, especially if you are planning to travel to jungle regions. A yellow-fever vaccine is strongly recommended for trips to the Amazon. The **Centers for Disease Control and Prevention** (www.cdc.gov; ✆ **800/311-3435**) warns that there is a risk of malaria and yellow fever in Lima and the highland tourist areas (Cusco, Machu Picchu, and Lake Titicaca).

Visitors should drink only bottled water, which is widely available. Do not drink tap water, even in major hotels. Try to avoid drinks with ice. *Agua con gas* is carbonated; *agua sin gas* is still.

As a tropical South American country, Peru presents certain health risks and issues, but major concerns are limited to those traveling outside urban areas and to the Amazon jungle. The most common ailments for visitors to Peru are common traveler's diarrhea; altitude sickness; or **acute mountain sickness (AMS),** called *soroche* locally; sun exposure; and dietary distress.

North American visitors can contact the **International Association for Medical Assistance to Travelers (IAMAT;** www.iamat.org; ✆ **716/754-4883**, or 416/652-0137 in Canada) for tips on travel and health concerns. The United States **Centers for Disease Control and**

Prevention (www.cdc.gov; ✆ **888/232-6348**) provides up-to-date information on health hazards by region or country. If you suffer from a chronic illness, consult your doctor before your departure. All visitors with such conditions as epilepsy, diabetes, or heart problems should consider wearing a **MedicAlert Identification Tag** (www.medicalert.org; www.medicalert.org.uk in the U.K.; ✆ **888/633-4298** or 209/668-3333), which will alert doctors to your condition if you become ill, and give them access to your records through MedicAlert's 24-hour hotline.

Deep vein thrombosis, or as it's known in the world of flying, "economy-class syndrome," is a blood clot that develops in a deep vein. It's a potentially deadly condition that can be caused by sitting in cramped conditions—such as an airplane cabin—for too long. During a flight (especially a long-haul flight), get up, walk around, and stretch your legs every 60 to 90 minutes to keep your blood flowing. Other preventative measures include frequent flexing of the legs while sitting, drinking lots of water, and avoiding alcohol and sleeping pills. If you have a history of deep vein thrombosis, heart disease, or another condition that puts you at high risk, some experts recommend wearing compression stockings or taking anticoagulants when you fly; always ask your family doctor about the best course

for you. Symptoms of deep vein thrombosis include leg pain or swelling, or even shortness of breath.

Insurance **U.S. visitors** should note that most domestic health plans (including Medicare and Medicaid) do not provide coverage abroad, and the ones that do often require you to pay for services upfront and reimburse you after you return home. Try **MEDEX** (www.medexassist. com; ✆ **410/453-6300**) or **Travel Assistance International** (www.travel assistance.com; ✆ **800/ 821-2828**) for overseas medical insurance coverage. **Canadians** should check with their provincial health plan offices or call **Health Canada** (www.hc-sc.gc.ca; ✆ **866/225-0709**) to find out the extent of their coverage and what documentation and receipts they must take home in case they are treated overseas.

For general travel insurance, it's wise to consult one of the price comparison websites before making a purchase. U.S. visitors can get estimates from various providers through **Insure-MyTrip.com** (✆ **800/487-4722**). Enter your trip cost and dates, your age, and other information for prices from several providers. For U.K. travelers, **Moneysuper-market** (www.moneysuper market.com) compares prices and coverage across a bewildering range of single- and multi-trip options. For all visitors, it's also worth considering trip-cancellation insurance, which will help retrieve your money if you have to back out of a trip or depart early. Trip cancellation traditionally covers such events as sickness, natural disasters, and travel advisories.

Internet & Wi-Fi   The availability of the Internet across Peru is in a constant state of development. How you access it depends on whether you've brought your own laptop, tablet, or smartphone, or if you're searching for a public terminal. Internet access is plentiful, particularly in the form of free high-speed **Wi-Fi,** which is available in most hotels, cafes in larger cities, and airports. Cybercafes (*cafés Internet,* or *cabinas*) can still be found in some areas, though they are not nearly as prevalent as they once were. Most hotels will have at least one public computer.

If you have your own computer or smartphone, **Wi-Fi** makes access much easier. Always check before using your hotel's network—many charge exorbitant rates, and free or cheap Wi-Fi isn't hard to find elsewhere, in urban locations, at least. Ask locally, or even Google "free Wi-Fi + [town]" before you arrive.

Savvy smartphone users from overseas may call using Wi-Fi in combination with a **Skype** (www.skype.com) account and mobile app.

Language   Spanish is the official language of Peru. The languages Quechua (also given official status)

and Aymara are spoken primarily in the highlands. (Aymara is mostly limited to the area around Lake Titicaca.) English is not widely spoken but is understood by those affiliated with the tourist industry in major cities and tourist destinations. Most people you meet on the street will have only a very rudimentary understanding of English, if that. Learning a few key phrases of Spanish will help immensely. Turn to Chapter 10 for those.

Legal Aid   If you need legal assistance, your best bets are your embassy (which, depending on the situation, might not be able to help you much) and the **Tourist Protection Service** (☏ **0800/4-2579** toll-free, or **01/574-8000** 24-hr.), which might be able to direct you to an English-speaking attorney or legal assistance organization. Note that bribing a police officer or public official is illegal in Peru, even if it is a relatively constant feature of traffic stops and the like. If a police officer claims to be an undercover cop, do not automatically assume that he is telling the truth. Do not get in any vehicle with such a person. Demand the assistance of your embassy or consulate, or of the Tourist Protection Service.

Your first move for any serious matter should be to contact your consulate or embassy (see "Embassies & Consulates," earlier in this section). They can advise you of your rights and will

usually provide a list of local attorneys (for which you'll have to pay if services are used), but they cannot interfere on your behalf in the English legal process. For questions about American citizens who are arrested abroad, including ways of getting money to them, telephone the **Citizens Emergency Center** of the Office of Special Consulate Services in Washington, D.C. (☏ **202/501-4444**).

LGBT Travelers
Although the Inca nation flag looks remarkably similar to the gay rainbow flag, Peru, a predominantly Catholic and socially conservative country, could not be considered among the world's most progressive in terms of societal freedoms for gays and lesbians. It remains a male-dominated, macho society where homosexuality is considered deviant. Across Peru, there is still considerable prejudice exhibited toward gays and lesbians who are out, or men—be they straight or gay—who are thought to be effeminate. The word *maricón* is, sadly, a commonly used derogatory term for homosexuals. In the larger cities, especially Lima and Cusco, there are a number of establishments—bars, discos, inns, and restaurants—that are either gay-friendly or predominantly gay. Outside those areas, and in the small towns and villages of rural Peru, openly gay behavior is unlikely to be tolerated by the general population.

There are a number of helpful websites for gay and lesbian travelers to Peru. **Gay Peru** (www.gayperu.pe) includes gay-oriented package tours, news items, and nightclubs and hotels (with versions in both English and Spanish). **Purple Roofs** (www.purpleroofs.com/southamerica/peru.html) has a decent listing of gay and lesbian lodgings, restaurants, and nightclubs throughout Peru.

If you're planning to visit from the U.S., the **International Gay and Lesbian Travel Association** (IGLTA; www.iglta.org; ✆ 800/448-8550 or 954/630-1637) is the trade association for the gay and lesbian travel industry, and offers an online directory of gay- and lesbian-friendly travel businesses. Many agencies offer tours and travel itineraries specifically for gay and lesbian travelers. **Above and Beyond Tours** (www.abovebeyondtours.com; ✆ 800/397-2681) is a gay and lesbian tour operator. **Now, Voyager** (www.nowvoyager.com; ✆ 800/255-6951) is a well-known San Francisco–based gay-owned and operated travel service.

Mail Peru's postal service is reasonably efficient, especially now that it is managed by a private company (**Serpost S.A.**). Post offices are open Monday through Saturday from 8am to 8pm; some are also open Sunday from 9am to 1pm. Major cities have a main post office and often several smaller branch offices. Letters and postcards to North America

or Europe take between 10 days and 2 weeks, and cost from S/7 to S/8 for postcards, S/9 to S/10 for letters. If you are purchasing large quantities of textiles and other handicrafts, you can send packages home from post offices, but it is not inexpensive—more than $100 for 10kg (22 lb.), similar to what it costs to use DHL, where you're likely to have an easier time communicating. UPS is found in several cities, but for inexplicable reasons, its courier services cost nearly three times as much as those of DHL.

Mobile Phones The three letters that define much of the world's wireless capabilities are **GSM** (Global System for Mobiles), a seamless satellite network that makes for easy cross-border cellphone use throughout most of the planet. If your cellphone is unlocked and on a GSM system, and you have a world-capable multiband phone, you can make and receive calls throughout much of Peru. (Mobile coverage in Peru, even in rural areas, is surprisingly good.) Just call your wireless operator and ask for "international roaming" to be activated on your account. Unfortunately, per-minute charges can be high.

There are other options if you're visiting from overseas but don't own an unlocked GSM phone. For a short visit, **renting** a phone may be a good idea, and we suggest renting the handset before you leave home.

North Americans can rent from **InTouch USA** (www.intouchglobal.com; ✆ 800/872-7626 or 703/222-7161) or **Bright-Roam** (www.brightroam.com; ✆ 888/622-3393). You can also rent an inexpensive cellphone once you touch down in Peru. In the International Arrivals terminal of Lima's Jorge Chávez International Airport (as you enter the baggage carousels area), you'll find young female representatives of **Peru Rent-a-Cell** (✆ 01/517-1856) offering inexpensive cellphones and plans (just $10 for the phone, up to a month, and incoming calls are free).

Per-minute charges for international calls can be high whatever network you choose, so if you plan to do a lot of calling home, use a VoIP service like **Skype** (www.skype.com) in conjunction with a web connection. See "Internet & Wi-Fi," above.

Money & Costs Frommer's lists exact prices in local currency (and occasionally in dollars, principally with regard to hotels that list rates in U.S. dollars). The currency conversions quoted below were correct at press time. However, rates fluctuate, so before departing consult a website such as www.oanda.com/currency/converter to check up-to-the-minute rates. At press time, US$1 equals S/3.4.

On the whole, although prices have risen in the past few years and Peru is slightly more expensive than its Andean neighbors Ecuador and Bolivia (but less expensive now than Chile and especially Brazil), Peru remains relatively inexpensive by North American and European standards. To those with strong currencies, Peru (outside of top-end restaurants and hotels) is likely to seem comparatively cheap. Peruvians tend to haggle over prices and accept and even expect that others will (politely) haggle, except of course in major stores and restaurants. In the bigger cities, prices for virtually everything—but especially hotels and restaurants—are higher, particularly in Lima. In addition, prices can rise in the high season, such as the Independence Day holidays (late July), Easter week (Mar or Apr), or Christmas, due to heavy demand, especially for hotel rooms and bus and plane tickets.

Peru's official currency is the *nuevo sol* (S/), divided into 100 *centavos*. Coins are issued in denominations of 5, 10, 20, and 50 *centavos*, and 1, 2, and 5 *soles*; bank notes in denominations of 10, 20, 50, 100, and 200 *soles*. The U.S. dollar is the second currency; some hotels post their rates in dollars, and plenty of shops, taxi drivers, restaurants, and

hotels across Peru will also accept U.S. dollars for payment. ***Note:*** Because many Peruvian hotels, tour operators, and transportation vendors charge prices solely in dollars, U.S. dollar rates are often listed in this book.

Peru is still largely a cash society. In villages and small towns, it could be impossible to cash traveler's checks or use credit cards. Make sure that you have cash (both *soles* and U.S. dollars) on hand. If you pay in dollars, you will likely receive change in *soles,* so be aware of the correct exchange rate. U.S. dollars are by far the easiest foreign currency to exchange. Currencies other than U.S. dollars receive very poor exchange rates.

Automated teller machines (ATMs) are the best way of getting cash in Peru; they're found in most towns and cities, although not on every street corner. ATMs allow customers to withdraw money in either Peruvian *soles* or U.S. dollars. Screen instructions are in English as well as Spanish. Some bank ATMs dispense money only to those who hold accounts there. Most ATMs in Peru accept only one type of credit/debit card and international money network, either Cirrus (www.mastercard.com;

☏ **800/424-7787**) or PLUS (www.visa.com; ☏ **800/843-7587**). Visa and MasterCard ATM cards are the most widely accepted; Visa/PLUS is the most common.

Be sure you know your personal identification number (PIN) and daily withdrawal limit before you depart. At some ATMs, your personal identification number (PIN) must contain four digits.

Travelers should beware of hidden credit- or debit-card fees. Check with your card issuer to see what fees, if any, will be charged for overseas transactions. Recent reform legislation in the U.S., for example, has curbed some exploitative lending practices. But many banks have responded by increasing fees in other areas, including fees for customers who use credit and debit cards while out of the country—even if those charges were made in U.S. dollars. Fees can amount to 3% or more of the purchase price. Check with your bank before departing to avoid any surprise charges on your statement.

Banks are no longer the place of choice in Peru for exchanging money: Lines are too long, the task is too time-consuming, and rates are often lower at *casas de cambio* (exchange houses)

THE VALUE OF THE PERUVIAN NUEVO SOL (S/) VS. OTHER POPULAR CURRENCIES

S/	US$	Can$	UK£	Euro (€)	Aus$	NZ$
1	0.29	0.42	0.20	0.27	0.42	0.45

WHAT THINGS COST IN PERU	S/
Taxi from Lima airport to Miraflores	S/55
Short taxi ride in town	S/5–S/10
Double room, inexpensive hotel	S/60–S/150
Double room, moderate hotel	S/150–S/350
Double room, expensive hotel	S/350–S/650
Three-course dinner for one without wine, moderate	S/65–S/95
Cocktail	S/16–S/20
Cup of coffee or bottle of water	S/3
Museum admission	S/5–S/20

or by using credit or debit-card ATMs or money-changers, which are legal in Peru. If you can't avoid banks, all cities and towns have branches of major international and local banks; see "Fast Facts" in individual destination chapters for locations. Money-changers, often wearing colored smocks with "$" insignias, can still be found on the street in many cities. They offer current rates of exchange, but count your money carefully (you can simplify this by exchanging easily calculable amounts, such as $10 or $100), and make sure you have not received any counterfeit bills.

Counterfeit bank notes and even coins are common, and merchants and consumers across Peru vigorously check the authenticity of money before accepting payment or change. (The simplest way: Hold the bank note up to the light to see the watermark.) Many people also refuse to accept bank notes that are not in good condition (including those with small tears, that have been written on, and even that are simply well worn), and visitors are wise to do the same when receiving change, to avoid problems with other payments. Do not accept bills with tears (no matter how small) or taped bills.

Making change in Peru can be a problem. You should carry small bills and even then be prepared to wait for change.

Packing Outside of a few high-end restaurants and clubs in Lima, Peru is overwhelmingly casual. You should probably be more concerned about packing the proper outdoor gear than the best duds to go out and be seen in. If traveling in rainy season, you'll want to be extra prepared for deluges in the highlands.

For more helpful information on packing for your trip, download our Travel Tools app for your mobile device. Go to **www.frommers.com/go/mobile** and click on the Travel Tools icon.

Passports Citizens of the United States, Canada, Great Britain, South Africa, New Zealand, and Australia do not require visas to enter Peru as tourists—only valid passports (your passport should be valid at least 6 months beyond your departure date from Peru, though in practice many travelers with as little as 3 months' validity are frequently permitted entry). Citizens of any of these countries conducting business or enrolled in formal educational programs in Peru do require visas; contact the embassy or consulate in your home country for more information.

White tourist (or landing) cards, distributed on arriving international flights or at border crossings, are good for stays of up to 90 days. Keep a copy of the tourist card for presentation upon departure from Peru. (If you lose it, you'll have to pay roughly a $5 fine.) A maximum of three extensions, at 30 days each for a total of 180 days, is allowed.

No immunizations are required for entry into Peru, although travelers planning to travel to jungle regions should see "Health," above.

Passport Offices:

o **Australia Australian Passport Information Service** (www.passports.gov.au; ☎ **131-232**).

o **Canada Passport Office,** Department of Foreign Affairs and International Trade, Ottawa, ON K1A 0G3 (www.ppt.gc.ca; ☎ **800/567-6868**).

o **Ireland Passport Office,** Setanta Centre, Molesworth Street, Dublin 2 (www.foreignaffairs.gov.ie; ☎ **01/671-1633**).

o **New Zealand Passports Office,** Department of Internal Affairs, 47 Boulcott Street, Wellington, 6011 (www.passports.govt. nz; ☎ **0800/225-050** in New Zealand or 04/474-8100).

o **United Kingdom** Visit your nearest passport office, major post office, or travel agency or contact the **Identity and Passport Service (IPS),** 89 Eccleston Square, London, SW1V 1PN (www. ips.gov.uk; ☎ **0300/222-0000**).

o **United States** To find your regional passport office, check the U.S. State Department website (travel. state.gov/passport) or call the **National Passport Information Center** (☎ **877/487-2778**) for automated information.

Pharmacies Prescriptions can be filled at *farmacias* and *boticas;* it's best to know the generic name of

your drug. For most health matters that are not serious, a pharmacist will be able to help and prescribe something. In the case of more serious health issues, contact your hotel, the tourist information office, or, in the most extreme case, your consulate or embassy for a doctor referral. Two of the biggest pharmacy chains, with locations in most cities, are Botica Fasa and Inka-Farma. Hospitals with English-speaking doctors are listed under "Doctors," above.

Police Losses, thefts, and other criminal matters should be reported to the nearest police station immediately. Peru has special tourist police forces (Policía Nacional de Turismo) with offices and personnel in all major tourist destinations, including Lima and Cusco, as well as a dozen other cities. You are more likely to get a satisfactory response, not to mention someone who speaks at least some English, from the tourist police rather than from the regular national police (PNP). The number for the tourist police in Lima is ☎ **01/225-8698** or 01/225-8699. For other cities, see "Emergencies" above and "Fast Facts" in individual destination chapters. Tourist police officers are distinguished by their white shirts.

Responsible Tourism
Sustainable, responsible tourism means conscientious travel. It means being careful with the environments you explore and respecting the communities

you visit. Two overlapping components of sustainable travel are ecotourism and ethical tourism. Traveling "green" and seeking sustainable tourism options is a concern in almost every part of the world today. Peru, with its majestic large expanses of nature, including the Amazon basin that covers two-thirds of the country, is a place where environmentally and culturally conscientious travel is not something to think about—it's the reality of the present and future. Although one could argue that any trip that includes an airplane flight or rental car can't be truly green, you can go on holiday and still contribute positively to the environment; all travelers can take certain steps toward responsible travel. Choose forward-looking companies that embrace responsible development practices, helping preserve destinations for the future by working alongside local people. An increasing number of sustainable tourism initiatives can help you plan a family trip and leave as small a "footprint" as possible on the places you visit.

The **International Ecotourism Society (TIES)** defines ecotourism as responsible travel to natural areas that conserves the environment and improves the well-being of local people. TIES suggests that ecotourists follow these principles:

o Minimize environmental impact.

- Build environmental and cultural awareness and respect.

- Provide positive experiences for both visitors and hosts.

- Provide direct financial benefits for conservation and for local people.

- Raise sensitivity to host countries' political, environmental, and social climates.

- Support international human rights and labor agreements.

You can find some eco-friendly travel tips, statistics, and touring companies and associations—listed by destination under "Travel Choice"—at the **TIES** website, www.ecotourism.org.

While much of the focus of ecotourism is about reducing impacts on the natural environment, ethical tourism concentrates on ways to preserve and enhance local economies and communities, regardless of location. You can embrace ethical tourism by staying at locally owned hotels or shopping at stores that employ local workers and sell locally produced goods. In Peru, it's a great idea to pick up artisanry such as textiles and ceramics from shops that ensure that the very artisans are well compensated for their labors. Many times those artisans are residents of poor rural communities and "fair trade" shops are increasingly seen. Many highlight the names of artisans and their home communities on their wares.

Volunteer travel has become increasingly popular among those who want to venture beyond the standard group-tour experience to learn languages, interact with locals, and make a positive difference while on vacation in Peru.

Deforestation is the main threat to Peru's fragile ecosystem. Farming has virtually wiped out most of the region's rainforests, and logging is a major threat. Such destruction has been devastating to many species, including humans, in the form of displaced indigenous tribes, and has led to drinking-water shortages, flash flooding, and mudslides. Though environmental awareness is growing, solving the region's huge environmental problems, including not just deforestation but the effects of overpopulation and industrial pollution, clearly remains an uphill struggle.

Peru has 72 million hectares (178 million acres) of natural-growth forests—70 percent in the Amazon jungle region—that comprise nearly 60 percent of the national territory. Peru has done a slightly better job of setting aside tracts of rainforest as national park reserves and regulating industry than have some other Latin American and Asian countries. INRENA, Peru's Institute for Natural Resource Management, enforces logging regulations and reseeds Peru's Amazon forests, and, in 2008, President García created the country's first

Ministry of the Environment. A handful of Peruvian and international environmental and conservation groups such as ProNaturaleza and Conservation International are active in Peru, working on reforestation and sustainable forestry projects.

Yet Peru is losing nearly 250,000 hectares (618,000 acres) of forest annually. The primary threats to Peru's tropical forests are deforestation caused by agricultural expansion, cattle ranching, logging, oil extraction and spills, mining, illegal coca farming, and colonization initiatives. Deforestation has shrunk territories belonging to indigenous peoples and wiped out more than 90 percent of the population. (There were once some 6 million people, 2,000 tribes and/or ethnic groups, and innumerable languages in the Amazon basin; today the indigenous population is less than 2 million.) Jungle ecotourism has exploded in Peru, and rainforest regions are now much more accessible than they once were, with more lodges and eco-options than ever. Many are taking leading roles in sustainable tourism even as they introduce protected regions to more travelers.

Besides sustainable travel to Peru's wilderness, national parks and reserves, and threatened areas, there are everyday things you can do to minimize the impact—and especially the carbon footprint—of your travels. Remove chargers from cellphones, PSPs, laptops, and anything else that draws from the mains, once the gadget is fully charged. Turning off all hotel room lights (plus the TV and air-conditioning) can have a massive effect; it really is time all hotels had room-card central power switches.

Green trips also extend to where you eat and stay. Vegetarian foods tend to have a much smaller impact on the environment because they eschew energy- and resource-intensive meat production. Most hotels now offer you the choice to use your towels for more than one night before they are re-laundered—laundry makes up around 40 percent of an average hotel's energy use.

Among Peruvian hotel chains, one stands out as a model for the industry. Although **Inkaterra** (www.inkaterra.com) operates just six hotels and lodges, it is a leader among green, sustainable tourism initiatives. The group, which began with a research center for scientists in the Amazon, takes environmental issues seriously: Its properties are carbon-neutral, and it operates a not-for-profit environmental organization, which actively monitors environmental deterioration in the Peruvian rainforest. The chairman of the group sits on the board of Conservation International. Other hotel groups, and particularly those operating ecolodges in the Amazon, are following suit, being careful to ensure that a healthy percentage of jobs

and benefits stay local and that the lodges' imprint on their fragile environment is minimal. In a country like Peru, with such a large tract of virgin rainforest and developmental needs, maintaining a balance between income generation/tourism and sustainable development is a huge ongoing challenge.

A source for environmentally sensitive hotels is **It's a Green Green World** (www.itsagreengreenworld.com), which lists green and eco-friendly places to stay, mostly ecolodges in the Amazon. **Responsible Travel** (www.responsibletravel.com, www.responsiblevacation.com in the U.S.) is one among a growing number of environmentally aware travel agents, with dozens of green Peru trips offered. **Vision on Sustainable Tourism** (www.tourismvision.com) is another excellent news hub. Carbon offsetting (not uncontroversial) can be arranged through, among others, **ClimateCare** (www.climatecare.org).

Safety Peru's reputation for safety among travelers has greatly improved and the country is more stable and safer than it has ever been. While some general warnings are required, for the most part, the majority of travelers will find Peru a very safe country with few of the overt threats to belongings or one's person that are sadly common in many parts of the world. Hopefully, the following warnings will seem over-the-top to travelers

who enjoy Peru without incident.

The most precautions, as in most countries, are required in the largest cities: principally Lima and, to a lesser extent, Cusco. In most heavily touristed places in Peru, though, a heightened police presence is noticeable. Simple theft and pickpocketing are not uncommon; assaults and robbery are rare. Most thieves look for moments when travelers, laden with bags and struggling with maps, are distracted. In downtown Lima and the city's residential and hotel areas, there is a risk of street crime. Occasional carjackings and armed attacks at ATMs have been reported, but they are very isolated incidents. Use ATMs during the day, with other people present. Street crime and pickpocketing are most likely to occur—when they do—at crowded public markets and bus and train stations. You should be vigilant with belongings in these places and should not walk alone late at night on deserted streets. In major cities, taxis hailed on the street can lead to assaults. (Use telephone-dispatched radio taxis, especially at night.) Ask your hotel or restaurant to call a cab, or use Uber or Easy Taxi, which have security protocol. Travelers should exercise caution on public city transportation and on long-distance buses, where thieves have been known to employ any number of strategies to relieve passengers of their bags.

You need to be vigilant, even to the extreme of locking backpacks and suitcases to luggage racks.

In general, do not wear expensive jewelry; keep expensive camera equipment out of view as much as possible; use a money belt worn inside your pants or shirt to safeguard cash, credit cards, and passport. Wear your daypack on your chest rather than your back when walking in crowded areas. The time to be most careful is when you have most of your belongings on your person—such as when you're in transit from airport or train or bus station to your hotel. At airports, it's best to spend a little more for official airport taxis; if in doubt, request the driver's official ID. Don't venture beyond airport grounds for a street taxi. Have your hotel call a taxi for your trip to the airport or bus station.

Peru's terrorist past seems to be behind it. The terrorist activities of the local insurgency groups Sendero Luminoso (Shining Path) and MRTA (Tupac Amaru Revolutionary Movement)—which together waged a 2-decade guerrilla war against the Peruvian state, killing more than 30,000 people—were effectively stamped out in the early 1990s. It has now been years since there were significant concerns about a possible resurgence of those groups. Though it remains a situation worth watching, to date the most populous (and traveled) regions of the country have

not been affected, and neither group is currently active in any of the areas covered in this book.

Senior Travel   Discounts for seniors are not automatic across Peru, though many attractions do offer a senior rate. Mention the fact that you're a senior (and carry ID with your birth date) when you make travel reservations; many hotels still offer lower rates for seniors. Many museums and other attractions also offer discounts; if a senior rate—often expressed as *mayores de edad* or *jubilados* (retired)—is not posted, inquire and show your passport.

Smoking   Smoking is still quite common in Peru, despite a widespread smoke-free policy implemented in 2011. In major cities such as Lima or Cusco, it is difficult to find smoky restaurants or hotels. In rural areas, the laws are less enforced.

Student Travel   Never leave home without your student I.D. card. Visitors from overseas should arm themselves with an **International Student Identity Card (ISIC),** which offers local savings on rail passes, plane tickets, entrance fees, and much more. Each country's card offers slightly different benefits (in the U.S., for example, it provides you with basic health and life insurance and a 24-hour helpline). Apply before departing in your country of origin. In the U.S. or Canada, visit **www.myisic.com;**

in Australia, **www.isiccard. com.au;** in New Zealand, **www.isiccard.co.nz.** U.K. students should carry their NUS card. If you're no longer a student but are still younger than 26, you can get an **International Youth Travel Card (IYTC),** which entitles you to a more limited range of discounts.

Taxes   A general sales tax (IGV) is added automatically to most consumer bills (19 percent). In some upmarket hotels or restaurants, service charges of 10 percent are often added. Foreigners who can demonstrate that they do not reside in Peru (generally all you need to do is show your passport) are exempt from having to pay the IGV tax at hotels. Some unscrupulous smaller hotels occasionally try to dupe guests into believing that they have to pay this 19 percent tax; this is flatly untrue.

Time   Peru is 5 hours behind GMT (Greenwich Mean Time). Peru does not observe daylight saving time.

Tipping   Whether and how much to tip is not without controversy. Visitors from the U.S. in particular tend to be more generous than locals and European visitors. Most people leave about a 10 percent tip for waitstaff in restaurants. In nicer restaurants that add a 10 percent service charge, many patrons tip an additional 5 percent or 10 percent (because little, if any, of that service charge will ever make it to the waiter's pocket). Taxi drivers are not usually tipped unless they provide additional service. Bilingual tour guides on group tours should be tipped ($1–$2 per person for a short visit, and $5 or more per person for a full day). If you have a private guide, tip about $10 to $20.

Toilets   Public lavatories (*baños públicos*) are rarely available except in railway stations, restaurants, and theaters. Many Peruvian men choose to urinate in public, against a wall in full view, especially late at night; it's not recommended that you emulate them. Use the bathroom of a bar, cafe, or restaurant; if it feels uncomfortable to dart in and out, have a coffee at the bar. Public restrooms are labeled WC (water closet), DAMAS (Ladies), and CABALLEROS or HOMBRES (Men). Toilet paper is not always provided, and when it is, most establishments request that patrons throw it in the wastebasket rather than the toilet, to avoid clogging.

Visitor Information
Within Peru, there's a 24-hour tourist information line, **iPerú (✆ 01/574-8000).** Peru doesn't maintain national tourism offices abroad, so your best official source of information before you go is www.peru.travel, the website of Prom Perú (Commission for the Promotion of Peru). Other helpful trip-planning websites include www.embassyof peru.org, the Embassy of Peru in Washington, D.C., and www.saexplorers.org, the South American Explorers website, which is especially good for trekking and adventure travel information.

The **Tourist Protection Bureau (Servicio de Protección al Turista)**, which handles complaints and questions about consumer rights, operates a 24-hour traveler's assistance line at ✆ **0800/42-579,** or 01/224-7888 in Lima.

USEFUL TERMS & PHRASES

Peruvian Spanish is, for the most part, straightforward and fairly free of the quirks and national slang that force visitors to page through their dictionaries in desperation. But if you know Spanish, some of the terms you will hear people saying are *chibolo* for *muchacho* (boy); *churro* and *papasito* for *guapo* (good-looking); *jato* instead of *casa* (house); *chapar* (literally "to grab or get"), slangier than but with the same meaning as *besar* (to kiss); *¡que paja está!* (it's great); *mi pata* to connote a dude or chick from your posse; and *papi* (or *papito*) and *mami* (or *mamita*), affectionate terms for "father" and "mother" that are also used as endearments between relatives and lovers (which can get a little confusing to the untrained outsider). The inherited indigenous respect for nature is evident; words such as *Pachamama* (Mother Earth) tend to make it into conversation remarkably frequently.

Spanish is but one official language of Peru, though. **Quechua** (the language of the Inca Empire) has been given official status and is still widely spoken, especially in the highlands, and there has been a movement afoot to add **Aymara** as a national language, too. (Aymara is spoken principally in the southern highlands area around Lake Titicaca.) Dozens of other native tongues and dialects are still spoken around the country as well. A predominantly oral language (the Incas had no written texts), Quechua is full of glottal and magical, curious sounds. As it is written today, it is mystifyingly vowel-heavy and apostrophe-laden, full of q's, k's, and y's; try to wrap your tongue around *munayniykimanta* (excuse me) or *hayk' atan kubrawanki llamaykikunanmanta* (how much is it to hire a llama?). Very few people seem to agree on spellings of Quechua, as you'll pick up on street signs and restaurant names in Cusco. Colorful phrases often mix and match Spanish and indigenous languages: *Hacer la tutumeme* is the same as *ir a dormir,* or "to go to sleep."

In addition to these primary languages, there are dozens of indigenous tongues and dialects in the Amazon region. At one time there may have been as many as hundreds of these isolated languages, though that number has dwindled to a few dozen, most of which are in danger of extinction.

BASIC SPANISH VOCABULARY

English	Spanish	Pronunciation
Good day	Buenos días	**Bweh-nohs dee-ahs**
Hi/hello	Hola	**Oh-lah**
Pleasure to meet you	Mucho gusto/Un placer	**Moo-choh goos-toh/Oon plah-sehr**
How are you?	¿Cómo está?	**Koh-moh eh-stah**
Very well	Muy bien	**Mwee byehn**
Thank you	Gracias	**Grah-syahs**
How's it going?	¿Qué tal?	**Keh tahl**
You're welcome	De nada	**Deh nah-dah**
Goodbye	Adiós	**Ah-dyohs**
Please	Por favor	**Pohr fah-bohr**
Yes	Sí	**See**
No	No	**Noh**
Excuse me (to get by someone)	Perdóneme/Con permiso	**Pehr-doh-neh-meh/Kohn pehr-mee-soh**
Excuse me (to begin a question)	Disculpe	**Dees-kool-peh**
Give me	Déme	**Deh-meh**
What time is it?	¿Qué hora es?	**Keh ohr-ah ehs**
Where is . . . ?	¿Dónde está . . . ?	**Dohn-deh eh-stah**
the station (bus/train)	la estación (estación de ómnibus/tren)	**lah eh-stah-syohn (eh-stah-syohn deh ohm-nee-boos/ trehn)**
a hotel	un hotel	**oon oh-tehl**
a gas station	una estación de servicio	**oo-nah eh-stah-syohn deh sehr-bee-syoh**
a restaurant	un restaurante	**oon res-tow-rahn-teh**
the toilet	el baño (servicios)	**el bah-nyoh (sehr-bee-syohs)**
a good doctor	un buen médico	**oon bwehn meh-dee-coh**
the road to . . .	el camino a/hacia	**el cah-mee-noh ah/ah-syah**
To the right	A la derecha	**Ah lah deh-reh-chah**
To the left	A la izquierda	**Ah lah ees-kyehr-dah**
Straight ahead	Derecho	**Deh-reh-choh**
Is it far?	¿Está lejos?	**Eh-stah leh-hohs**
Is it close?	¿Está cerca?	**Eh-stah sehr-kah**
Open	Abierto	**Ah-byehr-toh**
Closed	Cerrado	**Seh-rah-doh**
North	Norte	**Nohr-teh**
South	Sur	**Soor**
East	Este	**Eh-steh**
West	Oeste	**Oh-eh-steh**
Expensive	Caro	**Cah-roh**
Cheap	Barato	**Bah-rah-toh**

Basic Spanish Vocabulary

USEFUL TERMS & PHRASES

English	Spanish	Pronunciation
I would like	Quisiera	**Key-syeh-rah**
I want . . .	Quiero . . .	**Kyeh-roh**
to eat	comer	**koh-mehr**
a room	una habitación	**oo-nah ah-bee-tah-syohn**
Do you have . . . ?	¿Tiene usted . . . ?	**Tyeh-neh oo-sted**
a book	un libro	**oon lee-broh**
a dictionary	un diccionario	**oon deek-syoh-nah-ryoh**
change	cambio	**kahm-byoh**
How much is it?	¿Cuánto cuesta?	**Kwahn-toh kweh-stah**
When?	¿Cuándo?	**Kwahn-doh**
What?	¿Qué?	**Keh**
There is (Is/Are there . . . ?)	(¿)Hay (. . . ?)	**Eye**
What is there?	¿Qué hay?	**Keh eye**
Yesterday	Ayer	**Ah-yer**
Today	Hoy	**Oy**
Tomorrow	Mañana	**Mah-nyah-nah**
Good	Bueno	**Bweh-noh**
Bad	Malo	**Mah-loh**
Better (best)	(Lo) Mejor	**(Loh) Meh-hohr**
More	Más	**Mahs**
Less	Menos	**Meh-nohs**
No smoking	Se prohibe fumar	**Seh proh-ee-beh foo-mahr**
Postcard	Tarjeta postal	**Tar-heh-tah poh-stahl**
Insect repellent	Repelente contra insectos	**Reh-peh-lehn-teh cohn-trah een-sehk-tohs**
Now	Ahora	**Ah-ohr-ah**
Right now	Ahora mismo (ahorita)	**Ah-ohr-ah mees-moh (ah-ohr-ee-tah)**
Later	Más tarde	**Mahs tahr-deh**
Never	Nunca	**Noon-kah**
Guide	Guía	**Ghee-ah**
Heat	Calor	**Kah-lohr**
It's hot!	¡Qué calor!	**Keh kah-lohr**
Cold	Frío	**Free-oh**
Rain	Lluvia	**Yoo-byah**
It's cold!	¡Qué frío!	**Keh free-oh**
Wind	Viento	**Byehn-toh**
It's windy!	¡Cuánto viento!	**Kwahn-toh byehn-toh**
Money-changer	Cambista	**Kahm-bee-stah**
Bank	Banco	**Bahn-koh**
Money	Dinero	**Dee-neh-roh**
Small (correct) change	Sencillo	**Sehn-see-yoh**
Credit card	Tarjeta de crédito	**Tahr-heh-tah deh creh-dee-toh**

English	Spanish	Pronunciation
ATM	Cajero automático	**Kah-heh-roh ow-toh-mah-tee-koh**
Tourist information office	Oficina de información turística	**Oh-fee-see-nah deh een-for-mah-syohn too-ree-stee-kah**
Do you speak English?	¿Habla usted inglés?	**Ah-blah oo-sted een-glehs**
Is there anyone here who speaks English?	¿Hay alguien aquí que hable inglés?	**Eye ahl-gyehn ah-kee keh ah-bleh een-glehs**
I speak a little Spanish.	Hablo un poco de español.	**Ah-bloh oon poh-koh deh eh-spah-nyohl**
I don't understand Spanish very well.	No (lo) entiendo muy bien el español.	**Noh (loh) ehn-tyehn-doh mwee byehn el eh-spah-nyohl**
The meal is good.	Me gusta la comida.	**Meh goo-stah lah koh-mee-dah**
May I see your menu?	¿Puedo ver el menú (la carta)?	**Pweh-doh vehr el meh-noo (lah car-tah)**
The check, please.	La cuenta, por favor.	**Lah kwehn-tah pohr fa-borh**
What do I owe you?	¿Cuánto le debo?	**Kwahn-toh leh deh-boh**
What did you say?	¿Mande? (formal)	**Mahn-deh**
	¿Cómo? (informal)	**Koh-moh**

Numbers

English	Spanish	Pronunciation
one	uno	*ooh*-noh
two	dos	dohs
three	tres	trehs
four	cuatro	*kwah*-troh
five	cinco	*seen*-koh
six	seis	sayes
seven	siete	*syeh*-teh
eight	ocho	*oh*-choh
nine	nueve	*nweh*-beh
ten	diez	dyehs
eleven	once	*ohn*-seh
twelve	doce	*doh*-seh
thirteen	trece	*treh*-seh
fourteen	catorce	kah-*tohr*-seh
fifteen	quince	*keen*-seh
sixteen	dieciséis	dyeh-see-*sayes*
seventeen	diecisiete	dyeh-see-*syeh*-teh
eighteen	dieciocho	dyeh-see-*oh*-choh
nineteen	diecinueve	dyeh-see-*nweh*-beh
twenty	veinte	*bayn*-teh
thirty	treinta	*trayn*-tah
forty	cuarenta	kwah-*ren*-tah
fifty	cincuenta	seen-*kwen*-tah

English	Spanish	Pronunciation
sixty	sesenta	**seh-*sehn*-tah**
seventy	setenta	**seh-*tehn*-tah**
eighty	ochenta	**oh-*chehn*-tah**
ninety	noventa	**noh-*behn*-tah**
one hundred	cien	**syehn**
two hundred	doscientos	**do-*syehn*-tohs**
five hundred	quinientos	**kee-*nyehn*-tohs**
one thousand	mil	**meel**

Days of the Week

English	Spanish	Pronunciation
Monday	Lunes	***loo*-nehss**
Tuesday	Martes	***mahr*-tehss**
Wednesday	Miércoles	***myehr*-koh-lehss**
Thursday	Jueves	***wheh*-behss**
Friday	Viernes	***byehr*-nehss**
Saturday	Sábado	***sah*-bah-doh**
Sunday	Domingo	**doh-*meen*-goh**

SPANISH MENU GLOSSARY

GENERAL TERMS

Arroz   Rice
Asado   Roast
Café   Coffee
Camarones   Shrimp
Camote   Sweet potato
Carne   Meat
Cerdo   Pork
Cordero   Lamb
Ensalada   Salad
Fruta   Fruit
Huevos   Eggs
Leche   Milk

Lomo   Beef/steak
Mariscos   Seafood
Pan   Bread
Papas   Potatoes
Papas fritas   French fries
Pescado   Fish
Pollo   Chicken
Postre   Dessert
Queso   Cheese
Sal   Salt
Sopa (chupe)   Soup
Verduras   Vegetables

MEAT

Adobo   Meat dish in a spicy chili sauce
Alpaca   Alpaca
Anticuchos   Skewered meat
Cabrito   Goat
Carne de res   Beef

Chicharrones   Fried pork skins
Conejo   Rabbit
Cordero   Lamb
Empanada   Pastry turnover filled with meat, vegetables, fruit, manjar blanco, or sometimes nothing at all

Estofado   Stew
Lomo asado   Roast beef
Parrillada   Grilled meats
Pato   Duck

Pollo a la brasa   Spit-roasted chicken
Venado   Venison

SEAFOOD

Almejas   Clams
Atun   Tuna
Calamar   Squid
Cangrejo   Crab
Caracol   Snails
Conchas   Scallops
Corvina   Sea bass
Erizo   Sea urchin
Langosta   Lobster

Langostinos   Prawns
Lenguado   Sole
Mero   Grouper
Paiche   Large Amazon fish
Pejerrery   Silverside fish
Pulpo   Octopus
Tollo   Spotted dogfish
Trucha   Trout

FRUIT

Aguaymanto   Cape gooseberry
Camu Camu   Small Amazonian fruit high in vitamin C
Cherimoya   Custard apple
Cocona   Tree tomato
Fresa   Strawberry
Limón   Lime
Lúcuma   Eggfruit. Has a flavor similar to maple or pumpkin.

Manzana   Apple
Maracuyá   Passion fruit
Marañón   Cashew nut fruit
Naranja   Orange
Piña   Pineapple
Plátano   Plantain
Sandía   Watermelon
Tumbo   Banana passion fruit

VEGETABLES

Aceitunas   Olives
Lechuga   Lettuce
Mashua   Andean root vegetable with bright colors
Maca   Andean root, sometimes called Peruvian ginseng

Oca   Andean tuber, shaped similar to a carrot
Papa   Potato
Palta   Avocado
Tomate   Tomato
Yuca   Cassava or manioc

BEVERAGES

Agua   Water
    con gas   carbonated
    sin gas   still
Cerveza/Chela   Beer
Cóctel/trago   Cocktail

Gaseosa   Soft drink
Jugo   Juice
Leche   Milk
Refresco   Mixed fruit juice
Vino   Wine

PREPARATION

Caliente   Hot (temperature)
Cocido   Cooked
Crudo   Raw
El menu   Fixed-price menu

Frío   Cold (temperature)
Frito   Fried
Picante   Spicy
Vegetariano   Vegetarian

PERUVIAN FAVORITES

Adobo   Spicy Andean pork stew

Ají de gallina   Spicy/creamy shredded chicken, served over rice

Alfajores   Two layers of cookies filled with *manjar blanco*

Anticuchos   Beef-heart brochettes

Arroz con mariscos   Rice with seafood

Arroz con pato   Duck with rice

Carapulcra   A pre-Columbian dish of meat and dehydrated potato stew

Causa   Layered mashed potatoes with avocado, stuffed with chicken or tuna

Ceviche   Marinated raw fish

Chaufa   Chinese fried rice

Chicha   Fermented maize beer

Chicha morada   Purple-corn non-alcoholic beverage

Chifa   Peruvian–Chinese food

Choclo   Maize (large-kernel corn)

Chupe   Soup or chowder (*chupe de camarones,* prawn chowder, is the most common)

Cuy   Guinea pig. Can be roasted, fried, or cooked in a sauce.

Flan   Caramel custard

Humita   Ground corn steamed in a corn husk. Can be sweet or salty.

Jalea   Fried seafood with onion relish

Kiwicha   Andean variety of amaranth

Lomo saltado   Strips of beef with fried potatoes, onions, and tomatoes over rice

Manjar blanco   Sweetened condensed milk

Mazamorra morada   A typical dessert made of purple corn and dried fruits. Often served with rice pudding.

Pachamanca   Roast meat and potatoes, prepared underground

Paiche   Amazon river fish

Palta   Avocado

Palta rellena (or palta a la Reina)   Stuffed avocado (with chicken or tuna salad)

Panqueque   Crêpe

Papa a la huancaína   Boiled potatoes in a creamy and spicy cheese sauce

Papa rellena   Stuffed and fried potato

Parihuela   A thin seafood soup

Picarones   Deep fried donuts made from squash

Pollo a la brasa   Rotisserie chicken

Pulpo al olivo   Octopus in purple olive sauce

Quinua   Andean grain (quinoa), often in soup (*sopa de quinua*)

Rocoto relleno   Stuffed hot pepper

Salchipapas   French fries and sliced-up hot dogs

Sopa a la criolla   Creole soup (noodles or grain, often quinoa, vegetables, and meat)

Suspiro a la Limeña   A classic Limeñan dessert of *manjar blanco* and egg yolks topped with meringue

Tacu tacu   Refried leftover rice and beans

Tamal   Ground corn cooked and stuffed with chicken or pork, wrapped in banana leaves or corn husks, and then steamed

Tiradito   Ceviche-like strips of raw fish, marinated with *ají* peppers and lime but without sweet potatoes or onions, akin to Peruvian sashimi or carpaccio

Turrón de Doña Pepa   Traditionally prepared for the religious festivities of Señor de Milagros, this consists of anise-flavored cookies topped with cane syrup, sprinkles, and candies.

QUECHUA & QUECHUA-DERIVED TERMS

Quechua ("*Ketch*-u-wa") was the language of the Inca Empire, and it remains widely spoken in Peru and throughout Andean nations 5 centuries after the Spaniards did so much to impose their own culture, language, and religion upon the region. It is the most widely spoken indigenous language. Called *Runasimi* (literally, "language of the people") by Quechua speakers, the language is spoken by more than 10 million people in the highlands of South America. As much as one-third of Peru's 28 million people speak Quechua. Quechua speakers call themselves Runa—simply translated, "the people."

Quechua is an agglutinative language, meaning that words are constructed from a root word and combined with a large number of suffixes and infixes, which are added to words to change meaning and add subtlety. Linguists consider Quechua unusually poetic and expressive. Quechua is not a monolithic language, though. More than two dozen dialects are currently spoken in Peru. The one of greatest reach, not surprisingly, is the one still spoken in Cusco. Though continually threatened by Spanish, Quechua remains a vital language in the Andes and there have been new efforts to maintain it. Recent years have seen popular books and music translated into Quechua, helping inspire younger generations. Just Google "Michael Jackson's How You Make Me Feel in Quechua" to see what I mean.

Still, many Andean migrants to urban areas have tried to distance themselves from their indigenous roots, fearful that they would be marginalized by the Spanish-speaking majority in cities—many of whom regard Quechua and other native languages as the domain of the poor and uneducated. (Parents often refuse to speak Quechua with their children.) In some ways, the presidency of Alejandro Toledo, himself of indigenous descent, led to a new valuation of Quechua (and Aymara). Toledo said he hoped to spur new interest and pride in native culture in schools and among all Peruvians, and he had the Quechua language spoken at his 2001 inaugural ceremonies at Machu Picchu.

Quechua has made its influence felt on Peruvian Spanish, of course, which has hundreds of Quechua words, ranging from names of plants and animals (*papa,* potato; *cuy,* guinea pig) to food (*choclo,* corn on the cob; *pachamanca,* a type of earth oven) and clothing (*chompa,* sweater; *chullu,* knitted cap). Quechua has also made its way into English. Words commonly used in English that are derived from Quechua include coca, condor, guano, gaucho, lima (as in the bean), llama, and puma.

Common Terms

Altiplano   Plateau/high plains
Apu   Sacred summit/mountain spirit
Campesino   Rural worker/peasant
Chacra   Plot of land
Charqui   Dehydrated meat/jerky
Cocha   Lake
Huayno   Andean musical style
Inca   Inca ruler/emperor
Inti   Sun
Intiwatana   "Hitching post of the sun" (stone pillar at Inca ceremonial sites)
Mestizo   Person of mixed European and indigenous lineage
Pachamama   Mother Earth
Pucara   Fortress
Runasimi   Quechua language
Sacha   False
Soroche   Altitude sickness (hypoxia)
Tambo   In-transit checkpoint on Inca highway
Tawantinsuyu   Inca Empire
Viracocha   Inca deity (creator god)
Wawa   Baby

Try a Little Quechua

English	Quechua	Pronunciation
Yes	Riki	*Ree-kee*
No	Mana	*Mah-nah*
Madam	Mama	*Mah-mah*
Sir	Tayta	*Tahy-tah*
Thank you	Añay	*Ah-nyahy*

ETIQUETTE & CUSTOMS

Appropriate Attire   Many travelers to Peru are dressed head-to-toe in adventure or outdoor gear (parkas, fleece wear, hiking boots, and cargo pants). This is perfectly acceptable attire for all but the fanciest restaurants, where "neat casual" would be a better solution. In churches and monasteries, err on the side of discretion (low-rise pants, midriff shirts, peekaboo thongs, and anything else that reveals a lot of skin are not usually acceptable).

Avoiding Offense In Peru, you should be tactful when discussing local politics, though open discussion of the corruption of past presidents and terrorism in Peru is perfectly acceptable and unlikely to engender heated debate. Discussion of drugs (and coca-plant cultivation) and religion should be handled with great tact. Visitors should understand that chewing coca leaves (or drinking coca tea) is not drug use but a long-standing cultural tradition in the Andes.

In a country in which nearly half the population is Amerindian, expressing respect for native peoples is important. Try to refer to them not as *indios*, which is a derogatory term, but as *indígenas*. Many Peruvians refer to foreigners as *gringos* (or *gringas*) or the generic "mister," pronounced "*mee*-ster." Neither is intended or should be received as an insult.

On the streets of Cusco and other towns across Peru, shoeshine boys and little girls selling cigarettes or postcards can be very persistent and persuasive. Others just ask directly for money (using the euphemism *propinita*, or little tip). The best way to give money to those who are obviously in need of it is to reward them for their work. I get my scruffy shoes shined daily, and I buy postcards I probably don't need. If you don't wish to be hassled, a polite but firm *"No, gracias"* is usually sufficient, but remember to treat even these street kids with respect.

Queries about one's marital status and children are considered polite; indeed, women traveling alone or with other women should expect such questions. However, discussion of how much one earns is a generally touchy subject, especially in a poor country such as Peru. Although Peruvians might be curious and ask you directly how much you make, or how much your apartment or house or car or even clothes cost, I suggest that you deflect the question. At a minimum, explain how much higher the cost of living is in your home country, and how you're not as wealthy as you might seem. Ostentatious display of one's relative wealth is unseemly, even though Peru will be blissfully inexpensive to many budget travelers.

Gestures Peruvians are more formal in social relations than most North Americans and Europeans. Peruvians shake hands frequently and tirelessly, and kissing on the cheek is a common greeting for acquaintances; it is not practiced among strangers (as it is in Spain, for example). Indigenous populations are more conservative and even shy. They don't kiss to greet one another, nor do they shake hands as frequently as other Peruvians; if they do, it is a light brush of the hand rather than a firm grip. Many Indians from small villages are reluctant to look a stranger in the eye.

Using your index finger to motion a person to approach you, as practiced in the United States and other places, is considered rude. A more polite way to beckon someone is to place the palm down and gently sweep your fingers toward you.

Greetings When entering a shop or home, always use an appropriate oral greeting (*buenos días,* or good day; *buenas tardes,* or good afternoon; *buenas noches,* or good night). Similarly, upon leaving, it is polite to say goodbye (*adios* or *hasta luego*), even to shop owners with whom you've had minimal contact. Peruvians often shake hands upon leaving as well as greeting.

Photography With their vibrant dress and expressive faces and festivals, Peruvians across the country make wonderful subjects for photographs. In some heavily touristed areas, such as the Sunday market in Pisac or basically anywhere in Cusco, locals have learned to offer photo ops for a price at every turn. Some foreigners hand out money and candy indiscriminately, while others grapple with the unseemliness of paying for every photo. Asking for a tip in return for being the subject of a photograph is common in many parts of Peru; in fact, some locals patrol the streets with adorable llamas and kids in tow to pose for photographs as their main source of income. Often it's more comfortable to photograph people you have made an effort to talk to, rather than responding to those who explicitly beg to be your subject. I usually give a small tip (S/1–S/2) if it appears that my camera has been an intrusion or nuisance, or if I've snapped several shots.

It's not common except in very touristed places (such as the Pisac market), but some young mothers carrying adorable children in knapsacks and with flowers in their hair (and outstretched hands requesting a *propinita,* or tip) aren't actually mothers (or at least, not the mothers of the children they're carrying around); to tug at your tourist heartstrings and pockets, they have essentially "rented" the babies from real moms in remote villages. I don't think it's an especially good idea to reward this practice. If a very young woman has several children in tow, all dolled up for pictures and making the rounds all afternoon, she is very likely one of these rent-a-moms. Still, it does make for a great photo, and many feel it's worth the small fee.

Photographing military, police, or airport installations is strictly forbidden. Many churches, convents, and museums also do not allow photography or video, or they may charge a fee to take photos.

Punctuality Punctuality is not one of the trademarks of Peru or Latin America in general. Peruvians are customarily a half-hour late to most personal appointments, and it is not considered very bad form to leave someone hanging in a cafe for up to an hour. It is expected, so if you have a meeting scheduled, unless a strict *hora inglesa* (English hour) is specified, be prepared to wait.

Shopping Bargaining is considered acceptable in markets and with taxi drivers (which is why I use Uber and Easy Taxi apps in Lima!), and even hotels, but only up to a point—don't overdo it. Also bear in mind that many shops in large and small towns close at midday, from 1 to 3pm or 2 to 4pm.

Index

273